HISTORY OF CIVILISATION

The Etruscans

The Etruscans

MICHAEL GRANT

WEIDENFELD AND NICOLSON
LONDON

George Weidenfeld and Nicolson Ltd
91 Clapham High St   London sw4

ISBN 0 297 77748 3

Printed in Great Britain by
Fakenham Press Limited
Fakenham, Norfolk

To Anne-Sophie who suggested this book

CONTENTS

CONTENTS

ILLUSTRATIONS

xi

Cemetery of the Crocifisso del Tufo at Orvieto (*Photo: Fototeca Unione*)

Bronze Chimaera from Arretium (*Museo Archeologico, Florence. Photo: Alinari*)

Lamp of cast bronze from Cortona (*Museo dell'Accademia Etrusca, Cortona. Photo: Alinari*)

Bronze side-panel of chariot from Monteleone di Spoleto (*Metropolitan Museum of Art, New York*)

Terracotta seated statue from Murlo (*Palazzo Comunale, Siena. Photo: Mario Carrieri; by courtesy of Professor Mauro Cristofani*)

Head of a terracotta statue of Apollo from the Portonaccio temple at Veii (*Museo di Villa Giulia, Rome. Photo: Alinari*)

Braces for the teeth of Etruscans (*Merseyside County Museums, Liverpool*)

Mixing-bowl, probably from the Faliscan territory (*Vatican Museums*)

The Ponte Sodo at Veii (*Photo: Alinari*)

Amazon from the rim of a cauldron from Capua (*Reproduced by courtesy of the Trustees of the British Museum*)

Coin of an Etruscan-founded city in Campania (*Reproduced by courtesy of the Trustees of the British Museum*)

Ash-urn of pottery in the form of a hut (*Antiquarium Forense (Museo del Foro), Rome. Photo: Werner Forman Archive*)

Reconstruction of an Etruscan temple after Vitruvius (*Istituto di Etruscologia e di Antichità Italiche, Rome University*)

Gold bracelet from Praeneste (*Reproduced by courtesy of the Trustees of the British Museum*)

Silver-gilt bowl from the Bernardini tomb, Praeneste (*Museo di Villa Giulia, Rome. Photo: Pietro Roggero, Gabinetto Fotografico Nazionale, Rome*)

Bronze head of a siren from the rim of a cauldron, from the Bernardini tomb, Praeneste (*Museo di Villa Giulia, Rome. Photo: Deutsches Archäologisches Institut, Rome*)

Bronze bucket used as an ash-urn, from the Certosa cemetery near Bononia (*Museo Civico, Bologna. Photo: Scala*)

Gravestone from the Certosa cemetery (*Museo Civico, Bologna. Photo: Alinari*)

Foundations of grid-planned houses at Marzabotto (*Photo: Mario Carrieri; by courtesy of Professor Mauro Cristofani*)

Air view of Spina (*Photo: Alinari*)

MAPS

INTRODUCTION

The people who belonged to the Etruscan city-states lived in an incomparably beautiful part of the world, and they enriched it further by the creation of an imposing civilization that has every right to be considered along with its much better known Greek and Roman counterparts. The Etruscan way of life was intimately related to both these cultures, and yet it presents, at the same time, a series of notable divergencies from them. For what the Etruscans did and thought and made was surprisingly distinctive. For example, their artists and sculptors achieved masterpieces that still exercise a mesmeric effect. These works of art are the products of many borrowings and assimilations, and yet, at their best, they are paradoxically original, endowed with an alluring piquancy which is all their own and which does much to explain the peculiarities of the Etruscan psychology and temperament.

These Etruscan people also went through a unique process of political, social and economic development, about which much still remains to be said. No study of the ancient past, or of world history, can be complete if they are left out. Indeed, in many important respects, they are our own direct ancestors, since Rome, which gave us so much, had been given an enormous amount by the Etruscans.

However, the task of finding out about them presents a singular challenge. For one thing, unlike the Greeks and Romans, they have not left us any literature of their own. Even the extent to which they ever had one at all is uncertain; if they did, it dealt mainly with ceremonies and rituals. In any case it has not come down to us; instead, we have to rely on Greek and Roman authors for our literary information. But unfortunately the surviving Greek and Latin works that deal with the Etruscans tend to do so in a cursory fashion, and only when their concerns happen to impinge in some way or other upon Greek or Roman affairs. And even then, for the most part, the treatment given by

I

these writers is sketchy and ignorant, and, above all, suffers frequently, and indeed almost invariably, from the injection of hostile prejudices.

Much more, therefore, than when dealing with the Greeks or Romans, we are obliged to rely on material remains. Such remains, unearthed by generations of excavators, have yielded a great wealth of material. But what is not, perhaps, quite so widely known is that, although the Etruscans lived so long ago, this mass of evidence, and the number of sites to which it relates, increases and accumulates at a daunting, scarcely credible rate every single year and month, so that a book on the subject is likely to be out of date considerably before it even gets into print.

This intensely rapid progress means that the evasive Etruscans sometimes seem almost within our grasp, and yet the same phenomenon also involves certain serious difficulties. For one thing, there is no other subject whatever, from the entire range of themes relating to the ancient world, in which so cavernously wide a gap exists between the writings composed today by specialists for specialists, and those intended for an informed readership of wider dimensions. Works of the former type concerning the Etruscans (with splendid exceptions) tend to be much less palatable for the non-specialist reader than they might be, because of the use of unexplained technical phraseology and the too-ready assumption of general familiarity with specialist archaeological terms. Popular books on Etruscan themes, on the other hand, display a strong tendency to sink too low. Indeed, this branch of literature, over the past two centuries, has notoriously found room for an abundance of preposterous and almost lunatic theories.[1]

In addition, the archaeological evidence, despite its breathtaking rate of increase, remains patchy and tantalizing, providing information that is disconcertingly ill-proportioned. This is not merely because the climate of the country has failed to preserve any of the colourful clothes and other stuffs and materials for which the Etruscans were famous, for the same handicap applies to our studies of other ancient Mediterranean countries as well. What is much more serious is that the residences they reserved for their dead have survived a thousand times more frequently than the habitations of their living. Name any great cemetery that has been created in modern times: what would be our understanding of the civilization that produced it if we knew it from that burial-place alone?

Fortunately, however, this is not an entirely fair comparison, for it is at least consoling to the modern student of the Etruscans that they held a deep conviction of the need to look after their dead in a very thorough and conscientious fashion. This has meant that the tombs they made for them were often nobly constructed and lavishly equipped. Many of these graves, it is true, have been looted over the centuries, but many more managed to escape the attention of the plunderers and have survived to receive the attentions of excavators, operating with skills that improve all the time.

Even so, when our knowledge of a civilization depends so largely on its burials the picture is bound to be unbalanced; nor, in this particular field, are we always particularly well served by the auxiliary disciplines that help us to understand other ancient peoples. Etruscan coins, for instance, only start late, and inscriptions do not provide the material that they do for the Greeks and Romans. For one thing, the Etruscan inscriptions are far fewer in number. Luckily, we can at least read the letters they are written in, and by this means build up some sort of comprehension of what their writers intended to convey. But, as we shall see elsewhere, these messages are of a somewhat formalistic character and a limited significance, and we still cannot grasp the fundamental structure of the Etruscan language.

In setting down this last point I run the risk of incurring disapproval from those who have investigated the language so patiently, and with such interesting if not yet completely conclusive results. Experts on the civilization of the Etruscans sometimes become impatient if one too often describes them as 'mysterious', since all this additional information about them is emerging every day. Yet mysteries still remain. Etruscology is still by no means an exact science. However, having said that, may I withdraw the term 'Etruscology', and request its deletion?[2] 'Egyptology' and 'Assyriology' are equally objectionable; when we deal with the Greeks and Romans, we manage very well without speaking of 'Hellenology' and 'Romanology'. Besides, there is another strong objection to 'Etruscology'. It implies that the subject is self-contained and autonomous. Yet one of the principal gains of recent archaeological researches had been to emphasize the need to study the Etruscans within the framework of the whole Italian and Mediterranean civilization of their time.[3]

This necessity explains a feature of the present volume's plan, for the book, quite early on, devotes a considerable amount of space to the principal near-eastern and Greek influences that shaped the life and culture of the Etruscans. This is because, despite all their undoubted originality, many or indeed most of their characteristics are inexplicable (as modern research increasingly shows) unless seen in relation to the influences from the eastern Mediterranean that moulded their evolution. Yet if we have to enlarge our picture in order to see the Etruscans in the wider context of these external influences, it is imperative, next, to divide up the canvas into its component parts – that is to say, it is necessary to appreciate that, despite their common and peculiar language, these people did not just comprise an amorphous, unlike, in that respect, the city-states of the ancient Greeks. This of markedly independent and sometimes conflicting city-states – not unlike, in this respect, the city-states of the ancient Greeks. This conclusion has been recently insisted upon more than once, and yet most writers on the subject, even today, do not bear the point in mind nearly often enough. It is so much easier to follow the Greek and Roman authors who showed no interest in attempting the necessary distinctions and differentiations between these foreign, incomprehensible, hostile communities, and merely spoke of them as the 'Etruscans'. The Etruscan city-states have to be regarded, instead, as a group of separate units, each possessing its own sharp political and social distinctiveness and boasting a culture that displayed strong individual divergencies from the cultures of its neighbours. The most important of these states, in the days of Etruria's greatness, were Tarquinii, Caere, Vulci, Vetulonia, Volaterrae, Clusium and Veii,[4] which are therefore singled out for special discussion here.[5]

I have divided the book into two parts, of which the first deals with the question of how and why the life these people adopted had come into existence. This discussion includes not only an assessment of the foreign influences to which I have referred, but also that famous problem of the 'origins' of the Etruscans, seen nowadays not so much as the problem of 'where they came from' – or at least not only that, for one cannot fail to be fascinated by the question – as a field of study relating to the gradual formation of their civilization in Etruria itself. This first part takes the story up to the age when the Etruscan city-states became gradually established. Next, the endeavour is made to provide a general picture of the Etruscan expansion or presence outside Etruria itself, both in the southern and northern regions of Italy. The second part of the book seeks to present a geographical history or historical geography of the major Etruscan city-states, setting them on a firm territorial basis, one by one, in their own right, considering their histories and cultural achievements and pointing to the effects they exerted on the outside world. The last chapter seeks to sum up the conclusions that have been reached.

I referred earlier to the number of city-states that were important 'in the days of Etruria's greatness'. This attempt to distinguish between different periods of its history is yet another requirement frequently obscured by delusive Greek and Roman generalizations and preconceptions. For just as the Greeks and Romans mixed up one Etruscan city-state with another and made the whole country into a shapeless mass, so, too, they mixed and blurred the different periods of Etruscan history. Yet the Etruscans lasted for a very long time; were we studying a people or nation of the modern world, we should never assume that, just because we had discovered a piece of information about their existence in, say, the fifteenth century, it must also apply to their lives today – or vice versa. And yet very often remarkably little effort was made to apply this sort of historical, chronological method to the Etruscans. The result is that the Etruscans are treated as a timeless, unchanging phenomenon over a period of hundreds of years – like the ancient Egyptians, and with equally little justification.

Nowadays, happily, this erroneous tendency is being reversed. Modern scholars are presenting, instead, an Etruscan people or group of Etruscan city-states which possessed a history of at least seven centuries, and, during that period, quite as much as any other nation or community, they developed and evolved all the time. That, therefore, is how we should try to see them. True, we cannot supply much in the way of a connected narrative, but at all events we can distinguish one era in the history of the Etruscan city-states from another, and we must.

However, it would scarcely be useful to attempt this task over the whole seven hundred years of the process. This is too long-drawn-out and diversified a series of epochs for a rapid survey to yield any significant results. In any case, a very large part of the later period was a time of slow, prolonged and relatively uncreative decline. The earlier creative period was short, but that earlier period, as two recent writers have stressed, is what we first have to look at, if we are to understand what this civilization was all about. We must try to see what the Etruscans were like at the height of their achievement.[6]

In considering this achievement of Etruscan civilization, I have tried to present some of the results of modern research, and at times I have added a few suggestions of my own – but this I have done with all the diffidence conventionally required from an author's preface, and more. For Etruscan studies involve a formidable, overlapping range of complicated disciplines: archaeology, history, art-history, geography, geology, economics and sociology are only a few of them. In these exacting circumstances, I shall feel that this book has fulfilled its aim if it has added even a little to our awareness of the Etruscan city-states and their people, and if it has given the reader some encouragement to follow up the fascinating problems concerning their character and evolution that are arising all the time.

This book would never have been possible had it not been for the great deal of help that I have been fortunate enough to receive. In particular, I owe special thanks to the following: Mr C. H. Annis (and the Joint Library of the Hellenic and Roman Societies), Professor Giovannangelo Camporeale, Mr M. H. Crawford, Professor Mario Del Chiaro, Professor J. N. Coldstream, Professor Mauro Cristofani, Signora Karin Einaudi (and Fototeca Unione), Miss Flora Fraser, Mr Hugh Honour, Mr G. K. Jenkins, Ingegnere Carmelo Latino, Frau Adelheid Linden, Signor Piero Malvisi, Herr Wolfgang Mertz (and the Gustav Lübbe Verlag), Conte Fabrizio Niccolai Gamba, Professor Massimo Pallottino (to whom, among much else, I owe the ideas of Maps 8 and 9), Mrs Gunilla Rathsman, Professor A. E. Raubitschek, Dr David Ridgway, Mr J. C. A. Roper, Mr N. K. Rutter, Herr Heinz Scheiderbauer, Miss Vanessa Terry (and Penguin Books Ltd), Professor Mario Torelli, Dr D. H. Trump, and Mrs Patsy Vanags, whose comments on the manuscript I have found extremely helpful. I am also very grateful to Miss Paula Iley of Weidenfeld and Nicolson for her major editorial contribution, and to Miss Jane R. Thompson for her assistance.

Gattaiola, 1980   *Michael Grant*

Part One

THE FORMATION OF THE ETRUSCAN STATES

CHAPTER 1

ETRURIA AND ITS METALS

Etruria was the western part of central Italy, corresponding roughly to the modern Tuscany, together with the northern part of Lazio and including a western strip of Umbria. The country measured about 146 miles vertically, and about 94 horizontally, so it was about the size of Wales or West Virginia. To the west, it bordered upon that stretch of the Mediterranean known as the Tyrrhenian (Etruscan) Sea, and to the north it reached the Arno and the Apennine range beyond. At Etruria's southern tip, its limit was the Tiber, and the curving course of the same river formed its eastern frontier as well.

Etruria became important because of its metals. However, the terms 'Bronze Age' to cover, roughly speaking, the latter half of the second millennium BC, and 'Iron Age' to denote the period that followed, are somewhat misleading: the benefits of the 'Bronze Age' scarcely affected most of the inhabitants of central Italy until the second millennium was almost over. In consequence the last four centuries before 1000 BC are better defined as those of the 'Apennine Culture'. It was a civilization of a semi-nomadic, pastoral kind which brought a measure of cultural unity and comparative prosperity to a large part of the country for a considerable period.[1] 'Iron Age', too, is an unsatisfactory designation, because, although the introduction of iron in the tenth or ninth century BC proved of vital importance as farming was rationalized and intensified (because of its vital role in digging and cutting tools), it at first lagged far behind bronze, not replacing it as the common metal among the Italian population for a number of centuries to come.[2]

Nevertheless, it is still right to distinguish between two 'ages' in Etruria, with 1000 BC as their point of transition, because the new period witnessed great and growing transformations in the local way of life – for instance, burial customs changed, cremation replacing the burial of bodies (inhumation). And there were great material improvements. Organization and farming became much more efficient the size of the population must have considerably increased, and bronze belts, helmets, brooches and embossed buckets are indicative of skill and wealth. Then, in the eighth century, the whole process gained speed and momentum and the various parts of Etruria began to exhibit the cultural differences between one region and another which became so characteristic of the country's whole subsequent development.

Despite, therefore, the inadequacies of the terms 'Bronze Age' and 'Iron Age', they are salutary in that they pinpoint an important transition in Etruscan history. Moreover, they are also salutary for another and even more potent reason: these are the terms that lay special stress on metal – and so, in Etruria, they should, for metal was the creator of the Etruscan cities. In Greece, the factors that contributed to the all-important transformation of villages into cities were various. In Etruria, on the other hand, at all, or nearly all, of its earliest recognizable centres, there was one constant, dominant factor that exercised an enormous formative influence on this urbanization process, and that was the proximity of metal.

Etruria had other natural advantages. For millennia, its soil had provided summer and winter pasture for migrating flocks. Moreover, once the forests were cleared and the marshes and floodlands drained, it was second to no other land in fertility – as the ancient writers pointed out, recording some of the highest crop yields ever known in antiquity.[3] And effective light ploughs and methods of irrigation designed to profit from this opportunity were early in use. Furthermore, despite the hilly contours of this Etruscan territory, it possessed two important plains – the Maremma, fertile at that time and not yet marshy, running all down the coast, and the valley and plain of the River Chiana (Clanis), now drained, in the interior (Map 2).[4]

Yet none of these potential advantages would have come to fruition had it not been for Etruria's metals. Rash though such sweeping generalizations sometimes are, it can be asserted that the extraction and exploitation of the country's metallurgical wealth was, to an overwhelming extent, the determining factor not only in its urbanization but in the whole process of its development, and the cause of its rapid rise to prosperity.[5] For these metals aroused the keenest covetous interest among peoples in other lands, whose avid acquisition of them not only enriched themselves but also became immensely lucrative to the inhabitants of Etruria. Prompted by this urgent demand, the people of the rising Etruscan centres found the necessary stimulus to perform the various feats necessary to their evolution: clearing the forests (which supplied plentiful timber for their furnaces), merging their

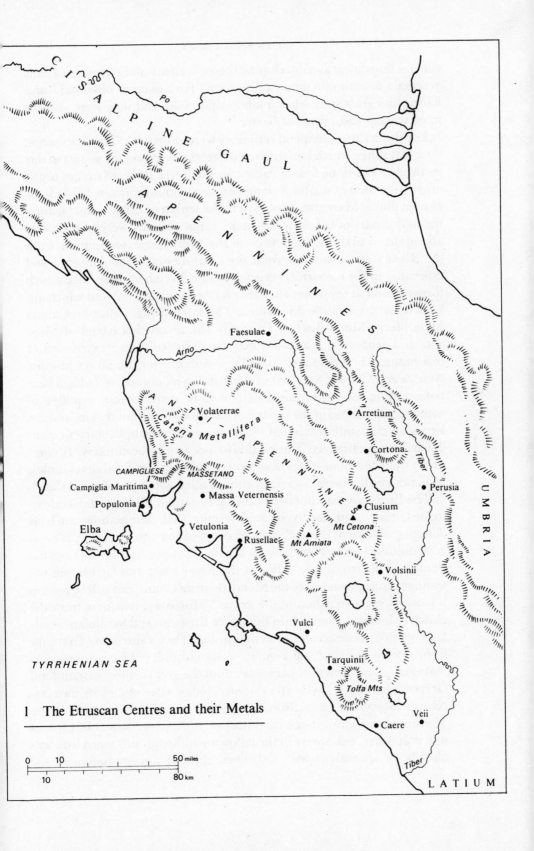

1 The Etruscan Centres and their Metals

CISALPINE GAUL

Po

APENNINES

Arno

Faesulae

ANTI Catena Metallifera APENNINES

Volaterrae

Arretium

Cortona

Tiber

CAMPIGLIESE

MASSETANO

Campiglia Marittima

Massa Veternensis

Perusia

UMBRIA

Populonia

Clusium

Elba

Vetulonia

Mt Cetona

Rusellae

Mt Amiata

Volsinii

Vulci

TYRRHENIAN SEA

Tarquinii

Tolfa Mts

Veii

Caere

Tiber

LATIUM

0   10   50 miles

10   80 km

villages into cities, and developing the agriculture and communications necessary to maintain them in existence. 'Then as now,' observed Luisa Banti, 'minerals were what made people rich. And they were also the most widespread article of barter.'[6]

For these Etruscan metal resources were enormous. The Apennines, the great range which half-encircled Etruria, were not the source of this wealth. It was to be found, rather, in the lower series of ranges much nearer the shores of the Tyrrhenian Sea, running down behind the coastal plain (Maremma) for most of the length of Etruria and forming the major part of the Anti-Apennine range. Metals were particularly abundant in that middle portion of the Anti-Apennines running from the River Cecina down beyond the Ombrone and the Albegna, and especially in the colourful, varied northern stretch of these hills, which thrust inland at this point almost as far as Saena (Siena) and which are known as the Colline Metallifere (Metal-Bearing Hills) or Catena Metallifera (Metal-Bearing Chain).[7] The metal-rich island of Elba, and in a sense even Sardinia, may be regarded as the extensions of this range. There was also metallic wealth farther inland on Mounts Amiata and Cetona, and farther south in the mountains of Tolfa. These resources of Etruria comprised the only considerable supplies of copper, iron and tin in the entire central Mediterranean region, and the Etruscan city-states exploited them on a scale which, by ancient standards, was prodigious. The local evidence can be seen today. It comprises multitudinous traces of workings, galleries, artificial caves, holes, trenches and furnaces, and waste dumps filled with piles of metal slag.[8]

The Etruscans had not been the first to exploit this metallic wealth – indeed, that need hardly be said, seeing that designations such as 'Copper' and then 'Bronze' Age are ascribed to cultures of the previous millennium. The early metalwork of a fine 'Copper Age' burial from the Ponte San Pietro, in the valley of the River Fiora not far beyond the southernmost extension of the Metal-Bearing Chain, can still be seen in a modern reconstruction of the grave.[9] Moreover, mariners from the eastern Mediterranean sought to acquire Etruscan and Sardinian metals later in this same second millennium BC. They came from Crete, or from one of the outlying centres of its culture (which we know as 'Minoan'), and then they came also from the great centres of mainland Greece, enjoying a civilization named today after one of its fortress-centres, Mycenae – a civilization which dominated large areas of the Mediterranean until its gradual decline in 1250–1200 BC. But it was not, it appears, until early in the following millennium – when iron was already, if sparsely, used, and when the full amalgamation of the hill-top villages of Etruria into cities and city-states was at hand – that the exploitation of these metals became much more systematic and impressive; this was apparently from about the middle of the eighth century BC.

To take these areas of Etruscan territory one by one, the most productive metal-bearing area in the whole region was to be found in two hilly nuclei opposite the island of Elba, in the immediate hinterland of the Etruscan port of Populonia. One of these zones was the Mas-setano, which takes its name from the town which was known to the Romans as Massa Veternensis and is now Massa 'Marittima' (although it is, and always has been, more than twelve miles from the Tyrrhenian Sea). In an annual display that the modern town offers, one can still note the remarkable profusion of metals produced in the area.[10] A little to the north-east and south of Massa, the traces of more than five hundred shafts and pits have come to light, together with smelting furnaces that look like old pottery kilns.[11] Some of these workings are of subsequent periods (Roman and medieval), but others apparently date right back to the beginnings of Etruscan wealth in the eighth century BC. The copper and, in due course, iron deposits of the Massetano played a pre-eminent role in establishing the prosperity of the Etruscan city-states.

No less fundamentally significant was the area adjoining the Mas-setano to the west, the Campigliese, which takes its name from Campig-lia Marittima (six or seven miles from the sea). On the slopes near Campiglia, once again, old open-cast mines, shafts and tunnels, and the remains of early smelting furnaces are visible, and these, too, go back to the eighth century BC. Copper supplies were abundant, and, a little to the south in the very same district, there was extensive iron.

Moreover, the Campigliese contained deposits of tin,[12] which were likewise of vital importance, since tin was needed to alloy copper, in the proportion of 8–15 per cent, to make bronze – and other sources of tin were very far away and hard to come by. The tin supplies of the Campigliese were not enormous – not enough, that is, to provide for Etruria's total requirement. But they were considerable all the same. A heap of selected tin ore has been found on the adjacent Etruscan site of Rusellae.

Another product of the Campigliese was alum, recalled by the name of Lumiere (Allumiere) di Campiglia, a place on a small jutting slope between Campiglia and the sea which has tombs of the early first millennium BC. Alum had long been used in the near east, sometimes as a medicine but more particularly as a mordant (binder) in the dyeing of fabrics and shoe-leather, both of which were leading Etruscan specialities.[13] The Greek name for alum, *strupteria*, has been plausibly recognized in the *turupterija* that appears in a text of the thirteenth century BC from Pylos in Greece, one of the centres of the Mycenaean culture.[14] The significance of dyes in the ancient world can easily be seen from the value attached by the Phoenicians, who succeeded the Mycenaeans in the control of the eastern Mediterranean waters, to the purple-producing mollusc known as the *murex* (and the Etruscans were fond of purple too).[15] It is true that the Roman writer Pliny the Elder, of the first century AD, in listing ancient territories where alum was found, does not include Etruria,[16] but that was only because Etruscan soil had ceased to provide alum by the time he was writing (though much later it did so again). However, the importance of Etruria's alum was not as great as that of its copper and iron, or even its more limited supplies of tin.

The Campigliese was only separated by a narrow channel from Elba, which was once again famous all over the Mediterranean world for the abundance of its metals. Early burials show that Elba's copper was already made use of at the beginning of the second millennium BC, but later the island's iron, which was renowned in ancient literature, gradually replaced copper as the principal local resource. Signs of its production appear in the mineral areas of Elba in the early years of the eighth century BC, and very nearly a hundred localities with remains of iron-workings have been found on the island. From *c.* 750–700 BC onwards it has been calculated that as many as ten thousand tons of iron were extracted annually over a period of at least four hundred years. The metal was mostly smelted and worked on the spot until wood-coal became exhausted,[17] after which the smelting had to be transferred to Populonia. Another and larger island, too, played an important part in teaching the coastal Etruscans how to work their metals. This was Sardinia, which was an island of expert miners and possessed very early links with Etruria:[18] bronze objects from Sardinian workshops were arriving at Etruscan harbours in the ninth and eighth centuries BC, at just about the time when Sardinia's own bronze working was at its climax.

On the mainland, the region extending north of Populonia included yet another tract of the Catena Metallifera enjoying great wealth in copper and iron. This was the valley of the River Cecina (leading up to Volaterrae), where exploitation of these resources was undertaken by the Romans in the last centuries BC and almost certainly by the Etruscans before them.[19] (Farther to the north, across the Arno, outside

Etruria proper, there were also metals in that extension of the Anti-Apennines and the Catena Metallifera known as the Apuan Alps.)

Moving into the interior of Etruria, we find other territories which likewise contributed substantially to the country's mineral production. One such region lay over thirty miles east of the Campigliese and just to the west of the highest reaches of the River Paglia (Pallia). This was the outcrop of hills rising to the massive beech- and chestnut-clad Mount Amiata, 5,690 feet high, the loftiest mountain in Etruria and the northernmost link in a chain of extinct volcanoes. This, too, was a wealthy storehouse of copper; and there was also some tin to be found and extracted.[20] Another product of Amiata was cinnabar, the principal ore of mercury – indeed, this was the speciality of the mountain, although the ore also occurred over a wider area, since it appears in almost all silver and lead deposits such as occur as a subsidiary feature in various regions of Etruria.[21] Cinnabar was used, Pliny tells us, as a medicine and a pigment, and he refers to the special importance the Romans attached to it. So too, no doubt, had the Etruscans. But, like alum in the coastal district, this was a speciality that counted less than the copper and iron which Mount Amiata also supplied. East of Amiata was Mount Cetona, which had likewise been a source of metals from at least the final years of the second millennium BC; its ancient mine-workings are still to be seen.[22]

However, it was another metallurgical centre altogether, in the opposite, southernmost region of the country, which apparently played the decisive part in the launching of the civilization of the Etruscan city-states as we know them. This was the area of the Tolfa Mountains, a not very high range straddling the land-mass between Lake Bracciano and the sea-coast near the modern Civitavecchia and dividing the volcanic area of southern Etruria into two sections. The high narrow plateaux of Tolfa are scored by the valleys and ravines of three streams which provided communications through thick woods of chestnut, beech and ilex, descending into the typical Mediterranean *maquis* of arbutus, mastic and broom. The mineral wealth of Tolfa, like that of other Etruscan centres, had already been recognized by the later years of the second millennium BC, an epoch from which important finds of bronze work and pottery have been discovered on the mountain, together with the remains of a village. Then, in Etruscan times, the Tolfa area became the focus of increasingly intense metallurgical development, as the tunnelling of many ancient mining shafts reveals, including one group rediscovered in the sixteenth century AD and exploited thereafter until recently.[23] It seems extremely likely that these supplies of copper, iron and tin from the Tolfa range produced, in the vicinity, the very first wealthy and powerful Etruscan city-states, formed by the amalgamation of villages;[24] it is now necessary to identify these city-states and to try to determine how they came into being and how they developed into centres that ranked among the most important powers of the ancient world.

CHAPTER 2

THE CREATION OF
THE ETRUSCAN CITIES

From Villages into Cities

So it was Etruria's resources of copper, iron and other metals and minerals which brought the country's historic civilization into being through the transformation of the earlier settlements and villages of the country into the cities and city-states of which their nation was from then onwards to consist. This point in the development of Etruria,[1] the most decisive stage in all its history, was reached in the eighth century BC (after preliminaries in the ninth): it was then that groups of adjacent villages – each group located upon a single, separate hill plateau of its own – merged to form larger units, which in due course evolved into cities and city-states. A single unit was easier for its inhabitants to defend than a group of separate villages, and more capable of organizing the irrigation of the surrounding countryside. Above all else, a unit under one control was better equipped to exploit local metal resources by instituting a manufacturing industry and a commercial organization able to deal effectively and profitably with the pressing external customers who wanted to acquire these metals.[2]

The exact processes by which the sets of adjacent villages came together can scarcely be reconstructed. But since each of the centres (as we can still see today) possessed a variety of cemeteries, usually numbering between two and four or five, the villages which each group of cemeteries served, and which later united to form a single larger nucleus, presumably fell, for the most part, within these numerical limits. It is possible to imagine an intermediate period in which the villages, while still retaining their own autonomy, had nevertheless gradually entered into co-operation with their immediate neighbours, so as to form a partial linkage.[3] Then, in the second stage, complete amalgamation was accomplished, and thus the process of forming cities and city-states was taken to its logical conclusion.

Ancient tradition maintained that many of the most important Greek cities of the eastern Mediterranean had come into existence through the same process of an amalgamation of villages. This is clearly correct, and is what happened, for example, at Athens and Corinth and Smyrna (Izmir), probably not before the eighth century, when a population explosion was taking place in Greek lands.[4] Aristotle noted the nature of the process: the village had been 'the first association of a number of houses for the satisfaction of something more than daily needs', and 'the final association, formed of several villages, is the city or state'.[5] We can also detect this kind of development at Rome, where, somewhat later than the earliest Etruscan communities (and in imitation of them), the villages on the Seven Hills likewise merged to become the city and city-state of the future.

As in Greece, so in Italy, such unions were encouraged and dictated by the facts of the country's geography.

This was especially true of Etruria, which formed a confusing succession of amply wooded hills or heights, nearly sixty in number, separated by plains that were mostly small in size, relatively isolated one from another, and often not too easily distinguishable from marshes. When a site was selected for urban development, or when groups of villages began to develop rapidly in that direction, this meant that a number of topographical requirements had been felt by the inhabitants to be adequately satisfied. Access to agricultural land was important, and access to metals an overriding essential. But defensibility was equally vital and to secure this the people of Etruria liked to locate their villages, and then their cities, on high plateaux that were protected by steep cliffs and looked down upon a junction of two ravines below.

In addition to defence, the ravines supplied riverside grazing, firewood, stone and clay. But they served an even more significant purpose, for they also provided the communications which formed the life-blood of the new cities, providing them with access to the goods and crops they needed and above all to the metals to which they owed their prosperity and their very existence. The history of Etruria is thus not only the history of its metals and cities but also of its ravines and rivers. The role that these rivers fulfilled is not always immediately obvious today. It is true that the Tiber and Arno are still substantial streams, but the Chiana (Clanis) has quite disappeared. And even the largest of the others – the Marta linking Lake Bolsena to Tarquinii and the sea, and the Fiora, Ombrone and Cecina flowing past Vulci, Rusellae and Volaterrae respectively – do not nowadays look very impressive: yet in Etruscan times they played an indispensable part.

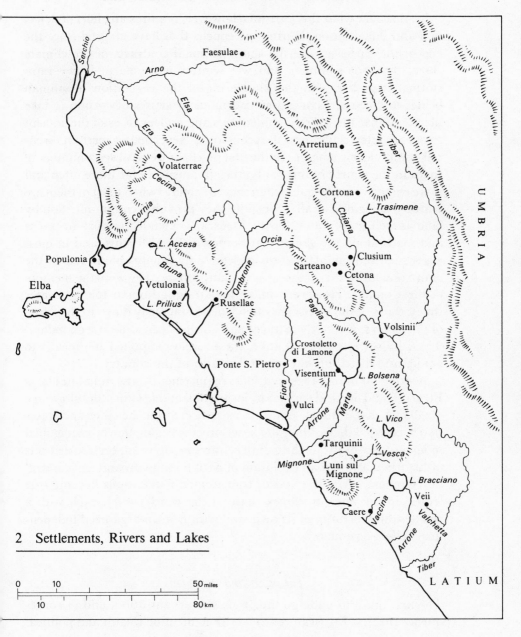

2 Settlements, Rivers and Lakes

To discover what this part was, however, requires an effort of detection and imagination. During the epochs that have elapsed since the end of the Etruscan age the sharp seasonal contrasts of the climate (long, dry, hot summers and wet winters with sharp, heavy rainstorms), together with the plundering of the vegetation by human beings and goats, have caused enormous processes of erosion to take place,[6] so that the courses, dimensions and appearances of the ancient rivers are often quite hard to reconstruct. Nevertheless, certain essential points clearly emerge. In the first place, as we shall see a number of times in the course of this study, the streams were far more often and more extensively navigable than they are today (when most of them are scarcely navigable at all). Secondly they provided communication by land as well as by water, for the Etruscans extended important tracks and roads along the slopes that bordered these streams, and in most cases such thoroughfares provided the only practicable routes in the entire region. In this activity, as in many others, they were the mentors of the Romans. However, unlike the straight Roman roads of later times, those of the Etruscans often wound sinuously down to the floors of the valleys, where their traces and cuttings can still be seen today.[7] Thus, by water and road alike, these valleys supplied the means to gather and distribute the mineral wealth of the country.

Bearing in mind these various requirements, the inhabitants of Etruria could not find very many locations suitable either for the groups of villages that initially came into existence, or for the cities and states that succeeded them. Once the latter process began, however, it gained momentum rapidly; as the eighth century BC drew on, certain districts of Etruria witnessed an explosion of both population and agricultural development.[8] And the new or transformed foundations became true 'cities' in the ancient, Greek sense of the word (*polis*), each with a surrounding territory of its own, and with its own organized independent self-government.[9]

Tarquinii and its Rivals

The first place to undergo the process of urbanization, and in consequence the first Etruscan centre to rise to metallic wealth and political power, seems to have been Tarquinii (the Etruscan Tarchnal and modern Tarquinia), in the southern part of the area. It was situated five miles from the sea, just over forty miles north-west of the Tiber. It was also scarcely ten miles from the minerals of Mount Tolfa which, at this stage, as archaeological links between the two areas unmistakably reveal, were under the control of Tarquinii.[10] At the very outset, therefore, there is a direct correlation between metals and Etruscan prosperity, and because Tarquinii formed the initial link it played a dominant role in the establishment of Etruscan civilization.

The villages which, in the earliest centuries of the last millennium BC, had existed on the site of the later Tarquinii can be more or less located by the positions of their burial grounds. A number of these settlements must have been distributed, in fairly close proximity to each other, over most of the plateau now known as La Civita or Pian di Civita, separated by a stream from the medieval and modern town of Tarquinia (formerly Corneto). La Civita was bounded and protected by steep limestone cliffs which fell away abruptly at its sides. A central depression divided the plateau into two parts; the western part stood out like the bows of a ship towards and above the River Marta, which, together with its tributaries, nearly surrounded the site. The Marta, small though it was, possessed a major, extensive drainage basin and, like other Etruscan streams, played a key part in the development of its region.

The villages on this site, much more advanced than any Italian settlements of the previous millennium, have a strong claim to be regarded as the most prosperous as well as the earliest pre-urban settlements in Etruria, so that the tenth and ninth centuries BC can almost be defined as the period of a 'Tarquinian civilization'.[11] A further village of substantial size has been identified on the ridge that was later to become Tarquinii's main cemetery, the great bastion of the Monterozzi plateau that stands between La Civita and the sea. Here traces of at least twenty huts have been found, both oval and rectangular, of competent construction. Moreover, the Monterozzi ridge appears to have started not only as a habitation site but as a burial ground fairly early in the first millennium BC, although perhaps the earliest graves of all are a group of tombs in the form of cylindrical pits or wells in another area, the hilly ground east of La Civita. These graves seem to date back to the ninth century. Here, as elsewhere, the cemeteries were placed outside the inhabited areas they served, on accessible hills or small knolls.

The chronological priority of the Tarquinian villages over other settlements in Etruria is confirmed by the skill – far superior to that of previous epochs – which their inhabitants displayed in working the bronze made from the copper that lay so near at hand on Tolfa. There is archaeological evidence of contact with south Italy and other regions of the Mediterranean even before the first foundation of Greek markets or colonies on Italian soil from the eighth century onwards – for example, bronze tripods, prior to that date, at Tarquinii already recall a Greek prototype. This might reveal the early presence of a Greek artist, but it is equally possible that the tripods were copied locally, from imported objects, by a native craftsman. The villages were also the production centres for stamped bronze shields, which began to be made as early as the ninth or eighth century BC. Moreover, people in these Tarquinian settlements were reproducing a kind of brooch that had long been known in the area but now reappears in considerably improved versions. These were some of the ways in which the local population was already benefiting – though modestly in comparison with what was to come – from the proximity and availability of local supplies of metals.

Some idea of the houses these people lived in can be obtained from the 'hut-urns' in which they interred the ashes of their cremated dead – urns in the shape of small square dwellings. It appears from these models that the actual huts, which were no doubt built of wattle and daub, possessed steep, thatched, wooden-ridged roofs, a wide rectangular window, and a circular hole in the roof for the smoke to escape through.[12]

The hut-urns date from various periods in the eighth century BC. And it was probably in the second half of the same century that the villages round Tarquinii completed their decisive transformation into the nucleus of a city-state. The chronological priority of the urbanization of Tarquinii, in advance of other Etruscan cities, is corroborated by foundation legends known to the ancients. The mythical Tarchon, believed to have established the principal cities of the Etruscans, was held to have founded, first of all, Tarquinii, which was said to have been named after him.[13] And it was the holy city of Tarquinii, through the agency of Tages, who supposedly rose from the ground in its midst, that claimed to have taught Etruria the rules regulating the relations between gods and men. Even if some of these stories were not very early in origin, they accurately reflect not only the earliness of the amalgamation of villages that created Tarquinii but also the seniority over other Etruscan cities which it possessed in consequence.[14]

This precocity of the Tarquinian settlements, however, was not manifested solely upon their own hills: it was also reflected in comparable, and almost equally ancient, developments at other villages in the fertile and increasingly well-cultivated surrounding region. To what extent these villages were politically subordinated to those destined to merge into Tarquinii cannot be determined, but they were at any rate under predominantly Tarquinian influence. Not surprisingly, there was a very early settlement of this kind, or more than one, on the Tolfa range itself – evidence of consistent habitation on its slopes dates back as far as the second millennium BC. There were also two settlements near the Mignone, which flowed between Tolfa and Tarquinii, and beside tributaries of that river. One of these habitation centres was at San Giovenale, on a crescent-shaped plateau of volcanic stone bounded by two gorges made by a tributary of the Mignone called the Vesca and by two of the Vesca's own offshoots. Here, too, the settlement goes back to before 1000 BC.[15] Not long after that date, however, it shifted to a site a little distance away, and the new village resembled those of Tolfa, from which it obtained its metallic livelihood.[16]

Farther to the west stood another early centre, or group of centres, at Luni sul Mignone, between the Vesca and another deep-set tributary of the Mignone, near the point at which the two streams joined the Mignone itself. Interested, no doubt, in the metals of Tolfa, visitors from Mycenaean Greece, or their intermediaries, had already deposited their traces at Luni in the thirteenth or twelfth century BC or even possibly earlier, leaving pottery and cutting the foundations for their huts in the local volcanic stone.[17] But the most remarkable discovery at Luni sul Mignone is a rectangular building, measuring eighteen yards by nine; its walls consisted of solid, irregular blocks of volcanic stone, and the foundations extended from four to six yards down into the ground. Archaeologists are certain that the remains of the building date from before 800 BC, which makes this the most ancient monumental structure in central Italy. Some scholars have conjectured that the edifice was a sanctuary, but it has now been argued that it was the residence of a ruler of the place.[18] In either case, its existence argues that, by the end of the ninth century BC, the urbanization of Luni had progressed a long way. The village or villages on the site must already have been transformed into something more advanced, the nucleus of a town or city – a transformation which was no doubt due to the accessibility of the Tolfa mines.[19] But a century or so later the place was destroyed by fire. This can only be seen in relation to the similar, and far more powerful, amalgamation of the Tarquinian villages which had taken place not far away. Whereas Luni sul Mignone may have originally served to guard the autonomous villages on the site of Tarquinii, the city which those villages then became would brook no rivals for miles around – and even relatively well established centres such as Luni sul Mignone could no longer survive.

The same message is conveyed by a similar fate that overcame other centres not far away. Whereas the Mignone area was vital because it was on the way to Tolfa's metals, the more immediate lifeline of the Tarquinian villages was the actual river beside which they stood, the Marta. This flowed down from Lake Bolsena, which occupied a volcanic crater twenty-three miles to the north-east. The Etruscans, who were worshippers both of springs and of standing waters, revered this lake as the place of their sacred origins. Like other Etruscan lakes and lagoons, it was navigable and rich in fish and in marsh-birds, and the region produced timber, reeds and canes for the construction of houses and of windbreaks. The lakeside was therefore thickly populated, as large ancient cemeteries show.[20] On the south-western shore, close to the point where the Marta issues from the lake, stood the village settlement of Visentium (Bisenzio). This site has disclosed many bronzes of Tarquinian origin and style, which indicate that Visentium belonged to the sphere of influence of Tarquinii;[21] indeed, the ancients often called Lake Bolsena the 'Tarquinian Lake'. Yet Visentium, once again, after flourishing actively in the second half of the eighth century BC, had no sequel whatever, but seems, like Luni, to have vanished off the face of the earth. Here, then, is a further illustration of the strong effect that the union of the Tarquinian villages exercised on adjacent communities, apparently eclipsing them by its dominant local strength and exploiting its proximity to the metals of Tolfa more successfully – aided by external spurs which will be indicated later.

But Tarquinii only remained pre-eminent for a short time; perhaps not more than a century. Thereafter, the leading position – and the control of the Tolfa metals which conferred it – passed to its south-eastern neighbour Caere (the Etruscan Cisra or Chaisr(i)e:[22] now Cerveteri), thirty miles north-west of Rome.

From about the ninth century BC, Caere, like Tarquinii, consisted of a group of villages – or possibly in this case only one on the actual site itself, with others scattered in the immediate neighbourhood. The central settlement was spread along the outermost spurs of the massive volcanic tableland extending south-westwards down to a plain leading to the sea, of which the shore was only three and a half miles from Caere. The valleys of two streams formed cliffs which bounded the habitation area on either side, meeting to form the little river Vaccina, known to Virgil as the river of Caere (*Caeritis amnis*), which has its estuary north of the modern town of Ladispoli. The location of Caere was no doubt originally chosen for its excellent supply of water, including medicinal springs for which the place became famous.[23] The site was also ideally placed at the junction between the coastal flats and the hills,[24] and the tongue of the rock on which Caere stood was a last outcrop of the metal-rich Tolfa Mountains. In the first centuries of the last millennium, as we have seen, they and their wealth had belonged to Tarquinii, but – although the Tarquinians may have retained part of the range – Servius, the commentator on Virgil, indicates a later boundary (the River Minio, now Mignone) which assigns it to Caere instead.[25] Archaeologists conclude from the nature of the objects found in their excavations that much of the ore-bearing region had passed, by the early years of the seventh century BC at the latest, from Tarquinian to Caeritan control, by which time the villages of Caere had already been amalgamated in a single city. It was linked to the mining centres by a number of roads, while streams in its territory, overlooked by further early hill-top sites, provided communications from Tolfa to the sea.

The nature of the historical convulsion that transferred the mining region from Tarquinii to Caere cannot be determined, owing to the sparseness of our records, yet that is what happened, and it decisively shifted the balance of power. As mentioned, there had been an early village at Caere from about the ninth century BC, but its greatness was only on the way when it secured access to these neighbouring metals, which soon transformed the settlement pattern. At first, there were two main burial places containing both pit-tombs for cremation and, later, trench-tombs for inhumation, and then cemeteries of the latter kind almost completely surrounded the central habitation area.

When Tarquinii lost part of Tolfa's mineral wealth in the eighth or early seventh century BC, its south-eastern neighbour Caere was not the only beneficiary. For another share of the metals, and the power they conferred, probably went to Tarquinii's neighbour on the other side, Vulci (in Etruscan, Velcha), lying thirteen miles away to the north-west and six miles from the sea. But this partial takeover only occurred after the site of Vulci had already had a considerable history – if only we were able to reconstruct it. The place stood on a flat hill admid a grandiose and desolate landscape in a loop made by the River Fiora (Armenta or Arnine to the Romans) and two of its tributaries. Steeply dropping scarps protected the place on the north-east side (where its acropolis was located), and to the east. From the existence of separate cemeteries providing material going back to the ninth century BC, it has been deduced that there had originally been about five autonomous villages on the site. They have not, it is true, yet been found, but they were evidently of some importance in the first part of the eighth century BC, and perhaps earlier.[26]

Conspicuous features of these early, pre-urban settlements of Vulci were objects of bronze, notably a hut-urn with a deep overhanging roof in hammered metal, and a bronze flask and sword. This evidence, supported by the fact that Vulci later became the seat of Etruria's most important bronze industry, makes it seem extremely probable that the villages on the site already possessed metal supplies of their own: their inhabitants could hardly have secured these supplies from other regions by trading, since they had nothing valuable enough to provide in exchange. On the other hand, it seems hazardous to suppose that these pre-urban villages at Vulci already had access to the metal of Tolfa, since in the early eighth century Tolfa still seems to have belonged to Tarquinii. It may be concluded, therefore, that the early Vulcentine settlements had contact with, and control of, valuable metals from another region altogether, namely Mount Amiata, which rose thirty miles farther up the River Fiora. It is true that this particular stream, unlike others, was not (as far as we know) navigable for any appreciable stretch. Nevertheless, the tracks following the course of its valley provided an obvious means of communication with the interior, and particularly with metal-rich Amiata.

The Fiora valley had known human habitation since early in the second millennium BC, notably at the Ponte San Pietro, where a Copper Age burial has been found. And graves of about 1000 BC, surrounded by impressive walls and surmounted by the mounds that were to become such a feature of the country's tombs, have now come to light at Crostoletto di Lamone, in the middle reaches of the valley.[27] The use of the valley as a thoroughfare, then, was nothing new, and the link that it provided with Mount Amiata was evidently the impulse that led to the union of the villages on Vulci's hill. This amalgamation seems to have taken place shortly before or after 700; and that, it appears, was the time when Vulci added further to its metal resources by taking over, together with Caere, part of Tolfa from Tarquinii, and thus becoming a joint heir of the Tarquinian pre-eminence (though Vulci may not have retained full permanent control of Amiata).

The villages on the future site of Vulci had already made themselves felt in the outside world. Burial-places at Capua in Campania have produced material very close to theirs, thus probably betraying their influence. Moreover, a statuette of the early eighth century BC found its way to Vulci from Sardinia. This was the time when the island's output of this kind of work was at its height, and its people may well have taught these Etruscans useful lessons about the working of the metal.[28]

The North-Western Centres

Another region which gained its early wealth from metals lay forty-five miles to the north-west of Vulci. This was Vetulonia (in Etruscan, Vetluna or Vatluna). Situated within a crook of the River Bruna and its tributaries, it stood upon a three-spurred hill 1,130 feet high with steep cliffs on three sides, amid a fertile area that now abounds in sweet wild grapes and game. Moreover, although the site is nine miles away from the coastline today, in ancient times the sea-lagoon Lake Prilius came up very close to its south-eastern side.

In the early first millennium BC there were two groups of cemeteries at Vetulonia containing pit-burials with cremation urns that were either in the form of huts or biconical (an un-Greek shape, in which the body of the vessel is an inverted cone, surmounted by a top that is an upright cone). The separation of these cemeteries indicates the existence, at the time, of two distinct villages, each of which must have attained considerable dimensions, though their traces have not survived.

Another necropolis very similar to these (and no doubt a very similar village also) existed on the banks of Lake Accesa, a little to the north-west of Vetulonia. This is significant, since the lake is on the outskirts of the rich and important metal-bearing zone of the Massetano, which the villages on the site of the future Vetulonia were uniquely well placed to exploit – and this is what they did, vigorously, by extracting and working copper and then iron.[29]

From this exploitation, predictable consequences followed. First, the region was already densely populated very soon after 1000 BC. Secondly, it became famous, in due course, for its rich profusion of locally worked bronze objects, for which manufactured bronzes from Sardinia – already arriving by the end of the ninth century BC – could serve as models. Thirdly, it was only a matter of time before the villages on the site were united into what was to become an important city-state: not, in this particular case, immediately after the access of wealth, and not as early as the amalgamations at Tarquinii and Caere, but scarcely later than that of Vulci, and at least by the seventh century BC.

Adjacent to Vetulonia, on its north side, was Populonia (in Etruscan, Fufluna or Pupluna), even closer than its neighbour to a great metal-bearing zone, since this site was only a dozen miles from the Campigliese region, which was so enormously wealthy in copper, iron and other metals. Famous for iron-working much later, Populonia was a centre for the working of bronze from at least the eighth century BC, when fine specimens of the art appear in its tombs. The local acropolis stood right on the sea, on a promontory nearly nine hundred feet high overlooking the Baratti Gulf. The ancient habitation site is still almost totally unexplored, but the early existence of two separate burial-grounds, one at the foot of the promontory and the other to the north-east, invites the conclusion that there were also, before the town existed, two separate villages which communicated with the mining hills in the immediate interior.[30]

The ashes lodged in these earlier burials were mostly deposited in trenches, but there is also a tomb in the form of a chamber, which is crowned by what is known as a 'false dome' (*tholos*), built of rows of overlapping stones that gradually close up to provide a conical summit. Later, false domes (often surmounted by mounds) became frequent in Etruria, but this is at present the earliest known example, dating apparently from the end of the ninth century BC or possibly from the beginning of the eighth.[31] It has been convincingly argued that the formula came to Populonia from Sardinia, for Sardinian false-domed monuments, in the shape of a truncated cone, display a similarity to the Populonian structure which, in view of the geographical proximity of the island and its close connections with Etruria, can scarcely be fortuitous.[32]

The false dome had a very ancient history in Sardinia as well as in many parts of the near east,[33] but the particular form in which the Sardinians transmitted the feature to Etruria had probably come to them in the latter half of the second millennium BC from western outposts of the Mycenaean civilization of Greece, to whose people this type of construction was familiar.[34] Indeed, it might be argued that Populonia had acquired the 'false dome' formula *direct* from the Mycenaeans, and not through Sardinia at all. But the time-lag between the disintegration or contraction of the Mycenaean world (*c.* 1250–1200) and the first known false-domed building at Populonia – which dates from at least four centuries later – makes it preferable to regard the Sardinians as intermediaries.

Nevertheless, when this architectural form did reach Populonia, it came to a place which would not find any part of the Mycenaean heritage too unfamiliar, for there is independent evidence that the early heirs of the Mycenaeans in the near east, before and after the turn of the millennium, had taken an interest in Populonia and its riches. Local tombs, situated in trenches, contained swords and brooches of types also found in south Italy, Sicily and the Aegean region, which go back to models of 1100–800 from Syria or Cyprus.[35] These objects were brought to Populonia by successors of the Mycenaeans interested in the metals of Etruria, operating via Sardinia or Sicily.[36] When, therefore, the people of Populonia adapted the Mycenaean formula of the false dome shortly before or after 800 BC, they were carrying on a tradition of contact with the eastern Mediterranean that was long-standing and may well have been more or less continuous.

In the light of these fruitful contacts it is not surprising that, during the initial centuries of the first millennium BC, the area around the two villages on the site of the future Populonia developed an exceptional density of population. Moreover in due course, as elsewhere in Etruria, the two settlements coalesced, perhaps completing their union not much later than the similar amalgamation of the Vetulonian site, in the seventh century BC. But the city of Populonia that emerged from this process remained unique among Etruscan centres (or rather, among those centres which eventually became city-states) because, in contrast to the others that are generally some miles inland from the Tyrrhenian Sea, it stood directly upon the coast. In consequence, it had a harbour of its own; this has recently been identified (and some of its underwater remains surveyed) just below the acropolis, in the Baratti Gulf which gave the port some shelter.[37]

The acropolis now lies unmistakably on the mainland, but in ancient times, and indeed until comparatively recently, the site formed a peninsula, as the geographer Strabo pointed out[38] – indeed, it was so nearly separated from the continent that it was virtually an island. That this was so is shown clearly on Renaissance and eighteenth-century maps, which reveal that the flat land which lies behind the eastern promontory of the gulf and now adjoins the estuary of the River Cornia (beside the modern town of Piombino) was then a large open lagoon or marsh (the Palude Caldana), almost an arm of the sea. This lagoon extended right round the acropolis to the coast on its north, where another stream seems to have joined its shallow waters as it debouched into the sea.

This island-like location makes it possible to explain another peculiarity of Populonia, for although the villages on its site, already prosperous, duly amalgamated in about the seventh century BC, Servius, the commentator on Virgil, remarked that as a city and city-state it was not so ancient as other cities of Etruria.[39] His information is indirectly confirmed by a historian of the first century BC, Dionysius of Halicarnassus, who omits Populonia from a list of north Etruscan towns which he provides for the sixth century BC. There is one good way of explaining how Populonia, while an early centre possessing considerable wealth, was nevertheless not an early city-state: in all probability its villages were associated with, or presided over, another category of community which is now beginning to be well known, namely that of the market (*emporion*). These *emporia* were commercial centres or outposts lacking city-state institutions and concentrating on trading activities.[40] It had been the custom of the Mycenaeans – who were so interested in the region – to establish markets of this type. Moreover, as we shall see in the next chapter, the Greek city-states, from the eighth century BC onwards, planted *emporia* of their own, very often on Mycenaean sites. Two such posts in the west, Pithecusae (Ischia) and Cumae (an *emporion* before it became a city-state), played an enormous part in stimulating the exploitation of Etruscan metals. As for the east, early Greek *emporia* included Al Mina on the Syrian coast, and it was Al Mina that fed Pithecusae and Cumae with goods and motifs from Phoenicea (Lebanon) and other near-eastern lands. It could also be relevant that Populonia had taken its name from the Etruscan god Fufluns (equivalent to Dionysus or Bacchus) – whose name, in turn, is likely to be an Etruscan form of the Greek Byblinos, the 'god of Byblos', the mercantile harbour on the Syrian coast.[41] But be that as it may, we can see the market-town of Populonia, with its unusual location and status, as a probable Etruscan link in this chain of Mediterranean *emporia*.

The availability of iron on the adjacent island of Elba also attracted the interest of Greek traders at least from the eighth century BC, since fragments of iron of that date, firmly traceable back to Elba mines, have been found at Pithecusae[42] – and Elba, like other islands, was called Aethalia from the smoke (*aithalos*) rising from its open-cast ironworks. Much earlier, however, as we have seen, Elba had also been famous for its copper, and in this connection it is noteworthy that Mycenaean tablets of the thirteenth century BC refer to *Aitaro*, which has been identified with Aethalia and related to Elba's role as a copper exporter.[43] The extent to which Populonia acted as an intermediary in these early relations of Elba with foreign lands in the second and early first millennia BC is not clear. It may well be that Elba also possessed an *emporion* (not yet identified) similar to that of Populonia. But anyway, outside interest in Populonia cannot fail to have been enhanced by its proximity to the metal wealth not only of the Campigliese but of Elba as well.

Volaterrae (in Etruscan, Velathri, now Volterra), thirty-four miles north-west of Populonia, was another major community of Etruria to be added to the list of those that owed their creation and prosperity to the availability of metals, for Volaterrae closely overlooked the metal riches of the Cecina valley. There are remains that suggest that as far back as the early second millennium BC it exploited this wealth, and although concrete evidence is not extensive it must be assumed that this was also the situation in Etruscan times a thousand years later.

The site of Volaterrae is an imposing and grandiose one, 'on the level summit', as Strabo records, 'of a lofty hill which is precipitous on all sides'.[44] A number of ancient cemeteries lie on the flanks of the hill, permitting the deduction that, as elsewhere, the plateau was originally occupied by a group of villages which subsequently amalgamated.[45] The cemeteries of seventh-century date at the north-western extremity of the acropolis are of interest because they include a type of tomb characteristic of north Italy – with which Volaterrae remained in close touch – comprising rectangular trenches lined with stone slabs.[46] These graves are not very rich, and there is no evidence that the place was particularly prosperous at the time. However, beside these cemeteries is the cliff of a gigantic picturesque landslide (Le Balze), into which large parts of these early burial-grounds are evidently fallen; so it would be rash to conclude, from our lack of information, that Volaterrae must have been insignificant in the eighth and seventh centuries BC. True, lying far to the north as it does, it was no doubt a later starter than the cities of southern Etruria, but at some stage it revived the exploitation of the Cecina metals and its villages joined together.

North-East and South-East

Clusium (Clevsin, today Chiusi) perched high on a rocky, volcanic spur, far into the interior of Etruria. It was forty-four miles north of Vulci: the metal-bearing wealth of Mounts Cetona and Amiata lay between Vulci and Clusium, nearer the latter. Accordingly, people on the site of Clusium controlled Cetona at an early date: already before 1000 BC the metals of the mountain had been exploited at the fortified village of Belverde,[47] and at some time during the course of the sixth century it would seem that the Clusines gained control of certain portions of Amiata as well.

However, it would be somewhat hazardous to group Clusium wholeheartedly with all the other leading Etruscan cities which primarily and initially owed their development and wealth to the possession of metals; for the villages that stood on the site of the later Clusium seem instead to have owed much of their original prosperity to agriculture. This was based on the remarkable fertility of the valley of the River

Chiana (Clanis), a tributary of the Tiber. Medieval marshes and modern irrigation have obliterated the river altogether. But in ancient times it was a considerable and even navigable stream.[48] At an early date the agriculture of the region was highly developed with the help of active drainage operations.

In addition to the settlements on the site of Clusium, there were at least six other early agricultural villages in the area, notably Poggio Renzo to the north, Sarteano to the south-east, and a settlement beyond Sarteano on Mount Cetona itself. However, in about 700 BC these centres were razed to the ground and absorbed by the new city of Clusium, which was becoming urbanized at just about this time by the union of the villages on its plateau. Previously the villages on the site of Clusium may have been Umbrian, though the land known as Umbria (Italic-speaking despite a measure of Etruscanization) was later understood as not extending so far to the west. Moreover, even in Etruscan times Umbrians ('Camertes Umbri') continued to form a part of the population of Clusium, which should therefore be classified as a bilingual community, like those in other fringe areas on the borders of Etruria.

A destroyer of certain centres in its territory, Clusium was also a founder of others. For the creation of a further Etruscan city, Volsinii (Orvieto), out of villages on the eastern shore of Lake Bolsena,[49] took place under Clusine impulse, in the late seventh or early sixth century BC. The Clusines were interested in this southern neighbour and off-shoot because of the great pan-Etruscan shrine of Voltumna on its territory. And, similarly, at about the same period, they turned north-wards and prompted the foundation of Cortona and Arretium (Arezzo) and Faesulae (Fiesole). So Clusium, it appears, was strong in commercial communications and in the capacity for expansion, under the stimulus of its wealth in farmlands and metals.

At Clusium, as we have seen, agriculture may have counted rather more than metals. Another relatively late starter, Veii (Veio), at the extreme south-eastern periphery of the country, seems, exceptionally, to have had no direct access to metals at all. Here agriculture and trading communications were the paramount causes of wealth and development – together with uniquely productive salt-beds at the mouth of the Tiber. The site provides occasional objects dating back to the second millennium BC, but permanent settlements only seem to have been established in the first, when there were at least three, and perhaps five, villages of oval huts, each with its own adjacent cemetery. These villages, each comprising between three hundred and six hundred inhabitants, were perched on a broad plateau consisting of two ridges and a southern outcrop (later the acropolis), and surrounded on three sides by sheer cliffs running down to the deep gullies of the River Valchetta (the ancient Cremera, a tributary of the Tiber) and one of its tributaries. The settlers not only lived on the plateau but farmed part of it. Their villages and cemeteries achieved a certain size, although, because of the region's lack of metallic resources, they are later and poorer than others in southern Etruria. Yet Greek pottery reached the place as early as 800 BC or very soon after,[50] actually in advance of the establishment of Greek trading-posts and colonies in southern Italy. The appearance of these pots at Veii is due apparently solely to the geographical situation of the place in the southernmost tip of Etruria, not far from the Tiber and nearest to the harbours of southern Italy, which the Greeks, although they had not yet established any regular posts there, were already beginning to frequent. The discovery of the pots at Veii does not seem to reflect any particular attraction exercised by the place in its own right. What attracted the Greeks was the metallic wealth of Etruria (of other Etruscan centres, that is to say, not of Veii itself), and it was because of this that the Greek trading-posts and colonies on and off the south Italian coast were planted from the mid-eighth century onwards. When they came into existence, they and their roving representatives offered enormous opportunities of enrichment to the Etruscans, and indeed supplied the major commercial, social and cultural impulse that created their civilization – providing, in particular, the decisive stimulus that caused them to amalgamate their villages into important city-states.

But the external impact on the Etruscans was twofold: it came not only from Greece but from the near east as well, and especially from Phoenicia. The two main influences on the creation of the distinctive Etruscan culture must now be described in greater detail, in an attempt to analyse and illustrate the peculiar blend of orientalism and Hellenism, combined with a distinct vein of native originality, which made that culture what it was.

CHAPTER 3

DECISIVE INFLUENCES FROM THE EAST

The Impact of the Near East

The people of Phoenicia, the maritime strip which forms part of the state of Lebanon today, played an outstanding role as transmitter of near-eastern customs, techniques and artistic themes throughout the Mediterranean and to the west. When the so-called Mycenaean civilization, based on Mycenae and other centres in Greece, had lost its expansive force in the years around 1250–1200 BC,[1] the trading vacuum was partially filled by the harbour cities of the Phoenician coast. The lead was taken by Sidon (Saida) from the early tenth century BC, followed shortly afterwards by Tyre (Sur) twenty miles to its south – both benefiting from the long maritime experience of their northern neighbour Byblos.

The Phoenicians possessed abundant wood from the mountains of Lebanon, which they used as fuel for the skilled working of metals and as timber for the building of ships. They were said to have been the first people who ever navigated by observing the stars, travelled beyond sight of land, sailed at night, and undertook voyages in winter-time.[2] In the ninth century BC they established tributary states on the island of Cyprus. The art of that island fuses Phoenician influences with those of the past Mycenaean age, in which Cyprus had already served as an important distribution centre during the fourteenth century BC. Using Cyprus as a staging point, or employing more direct routes, the Phoenicians moved rapidly into the wider Mycenaean inheritance, and their commercial bases appeared on the coasts of the Aegean islands and as far afield as north Africa. On that coast, Tyre founded its renowned colony Carthage in the late ninth or early eighth century BC. A foundation much more substantial than the usual Phoenician trading-post, Carthage soon asserted its independence from its founders and became the leader of Phoenician power in the western Mediterranean and one of the largest cities in the world.[3]

The activities of the Phoenicians also extended right up to the south coast of France and over to the shores and islands of Spain. Their first Spanish market, designed to keep Greeks away from vital Spanish metals, was on the Balearic island of Ebusus (Ibiza, traditionally founded in 654–653 BC),[4] and their settlement at Gades (Cadiz) gave them access to the gold, silver and copper of Tartessus at the mouth of the River Guadalquivir.[5] Indeed, Tartessus itself may also have come under temporary Phoenician occupation a few years later. On the way to these Spanish outposts, other Phoenician (later Carthaginian) trading-posts were established in the central Mediterranean area, not only on the island of Melita (Malta), but also in Sardinia, where their first settlement was at Nora, founded in the eighth or possibly the ninth century near the southern extremity of the island.[6]

The north and east coasts of Sardinia naturally had close connections with Etruria, and one community on the eastern side of the island, that of the Aesaronenses, even had an Etruscan name.[7] However, it was a Phoenician port established not long afterwards on the west coast of Sardinia, Tharros, which evidently had the closest links of all with the Etruscans. This western shore of the island faces away from Etruria, but it faces towards Spain, where gold came from, and that is why it had such extensive dealings with the Etruscans, who hankered after this metal in exchange for their own copper, iron, tin and agricultural produce. Situated on a peninsula beside a gulf and possessing easy access to fisheries and salt-beds, Tharros was the wealthiest of all the Sardinian cities, and, in particular, its workshops of imported gold, silver and precious stones were apparently the largest in the whole Carthaginian west.[8]

After the Phoenicians and Carthaginians had begun to establish their trading-posts in Sardinia, they planted others in western Sicily as well. The first of these foundations was Motya (Mozia, near Marsala), probably after 700 BC. There were also Phoenician and Carthaginian trading-quarters in Etruria, notably at Punicum (meaning 'Carthaginian'), which was a port of Tarquinii, at Pyrgi a port of Caere, and apparently at Rome.[9] Moreover, the Phoenicians may, much earlier still, have had a commercial foothold on the island of Pithecusae (Ischia) beside the Bay of Naples, before the Greeks arrived there in the early eighth century BC.[10]

Like the Greeks, who predictably denounced them as pirates – just as they denounced the Etruscans as well – the Phoenicians located many of their western trading-stations with a view to the acquisition of metals. The Phoenicians acquired silver in south-eastern Asia Minor, and

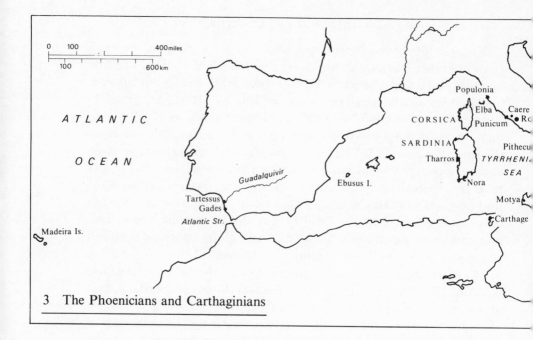

3 The Phoenicians and Carthaginians

copper in Cyprus (which owes its name to the metal, smelted there from the middle of the second millennium BC).[11] Their western outposts were eager for further, nearer supplies of copper, and they needed tin to convert this copper into bronze; but tin, in sufficient quantities, was hard to get. Probably their main source of the metal was northern Spain, but they also obtained it from France and south-west Britain (Cornwall).[12] The Etruscans, too, were eager to have this tin, as well as the silver that the Phoenicians and Carthaginians could acquire for them from Spain. For although they had a certain amount of both metals, it was not enough,[13] and they were always ready for more gold.

Owing to these close contacts between the Phoenicians and the Carthaginians on the one hand and the Etruscans on the other, it is likely that some of the numerous near-eastern objects that made their way to Etruria, and the many near-eastern motifs that in the later eighth and seventh centuries so strikingly and increasingly dominated its art, came to the country, not through Greek intermediaries, but *direct* from Phoenicia or from Phoenician–Carthaginian settlements and outposts in the west. So, perhaps, did the names of some of the Etruscan gods: Sethlans, the patron of metalwork (corresponding to the Greek Hephaestus and Roman Vulcan) recalls the Sidonian name Sethlos,[14] and Fufluns (Dionysus, Bacchus), after whom Populonia (Fufluna or Pupluna) was named, may be etymologically akin to the name of the

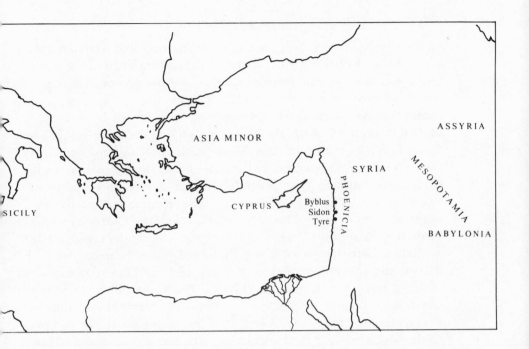

Phoenician town of Byblos – appropriately enough in the latter case, since the Etruscans at first imported wine, and probably olive oil as well, from Phoenicia. The extent to which these and other borrowings from the near east came to Etruria indirectly through Greek inter-mediaries, or directly without any such mediation, is disputed, but at all events a great deal of the Etruscan civilization was derived, in one or other of these two ways, from the Phoenician region.

This assertion is in no way contradicted by the bewilderingly varied character of the near-eastern elements in the Etruscan way of life, for the art and culture that could be seen in the Phoenician cities and markets, and was distributed by them to many far-off destinations, was equally varied. The Phoenicians, at the centre of a huge cultural melting pot, obtained their aesthetic ideas from a great number of different sources and were tireless pickers-up of the customs, methods and arts of surrounding lands. For example, they had learnt the tech-niques of mining metals from Egypt, with which they maintained close contact, and it was from Egypt once again that they had mastered the arts of gold *repoussé* and granulation (the application to the gold surface, while it was hot, of minute spheroidal grains of gold, in rows or zones),[15] which they passed on, once again directly or indirectly, to Etruria – together with some of the gold itself.

Objects normally labelled 'Phoenician', though compounded also of various Syrian, Cypriot, Egyptian, Mesopotamian and Assyrian influences, were already reaching Etruria in the second half of the eighth century BC and became more numerous still around 700. Likewise of near-eastern origin were the great Etruscan mound tombs, consisting of chambers erected on shallow drums and surmounted by a rounded mound (*tumulus*) of earth. The closest parallels to these tombs are to be found in various parts of Asia Minor and adjoining regions,[16] from which the idea found its way to Etruria – partly through contacts with the island of Sardinia, from which the Etruscans apparently learnt how to equip such tomb-chambers with false domes, but partly also, perhaps, from Syria or Phoenicia, without any such Sardinian intermediaries. Within the tombs, objects of varied near-eastern character are found. Ostrich eggs were brought from Egypt to be decorated with designs and attachments and to serve as vessels, and Egyptian varieties of finger-rings, too, some with elliptical bezels, had likewise become common in Etruria before 700 – in this case unmistakably through Phoenician intermediaries. The ivories found in Etruria are also particularly suggestive of the Phoenicians, who brought the material from Asia and west Africa and were famous for their engraving of it, once again characteristically incorporating motifs from various surrounding cultures. The Etruscans imported all these products and perhaps their artists as well, or enough of them to teach Etruscans how to copy or adapt the work for themselves.

In the first half of the seventh century BC they also imported bronze receptacles of a kind that is found at near-eastern and Greek centres. These include tripods, conical stands, and cauldrons with protrusions or handles fashioned into the heads of lions or griffins.[17] These objects, and particularly the cauldrons, were until recently ascribed an origin to the north-east of Asia Minor, but recent research has correctly reassigned their inspiration to northern Syria;[18] the earliest of the tripods made in Etruria (*c*. 675) show certain north Syrian features hitherto unrecorded in Greek markets or cities.[19] Moreover, in Etruria, as elsewhere, such objects were also imitated locally, not only in bronze but in terracotta or unpurified clay. Their impressiveness suggests that they were intended for sanctuaries, or for the mansions and tombs of potentates and the new rich.

Other Phoenician imports into Greek and Etruscan lands included glasswork (a speciality of the Phoenicians) and near-eastern and Babylonian textiles[20] (often imbued with the famous Phoenician purple dye of the *murex*), although, unsurprisingly, no trace of such fabrics has survived.[21] An even stronger influence was exerted on Etruria by the

Phoenician and Syrian alphabet. In its homeland, this had already developed to full maturity before the end of the second millennium BC, serving a literature that has not survived. This form of writing, the greatest of the Levant's legacies to the world, then spread, with the addition of vowel-signs, to all subsequent users of alphabetic scripts – in the first place to the Greeks, and then to the Etruscans and Romans; in this context, the role of the Greeks as intermediaries with Etruria is unmistakable.

The abundance and diversity of near-eastern influences upon the art of the Etruscans show that they were remarkably diligent learners, absorbers and borrowers, like the modern Japanese.[22] The art of the Greeks, too, went through an enormously influential 'orientalizing' period from *c*. 700, in succession to the epoch when they had covered their vases with 'Geometric' designs; but the Etruscans were far more uncritical than the Greeks in taking over near-eastern artistic ideas. For one thing, they had no strong artistic tradition or roots of their own: early Etruscan minds and senses were fresh and malleable. Besides, they were temperamentally quite different from the Greeks. The eastern objects that came to them, especially if these displayed an element of exaggerated fantasy, produced a special sort of enthusiastic creative response – just at the time when, owing to the enormous demand for their metals, they had acquired the necessary material resources to indulge their tastes as luxuriantly and extravagantly as they wished. The orientalizing seventh century that ensued in Etruria is sometimes dismissed as a period of transition, as it was in Greece. But if we can manage to avoid looking at the Etruscans through exclusively classical eyes, there is a case, instead, for regarding this epoch of ebullient, effervescent orientalism as their climactic epoch.

The Phoenicians and their western descendants, then, owing to their desire for Etruscan metals, fulfilled a decisive role in the transmission of the near-eastern elements that subsequently played such a vital part in the development of Etruria. As has been suggested, some of these objects and motifs and ideas no doubt came to the country direct from the Phoenician communities of the near east or their western offshoots: but we have reason to believe that many more of these borrowings came through Greek intermediaries, who must now be discussed.

The Greeks in South Italy

The Phoenicians may have had a trading-post or -quarter on the island of Pithecusae (Ischia), off the Bay of Naples, or they may not. What is

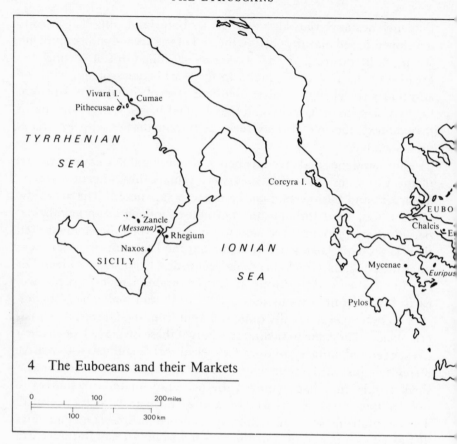

4   The Euboeans and their Markets

certain, however, is that if it existed it was superseded by a Greek
market there, followed by another at Cumae on the mainland opposite.
The businessmen at these markets, eager for the metals belonging to the
Etruscans, not only acquainted them, in the process, with Greek civilization, but also helped to transmit to them many of the near-eastern
cultural elements that have been mentioned in the foregoing pages.

The Greek markets at Pithecusae and Cumae were founded in the
eighth century BC, and it is no coincidence that this was the very time
when the Etruscan villages were uniting into cities – cities which were
able to achieve the co-ordinated organization necessary for arranging
the immensely lucrative, transforming business deals for which their
metals gave them such ample opportunities. Recent excavations have
revealed that pottery from Greek lands had already been present on the
fertile island of Pithecusae in the late fifteenth and/or early fourteenth
century BC during the age of the Mycenaean civilization. These objects

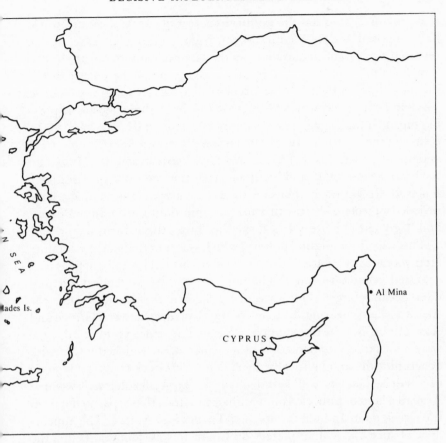

have been found upon the steep, defensible promontory of Monte Vico
above Lacco Ameno (the Roman Heraclium) at the north-western
corner of the island, beside a partially protected bay and a fruitful strip
of soil to which Strabo refers.[23] Moreover, another Mycenaean
trading-post has been detected on the adjoining islet of Vivara, nearer
the mainland, south of Cumae.[24] The Mycenaeans' staging point on the
way to these far-off outposts may well have been the island of Lipara
(Lipari), close to the Sicilian Strait, where similar objects have been
found. So the quest for Etrurian metals was already under way during
the second millennium BC: that was why the Mycenaeans established
themselves on these three islands. Etruria was still far away, even from
Pithecusae and Vivara, but the Mycenaean traders could not establish
markets any nearer owing to harbourless coasts and hostile hinterlands –
though the Etruscans themselves may have founded a complementary
market at Populonia to help deal with their Greek trade.

41

By about 1250–1200 the political centres of the Mycenaean world had collapsed and its Mediterranean trading gradually ceased, to be renewed slowly and tentatively, as the last millennium began, by the Phoenicians – and by the Greeks as well. One of the chief cultural manifestations of the dawning Greek revival was its well-proportioned 'Geometric' pottery, which began to reappear in about 900 BC, displaying meander and zigzag patterns in horizontal bands (to which, in the course of the eighth century, conventionally drawn figure scenes were added). It was at this period that contacts between southern Italy and Sicily on the one hand, and Etruria on the other, began to be tentatively renewed. Recent excavations north of Syracuse, in eastern Sicily, have revealed objects of Etruscan workmanship dating from about 800,[25] and 'Geometric' pottery has turned up in southern Etruria.

This widely circulating pottery, which was imitated in the west until after 700, is constructed of coarse red clay covered by a slip of finer clay coloured yellowish-white.[26] The pots were at first of modest size and later became larger. One category is known as 'Cycladic' after the Aegean islands bearing the name of the Cyclades, between Greece and Asia Minor, but the designation is misleading, since vases of this type were to a large extent made at the centre upon which the Cyclades geographically and politically depended – the Greek trading city-state of Chalcis. Chalcis was situated on the large, fertile, well-wooded Aegean island of Euboea, commanding the strait that separated it from the Greek mainland not far north of Thebes and Athens. The appearance of such Chalcidian pottery on Etruscan soil (followed before the eighth century was over by the appearance of local copies) reflects the special position of Chalcis at this time,[27] and entitles it to a leading place in the development of Etruscan civilization. Its imposing location made it one of the very first of the new Greek cities which became able to resume the Mediterranean trading that had been cut off after the end of the Mycenaean age. Chalcis also controlled a small but very productive agricultural zone, the plain bordering on its maritime neighbour Eretria, which moved onto a new site early in the eighth century BC and was concerned, like Chalcis itself, with western commerce.

Euboean exports extended widely throughout the eastern Mediterranean, offset by the influx of a wealth of near-eastern jewellery, showing novel motifs and techniques of exotic origin. Such exchanges were enormously facilitated by the establishment, in about 825–800, of a marketing- and trading-post (*emporion*) at Al Mina – probably known to the Greeks as Posidion – on the coast of northern Syria at the mouth of the River Orontes.[28] Excavations at Al Mina reveal, as one would expect, that it was in close touch with its commercial neighbours the Phoenicians, both in their own homeland and at its offshoot communities on the island of Cyprus.[29] But it also emerges from the finds that, at least until the last decades of the eighth century BC, the people of Chalcis and Eretria in Euboea (and their dependants in the Cyclades) had a virtual monopoly of the Al Mina trade. They found it enormously profitable because of the gold, silver and pale gold (electrum) they were able to acquire in the area and dispatch to their Greek homelands.

In order to obtain these precious metals from their near-eastern neighbours, the Greeks obviously had to provide other things in exchange – and for these they had to look, and move, to the west. On the western route, therefore, the Eretrians, early in the eighth century BC, planted a trading-station at Corcyra (Corfu) off the coast of north-western Greece, with holdings on the mainland opposite which enabled them to control the strait. But that was scarcely even half-way to their ultimate objective, which was the metallic wealth of Etruria (a resource of particular interest to the Chalcidians, since they themselves were famous as metal-workers; a foundry of *c.* 900 BC has been found at Lefkandi near the city, deriving its copper from the prolific resources of Cyprus). In order, therefore, to achieve access to these Etruscan metals, the Chalcidians set out to establish a market in Italy itself, in the south-west of the country, which was as near to Etruria as they (like the Mycenaeans before them) could get, owing to the hazards of settling any farther up the unwelcoming coast. They were joined in this venture by a smaller number of Eretrians and by some people from Cyme, which is probably not the city of that name in western Asia Minor (Aeolis) but once again a place in Euboea, a little town (or group of villages) that worked metals.[30]

The trading-post these travellers established was on the island of Pithecusae, on the same north-western promontory of Monte Vico where the Mycenaeans had left their goods more than four centuries earlier, and where Phoenicians, too, had possibly established a market in the quite recent past. The Greek post, too, was a trading-centre (*emporion*), of the same kind as Al Mina in Syria, of which the Chalcidians had likewise been the founders – that is to say, Pithecusae was not a fully organized and institutionalized Greek 'colony'. We are not yet in the fully colonial age of the Greeks; that did not begin until about the 730s BC, whereas the cemetery of Pithecusae, beneath its early habitation area, has disclosed Greek material going back to at least 775 or 770.[31]

This material, not unexpectedly, includes both Greek 'Geometric' pots and vases of the eighth-century types associated with Chalcis in Euboea, and local copies also occur (the name of Pithecusae, which was originally that of the Monte Vico settlement rather than the whole island, is related by Pliny the Elder to a Greek word meaning 'jars').[32] One such pot displays an inscription in the Chalcidian form of the Greek alphabet,[33] while another, no less revealingly, shows a picture of a shipwreck – perhaps the earliest 'Geometric' figurative painting that has been found anywhere in Italy, and a testimony to the far-reaching nautical operations involved in the Euboeans' commercial drive. Other finds include objects displaying near-eastern motifs; among them are sealstones of the third quarter of the eighth century BC from the corner of the coast where Syria and Asia Minor meet, and no less than fifty scarabs (beetle-shaped seals or gems) of Egyptian or Egypto-Phoenician design. Some of these objects are local copies, but others are imports – and it is highly probable that these had been brought from that other Euboean-dominated commercial post at Al Mina on the Syrian coast.[34] An amphora which has also been found at Pithecusae is of local fabrication, but bears an inscription in the Aramaic language of Syria.[35]

These discoveries are profoundly relevant to the present book, for there is ample evidence that the island market of Pithecusae was in almost immediate and intensive contact with Etruria, on which it exercised a most powerful formative influence. Greek 'Geometric' vases of this period, displaying Euboean shapes and decorative patterns, are found at a variety of sites in southern Etruria and show the link between that country and Pithecusae in unmistakable fashion. Once more, of these objects some were no doubt imported to Etruria from Pithecusae, but copies were also made at Etruscan centres. The same can be said of scarabs of Egypto-Phoenician type that have likewise come to light in the southern part of Etruria. The correspondence between material found at Pithecusae and Etruscan sites is exact and remarkable.[36] Indeed, without discounting the possibility of some direct contacts between Phoenicia (or its outposts) and Etruria, it seems necessary to conclude that Pithecusae, by means of its Syrian contacts, was the source, or provided the prototypes, of a great many, and perhaps the majority, of the first oriental objects found in the rising Etruria of the eighth century BC.

There is other evidence, too, of the trading links between Etruria and the island market: a piece of iron in its natural state (haematite) which has now been found at the earliest levels of Pithecusae has been proved to originate from the Etruscan island of Elba. The metal had been brought from Elba to be worked at Pithecusae, and remains of the Pithecusan iron-workings – blooms and slag and bellows mouth-pieces – have survived. This, then, more than the fruitfulness of the soil cited by Strabo, was the reason why the trading-station at Pithecusae was founded – to secure the metals, not only iron but copper as well, which the Euboean traders so greatly coveted. Indeed, on that habitation site of the eighth and seventh century at Pithecusae, every building but one, out of those that have hitherto been located, was concerned with the workings of bronze or iron – that is to say, of metals from Etruria.

What tempted the Etruscan leaders to supply these Euboean visitors with iron or copper was, above all else, the prospect of gold in return, as the passion for gold work displayed in Etruria's eighth-century tombs abundantly demonstrates. No doubt, the Etruscans could obtain some gold from the Carthaginians in Sardinia, but not enough for them, and more gold was what the Euboean traders at Pithecusae provided. They, for their part, had first obtained this metal from their other market at Al Mina, which possessed access to the gold mined in a number of near-eastern territories (including the mysterious Biblical Ophir from which the Phoenicians drew their supplies). When the gold had been brought to Pithecusae, it was worked there on the spot; Strabo's word *chryseia*, ascribed to the island as one of its principal assets, refers not, as had been supposed, to gold-mines, which Pithecusae does not possess, but to gold-workings. Indeed, it has been concluded from the excavations that some, and perhaps a good deal, of the splendid gold jewellery of eastern styles that appears in the grandiose Etruscan tombs of the seventh century BC had actually been worked and made at Pithecusae – by Euboean artists and craftsmen, but to Etruscan tastes – before being dispatched to Etruria.[37] The island settlement was an industrial as well as a commercial centre.

Having gained confidence by establishing themselves at Pithecusae, the Euboean Greeks sought an even more effective base for their profitable Etruscan contacts by planting a second such market on the mainland twelve miles away. The settlers came from Pithecusae, and they were once again joined by a small contingent from Cyme in Euboea, who gave the new post its name of Cumae (now Cuma). It can be deduced from the character of the pottery and other objects found on the site that the date of the new enterprise fell between 750 and 725 BC. It is uncertain whether the new Greek traders and craftsmen ousted the natives of the place or let them stay – the lofty, isolated acropolis of Cumae, adjoining a safe beach or even perhaps a sheltered harbour,[38] had been inhabited by a native population since the tenth century BC.

Cumae possessed its own beds of mussels, and it enjoyed excellent facilities for catching large fish. But the new trading-post principally owed its creation, once again, to the Euboeans' interest in Etruscan copper and iron. Ancient suggestions that Greek Cumae was founded before the Etruscan civilization began have therefore to be qualified: the metals of Etruria were already known at the time when the market at Cumae was established, and there were already people in that country, with traditions of their own, who had to be negotiated with by the Greek Cumaeans in order to obtain its metallic wealth. And yet, conversely, it was partly because of Cumae, pursuing on a larger scale the enterprise started at Pithecusae, that the enormously wealthy Etruscan civilization, in the form in which we know it, burst upon the world in the years before and after 700. It was sometimes a two-way traffic: large parade shields in Cumaean graves seem to have come from Etruscan workshops. But Cumae's spectacular Fondo Artiaco tomb (*c.* 730)[39] contained gold work which, although it looks thoroughly Etruscan, may well, like similar gold objects from Pithecusae, have been made on the spot – in this instance, for a local resident, the man who is buried in the grave, but in other cases, and more frequently, for export to Etruria.

So a picture begins to be apparent, not only or precisely of separate Etruscan and Greek communities in Italy (though separate, in many ways, they certainly were), but also of the close interlocking and interaction of the two sets of communities within a single, massive, historical, cultural and economic central Mediterranean unit; that is the scenario emerging persistently from each successive stage of current research.

Next, from *c.* 730–725 onwards, the Greek trading-posts in Italy were followed up by 'colonies', fully organized and institutionalized units set up by settlers from overpopulated city-states of Greece to form regular expatriate city-states on their own account, engaging in trade and possessing tracts of agricultural land. By the agency of these colonies, the links of the Greeks with Etruria, and their commercial and cultural penetration of that country, were further intensified and deepened. This was mainly, as before, because of the Greek desire for metals. How the traffic was actually conducted we do not know. Either the colonists themselves went on journeys to the Etruscan centres, or they provided facilities for passing Greek traders on their way through from the eastern Mediterranean to do so, enabling them to stop and revictual *en route*. There were evidently Etruscan traders in more southerly Italian

5   Greek South Italy and Sicily (Magna Graecia)

waters, too, since they were denounced as pirates in a Homeric hymn that may be of eighth-century date, as well as by early local colonists and subsequent Greek settlers on the island of Lipara (the modern Lipari).[40]

Pithecusae was not converted into a colony, because it had become largely superseded by Cumae (and was evacuated for a time, like the rest of the island, after an eruption, probably at the end of the sixth century BC). But Cumae itself became one of the earliest and

47

most powerful of the new colonial city-states. It enjoyed highly fertile volcanic soil, which encouraged a flourishing grain trade. It may also have been the place that inaugurated Italy's cultivation of the olive and vine and taught both these essential skills to Etruria.[41] Moreover, traders from Cumae seem to have given the Etruscans their alphabet.

Many other Greek colonies, too, were rapidly founded, not only in southern Italy but in Sicily as well. At first the lead was still taken by the city that had initiated the original trading-posts, Chalcis in Euboea. It was Chalcidians who established colonies on the Straits of Messina between Italy and Sicily which were so vital for the transmission of goods from Etruria – at Naxos and Zancle (Messana, now Messina) on the Sicilian bank of the straits, and at Rhegium (Reggio Calabria) on the Italian side.[42]

Bypassing the Phoenicians and their western outposts, Chalcis had established a stranglehold over this Etruscan trade, thus making itself, one may be sure, unpopular with a number of other Greek city-states. One way, however, in which these might side-track Chalcidian dominance was by developing an overland route northwards to Etruria, and this was the achievement of Sybaris (near Sibari) in south-eastern Italy, a colony founded in the 720s BC by Peloponnesians for the exploitation of a rich and fertile plain at the mouth of a river. At the height of its luxurious career – which brought the epithet 'sybaritic' into existence – Sybaris controlled no less than twenty subject cities. It was described by the Greek historian Timaeus as having been a friend of the Etruscans,[43] and archaeological discoveries in the area confirm this association, as well as indicating the land route that was needed to maintain it. This route passed by way of Posidonia (Paestum) at the mouth of the River Sele (Silarus) – a settlement which was described as partly Etruscanized,[44] and served to protect Etruscan communications with Sybaris. The Sybarites also had close connections with the eastern Mediterranean, and particularly with the great city of Miletus (now Yeniköy) in Ionia (Asia Minor),[45] a country which made an enormous contribution not only to Greek but also to Etruscan culture. Milesian woollen goods – though there is obviously no trace of them today – played a large part in the Sybarites' trade with Etruria, which was so deeply interested in fabrics and was amply equipped with the minerals (alum and cinnabar) needed for dyeing them.[46] But when Sybaris was destroyed by its neighbour and rival Croton (Crotone) in 510 BC, the Etruscans, whose relations with Campania were also weakening at this very time, had to seek their commercial openings elsewhere.

Corinth, the Eastern Greeks and Athens

These connections described so far only formed a small portion of the Etruscans' complex relations with the Greek world, for not long after the foundation of the first Greek colonies in Italy, a large part of the task of transmitting external cultural influences to Etruria in exchange for metals was already being undertaken by a new Greek colonial power which had come to the fore in mainland Greece itself. This was Corinth, which, like the earliest Etruscan city-states themselves, was formed out of the union of a group of villages in the eighth century BC. The unique location of the place on its isthmus enabled it to face both east and west and gave it a remarkable and long-lasting opportunity to dominate Mediterranean trade and culture – and, in the process, to reinforce powerfully the Greek and near-eastern impact on the cities of Etruria. In particular, in c. 734, the Corinthians established a colony at Syracuse in eastern Sicily which subsequently became the richest of all Greek cities, exploiting its agricultural hinterland with unprecedented skill and serving as a valuable intermediary for Corinth's Etruscan trade.

Corinthian Syracuse was able to keep outside the sphere of influence of the Euboean colonies in Sicily, and before long Corinth itself was able to gain a decisive advantage over them and their founders, Chalcis and Eretria. For in the later years of the eighth century BC, those two cities fell out with one another and clashed in a long and bitter war for the fertile plain that lay between them, the first Greek war of which we have any real knowledge.[47] After each had received support from a number of allies the Eretrians were finally defeated, but Chalcis, too, found itself exhausted by the war, and was thenceforward doomed, not only in its own region but in the west as well, to be eclipsed by the rapidly increasing prosperity and expansion of Corinth. There had long been trouble between Corinth and Eretria, whose colony at Corcyra the Corinthians had displaced (c. 733), but Corinth and Chalcis had hitherto co-operated, and even now this co-operation did not entirely cease.[48] Yet it was the trading might of Corinth that thenceforward prevailed. On the Syrian coast, for example, Al Mina, from the beginning of the seventh century onwards, handled Corinthian pottery to the exclusion of the previously dominant Euboean (Chalcidian) wares. It was the same story in Italian waters, where the impact of Corinth on the Etruscans was enormous – for the Corinthians were establishing their commanding Mediterranean position at precisely the time when Etruria was opening up widely to external contacts, and for nearly a

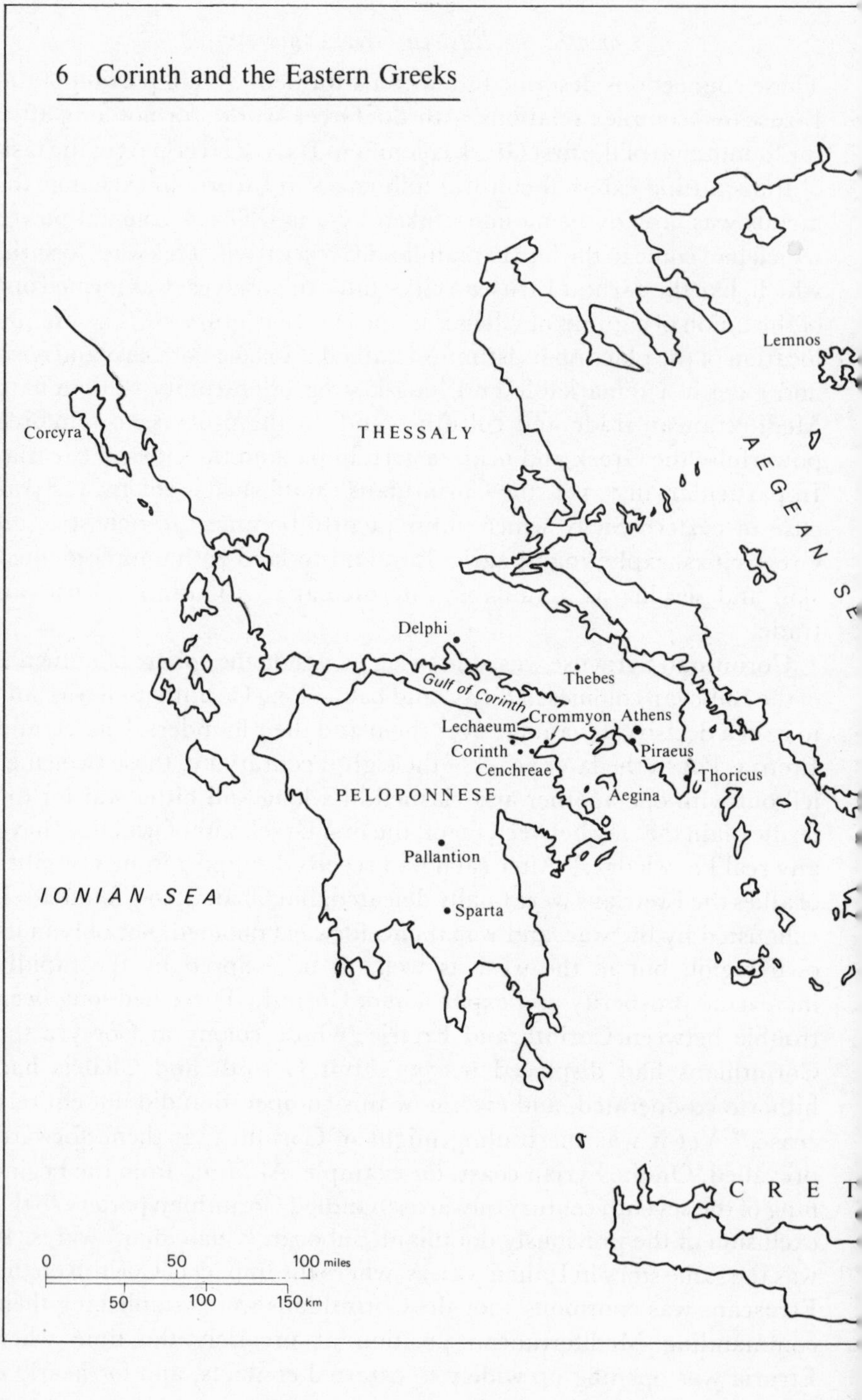

6   Corinth and the Eastern Greeks

Lemnos

Corcyra

THESSALY

AEGEAN SEA

Delphi

Gulf of Corinth

Thebes

Crommyon   Athens

Lechaeum

Corinth

Cenchreae

Piraeus

Aegina

Thoricus

PELOPONNESE

IONIAN SEA

Pallantion

Sparta

CRET

| 0 | 50 | 100 miles |
| 50 | 100 | 150 km |

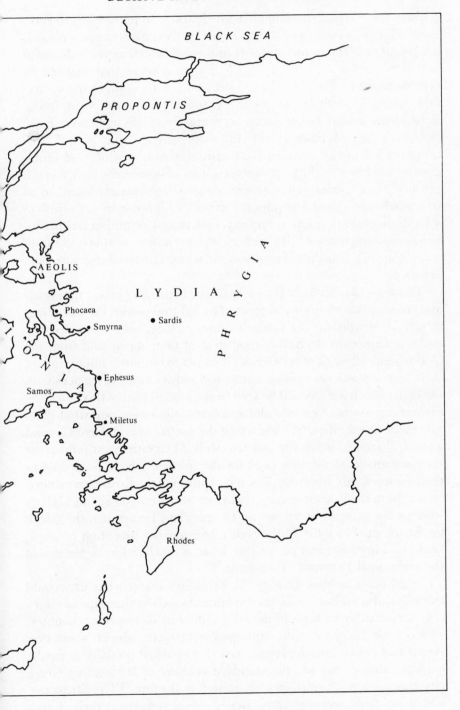

BLACK SEA

PROPONTIS

AEOLIS

L Y D I A

PHRYGIA

Phocaea

Smyrna

Sardis

IONIA

Ephesus

Samos

Miletus

Rhodes

century they virtually monopolized its market. In particular, an enormous effect was exerted on Etruscan art by Corinthian artists, notably the painters of the numerous pots and vases which Corinth designed and fashioned and sent out to Etruria, in a drive that reached its crescendo after *c.* 625. The Etruscans particularly enjoyed the bizarre and fantastic designs on some of these pots, and soon imitations of them were being made on a massive scale in Etruria itself, laying the foundations of the Etruscan orientalizing style.[49] The imitators learnt the art from the Corinthian local visitors and immigrants, and Pliny the Elder preserves a story of how, in the later seventh century BC, a Corinthian aristocrat named Demaratus (described as father of Rome's King Tarquinius Priscus), emigrating from Corinth to Tarquinii to escape political tyranny, took three Corinthian artists with him as his companions.[50] Demaratus thus became a notable example of a new class of trading noblemen, around whom clustered craftsmen and artists.

The designs of some of the early Corinthian vases reveal that trade and colonization were now supported by fighting power. For one thing, we are shown pictures of Corinth's famous long, low, lean warships, and the Etruscans derived a good deal of their naval skill from the Corinthians (though other Greek cities played a part), improving on their own already developing native techniques and experiences with the help of such aid. As will be seen in the second part of this book, the earliest city-states of Etruria all had ports of their own, and what Plato said of the Greek cities, 'We live round the sea like ants and frogs around a pond,'[51] applied to the Etruscans as well. Their cities were famous for their command of the seas (and for the 'piracy' which, according to their enemies, this involved). The naval power of the Etruscans reached its height in the years immediately before and after 600 BC, and Italy's western sea came to be known as Tyrrhenian (Tyrsenian), the Greek for Etruscan. Pliny the Elder even attributes the invention of ships' beaks to a mythological personage, Pisaeus, declared to be the son of the archetypal Etruscan, Tyrrhenus.[52]

In all this maritime activity the Etruscans learnt what they could from Corinth, and so it was also on land. As well as warships Corinthian vases display pictures of the fully armed infantrymen or 'hoplites' (from '*hopla*', 'arms'), who, equipped with heavy shield, short iron sword and spear, and deploying in a close-packed phalanx in battle, became, after *c.* 700 BC, the standard soldiery of the leading Greek city-states – with Corinth once again well to the fore.[53] The Etruscans, whose soldiers were already better equipped than their Greek counterparts because of the readier accessibility of copper, followed their lead. The existence of warriors wearing partially hoplite arms and armour is demonstrated by finds in the Tomb of the Warrior at Tarquinii of about 730 BC,[54] and the first complete bronze armour of which we are aware, apparently imported from Etruria, appeared at Rome in about 650. Vase-paintings from about the same date confirm the completion of the evolutionary process, and from that time onwards many artistic representations of Etruscan warriors indicate that the Greek hoplite panoply had now become standard. But the social backgrounds of the two sets of armies remained somewhat different. The Corinthian and other Greek soldiers had been products of a rising middle-class, whereas a similar class, though not altogether lacking, did not achieve anything like the same strength in Etruria. It is probably right, therefore, to conclude that the earliest Etruscan hoplites were not so much relatively independent citizens as groups of clients and dependants of the wealthy upper class.

During the same period of Corinthian influence, the Etruscans were also affected by the cultural trends of the southernmost Greek islands,[55] but subsequently most of all – following and overlapping the Corinthian phase – by Greeks of western Asia Minor, the Ionians. Ionia, in the central region of that coast, had been settled by refugees from the Greek mainland, convulsed by invasions and other disturbances, at the beginning of the first millennium BC or a little earlier. After 800, their villages amalgamated into cities like those of mainland Greece and Etruria. The civilization of these Ionian city-states developed precociously and splendidly, incorporating not only survivals from earlier civilizations of Asia Minor such as that of the Hittites but also some of the cultural advances that had subsequently been achieved in the same area by the kingdoms of Phrygia and Lydia.[56] In due course these various influences were transmitted by the Ionians, first of all across the Aegean, and then to the Greek and Etruscan west. Miletus, the greatest of their colonizers, had commercial contacts with Etruria through Sybaris. Another Ionian centre which exerted a similar impact was the island city-state of Samos, from which extensive finds, especially metalwork in which its craftsmen specialized, have turned up (and were imitated) in various Etruscan centres,[57] while Etruscan pottery has also been found at Samos.[58] In 638 a Samian sea-captain, Colaeus, piloted his ship to the farthest confines of the Mediterranean and even right out into the Atlantic beyond, returning with a fabulously rich cargo.[59]

This adventure excited another Ionian city, Phocaea; its people had

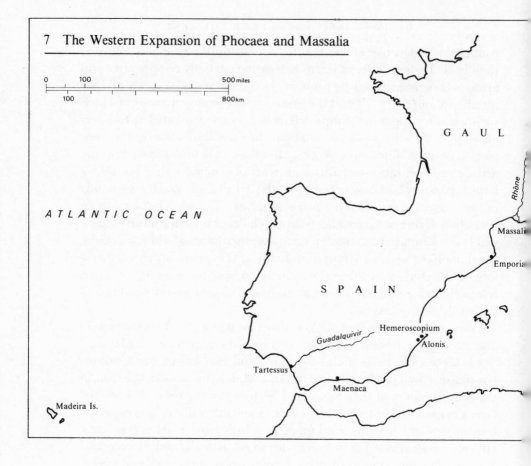

poor arable land but a fine harbour, and proved to be intrepid mariners. They sailed in swift war-galleys, resistant to the winds, called
penteconters or 'fiftiers' because of the number of oars they carried;[60]
and they now proceeded to take the lead on their own account in
western Mediterranean trade and colonization,[61] thus gaining, in their
turn, a reputation for 'piracy', like the Phoenicians and Etruscans[62]
before them. Before long, the shores of southern France and eastern
Spain were thickly studded with Phocaean colonies. The greatest of
these settlements was Massalia (the Roman Massilia, now Marseille),
established in about 600 and soon famous for its olives and vines – but
above all it was known for its harbour, judiciously located near the delta
of the Rhône, which was the major communication route of the
country.[63] Massalia not only became a great rival of Carthage, but
inevitably came into close contact with Etruria. Still more significant,
from the point of view of the Etruscans, was another Phocaean colony

54

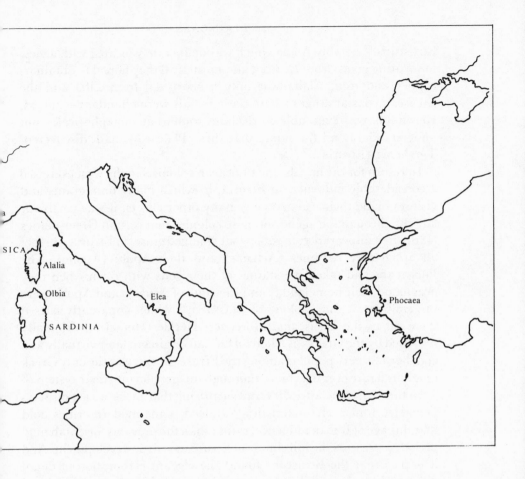

SICA
• Alalia
• Olbia
Elea
SARDINIA

• Phocaea

even nearer at hand; this was Alalia (now Aleria) in eastern Corsica, just opposite the shores of Etruria itself. A decade or two after the foundation of Alalia in about 560, Phocaeans and other Ionians began to reach the central Mediterranean area in ever greater numbers when the capture of their homeland by the Persians brought floods of refugees to the west.

The Phocaeans were in the western Mediterranean for metals:[64] Massalia was primarily founded in order to acquire them, especially tin, from France, Spain and Britain. This ambition was one of the factors that led eventually to a direct clash with the Etruscans, whose pottery, found in large quantities in northern Spain and southern France from the early seventh century onwards,[65] shows a keen attempt to compete with Massalia. Nevertheless, Massalians and other Phocaean colonists may also have sometimes been the carriers of these Etruscan wares. Some of the colonies clearly co-operated with the

Etruscans,[66] notably Alalia which was deliberately located with a view to securing goods from Etruria; and most of all they hoped to obtain its copper and iron. Alalia was only a short sail from Elba and the Etruscan coastal ranges where these metals were abundant – indeed, Herodotus was even able to declare, somewhat metaphorically but understandably all the same, that these Phocaeans had 'discovered' Tyrrhenia (Etruria).[67]

In return for the metals, the Phocaean colonists in the west exercised a considerable influence on Etruria, to which many immigrants and visitors made their way. Among many other effects, it was partly, or largely, through the agency of these colonies that certain Greek deities made their appearance, in somewhat changed guise, in Etruria – first of all apparently Artumes (Artemis) and then Apulu (Apollo). The Phocaeans had taken the statues of their gods with them when they evacuated their homeland,[68] and the cults of Artemis and Apollo were pre-eminent at their colony of Massalia,[69] which apparently passed them on to the Etruscans. Moreover, Herkle (Heracles), originally regarded by the Greeks as a hero of human origin but later virtually as a god, became very popular among the Etruscans and was the only Greek religious figure ever to achieve thorough integration into their system.[70]

In these circumstances, it is not surprising that Etruscan art displays pervasive Ionian characteristics.[71] Indeed, some modern critics hold that this age of Ionian influence, rather than the previous 'orientalizing' period, represents the full climax of Etruscan artistic development. And it is true that the Etruscans found the elegant elaboration of detail displayed by these skilful Ionian artists, and the soft modelling and curvilinear rhythms which they favoured, very much to their taste; they were captivated by the Ionians' sharp eye for what was essential and by their eager desire to grasp the immediate, momentary impression.

When, therefore, in the mid-sixth century BC, the Etruscans began to apply Greek terracotta plaques and other decorations to the exteriors of the temples which by now they were actively building, their models, though altered in the process, were taken straight from the Ionian cities.[72] In the same way, once again after modifications, the themes and styles of the tomb-painting at Tarquinii of the same epoch were adapted from Ionian vases, and Ionian, once again, were the proto-types of the earliest gems cut in Etruria, shortly before 500.[73] The Ionian artists who flocked into Italy – especially after the Persian conquest of their country – found it easier to establish their homes and workshops in Etruria than in the Greek colonies, which already had traditions of their own and did not want to change them. Almost at once local Etruscans learnt the techniques of these visitors, so that it is often hard to tell whether a piece of work is by an Ionian or an Etruscan hand.

Just as Ionians came to Etruria, so, conversely, an Etruscan city-state may have had a trading-post or base on the north Aegean island of Lemnos. A grave-stone that has appeared on the island, probably belonging to the early sixth century BC, displays not only a relief of a warrior not unlike certain reliefs of northern Etruria, but a long inscription[74] which, although indecipherable, is written in letters, and a language, that are unmistakably close to those of the Etruscans.[75] Moreover, there was an ancient tradition that the people from Thessaly (northern Greece) who were regarded as the original Greek settlers on Lemnos should be identified with 'Tyrsenians' or Tyrrhenians (Etruscans). Thucydides spoke of people on the adjacent mainland, too, who were 'of Tyrrhenian race'.[76] He strangely added that this was the race that once lived in Lemnos – and Athens! But this last link had been invented by his source, since it was convenient to Athenian politicians, providing them, on the fictitious grounds of relationship, with a plausible way of legitimizing their forcible seizure of the island in c. 500 and its colonization fifty years later.

These cryptic pieces of evidence have been frequently employed to justify the view that the Etruscans were immigrants from the east. But it seems more likely that the Lemnian inscription testifies to exactly the opposite state of affairs – namely the presence on the island of a trading-post or market belonging to one of the Etruscan states,[77] analogous to the Greek *emporia* at Pithecusae and Cumae and to Greek and Phoenician commercial quarters in Etruria itself. Lemnos was a suitable place for such a post – indeed, it had already been employed as such by the Mycenaeans, on whose inscriptions its name appears[78] – for it was a metal-working centre, and for that reason it shared the Greek name 'Aethalia' ('smoky') with Elba. Pliny the Elder classified a monumental tomb on the island of Lemnos with the grave of Lars Porsenna at Clusium.[79] Moreover, the Lemnians, just like (other) Etruscans, had a reputation as pirates; women from Brauron (near Athens) were said to have been raped by Tyrrhenian pirates at Lemnos, and it is tempting to regard the Tyrrhenian pirates who kidnapped the god Dionysus in the seventh Homeric hymn[80] as Lemnian seamen. The central Aegean was no doubt a leading region of Etruscan trade or 'piracy', and indeed Etruscan artefacts are increasingly coming to light in the area,[81] where they were probably distributed by the traders of Lemnos. Such objects still remain rare, because the Greeks principally sought Etruscan raw materials in exchange for their finished products;[81] however, Etruscan pots and bronzes are found as far afield as southern Russia.[82] Here again Lemnos was particularly well suited to act as an intermediary, since it lay close to the approaches to the Black Sea and the settlements the Ionians had planted on them.

In the course of the sixth century the relative positions of the various Greek states in the Aegean area, and in the western Mediterranean region as well, underwent a radical change, affecting Etruria and many other lands. This was because of the rise of Athens, whose role at Lemnos we have seen. Originally, Athens, like Corinth and the cities of Ionia and Etruria, had been brought into existence by the amalgamation of its constituent villages. In the ninth and eighth centuries, the place had produced fine 'Geometric' pottery, and then late in the seventh, as the Athenian people's unique artistic talents began to develop further, their superb 'black-figure' vases, with the figures standing out darkly on warm orange-red Attic clay, began to exert a powerful challenge. After 600 BC, during a time of rapid political and economic evolution at Athens, these 'black-figure' wares became a serious threat to the Corinthian export trade,[83] completely superseding it in Etruria and elsewhere by 550. Twenty years ago, a list was made of no less than 1,560 Attic 'black-figure' vases found in Etruria, and now there are many more.[84]

Towards the end of the 'black-figure' period, the more virile and humanistic Attic manner had replaced the Ionian style as a fashion for the Mediterranean world. First, between c. 540 and c. 520, came a brief transitional period at Athens when the Ionian style, in sculpture and painting alike, came under strong influence from the rising Attic style and the two intermingled. This, in Etruria, was the period of the wonderful life-size terracotta statues of Veii and Caere, in which the Etruscan talent for absorbing and renovating complex external influences appeared at its best, challenged by the joint impact of the Ionian and Attic spirits. But then came a curious change in the cultural relationship between Athens and Etruria. There followed, in Greece, the absolute pre-eminence of the famous classical Attic style, the style of the 'red-figure' vases, starting in c. 530, continuing throughout the fifth century BC, and producing a series of masterpieces, as Athenian artists were also doing in other media. Yet at this very time of cultural triumphs, there is also a marked weakening in the entire Greco-Etruscan cultural nexus. True, it can be seen that the Athenians had a certain respect for Etruscan art, not so much from the fact that the occasional Etruscan bronze has turned up in Athens,[85] but because at least three sixth-century Attic vase shapes are of Etruscan origin.[86]

Conversely, too, Athenian 'red-figure' pottery continued to pour into Etruria, and the Etruscans attempted a large number of imitations of Athenian vases. Yet they are mostly of mediocre provincial quality and display no sympathetic inspiration. For Etruscan interest in the great Athenian artistic achievement of this epoch remained very sparse; in sharp contrast to the passionate enthusiasm that earlier movements of Greek art had inspired in the hearts of the Etruscans, the golden age of Athenian art hardly influenced them at all. As we have seen, they had admired the exotic fantasies and bizarre subtleties of the orientalizing Corinthian phase of Greek art, and then the delicate elaborations of the Ionian manner as well; these styles had made their own art what it was. But the mature, classical, art of the fifth-century Athenians kindled no spark in their spirit. It found, certainly, a good many second- or third-rate Etruscan imitators. Yet their serious artists reacted to the new manner by just ignoring it, continuing instead to display variants of the styles that had fascinated them previously.

This sudden guillotine that descended on Etruscan art, weakening the best Greek links just when Greece was attaining its highest achievements, is a curious phenomenon which has been variously explained. Some have suggested that the succession of political and military failures by the Etruscan city-states during the later sixth and fifth centuries BC was responsible; and it is true that the leading Greek states of Italy, Cumae and Syracuse, were perilously alienated, that Samnites and Gauls then eliminated Etruscan influence in north and south respectively, and that these setbacks meant that the Etruscans now had less money to invest in their art. But there was also a psychological factor that cannot be ignored: much as the Etruscans had loved the more fantastic and stylized manners of earlier Greek art, the ripe, classical, naturalistic humanism which now pervaded Athenian culture and art left them quite cold.[87] This is a matter which now needs discussion, if a correct balance between their Greekness and un-Greekness – the two contradictory, complementary keynotes to their achievement – is to be struck.

CHAPTER 4

THE 'ORIGIN' OF THE ETRUSCANS

Un-Greek Features

So the marriage of Greek and Etruscan minds and tastes continued as long, and only as long, as Greek art favoured either the uninhibited fantasy of Etruscan orientalizing design or the element of decorative stylization which still remained apparent in the delicately flowing products of Ionia. Feeling free to draw upon Greek art in eclectic and arbitrary fashion, as and when they wished, the Etruscans revelled in its more bizarre and early aspects. On these they lavished a coarse vigour all their own, and at times a vulgar gaiety too, which saw no merit in classical moderation. They themselves, moreover, had a special taste for the grisly and eerie, and their portrayals of horrific gladiatorial sports and other scenes of slaughter show that brutality and cruelty did not come amiss to them. They were temperamentally different from the Greeks, and in consequence had different needs and customs.

We saw that the humanism of classical Athenian taste, as displayed on the Attic 'red-figure' vases, evoked little response from leading Etruscan artists. One overriding reason why the Etruscans were not humanists was that their religion told them that humankind was wholly under the thumb of the divine power. They felt an uncompromising certainty, with none of the loopholes permitted by Greek speculation, about the shattering totality of this power, and the nonentity, surrender and abdication of human beings before its might. And, in consequence, they showed no interest in the idealization of the male and female forms that was one of the greatest achievements of fifth-century Athenian art. Nor did they see the slightest point in the naturalist forms in which the Athenians clothed this idealism. Thus Greek nudity, for example, had no appeal for them.[1]

Far from requiring the delineation of the human body, whether idealized or realistic, the Etruscans' own conception of art involved highly formalized, dream-like patterns, and, sometimes, grotesquely caricatured exaggerations and elongations. The balances and pro-portions, the clear frameworks and logical formal principles that were the essential features of Attic classicism held no interest for them at all.[2] The Etruscans would have preferred Picasso to Raphael; and it is in no way surprising that a number of twentieth-century painters and sculptors (notably Giacometti, Marino Marini, and Modigliani, who origi-nated from Etruria) have drawn more inspiration from Etruscan than from Athenian art.

Not only were the temperaments and character of the Etruscans quite dissimilar from those of the Greeks, but many features of their geographical situation and environment were equally different – including the various materials from which they made their buildings and works of art. Their whole history and background were no less divergent. Pre-urban Italy, from which they inherited so much, was not at all the same as prehistoric Greece, and stress has been laid already on foreign ingredients from the un-Greek near east. Certainly it is true, and remarkable, that the Etruscan absorption of Greek art was a 'cultural invasion of a scale, intensity and duration for which no parallel readily comes to mind'. Yet it has also been said, perhaps provocatively but with some justification, that 'in spite of its habitual connections with Greece, the art of Etruria is really very little Greek'.[3]

Some of the dissimilarities, as we have seen, came to a head when Greece, under Athenian leadership, turned resolutely to humanistic and classical ideals. Yet, on closer inspection, the rift was not new. For in spite of the Etruscans' manifold borrowings from the Greeks, there had also been very marked differences all along. Examples are easy to find: for one thing, Etruscan temples deviated from those of the Greeks. The most typical features of the Etruscan shrines – their lofty pedestals, their strong frontal emphasis, their roomy porches designed to enable the people to come and meet the gods, their closed back walls, their uncolonnaded side-walls, their reliance on wood as the constructional material – were all near-eastern rather than Greek. The shapes of the Etruscan tombs, too, in all their variety and emphasis, stand out at once as conspicuously un-Greek,[4] and so do all the decorative wall-paintings in these tombs – indeed, the Greeks did not have any such burial-places of their own to paint. Etruscan statuary, too, was different, for it was exclusively funerary; moreover, it was not of stone, but of terracotta – and even when stone was used (in the few places where it was available) the results, despite the obvious employment of

61

Greek models, look disconcertingly unlike them. In the field of ceramics, for reasons we have noted, the Etruscans did not derive much artistic benefit from the influx of the 'red-figure' vases that dominated Greece; but long before that, the most characteristic form of Etruscan pottery, the black *bucchero*, with its designs often imitated from metalwork, had looked very un-Greek.[5]

Small Etruscan bronze figures are often instantly recognizable as Etruscan, and not Greek, because of the characteristic poses and the emphatic gestures and facial expressions they display, revealing those unclassical distortions which the Etruscans enjoyed. A well-known Athenian, Critias (d. 403 BC), singled out their household bronzes and metal objects as exceptionally good,[6] and he could have added that they had always been markedly distinctive. So was their gold jewellery, for which they were able to use imported gold with a lavishness that must have shocked the Greeks – or moved them to envy. It is true that much of this jewellery makes use of Greek motifs, but even if sometimes worked at Greek markets such as Pithecusae and Cumae, it does so in a highly original fashion and with new technical skill. Filigree techniques are brought to an unheard-of degree of refinement, and granulation is employed to render figures in outline or silhouette in a way never encountered in Greece.

Evidently, then, to dismiss the culture of the Etruscans as a mere provincial variant of Greek civilization is wrong (and the same is true of other artistic peoples on the Hellenic fringe, notably the Scythians, Thracians, Celts and Iberians). The art-historian Bernard Berenson, under the heading 'The Originality of Incompetence', declared that if anything good could be found in Etruscan art this was only insofar as it was Greek.[7] That ignores the extent to which the Etruscans, for all their apparently docile borrowings, persistently maintained a markedly independent approach, attempting and achieving something altogether different. Uninterested in the classical principles of propriety, they went all out to capture the instant, unrepeatable visual flash. What they wanted – and this had been true of some of the Ionian artists they admired – was the spirit of the moment rather than any permanent philosophical truth. In a world of overpowering divine forces, what had gone before or would come after did not interest their artists. Instead, they expressed the world of their own imaginings by inconsequential improvisations, characterized by force and fantasy and charm.

Take the two figures reclining on the famous sarcophagus from Caere: many recognizable Greek artistic formulae are called into play.

Yet this framework is remoulded, and its concepts adjusted, to provide a wholly non-Hellenic atmosphere of restlessness and disturbance – an atmosphere which is deliberately enigmatic and equivocal, alien from the harmonious equilibrium sought by Attic contemporaries. Moreover, the Etruscans themselves must have looked extremely un-Greek. About their ethnic components it would be unwise to generalize too sweepingly, first because such artistic representations of their features as have come down to us contain conventional and therefore unrealistic elements, and secondly because – like most other peoples, ancient and modern – they must have comprised a most complicated racial mixture. But they dressed entirely differently from the Greeks, and more ostentatiously; experts have noted a number of basic contrasts. Among these, the Etruscans' more varied and extensive employment of mantles and hats is a conspicuous example, and another is provided by the special forms of their shoes and sandals – for which they were famous, exporting their footwear far and wide.[8]

Etruscan women in particular were readily distinguishable by the long, un-Greek braids of hair that extended down their backs; but that was only one, and the least, of the striking differences between Etruscan and Greek women. All the ancient library sources agree, and wall-paintings and reliefs of banquets and other festivities abundantly confirm, that the women of Etruria, or at least the more important of them, enjoyed far greater freedom than their Greek counterparts. The stupendous jewellery with which they were loaded conveys the message; and so does the portrayal of Etruscan husbands and wives side by side in egalitarian fashion. Stories of the prominent role played by legendary Etruscan ladies such as the forceful Tanaquil (Tancvil), alleged to have spurred on her husband Tarquinius Priscus to the kingship of Rome in the late seventh century BC, authentically reflect the power that such women possessed. Tanaquil was also said to possess a knowledge of divination – an Etruscan speciality – and she was credited with an expert acquaintance with medicine,[9] a profession in which Etruscan men, too, were known to excel.[10] There were Greek males who knew both divination and medicine, but very few Greek females indeed. The elevated position of women in Etruria went back, in some degree, to the social conditions of pre-urban Italy, when it is possible to deduce from burials that women were not, in general, regarded as inferior to men, though not perhaps quite equal to the most glamorous of the warriors.

But this difference in women's status was only one aspect of a far wider divergence between the social evolution of the Etruscans and that of the Greeks. Apart from their more liberal attitude to women, it was usually the Etruscans who were the less progressive of the two. In particular, their class structure never achieved, or attempted, the same approach towards democracy. Thus, as we have seen, what may roughly be described as the middle groups of society always remained relatively weak, in contrast to the powerful part played by such groups in Greece.

The religious devotion of the Etruscans, too, which was one of their most conspicuous characteristics, assumed very un-Greek forms. Not only did they have a far stronger sense of their subordination to the will of the heavenly powers, but, in contrast to Greece, their religion was uniquely centred on sacred writings, supposedly emanating from supernatural sources. However – and this also was by no means Greek – in spite of all this careful definition, they remained vague about the number, attributes, sex and appearance of the gods and goddesses, since they did not articulately visualize them in human shape.[11] At the same time they had a very real and terrifying sense of these deities' presence in their temples, and they were convinced of continual divine intervention. As the Roman writer Seneca the Younger significantly pointed out, whereas rational explanations for lightning were put forward elsewhere, the Etruscans inevitably preferred a supernatural and miraculous one.[12] They retained the sort of magical, mystical, illogical interpretation of phenomena which the Greeks had early begun to discard in favour of a gradually strengthening rationalism that remained meaningless to the Etruscans. Like romantics and Freudians of later ages, the Etruscans believed that there are mighty spheres of activity in which reason does not and cannot penetrate at all. This was why they placed such enormous and peculiar emphasis on divination, erecting it into a complex and cumulative system founded on the recorded precedents of centuries and the teachings of successive generations of experts.[13]

The Etruscans also maintained a very un-Greek attitude to the after-life. Most Greeks, in their various ways, believed in a life after death, but their views included nothing to compare with the intense conviction of the Etruscans that death was not a real break in continuity at all but a prolongation and perpetuation of life on earth. That is the motivation behind the innumerable, varied, and grandiose tombs which contribute so enormously to our knowledge of the beliefs, customs and arts of the Etruscans. These graves, once again, create a non-Greek impression. For one thing, there is the immense wealthiness of the treasures deposited in their chambers, more akin to the practice of the ancient Egyptians than the Greeks, and then there are all their brilliantly colourful wall-paintings, especially at Tarquinii. Yet the tombs have caused a serious misconception to arise in modern times: namely that the Etruscans stood in dread of what would happen to them after death. This, for example, was the view of the writer-politician Gabriele D'Annunzio. He based his opinion partly on the numerical abundance of Etruscan tombs, compared with the apparent scarcity of dwellings for the living. But it was a mistaken conclusion, because there are only more of the former than the latter because more have survived destruction. Nor is the belief that Etruscans feared the after-life confirmed by the horrific infernal demons depicted on the walls of their graves: this was a late development, and was not in the least characteristic of the great age of Etruria that is the subject of this book. On the contrary, the remarkable wall-paintings of the tombs of this golden epoch habitually depict occasions of lively festivity. There are pictures, for example, of numerous banquets, and many scenes of the music and dancing to which the Etruscans were so addicted – no feast was complete without them.[14] The unrestrained gaiety of these paintings, all metaphors for a happy activity after death, startled George Dennis when he saw them before writing his admirable *Cities and Cemeteries of Etruria* (1848): 'Can these scenes of feasting and merriment,' he asked, 'this dancing, this piping, this sporting, appertain to a tomb? ... On the inner wall, one fellow is playing the fife, though not moderating his saltatory action a whit on that account.'[15]

D. H. Lawrence, on the other hand, in his *Etruscan Places* (1952), exulted in these uninhibited manifestations, which he contrasted with what he regarded as the bleakness of Etruria's eventual conquerors, the Romans. He might equally have drawn a contrast with the Greeks, because there is also something strangely un-Greek about these Etruscan celebrations. True, the Greeks also liked music and dancing; yet they felt nothing like the Etruscans' urgent need to project the pleasant things of life into the after-life by surrounding the dead person's remains by these painted representations of festive happiness.

Moreover, the paintings in the Etruscan tombs depict not only banquets and the like but also mythological scenes, and these, too, deviate considerably from Greek tradition.[16] They regularly reproduce what profess to be Greek myths, but it soon becomes very clear indeed that the myths have become strangely altered, distorted and Etruscanized in the process.[17] And the same applies strongly to the incised designs on Etruscan mirrors.

But the biggest and most conspicuous contrast with Greece is provided by the Etruscan language. No literature in this language has come down to us, and whether there was much, or any, early literature at all is disputed. About ten thousand Etruscan inscriptions have been found, but only four or five of them are of more than a hundred words long; and of the rest, scarcely a dozen contain more than thirty. The earliest examples date from the late seventh century BC, but only a very few of any real historical value are earlier than about 400.[18] Some partially Etruscanized regions of Italy, outside Etruria itself, seem to have been more or less bilingual at this time, notably Latium and Rome and the Faliscan territory to its north. In all these areas, Etruscan, spoken by the rulers, had to contend with quite different Italic tongues spoken by the rest of the population. But in Etruria itself, except in certain fringe areas such as that of Clusium (Chiusi), Etruscan (in one dialect or another) was evidently the language of virtually the entire people of Etruria.

Since the Etruscan letters were adapted from a Greek alphabet learnt from Cumae, it is at least possible to read them. It seems that the language must have bristled with clicks and hisses, and we are able to tell, in approximate terms, what many of the inscriptions are about. The two longest, comprising 1,190 and 300 words respectively, are a liturgical text and a prescription for funeral ceremonies; and most of the others contain repetitious religious formulas, epitaphs, or enumerations of proper names and titles. Because this measure of understanding has been attained, specialists tend to resent the suggestion that we cannot translate Etruscan or that it is a mystery.[19] Yet the fact does remain that the structure of the language is, so far, not recognized or understood – that is to say, despite the advances achieved by various methods of interpretation,[20] we still do not even know the linguistic group to which it belongs, or the other languages, if any, which may be related to it. On this last subject, the most fanciful and improbable relationships have been suggested over the years: for example, links with Irish, Finnish, Albanian and Basque have been claimed, but in all cases with insufficient justification.

What can now be regarded as fairly clear, however, is that Etruscan, despite the admission over the centuries of Italian (including Latin) and then Greek loan-words and names, was not one of the Indo-European family to which those tongues belonged. According to the definition preferred by Massimo Pallottino, Etruscan was a language 'whose origin is basically non-Indo-European, or at least whose structure cannot be described in terms that are typical of the Indo-European languages'.[21] When, therefore, Dionysius of Halicarnassus, writing in

8   The Languages of Ancient Italy

0   50   100 miles
50   150 km

RAETIAN

Venetic

LIGURIAN

ETRUSCAN

Tiber

Faliscan

Rome
Latin

Italic

Messapian

SARDINIAN

Note:
Hatched areas = speakers of non-Indo-European languages
White areas = speakers of Indo-European languages

SICAN

Sicel

the first century BC, declared that Etruscan was unlike all known languages,[22] he may well have been right. This linguistic isolation helped to make the Etruscans feel that they stood apart and formed a separate unit or nation – which they called *Rasna* or *Rasnea*, transliterated by the Greeks as Rasenna.[23]

The extreme difference of their language from Greek or Latin struck not only Dionysius but numerous other people in the ancient world as well. Why it should also surprise many modern students is not so clear;

67

such a reaction suggests that we are seeing the matter too exclusively through Greek and Roman eyes. It is important to realize that at the time of Etruscan power and wealth, about half of Italy spoke Indo-European languages, but the other half did not. Roughly speaking, the speakers of Indo-European tongues lived to the east and south of the River Tiber,[24] and the people of non-Indo-European speech dwelt to its west and north. Although language and race do not invariably coincide, this configuration suggests that, at some prehistoric date which remains disputed, perhaps in small groups over many centuries, the speakers of the Indo-European languages came westwards from across the Adriatic and pushed farther into Italy itself – as far as the Tiber, where the process stopped.

On the other side of the Tiber, Etruscan was not the only non-Indo-European language in Italy which remained fundamentally untouched by this westward Indo-European expansion: other such tongues apparently included Ligurian in the whole of the north-west, perhaps north Picene on the Adriatic above Ancona, and Raetian on the north-eastern fringe, as well as Sardinian on the island of that name, and probably Sican in west Sicily. We do not know the basic features or relationships of any of these languages, any more than we know those of Etruscan. But it seems fairly certain that they were all non-Indo-European, and that some of them at least were established in Italy before the Indo-European tongues began to be spoken in the country.[25] (In Greece, likewise, various pre-Greek, non-Indo-European languages continued to be spoken in historical times.)

Where did the non-Indo-European tongues of Italy come from? It is quite impossible to say, and this applies to Etruscan as much as to any of the others. This is one of a number of aspects of the Etruscan civilization of which we know little or nothing. Another relates to the separate question of where not Etruscan, but the Etruscans, came from. But before pursuing the question further it is necessary to consider, briefly, the reasons for our far-reaching ignorance about this people and their fundamental institutions.

Greek and Roman Alienation

One principal obstacle to finding out more about the ancient Etruscans comes from the very inadequate and dismissive 'press' they received from the Greeks, and from the Romans as well. The causes behind this inadequacy are fairly clear: the Etruscans were alien to the Greeks and Romans and they were enemies. The Etruscans called themselves a separate people because their customs were in many ways so extremely different, and in particular because their language was utterly foreign. Besides, over a very long period, from the later sixth century BC onwards, they were enemies of leading Greek states such as Cumae (despite previous fruitful contacts) and Syracuse (a struggle immortalized by the Greek poet Pindar).[26] And then the city-states of the Etruscans, one by one, or group by group, were locked in deathly combat with the Romans.[27] Moreover it was, for the most part, only at the climactic moments of such clashes that the Etruscans were mentioned by the Greeks and Romans at all – when an Etruscan city-state impinged, that is to say, on their affairs, and fought against them. The result is that the Etruscans appear in classical literature in an entirely secondary capacity, and in a pejorative light. This attitude, reflected perfectly in T. B. Macaulay's *Lays of Ancient Rome*, cannot begin to do them justice, or explain the enormous influence they exercised on the life and development of the Mediterranean region.

Those are the two factors – alienness and downright hostility – which made it impossible for balanced accounts of the Etruscans to emerge from the literatures of Greece and Rome. This highly critical, unhelpful Greco-Roman tradition is already apparent as early as certain of the so-called Homeric hymns, written from the eighth century BC onwards, and then, to a very marked degree, in the writings of Greek historians of the fifth and fourth centuries. And the same theme of Etruscan foreignness and nastiness is retained and elaborated, with vigour and insistence, by writers of Roman times.[28]

There are three main points of attack: the Etruscans are cruel, they are 'pirates', and they live too luxuriously and extravagantly. That they were cruel, on occasion if not by habit, is evidently true. Their wall-paintings suggest it, and there is an ugly tale of the Caeritans' brutality to prisoners after the battle of Alalia – though parallels from Greek and Roman history would not be too hard to find. No doubt the Etruscans were also sometimes treacherous as well, as the Greek tradition insists; but people always say this about their enemies. Likewise, the charge that they were 'pirates' merely meant that they were enterprising merchants who challenged the Greeks for the command of the seas.[29] The same accusation was levelled against other enterprising maritime communities, notably the Phoenicians and the Phocaean Greeks. No doubt there was a measure of truth in all such charges, because these adventurous seamen were presumably not too meticulous in their observance of human rights. But the declamation of the term 'pirates' as a general parrot-cry or label merely serves to obscure historical enquiry.

   The other repeated accusation, that the Etruscans were too luxurious
and loose-living, is very understandable, because the leading classes of
their city-states evidently enjoyed a material standard of living higher
than that of the vast majority of Greeks (except possibly at a few rich
centres such as Syracuse) and superior to that of any Romans whatever
until centuries after Etruscan power and wealth had declined. However, the charge habitually goes into further detail, declaring that the
Etruscans were degenerate and liked orgies, that their women were
prostitutes and their slaves too smartly dressed. As to the orgies, the
paintings at Tarquinii leave us in no doubt that the Etruscans enjoyed
excitingly animated parties – though pornographic representations,
while not wholly absent, occur more rarely than in Greek or Roman art.
   With regard to Etruscan women, the Roman comic dramatist
Plautus wrote about their whoredoms in a play.[30] They certainly lived
more free and open lives than their counterparts in Greece and Rome,
where people were shocked, in particular, to see Etruscan women
reclining at dinner-parties alongside the men, a practice familiar to
Etruria long before the Greeks and Romans considered it possible.[31] As
to Etruscan female morals, since the general standard of living among
the dominant class was so high and convivial, no doubt there was some
laxity, and perhaps a good deal of it. But surely the great historian
Theodor Mommsen was adhering somewhat too closely and prejudi-
cially to his Greek and Latin forerunners when he pronounced that the
depravity of Etruscan women 'in no way fell short of the worst immoral-
ity of Byzantium and France'.[32]
   As to the slaves dressing too well, the same criticism was made of all
Etruscans, not forgetting their beautiful shoes. Indeed, Etruscan men
were generally much too soft, said the hostile Greeks and Romans: it
was complained that they even took costly and artistic objects with
them on military campaigns.[33] And they were accused of being fat –
with justice, no doubt, in some cases, to judge from the heavy figures
who recline on the sarcophagi of Volaterrae and Clusium, with every
appearance of self-satisfaction. But they belong to the time of the
decadence, and even if the high living of early times, too, had already
resulted in cases of overweight – for all we know, it may have been
respected as a visible sign of prosperity – the vast political, military and
economic strength of the early Etruscan city-states does not leave the
impression of a universally obese nation.
   The Romans loved to say that the cause of the Etruscans' political
and military collapse had been their excessive luxury. This, of course,
was a well-known ethical theme, which countless moralists (including

innumerable modern novelists and film-writers) have detected as a reason for the downfall of the Roman Empire as well. But orgies had nothing to do with the decline and fall of Rome (indeed, they were much rarer in declining Rome than in earlier and more successful days), and they were irrelevant to the eclipse of the Etruscan city-states as well. The whole theme was just another of the Etruscan topics on which the Greeks and Romans were ignorant.

Did They Come from Asia Minor?

With regard to the Etruscans' earliest origins, as in respect of their eventual decline, Greek and Roman interpretations and diagnoses are likely to be ill-informed and fallacious and to leave us in the dark. However, the problem of these origins is one that cannot be avoided, since it is apparently of wider general interest than any other aspect of this people – despite the protests of many modern experts who prefer not to ask where they came from but rather to concentrate on the factors that contributed to their formation as an important nation in Italy.[34]

Where the Etruscan language came from we cannot say, but in any case where the Etruscans themselves came from need not necessarily be the same question, since language and race need not coincide (witness America, where millions who are not of Anglo-Saxon origin nevertheless speak English as their first language). The starting-point in this enquiry about their beginnings is a famous passage in the Greek *History* of Herodotus, written in the fifth century BC. Herodotus quotes a story giving their place of origin as Lydia in western Asia Minor. Lydia was not Greek, but was well known to the Greeks because it lay immediately behind their own cities on the Ionian coast, which were subordinated, in the sixth century BC, to the Lydian King Croesus until Lydia and Ionia alike fell to the Persians in the second half of the same century. In giving his account of the origin of the Etruscans, Herodotus twice remarks that he is quoting Lydian sources. On their authority, he tells of what was done by a legendary King of Lydia, Atys, the son of Manes, when he was confronted by a prolonged and desperate national famine:

Atys divided the population into two groups and determined by drawing lots which should emigrate and which should remain at home. He appointed himself to rule the section whose lot determined that they should remain, and his son Tyrrhenus to command the emigrants. The lots were drawn, and one section went down to the coast at Smyrna, where they built vessels, put aboard all their household effects and sailed in search of a livelihood elsewhere. They passed many countries and finally reached Umbria in the north of Italy, where they settled and still live to this day. Here they changed their name from Lydians to Tyrrhenians after the king's son Tyrrhenus, who was their leader.[35]

How much historical truth does this story contain? It seems necessary to reject it altogether and completely. But whoever does this must of course show how and why the fictitious tale came to be invented and told.

In the first place, it has to be emphasized that the Greeks (like the Romans after them) were passionately fond of allotting imaginary origins to peoples and cities. As a result, there was a whole host of literary works entitled *Origins*, as the historian Polybius pointed out in the second century BC, remarking on the extraordinary degree of popularity that this type of work still enjoyed.[36] Every Greek city-state had a founder or founders invented for it, drawn from the infinite range of mythology or pre-history. This 'foundation industry' showed no interest in what had actually happened, or in archaeological evidence; it was simply part of a learned, traditional, literary form of entertainment and controversy that lasted for centuries.

In particular, there was a whole industry devoted to finding such origins for non-Greek peoples and places on the fringes of the Greek world. For these communities the Greeks, practising a sort of mythological imperialism, very often invented legendary Greek founders. This practice was applied with remarkable thoroughness to those coastal towns of Etruria with which the Greeks were in particularly close contact, notably Etruscan Caere, Pyrgi, Telamon, and Orbetello (Cosa) as well as semi-Etruscan Pisae, and some other Etruscan towns in the interior, for instance Cortona – even though not one of these places preserves the slightest archaeological trace of having such Greek beginnings, and in no case is such an origin probable.

Insight into this whole myth-making process, and understanding of the 'principles' that dictated it, can be obtained by studying Rome, which was at one time a quasi-Etruscan 'fringe' city itself, and is, for obvious reasons, the place to which the largest amount of story-telling was subsequently devoted. Indeed, no less than twenty-five separate or partially separate Greek accounts of the origin of Rome can be recorded, and every one of them is quite unrelated to historical fact.[37] But these versions of Rome's beginnings are of value all the same, because they throw light on one of the principal methods favoured by such foundation-seekers. For many of the tales in question are based on supposed etymological links between the names of Roman sites or persons and suggestively similar names occurring in other lands. The analogies are fortuitous and quite without sound foundation, but the search for them was fashionable and indeed predominant in antiquarian circles.

At Rome, this method is illustrated by the story of the legendary Greek King Evander in the magnificent and moving eighth book of Virgil's *Aeneid*. Evander is seen to be ruling over Rome's Palatine Hill before Rome itself was ever founded. Why is he there? Merely because a minor deity named Evander was worshipped at a place named Pallantion in Arcadia in the Peloponnese, and its name seemed, quite wrongly, to bear a significant resemblance to 'Palatine' – or, according to a variant theory of the same futile calibre, because 'Palatine' resembled the name attributed to Evander's mythical grandfather, which was 'Pallas'.[38] And then, for good measure, Evander is made to establish the Roman festival of the Lupercalia, believed to have been derived from *lupus*, the Latin for 'wolf'; this act was ascribed to him because, in his original Greek homeland, his name was linked with the worship of Pan 'Lycaeus' – an epithet conjecturally associated with *lukos*, the Greek word for wolf.[39] Furthermore, Evander (Euandros) means 'strong man' in Greek, and Rome (Rhome) means 'strength' in the same language. These bogus etymological explanations for Roman and national origins are very far indeed from exceptional. On the contrary, they were multiplied universally and applied to any number of cities and peoples.

In the case of one of the accounts of Rome, a refinement was added. The Trojan hero Aeneas, who found Evander on the site of the city, had from an early date played a large part in Etruscan mythology, and his cult had then moved on to Rome, where his story became one of the rival tales explaining its beginnings. At a much later date, this version of Rome's foundation proved particularly fashionable among the Greeks, for they apprehended the non-Greek character of the city, and did not, this time, want to 'annex' its origins, because it had in historical times (from the third century BC onwards) emerged as an enemy of the Greeks. It seemed desirable, therefore, to make sure that speculations about the city's 'origin' reflected this situation. To attribute the 'origins' of places to heroes who had figured in Homeric accounts of the Trojan War was particularly customary, and in the case of most communities, therefore, warriors on the Greek side were selected; but in view of Rome's historic alienness and hostility to the Greeks they preferred, in this instance, to fasten upon a founder who had fought against them in that conflict, one of the Trojans – among whom Aeneas was particularly eligible, since he had for so long played a part in the religious tradition of Rome.

Now the Etruscans attracted especial interest among those engaged in the pursuit of origin-hunting. And it did not seem to be enough to ascribe mythical origins to their individual cities: their separateness and distinctiveness as a nation, speaking a single alien language, also seemed to cry out for some sort of explanation.[40] Yet when we look into the explanation that was fabricated by Herodotus' informants, we find not only an overall account that directly contradicted those proposed for the individual cities, but the very same unmistakable, wholly fallacious procedures that were applied to the Romans and so many others. First, the explanation is based on the same kind of preposterous etymological 'links'. In particular, a connection had evidently been invented between the Tyrrhenians (Etruscans) and a town in Lydia called Tyrrha – a place associated with the name of King Gyges, who virtually founded the Lydian national state in the seventh century BC. There is no true connection at all between the Tyrrhenians and Tyrrha, but by ancient standards of etymological deduction these names looked quite close enough for a link to be erroneously assumed – and that is what evidently happened.[41] This, then, is the source of the story heard by Herodotus, indicating that the Etruscans came from Lydia.

Moreover, this invention was facilitated by a second fabricated analogy of the same type which brought into the picture a group of persons known as the Tyrrhi. They, too, were believed to have come to Italy from the east, and indeed ultimately from Asia Minor. The name of the Tyrrhi was preserved in the town of Tyrrheion (or Thyrium) in Acarnania in north-western Greece, where some of them had supposedly stopped *en route* for Italy. They called themselves 'Dardanians', that is to say claimed descent from the legendary King Dardanus of Troy, or rather, more generally, from peoples in that region of north-western Asia Minor from which they believed they had originally came. Their subsequent presence in Italy is mirrored in the legendary figure of Tyrrhus, whom Virgil depicts as a shepherd of Latinus, the King of the Latins, just south of Etruria.[42] These Tyrrhians or people from Tyrrhium had no ethnic or etymological connection with the Tyrrhenians (Etruscans), but it was very easy indeed, and all too likely, for the two names to become confused and erroneously identified.[43]

A second reason why the Greeks and others were ready enough to suppose that the Etruscans had come from Lydia was that the Lydians, although foreigners, could be fitted all too easily into the Greek mythological framework. For in the century before Herodotus they had been the first foreign people to be regarded as Hellenized, under the leadership of Croesus – described by Herodotus at great length[44] – who had reduced the Ionian Greeks to subjugation (before the Persians did the same) so that they became dependants of his kingdom. And myth, as so often, was made to follow history, since it was declared that the Greek mythological personage Tantalus had once reigned in Lydia, and that another even more eminent Greek hero, Heracles, had once resided there.

Thirdly, the Lydians had been enemies of the Greeks – a hostility which (together with their Greek connections) fitted them excellently to be regarded as the forebears of the Etruscans, hostile yet partially Hellenized like themselves. Furthermore, there was a special reason why the Lydians might have told Herodotus, or his source, of their claim to have originated and founded other peoples. For the historian's contemporary, Xanthus, was a Lydian who wrote (in Greek) offering the most sweeping claims imaginable of this very kind, declaring even that the first man on earth (Manes) had been a Lydian, that his descendants had reigned there long before the time of Heracles, and that not only Tantalus but the founders of other towns in Asia were also Lydians.[45] Xanthus had given Lydia the reputation of a founder of foreign communities on the most sweeping scale. Dionysius of Halicarnassus informs us that Xanthus did not believe the story that the Etruscans, too, were of Lydian origin.[46] But it was he who had helped greatly to create the atmosphere which brought such stories so abundantly into being, so that it only needed an alleged etymological resemblance or two to touch them off. And that is how Lydia's claim to have founded Etruria was first put forward – probably in the earlier sixth century BC, when both peoples were at their height.[47]

Although at least four genealogies, all different and contradictory, were attributed to Tyrrhenus, the leader of the fictitious immigrants, phil-Hellenic Etruscans swallowed the story of their Lydian origins eagerly and were still referring to it many centuries later. Etruscan businessmen visiting Asia Minor also remained happy to claim such ingratiating Lydian connections:[48] it even proved possible to associate the Lydian monarch Atys of Herodotus' story with a mythical King of Alba Longa of the same name – and a link with Atia, the mother of Augustus, was also convenient.

It must be noted, and is too often forgotten, that Herodotus, as befitted such a deeply intuitive historian, did not necessarily accept the tale as true. What he said, and he said it twice, was that he had learnt the story from the Lydians. As if to reinforce his own willingness to disown it he elsewhere offered a different version of Etruscan origins altogether (ascribing them instead to Phocaean Greeks).[49] This caution now seems justifiable, for when the matter is looked at in the light of our present knowledge of the Lydian civilization, the alleged Etruscan connection with that country is unimpressive. True, there are some resemblances between their two cultures. This is what one would in any case expect, since artistic and cultural influences from every part of the near east flooded into the Etruscan world from Al Mina and eastern Greece, including the coasts and adjacent islands of Ionia, among which it is obvious that Lydian influences must have played some part. For example, there were musical links: the Etruscan double pipe, almost a national instrument, was supposed to come from Lydia – though its neighbour Phrygia was mentioned as an alternative source.[50] Dice, which are often found in the tombs of wealthy Etruscan women, were said by Herodotus to have been invented by Lydians. And the women of both countries, he heard, were equally engaged in prostitution. But as previously suggested that is merely the sort of story that arises when women enjoy freedom – and in any case Herodotus may only have picked it up as part of a malicious tradition of the Ionians about their Lydian oppressors.

Grave-mounds, too, appear in Lydia as well as Etruria, but Lydia is only one of several countries of Asia Minor in which they occur, and there is nothing specifically Lydian about them.[51] Then again the name of the mythological Etruscan hero Tarchon seems to echo the name of an Asian god Tarku, but he, too, was not especially Lydian – nor was the rest of Etruscan religion. A single Lydian dedicated a single Etruscan cup (Pactyes at Graviscae, the port of Tarquinii)[52] – but so did many other foreigners from other countries. Most significant of all, the structural relationship of the Etruscan language with that of the Lydians (which survived for many centuries) was either non-existent or at most very tenuous indeed.[53]

To sum up, then, the analogies between the two peoples amount to a diminutive total in comparison with the enormous debts owed by Etruscan life, art and civilization to other near-eastern lands, especially Syria and Phoenicia. If the Etruscans had really come from Lydia, which had a distinctive and elaborate culture, the failure on their part to retain any appreciable portion of that heritage would indeed be hard to understand. Why, among their many demonstrable near-eastern borrowings, would they not have brought with them or imported more, many more, specifically Lydian customs and objects, not to speak of the language? These points were made by Dionysius of Halicarnassus, who observed: 'I do not believe that the Tyrrhenians (Etruscans) were a colony of the Lydians. For they do not use the same language as the latter, nor can it be alleged that, though they no longer speak a similar tongue, they nevertheless still retain some other indications of their mother country. For they neither worship the same gods as the Lydians nor make use of similar laws or institutions.'[54] Dionysius was something of an expert on the Etruscans, on whom he promised a separate monograph,[55] and, although his dislike of them encouraged him to deny them a pedigree, this contradiction of the story quoted by Herodotus must be given some weight.

Herodotus' tale of Lydian origins raises another major difficulty too. Whereas the Etruscan civilization as we know it started in the eighth century BC under the explosive impact of Greek and near-eastern influence, the historian's source, to judge from the genealogical framework he attaches to the story, ascribes the supposed migration of Tyrrhenus from Lydia to Italy to a period some five centuries earlier – in about 1250 BC, at about the time when the Trojan War was supposed to have taken place, preceding the decline or disintegration of the Mycenaean civilization.[56] Indeed, according to some versions, the Etruscans had arrived in Italy earlier still, since Virgil, for example, imagines them well established in the country by the time of the arrival of Aeneas, in flight from conquered Troy.

In connection with this chronological pattern, much interest has been aroused by the appearance, in Egyptian records, of wandering, plundering 'northerners coming from all lands', often described nowadays as 'sea-peoples'. These marauders, indicated as TRSW (?TWRWS), SHKLSH and SHRDN, who attacked the Egyptian coastline in about 1200 BC have been tentatively identified with Tyrsenians (Tyrrhenians), Sicels (east Sicilians) and Sardinians respectively; and the *Tariusha* on a text of the thirteenth century BC emanating from the Hittite kingdom that ruled most of Asia Minor at that time have been equated with the Tyrsenians once again. But it remains impossible to accept these identifications with any confidence.[57] Moreover, even if they were correct, the appearance of sea-going 'Etruscans' off the Egyptian seacoast or in Asia Minor during the thirteenth century BC does nothing to explain why and how their urban civilization in Italy only became prominent in the eighth. A gap of time representing 'stages on the journey' is too tenuous an explanation to seem convincing when the gap is as long as five centuries.[58]

But should we nevertheless utilize the Herodotean account, despite the curious loss of this half-millennium, and for all its weaknesses, as valid evidence for *some* large-scale immigration from the east into Etruria (not necessarily yet of 'Etruscans', and not necessarily from Lydia) soon after the supposed epoch of the Trojan War, during the later centuries of the second millennium BC? Were the Etruscans, as we know them hundreds of years later, descended from people who had moved together into Etruria from some near-eastern land at that much earlier date? There are certain points which, at first sight, might seem to favour such a conclusion. For there was, despite continuities, a very substantial cultural break in Etruria and central Italy at the turn of the second millennium, during the transitional period spanning what are described as the Bronze and Iron Ages. There were new burial customs, a great advance in metallurgy, and a whole new way of life (and the changes may even be dimly reflected in Etruscan traditions that a new era had begun in the eleventh, tenth or ninth century BC).[59] True, to think of the Etruscans as the earlier inhabitants driven into Etruria at this time by new 'Iron Age' invaders from the east is implausible, since survivors of this type are habitually driven into the poorer areas and not permitted by their pursuers to settle in regions of outstanding fertility such as Etruria. It has alternatively been suggested, however, that Herodotus' alleged migrants into Etruria were themselves, as his source suggested, invaders *en masse* from the east (if not actually from Lydia) who had brought about this shift in the central Italian cultural pattern – migrants who had crossed the Adriatic, had made contact with the metal trade on Italy's Adriatic coast-line (where it had flourished primarily until then), and then had moved westwards to exploit the even larger supplies of metals in Etruria. There was, we have seen, a cultural break in the country at this time, yet it is notoriously unwise to deduce physical migration from such a break. Furthermore, it is very hard indeed to believe that the efficient organization required for such a vast operation, involving both mass movement and subsequent settlement, can have existed at that date, especially among people whose culture was still not very highly advanced. Even the armada ascribed by Homer to the (more advanced) Greeks who sailed off to the Trojan War is too large to be credible,[60] and they did not settle.

There is also another reason to doubt whether Etruria can have been occupied by immigrants from the east towards the end of the second millennium BC. For a large element in the culture of Italy and Etruria during the centuries before and after 1000 BC has a central European rather than an east European appearance. In other words these features, it has been argued, may have arrived in Etruria at about that

9   Burial Customs in Pre-Urban Italy

Note:
Hatched areas = regions where inhumation prevailed
White areas = regions where cremation prevailed

time, not from the east, across the Ionian (Adriatic) Sea, but from the north across the Alps. This must be true, in particular, of the introduction of cremation tombs (in contrast to the inhumation rite which had previously been universal). In these tombs the ashes were contained in cinerary urns arranged in cemeteries known as urnfields,[61] of which the Italian examples present an unmistakable analogy with the urnfields of the Danubian area that have given their name to a whole great second millennium 'urnfield' culture,[62] based on the control of vital commodities

79

such as copper (which these central Europeans were experts at working) and salt. The cremation tombs of Etruria seem to reflect the influence of this civilization.

These northern elements in central Italian life weaken still further the belief that there was a mass migration into Etruria from the east in the last centuries of the second millennium BC. Do they, however, suggest that there was a mass migration from the north, across the Alps, as well or instead? Once again, this is scarcely likely. There is the usual peril of deducing ethnic movements from customs, and the further difficulty of envisaging such a mass operation. And, thirdly, although cremation in urnfields prevailed across the Alps, it is by no means certain that this was the route by which the practice reached Italy, owing to the disconcerting fact that it seems to have spread through the peninsula from south to north.[63] Nor, in conclusion, can anything be deduced from the statement of ancient writers that the Raetians of the north-eastern Alps were of Etruscan origin;[64] for this statement is apparently based on an alleged resemblance between the two languages, which would be no argument for immigration, since language and race do not, as we know, always coincide. This claim in any case seems quite insubstantial; both tongues appeared to the Greeks and Romans very foreign, and that was enough to prompt them to the facile comparison.

In conclusion, then, there is no clear evidence for a mass migration into Etruria just before or after the end of the second millennium BC, either from the east or from the north. But in any case, leaving that question aside, should the people who lived in Etruria at that time already be described as 'Etruscans'? Perhaps the point is without much substance, like an attempt, for example, to define when the British started to be British, or the Americans American, or the French French.[65] However, if the question has to be considered, there are arguments on both sides. In favour of already using the term 'Etruscans' at that early period is the turning-point of customs and culture which, as we have seen, had marked its commencement. Against doing so is the fact that there was an equally (or more) decisive turning-point a quarter of a millennium later, in c. 750–700.[66] This second transformation comprised a whole series of more or less simultaneous economic, social, cultural and political explosions – including, once again, a burial change, involving (except in parts of northern Etruria) a fairly general reversion to inhumation.

Once again, it must be asked if these are changes that require a single massive immigration to explain them. And the answer, once again, is that they do not, for they are all thoroughly accounted for by the successive or simultaneous trading-contacts with the outside world – so eager to acquire Etruscan metals – that were described in the last chapter: contacts with Pithecusae and Cumae and other south Italian centres; with the Phoenicians and all the near-eastern cultures whose products they channelled; with Corinth and Ionia and Athens. The immediate, remarkable progress of the newly urbanized Etruscan city-states is fully explained by these external contacts, and the metals which invited them, without the need to assume any single mass movement of population.[67]

Another favourite theory, among those who see the difficulties in a single mass immigration but still want to cling to a single immigration of some kind or other, envisages the arrival by land or sea, again once and for all, of an intrepid, invading élite – a small ruling group, a few thousand or a few hundred strong, who took over the country by ruthless determined action, like the Normans in Sicily and England or the Spaniards of Cortes in Montezuma's Mexico. To such enterprises, it is suggested, the logistic objection should not be regarded as insuperable. It is certainly tempting to apply some such formula to places like Clusium, where a subject population belonging to another race (the Camertes Umbri) continued to exist under Etruscan domination. But elsewhere in Etruria the Etruscan language became practically universal, and it is hard to imagine that a comparatively minute ruling group could have brought about this result, any more than the Normans or Spaniards did. Besides, Normans and Spaniards took over unitary going concerns and existing administrations which could be bent to their purposes, whereas these hypothetical Etruscans would have entered a totally divided and far less advanced country filled with geographical obstacles. It is impossible to entertain the idea of a single, neat, intrepid operation.

The Products of Many Movements

There is nothing, therefore, to suggest that the Etruscans came into their country by any single movement, either in c. 1250–1000 or in c. 750–700. Must we therefore accept the view put forward by Dionysius of Halicarnassus that they never came into Etruria at all – that they had been there forever and were indigenous? After his denunciation of the theory of immigration from Lydia, he concludes: 'Indeed, those probably come nearest to the truth who maintain that the Etruscan nation migrated from nowhere else, but was native to the country.'

For all his knowledge of the Etruscans, Dionysius' motive is suspect, because what he wanted to do was to deny them the fashionable Greek-style pedigree which an external origin would have permitted them.[68] Nevertheless, he has been supported by modern followers who see the Etruscans as indigenous remnants of communities that had once inhabited the entire Mediterranean basin. One difficulty about this theory has already been mentioned: peoples submerged by invaders do not remain in such fertile lands. But there is also another major difficulty. To envisage the whole Etruscan civilization as an entirely static, leftover, archaism of this kind requires the supposition of a hermetically sealed community over a period of many troubled centuries – a supposition that does not make sense, besides clashing with the fact of Etruscan energy and activity and ebullience. The various stages of the later second and early first millennium BC must have been filled with every kind of disturbance and upheaval. This our archaeological evidence reveals clearly, showing much destruction by the hand of man and by fire – and such fragments of literary information as we possess present the same picture and fill it out a little. But the archaeological and literary evidence alike is both fragmentary and fortuitous, and leaves us with a strong suspicion that it only shows us the top of the iceberg: the convulsions were surely a hundred times more numerous than we know anything about – inside Etruria and in other parts of Italy as well, and even in other countries that were in touch with them and impinged on them.

These convulsions must inevitably have involved a very large number of separate displacements and movements of population at different times, from one part of Etruria to another and from outside the country to within its borders and the reverse. There was no single migration by a small group, but many: the correct picture is one of almost continuous, widespread movements by such groups, displaced or prompted to migrate by the convulsions of those successive centuries.[69] These convulsions comprised both the infiltration and diffusion, peaceful or otherwise, of repeated shiploads by sea, and the purposeful or hopeful roaming of little isolated bodies by land.[70] In terms of race, there was no doubt profound, incessant mixture and cross-fertilization right from the very beginnings, and when the archaeologists report that the peoples of Italy, in the early first millennium BC, are shown by their artefacts to have formed ethnic mixtures, this (although involving a dangerous argument from material objects to racial distinctions) is totally unsurprising. The same situation existed in Greece, with its 'many tribes and pockets of settlement and culture'.[71]

In anticipation of fuller discussions in the chapters to come, the small groups whose movements made up the historic Etruria may perhaps be divided roughly into several categories. Movements inside Etruria itself can be listed as follows:

1 The amalgamation of groups of adjacent villages into the Etruscan cities and city-states of the future must have caused a good deal of physical movement and uprooting.

2 When the cities became strong, they often destroyed other settlements in their vicinity, whose populations were presumably not all killed, but in some cases went to other places in Etruria.

3 The bilingual situation that existed at Clusium suggests that a small or fairly small Etruscan group had entered the place and seized control.

4 Some of the Etruscan cities seem to have been founded by others: for example, Arretium, Cortona and Perusia were established by Clusium, and Populonia seems to have been an offshoot of Vetulonia and may have received some Volaterran settlers as well. Once again, movements of population must have been involved – or at least of small pioneering groups, not necessarily as organized and systematic as the founder-settlers of Greek colonies.[72]

5 We have evidence of Etruscan cities, singly or in coalitions, fighting against one another, or at least of their citizens undertaking such action. This is shown, for example, by wall-paintings from the François tomb at Vulci and inscriptions (*elogia*) from Tarquinii. Such wars must have meant that people were displaced from their homes and went to other Etruscan centres.

6 Sometimes, too, adventurers from different Etruscan towns banded together, notably, it has been suggested, Avle Feluske from Vetulonia and Hirumina of Perusia – two men whom an inscription from the former town seems to describe as companions. Once again, such alliances no doubt involved movements.

7 Etruscan and other artists and craftsmen evidently moved from one Etruscan town to another, not only singly but in groups as well.

Even such purely internal movements must have caused substantial displacements of population; but it is equally clear that similar groups infiltrated into Etruria from outside. If there was a 'long march' of people from various races, including Etruscans, into Campania in 525–524 BC, why should there not, on other occasions, have been comparable marches *into* Etruria, of which our fragmentary record has left no trace? Perhaps sometimes such marchers were mercenaries or comprised private armies such as remained common in Greece as well until the end of the sixth century BC. The fact that the Etruscans took over so many personal names from other Italian peoples (in addition to the converse process) provides a further sign of such infiltrations. The Sardinian influences brought to bear upon the Etruscan coasts opposite the island may have been partly the product of immigrants. Conversely, the Etruscans themselves must have sent many people, individually or in groups, south to Campania and Latium and north to the Po valley. In the latter zone, Virgil describes how at Mantua these Etruscan immigrants took their place among an extraordinary mixture of other peoples. And then private wars, such as the campaign conducted against neighbouring Etruscan Veii by the Roman clan of the Fabii, were just the sort of event to involve transfers of inhabitants. Rome, of which we know most, provides several other pieces of suggestive evidence as well. Some of the people of conquered Alba Longa came to live in the city and its territory, and Vulcentines under Mastarna and the Vibennas did the same – hence, perhaps, the Vicus Tuscus (Etruscan Street) in the city. Later on, a Sabine, Attus Clausus, brought five thousand of his clan and dependants to live on Roman land. If only we knew more about Etruscan city-states, this is just the sort of thing that we should find happening there as well. Tens or hundreds of individual traders, too, were constantly passing not only from one town of Etruria to another, but into the country from outside. Indeed, there were whole Greek quarters or trading-posts at ports belonging to Tarquinii and Caere, and similar Carthaginian quarters at another Caeritan port (as well as at Rome). We may rightly suppose these harbour towns to have received a constant influx, temporary or otherwise, of businessmen of many different races from the countries concerned.

Much of this evidence, it is true, is relatively late, from the sixth and fifth centuries BC, but we also have evidence of far earlier Greek and Phoenician visitors and traders and artists. Indeed, they were the making of Etruscan civilization; as we now know, the process involved the actual arrival of foreign artists and craftsmen, sometimes in groups, as early as the eighth and seventh centuries BC. Moreover, we can surely infer the existence of these movements, and all the other kinds that have been described, into the much earlier and dimmer past. They, and the intermarriages resulting from them, must have been going on right back to the times when people were first able to move about.

This picture therefore does not readily permit the assumption of a single huge immigration into Etruria in the later second millennium or the eighth century BC or both. The scene is rather one of continually moving, infiltrating small groups, of the most varied origin and race and character, over a very great number of years. It was this swirl of roaming and trekking people that ended up as the Etruscan nation. The

universality of the Etruscan language in the country is no objection
to the diversity of this picture. It was one of the strong, persistent
languages, like our own. The immigrants or infiltrators or itinerant
visitors made it their business to learn it, just as the immigrants to
America learnt to speak English.

CHAPTER 5

EXPANSION TO THE SOUTH

Campania

The Etruscans expanded far beyond Etruria, both to the south and the north: recent research increasingly shows that these were not merely colonial extension areas, but, despite even stronger Greek influences than in the homeland, integral parts of the territory of Etruscan civilization, belonging to the same social and cultural community and undergoing the same formative processes from the beginning.

The central point of the southern region of this civilization was Capua, which is now Santa Maria Capua Vetere. Destined to become the second city of peninsular Italy and its leading manufacturing centre, Capua was in the interior of Campania, twenty miles inland from the Greek city-state of Cumae which played such an enormous part in the opening up of the region. Recent investigations have revealed an unbroken development on the site of Capua from at least c. 800 BC onwards, with a necropolis of the eighth century at Sant'Angelo in Formis nearby, beside a much revered sanctuary of Artumes (Artemis, Diana) on Mount Tifata. Settlement on the Capua site seems to have evolved on very similar lines to those of pre-urban Etruria, initially based, no doubt, on a group of adjacent autonomous villages. This date fits in very well with an assertion by a Roman historian of the first century AD, Velleius Paterculus, that Capua was founded 'by the Etruscans' in c. 800 BC;[1] he thus contradicts Cato the Elder, who said that the Etruscans had only founded the place in about 500. Cato's statement probably refers to an enlargement or reorganization. Relevant, too, is a story that Cacus, a prominent figure in Etruscan legend, fled from Tarchon (the mythical founder of Tarquinii) and established a kingdom on the River Volturnus or Vulturnus;[2] for the Volturnus (now Volturno) flows past Capua, which stood beside its ford on an important north–south route. The name of the river is Etruscan, like those of two others nearby – the swampy Clanius (Regi

86

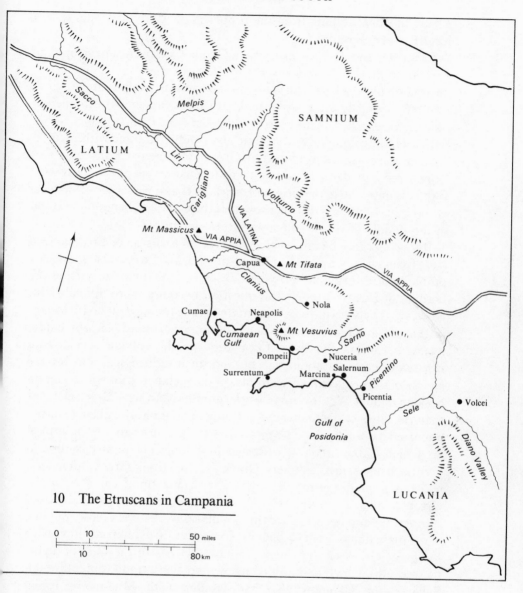

10 The Etruscans in Campania

| 0 | 10 | | | | 50 miles |
| | 10 | | | | 80 km |

Lagni) forming a barrier a little way south of the city,[3] and another,
Clanis or Glanis, which was the former designation of the Liris (Liri);
these names are derived from, or akin to, the Clanis (Chiana) which
was the river of Clusium in Etruria. As for the Volturnus or Vulturnus,
it was named after Capua itself, which was called something like
Volturnum in Etruscan – though 'Capua' (Capeva), too, was an

87

Etruscan word, coming from the proper name Capys[4] belonging to a local Etruscan family.

From at least c. 800 onwards, then, Capua underwent a development parallel to that of the cities of Etruria at the same time. Thereafter – once again like the Etruscan centres – it became urbanized in the eighth century or shortly afterwards, making early contacts with the neighbouring Greek (Euboean) centres Pithecusae and Cumae, which as has been seen were founded at that time and conducted trade with Etruria. Indeed, the ceramics produced by Greek craftsmen at Pithecusae and Cumae recur in identical form not only in Etruria, but at Capua as well. Capua is only unlike the cities of Etruria in that it was situated on level ground, in common with other towns of the Campanian region; it stood in the middle of very fertile agricultural territory.

But when can it be said to have become an Etruscan or Etruscanized city? Even when we are considering the cities of Etruria itself, this is a problematical question; but when we come to Capua, far outside the borders of Etruria proper, the question becomes more difficult still. However it may perhaps be legitimate to date the start of the Etruscanization of Capua to the time when it became urbanized – at which date it also became a city-state. Excavation on the site has revealed an Etruscan helmet of about 650 BC and an inscribed seal and bronze figures of the next century, examples of the metalwork for which Capua became famous. Yet this metalwork contains a stronger Greek element than the cities of the homeland, although presumably utilizing copper imported from Etruria. The terracotta temple decorations – a form of art which Capua may have started producing before any centres in Etruria itself – also look very Greek. These strong Greek influences, which militated against complete Etruscanization,[5] came from the Greek colonies in south Italy. With Cumae, relations were probably competitive and hostile, since the two places were so very close. But one of the main functions of Capua was to protect Etruscan trade links with the great Greek city of the south-east, Sybaris in the Gulf of Taras (Tarentum), which maintained its own northern trade-route; through Sybaris, the Capuans also had contact with Miletus in Ionia. Moreover, although Sybaris was destroyed in 510, Capua's connection with Miletus perhaps survived, for the Capuans borrowed the 'gridiron' system associated with the famous Milesian town-planner Hippodamus, who was one of the colonists and perhaps the designer of a new pan-Hellenic foundation in 443 at Thurii, beside the place where Sybaris had formerly been.[6]

By what routes did the Etruscans come to Capua and Campania?

Clearly they came, in the course of time, both by land and by sea; but there is some reason to suppose that their initial arrival in Capua was by land.[7] It is true that the place may have possessed a small harbour at the mouth of its River Volturno,[8] yet it was Capua's rivals, the Cumaeans, who controlled the sea. And there was a direct and easy land-route from Capua northwards: it ran along the river valleys of the Garigliano, the Liri (Liris), and its tributary the Sacco (Trerus), and the Sacco led up to the Aniene (Anio), which flows into the Tiber.

The Etruscans had many other settlements in Campania too. One was Nola (perhaps the Etruscan Nuvla), an important road-station seventeen miles to the south-east of Capua, which had probably founded it; the Etruscan origin of Nola was confirmed by Cato the Elder.[9] Acerrae (Acerra), west of Nola, also has an Etruscan name, which is the same as that of a town in north Italy (just as the Etruscan name of a local stream, the Melpis, is reminiscent of Melpum in the same region). On the other side of Vesuvius, Etruscan finds have now come to light at various points in the Sarno (Sarnus) valley. Discoveries at Pompeii, for example, include fragments of Etruscan-type black *bucchero* pottery (probably of local manufacture) and have also provided graffiti in Etruscan characters, thus confirming Strabo's testimony to a period of Etruscan settlement or control, which evidently started well before 550 BC and was accompanied by strong influence from Pithecusae and Cumae.[10] Pompeii was an important communications link, providing a harbour for Nola and other Etruscan towns in the neighbourhood. Etruscans were also reported to have settled in the Phlegraean Fields behind the northern part of the bay, and in Surrentum (Sorrento) at its southernmost extremity, where there was a temple of Athena 'Tyrrhena', the goddess whom the Etruscans called Menrva and the Romans Minerva.[11]

More remarkable still, recent and extensive finds confirm a very important Etruscan zone farther to the south-east, in the Gulf of Salerno. Here, contacts with Etruria are demonstrated as early as the ninth century BC and were maintained and increased by a process of steady expansion; it is in this region (as well as the Surrentum area) that the earliest-known Etruscan inscriptions of Campania have been found, dating back to the years after 600. An important Etruscan site has been identified at Fratte di Salerno, a suburb a little inland of Salernum (Salerno), which lay on the trade-route to the Greek south, and the Etruscan connection is recalled by the name of Cava dei Tirreni (the Cave of the Tyrrhenians) nearby. In this remoter region, the link with Etruria was probably created and maintained not by the land-route but by sea, through the adjacent port of Marcina (Vietri sul Mare).[12]

But the outstanding site in the area is Picentia (Pontecagnano),[13] to the south-east of Salernum on the little River Picentino, just inland from the major road to the south; Pliny the Elder confirmed the Etruscan character of the Picentine region.[14] The objects found in the large cemeteries of Pontecagnano offer the entire time sequence famil-iar from Etruria itself, right from the ninth century BC down the middle of the sixth, including some very rich tombs of c. 700, seventh-century vases, brooches, cups, and an inscription from Phoenicia. Apart from certain influences of a local character, this distant centre is virtually indistinguishable from those of Etruria in the same period, and greatly enlarges our knowledge of this early Etruscan presence in Campania. Once again, it must have been by sea that Pontecagnano maintained its earliest communications with Etruria, which go back as far as the ninth century BC and reveal contacts with the coastal Etruscan area in particular[15] – though later, no doubt, land links were also established.

East of Pontecagnano, on the site of a settlement that had been in existence since the previous millennium, was another Etruscan centre, Volcei (the modern Buccino), overlooking the Diano valley which led south to the Etruscophile Greek city of Sybaris. Volcei was located on a tributary of the River Sele and formed an inland thoroughfare between the Ionian (Adriatic) and Tyrrhenian Sea.[16] It is obvious that the name of the place echoes that of Etruscan Vulci, whose people may have played a part in its foundation. The later coinage of Campanian appearance inscribed 'Velecha' may perhaps have been issued at Vol-cei.[17] Further issues are inscribed 'Uri' or 'Urina' (perhaps the equiv-alent of the Greek 'Hyria'). The dies of these coins, of late fifth- or early fourth-century date, are shared with others bearing the name of Nola, and were apparently issued at the Greek city of Neapolis (Naples), so that 'Urina' is evidently one of the Etruscan centres in the area, near (or identifiable with) Nola. Since Aurinia (Saturnia), from which 'Urina' probably derived its name, was in the territory of Vulci, it may be that people from Vulci, once again, had some hand in the establishment of the Campanian centre. The place of issue of other Campanian coins bearing the name of 'Velsu' may have been a town that took its name from Etruscan Volsinii, but it cannot be identified.[18]

These links with Vulci and Volsinii will be discussed later when the influences of these and other cities of the homeland – influences for which there is a great deal of evidence over and above these fragmentary coinages – can be analysed in greater detail. And it will also be suggested later that the influences are indeed those of individual cities, and not pan-Etruscan, for this is an important point about the nature of the Etruscan connection with Campania: it was a series of contacts made and maintained by this or that Etruscan city-state or its members. The ancient idea of a federation of twelve Campanian colonies (if indeed there even were twelve), founded in unison by the no less dubious total of twelve cities of Etruria, is far too neat, schematic and symmetrical.[19]

The Etruscan golden age in Campania did not last very long. The inevitable rivalry between the Etruscans and their Greek neighbours in the country, and particularly between Etruscan Capua and Greek Cumae, which were far too near to one another for comfort, came to a head in the later sixth century BC. Another Greco-Etruscan clash occurred in c. 525–524 BC when a force of Etruscans and others outside the country invaded Campania. This was the 'long march', already mentioned, in which an Etruscan contingent (coming from Spina and probably Clusium) was joined by some of Etruria's Italic neighbours, including, it seems, a contingent from Ardea in Latium. Aristodemus, the ruler of Cumae, repelled the invaders, although some of them no doubt stayed on to make further trouble. With the help of other Latins who were not on good terms with the Ardeans, Aristodemus subsequently inflicted a further defeat on his Etruscan enemies at the Latin town of Aricia some time between 506 and 504 BC.[20] And so, by the end of the sixth century, the Campanian Greeks of Cumae had consolidated their position against their Etruscan neighbours.

This process continued when King Hiero I of Syracuse defeated the Etruscans together with their Carthaginian allies off Cumae in 474, once again with the help of a Cumaean force, and the Syracusans led a further expedition against them in 454–453.[21] Capua and the other Etruscan settlements in Campania had proved no match for the Greeks. Yet Cumae did not emerge as the winner after all, for Capua and Cumae alike succumbed, within the period of a few years (c. 430–423), to backward but hard-fighting central Italian tribes, the Samnites. It was they whose descendants in the area, profiting by the local civilizing influences, became a new Campanian nation.

Rome

Capua had thrived as long as it was able to maintain its land route to Etruria through Latium; one of the reasons why it ceased to flourish in the fifth century BC was that this lifeline had been severed. The power that severed the line was Rome, for Rome was the key to the communications between Etruria and Campania, and for a part of the seventh and almost all the sixth century BC it was governed by Etruscans and was to a large extent an Etruscan city.

Although Rome's early development is encrusted in legend, the subsequent importance of the place means that we possess some reliable archaeological material about its beginnings as well as some not wholly unreliable literary information. This evidence enables us to understand the sort of processes that were no doubt also taking place at other, more completely Etruscan, cities as well. The site of Rome enjoyed a good water-supply at all seasons and was within easy reach of fertile soil. Its river, the Tiber, the largest river of the peninsula and the boundary between Etruria and Latium, was navigable in its lower reaches. Thirteen miles from the Tyrrhenian Sea – near enough for ready access to its waters, yet far enough to provide warnings of sea-raiders – was the lowest of the river's practicable crossing-points, beside its left or southern bank at Rome. The crossing also coincided with the most convenient and important of Italy's few longitudinal land-routes, connecting Etruria with Latium and Campania. Moreover, the site commanded easy progress down and up the Tiber's stream. Downstream along the river itself and the road that ran beside it, there was access to precious, coveted salt-pans on the coast. Upstream and inland, the continuation of the same 'salt road' (Via Salaria) up the Tiber valley led by fairly easy passes into the central regions of Italy bordering on Etruria.

Yet this strategic position of Rome for all its advantages was also perilously likely to arouse the covetousness of others, and its inhabitants needed protection. They were given it by the cliff-protected hills or hillocks on which they planted their settlements. These eminences were a hundred to three hundred feet above sea-level and safely raised above the river's floods – a series of flat-topped spurs divided by ravines that were much steeper than they are today; most of the hills were already occupied during the second millennium BC.[22] It is also possible that at this period the occupants of the future Rome already spoke the Indo-European tongue which later became Latin and which, as we have seen, was structurally unrelated to the Etruscan speech just across the river. Once the habitation of the Roman hills had begun, it may have continued without a break. As in Etruria, however, new and more advanced materials and customs began to be seen there at the start of the first millennium BC. At this juncture, there were probably small-scale movements and displacements of the region's population, with groups coming in, for example, from a fertile extinct volcano, the Alban Mount (Monte Cavo), thirteen miles to the south-east; other pioneering groups no doubt also converged on Rome at different times. From about the tenth century BC onwards, new or renewed villages, not dissimilar from those on the hill-sites of Etruria, were in existence on several of the hills of Rome. At this period, the local inhabitants cremated some of their dead and buried others.

In later, literate times, efforts were made to fix a time for Rome's foundation; and after various other suggestions had been made, it was assigned to 753 BC. This date henceforth remains canonical, yet it had only been arrived at by a series of wholly arbitrary synchronizations,[23] and it was probably, in fact, rather later – some time after the similar processes of development in southern Etruria – that the villages on the Palatine, Esquiline and Caelian Hills of Rome joined together, perhaps gradually. Then, in c. 625 BC, the low-lying water-logged area later known as the Forum, which lay between the hills, was systematically drained in order to form a general meeting-place. Moreover, in about the same period, the two northernmost Roman villages, upon the Quirinal and Viminal Hills, were united with the growing township.

At the same period, according to tradition, the first bridge was built across the River Tiber at Rome, supplying a direct and unprecedented land-link between Etruria to the north and its Campanian settlements to the south; it was this land-link that attracted Rome's Etruscan neighbours.[24] Indeed, the new city and its rapid development were very largely, if not entirely, due to the Etruscans and to their interest in its potentialities as a staging-point towards Campania. Ever since the eighth century BC, when the Etruscan city-states were first taking shape, Rome had been in ever closer contact with a number of them, and had increasingly assimilated their material culture with its own.

Rome and the Etruscan city-states were evidently subject to the same external cultural influences: we find in the Roman cattle-market, beside the river – near the altar of Heracles to which Greek and Carthaginian and no doubt Etruscan traders came – fragments of eighth-century pottery from the Greek trading-post of Pithecusae[25] which had done so much to stimulate Etruscan beginnings as well. Other excavations at Rome have also provided objects of Egypto-Phoenician appearance dating from before and after 600 BC, of precisely the types that Pithecusae and Cumae were exporting extensively to the Etruscans. There is also evidence of direct Etruscan influences: the drying-out of the Roman Forum in the same period which was effected by the construction of an impressive drain, the Cloaca Maxima, was a characteristically Etruscan kind of operation. It was at just about this period, too, that the first pottery and metalwork from the nearest cities of southern Etruria, just across the river, began to make their appearance at Rome: a tomb on the Esquiline Hill was found to contain Etruscan-type armour of about 600 BC. With the aid of Etruscan immigrants and visitors – confirmed by the existence of the previously mentioned Vicus Tuscus (Etruscan Street) – the place was on the way to becoming an Etruscan town and city-state. Yet Rome was not just an Etruscan colony and foreign dependency, but a centre with a rich Etruscan-type culture in its own right.[26]

In the same years before 600, the first structure built on stone foundations replaced earlier huts and burials in the Forum. The building was known later on as the Regia, and perhaps that was its name already. The word comes from *rex* (king), so the Regia must originally have been the residence of the King of Rome; the fact that the city had at first been ruled by kings was unanimously asserted by subsequent ancient historians. It was also recorded that, whereas the Roman monarchy itself pre-dated Etruscan domination, an Etruscan dynasty took over in the later seventh century BC – by peaceful agreement, according to Roman tradition, although this may be little more than a patriotic device to scotch the uncomfortable idea that Rome had once been forcibly subjected to foreigners.

The first Etruscan ruler was named as Tarquinius Priscus. The traditional dates of his reign are 616–579 BC, and here Roman tradition harmonizes with the evidence of archaeology, which ascribes the decisive stages of Rome's urbanization to the last quarter of the seventh century. The new monarchs appear to have left their earlier residence in the Regia, which became a religious sanctuary, in order to reside instead upon the precipitous, defensible acropolis of the Capitoline Hill. Subsequently, Rome came under the control or influence of other Etruscans, Mastarna (Servius Tullius?) and the brothers Vibenna from Vulci, and Lars Porsenna of Clusium, who will be discussed when we come to consider their places of origin; and finally, according to tradition, there was a second Tarquin (Tarquinius Superbus), before Rome became a native Republic.

As the archaeological evidence confirms, the Etruscan impact on the city, already strong in the seventh century BC, grew more powerful still in the sixth. But just how Etruscan, at this stage, did the place become? It was not as Etruscan as the cities of Etruria itself, because

Latin was the tongue that its population continued to speak, and they retained many of their own national customs;[27] rather, Rome fell into a special category, of which we shall hear more later, of Etruscanized but still Italic-speaking communities. Yet Etruscan influence penetrated very deep into Roman society. The sacred area of Sant'Omobono near the port contained sixth-century Etruscan statues,[28] and the temple of Jupiter, Juno and Minerva (Tinia, Uni and Menrva to the Etruscans, and Zeus, Hera and Athena to the Greeks) was the largest temple of the Etruscan style and form ever built anywhere; its triple structure was a formula found in other Etruscan cities as well, and it was decorated with Etruscan sculpture by Vulca of Veii.[29] The institutions of Rome, too, for all their basic Latin character, continued to embody thoroughly Etruscan features. Their religion and mythology, for example, including the myth of Aeneas, were pervaded by such Etruscan elements, and so was their calendar, their ceremonial, agriculture, art and costume. All this represents a far deeper cultural penetration than is allowed by chauvinists such as Livy, who prefer to dwell on the theme of Etruria absorbed by Rome rather than on the earlier domination of Rome by Etruscans.

No doubt the majority of the local population were relatively unaffected, since what they, like their underprivileged counterparts throughout world history, had to concern themselves with was the problem of bare subsistence: they remained relatively unsusceptible to external cultures. And yet it is evident that, even though Rome's Etruscan rulers never succeeded in wholly imposing their language, the influence they exercised on Rome was deeply pervasive – so pervasive, indeed, that Dionysius of Halicarnassus flatly calls it an 'Etruscan city'.[30]

Latium

The Etruscans wanted and needed a sympathetic régime at Rome because it was a key point on the land-route to Capua and their other Campanian centres. But in order to get to Campania it was still necessary for them, after crossing the Tiber at Rome, to traverse more than another hundred miles. This intervening country was Latium – the south-eastern half of what is called Lazio today.

Latium was a well-watered region consisting of plains furrowed into gullies and undulating folds, inhabited, as the first millennium BC began, by roving groups of men and women who spoke, like the Romans, some version of the Indo-European Latin language and were

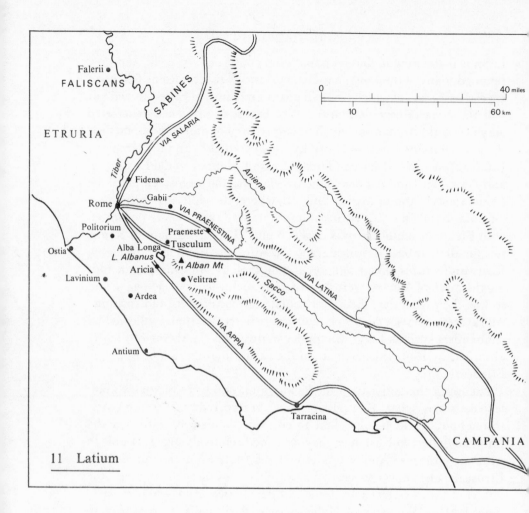

11 Latium

descended from people who had possessed some contact with the
Mycenaean civilization.[31] Those who moved in and settled on the site of
Rome included some, as we saw, who came from the Alban Mount not
far away. This peak was a natural fortress some three thousand feet in
height, dominating a semicircle of cone-shaped hills. The mountain
was a former volcano that had ceased to be active some thousands of
years earlier; but before it became quiet its eruptions had fertilized the
earth with phosphate and potash deposits, enriched by decaying leaves.
All that was needed was drainage of the water-logged soil, and then it
would be a fertile country.

By the first years after 1000 BC, the settlement of the Alban hills,
perhaps by small groups of migrants from the coastal area, was
approaching completion, and nomadism was gradually giving way to

intensive agriculture as irrigation began to develop. On the shores of
the Alban Lake, beside the mountain, stood the village or villages of
Alba Longa (Castelgandolfo). It was famous in Virgil's legends as the
parent city of Rome; whether there is truth in this tale is uncertain.
Alba Longa was in a position to control one of the main thoroughfares
to south Italy, the later Via Appia, and it controlled also a regional
sanctuary of the sky divinity Jupiter on the Alban Mount, so that in the
tenth century BC it was already the centre of a loosely knit association of
Latin villages. Cremation urns in the form of huts may have been used
in Latium first (before the introduction of inhumation in the eighth
century BC) and then borrowed by the southern Etruscan centres. But,
conversely, material influences from Etruria gradually became strong
in the Latin region. Moreover, the names of certain legendary Alban
kings are etymologically Etruscan, notably Capys, reminiscent of
Etruscan Capua, and Tarchetius, who was said to have consulted an
oracle in Etruria.[32]

There was also a story that an Etruscan King Viba (or Vibe) – the
name is related to that of the Vulcentine house of the Vibennas – had
come from Veii to visit his counterpart Amulius at Alba Longa.[33] So
Alba Longa had Etruscan contacts, and may well have become partly
Etruscanized. Yet the existence of its separate monarch, Amulius,
reminds us that these Latian cities – however many Etruscan visitors or
even immigrants they received – do not seem to have been colonial
dependencies of the cities of the Etruscan homeland but rather formed
an autonomous part of the same cultural sphere.

In this respect the destiny of Alba Longa was similar to that of Rome;
but in due course the balance of power shifted from Alba Longa to the
Roman hills, with their even better strategic position, and finally the
Romans conquered the place. The ancient literary tradition ascribed
the event to the first half of the seventh century BC, but archaeologists
prefer a date fifty years later, or more, when Rome, itself under Etruscan rule, had begun to assume an expansionist policy. After the annexation of Alba Longa it was recorded that survivors of its downfall, under
their leaders, moved to Rome; this shows the sort of local population
movement that must often have taken place in Etruria itself, and has to
be taken into account when considering Etruscan 'origins'.

Another significant link in the Etruscan line of communications to
Campania running through Latium was Praeneste (Palestrina).[34] This
settlement stood commandingly on an isolated ledge 1,350 feet above
sea-level, crowned by a citadel rising 1,200 feet higher, in a vital
position dominating the plain joining the Aniene (Anio) and Sacco

(Trerus) valleys that provided the main landward route towards the south. Praeneste boasted an unusual number and diversity of foundation myths insisting on its legendary heroic links, and indeed the place was of venerable origins. Excavations have now shown that the great leap forward, involving urbanization, the diffusion of new ideas, and the first influx of foreign materials and artisans, took place in the latter half of the eighth century BC[35] – just at the time when the Greek markets at Pithecusae and Cumae in Campania were trading with Etruria and developing its civilization. By that time, what is nowadays described as the 'Latian culture' may be said to have established itself fully in the region, particularly at Praeneste. It was a mixed culture,[36] deriving some of its elements from local Italian traditions dating back to the pre-urban epoch but also displaying extraordinary resemblances to the civilization of the cities of southern Etruria. Just as that civilization was based on a blend of Greek and near-eastern influences emanating from Pithecusae and Cumae, so was the civilization of Praeneste. Indeed the contents of its remarkable graves of the mid-seventh century BC, the Barberini and Bernardini tombs – far richer in jewellery and metalwork than anything of the same period at Rome – are startlingly similar to the finds in south Etruscan cemeteries, notably at Caere.

Seeing these objects from Praeneste, one understands how it was that, before the sixth century BC, the Greeks could not manage to distinguish between Etruria and Latium. Indeed, so far do these resemblances go that it is becoming preferable to avoid talking of Etruscan 'influences' at such centres as Praeneste, but to say instead that they can only have produced this culture there by drawing separately, directly upon the same Greek and near-eastern cultural sources as the cities of the Etruscan homeland. That is why, in the political field, Alba Longa (though at least partly Etruscanized), existed as a city-state on its own account; and the same evidently applied to Praeneste. However, since the two regions were so indissolubly bound together, there must have been Etruscans continually coming and going – and possibly, at one stage at least, a sort of domination by some of the cities of Etruria which anti-Etruscan historians like Livy were at pains to conceal. There were even ancient traditions of Latin towns being established according to the well-known Etruscan rituals for such foundations, and for all we know Alba Longa and Praeneste may have been among them.

The communities that emerged from these processes retained a dual culture. The word 'Vetusia' on a silver cup from the Bernardini tomb at Praeneste is an inflexion of an Etruscan name, though whether this was masculine or feminine is uncertain.[37] The Latin alphabet, too, was derived from the Etruscans. However, as we have seen, the language of the Latins was not, and it so happens that the oldest known inscription in that language likewise comes from Praeneste, where it appears on a gold brooch of the late seventh century BC.[38] We must think, then, of this place as another example (like Rome) of a dual culture, in which the population continued to speak Latin while, at the same time, a good deal of Etruscan speech was also heard.[39]

The same was no doubt true of Gabii (Castiglione) – another transit centre on the way to Campania, commanding the road between Praeneste and Rome. Here, extensive recent discoveries have revealed a cult-centre of the first importance belonging to the seventh and sixth centuries BC. And other towns a few miles farther south may well have Etruscan names: one is Tusculum, 2,200 feet above sea-level, a powerful place in early Latium, once again on a major route to the south. Although excavations have so far not confirmed that Tusculum went through a period of Etruscanization, its name seems to come from *Tuscus*, Etruscan. The name of Tarracina (Terracina) is also probably Etruscan, recording a connection with Tarquinii.[40]

The people of Ardea, too, were sometimes regarded as Etruscans, and evidently were Etruscanized, or came under Etruscan control;[41] their legendary leader Turnus, so well-known from Virgil's *Aeneid*, bore an Etruscan name related to 'Tyrrhenus'. The people described by Virgil as 'Daunians',[42] who joined Etruscan contingents from Spina and probably Clusium in the 'long march' into Campania in 525–524, are likely to have been men of Ardea rather than the Apulians of south-east Italy who were later more generally known by this name.[43] Another city of Latium, Antium, was used or occupied as a harbour by Etruscan 'pirates' or traders, and it was recorded that the Volscian people, an Italic-speaking group of tribes from the interior which at one time made Antium their principal centre, were for a period under Etruscan control.

These were all places of vital concern to the Etruscans, seeing that Latium was the bridge to Campania. They were especially concerned with a place very near to them indeed, only ten miles south of Rome; this was Politorium (Castel di Decima), right beside the Tiber itself, one of a dense line of settlements on the Rome–Ostia route. Recent excavations at Politorium have revealed a prosperous town with many fine tombs dating from the last decades before 700 BC.[44] The discoveries of this date include artefacts of Etruscan appearance, among them a bronze providing our earliest known Italian representation of the myth of Aeneas,[45] which was so prominent in Etruria. Perhaps it should be deduced from these remains that people from Etruria were present at Politorium; but, whether this was so or not, it seems once again that a prosperous culture of the Etruscan type was here in its own right, maintaining direct links both with Etruria and with Greek markets such as Pithecusae in the south. Moreover, the residential centre beside the tombs at Politorium discloses a differentiation between the social grades of the dead which bears witness to at least the preliminary stages of an urban society. Yet the tombs stop abruptly in *c.* 630–620, when the site seems to have been abandoned. It seems likely that the Romans obliterated the place, in the course of their advance to establish a settlement at Ostia on the Tiber mouth in pursuit of the salt they contested with Veii.[46]

Towards the end of the sixth century, the power and civilization of the Etruscans in Latium continued to weaken, at the same time as it deteriorated in Campania. The battle of Aricia, lost against a combined force of Latins and of Campanians from Cumae (*c.* 506–504 BC), was one of the principal landmarks. After 500, any political influence that the city-states of the Etruscan homeland may have exercised in the region was no more, and their commercial and cultural influence likewise waned as first Latins and then Romans assumed commanding positions.

This was the end of an epoch in which the states of both Latium and Campania had virtually formed part of the same politico-economic zone as the states of Etruria. Indeed, Dionysius of Halicarnassus declared that all western Italy had been known as Tyrrhenia;[47] and Livy, following Cato the Elder,[48] was inspired to declare that almost the whole of Italy from the Alps to the Straits of Messana had at one time been under Etruscan sway.[49] Even if this was, as we have now seen, something of an over-simplification at least as far as southern Italy is concerned, it is possible to see how such an observation could be made: the influence of the Etruscan way of life had extended very widely and deeply, to such an extent, indeed, that (despite differing emphases) the cultures of the principal regions can sometimes only be distinguished with difficulty. But Livy was referring to the north of Italy as well as to the south, and it is to the north that we must now turn.

CHAPTER 6

EXPANSION TO THE NORTH

The Inland Centres

The powerful presence of Etruscan culture in north Italy, across the Arno and the Apennines, was a phenomenon comparable to the extension of its presence into Campania in the south,[1] though once again it is always hard to say to what degree this connection may have involved political subordination to one or another Etruscan city-state as well as commercial and cultural contacts. As in Campania, the northern centres sometimes seem almost as Etruscan as those of Etruria and subject to the same processes of development. Yet, once again, there were also direct influences from the city-states of Etruria, or people belonging to them. When we come to discuss the northern Etruscan states, in particular Volaterrae and Clusium, we shall see that it is largely they, owing to their geographical situation – and not any federal initiative – that may be credited with such connections.

The earliest and principal Etruscan centre in northern Italy was the place the Romans later called Bononia (the modern Bologna); the Etruscans knew it as Felsina.[2] The considerable group of villages which clustered together on the site shortly before or after 900 BC was located on rising ground above a very fertile and densely populated plain beside the River Reno (Rhenus) – at that time a tributary of the Po – while another stream was adjacent to the settlements on the other side. Although not located with a view to defence, they were remarkably well placed for communications, being in easy reach of the great River Po, by far the most important river in Italy, and possessing ready access also to the Adriatic Sea, into which the Po debouched.

Like the centres of the Etruscan homeland, Bononia was developed, and became a prosperous city and a city-state, because of its proximity to metals. Iron could be extracted from the neighbouring Apennines as well as from other mountainsides in northern Italy.[3] The copper and gold of the region may also have been exploited: copper lumps of the

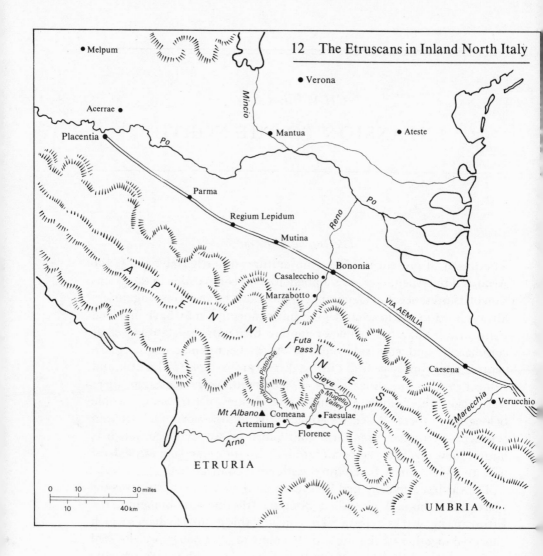

Melpum

Verona

Acerrae

Mantua

Ateste

Placentia

Mincio

Po

Parma

Regium Lepidum

Reno

Po

Mutina

Bononia

Casalecchio

VIA AEMILIA

Marzabotto

A P E N N I N E S

Futa Pass

Ombrone Pistoiese

Sieve

Caesena

Zambra

Mugello Valley

Marecchia

Verucchio

Mt Albano▲ Comeana

Faesulae

Artemium

Florence

Arno

ETRURIA

0   10   30 miles
10   40 km

UMBRIA

sixth or fifth century have come to light in the Po valley. In addition, Bononia's culture persistently reflected Transalpine tendencies, since it stood at the meeting-point of two commercial routes that led to metalworkings across the Alps.[4] Not surprisingly, then, it became the location of a major bronze-working industry, the leader among a number of such industries in the Po valley. A very large bronze find, of a date shortly before or after 700, comprised objects that were apparently valued according to weight and thus functioned as forerunners of coinage.[5]

This access to metals was one of the two vital factors in the evolution of Bononia from a group of villages to an important city. The other was its access to Etruria. The villages stood at the mid-point of the Reno valley, at the entrance to easy passes into Etruria which it provided with its main route to the north. It was under this Etruscan impulse, then, that the villages amalgamated early in the eighth century BC; by 750 the new centre was already at the height of its expansion and economic power.

The process of development was a complex one. Like the centres of Campania and Latium, Bononia may almost be regarded as part of Etruscan territory from the very start of the formation of the Etruscan people.[6] There was no question of a single, massive immigration by Etruscans – though it is perfectly possible to envisage the Etruscan pioneers arriving singly or in groups.[7] However, the Etruscanizing process at Bononia took a long time. The extravagant outburst of wealth that characterized the seventh-century development of the Etruscan cities is not to be found here: apparently the Bononians did not have an aristocracy as grandiose as theirs, although Bononia must have included quite a prosperous upper class, probably of merchant origin.

From about 600 BC, Bononia began to produce a great series of *situlae* – bronze buckets in the shape of truncated cones with figured reliefs. These buckets are also found in the Alpine regions, in Austria, and particularly in Slovenia, and it has been suggested that Bononia borrowed the forms and techniques of its buckets from those territories.[8] The designs of the vessels from Bononia, however, display a special style and iconography all their own.[9] At about the same time, Bononia began to produce gravestones that are likewise of a peculiar and characteristic type, in the form of horse-shoes.[10]

Despite these un-Etruscan elements, it was at about this period that Etruscan culture, in many of its material aspects, first established itself firmly at Bononia. Within this predominantly Etruscan aura, like the centres of Latium and Campania, it apparently enjoyed an autonomous Etruscan existence as a city-state, remaining politically independent of the homeland centres.[11] In the middle of the fourth century it succumbed to invading Gauls, one of whose tribes, the Boii, gave it the name of Bononia which henceforward replaced that of Felsina.

A little to the south of Bononia was another Etruscanized settlement at Casalecchio di Reno. Like Bononia, of which it appears to have been a sort of colonial extension,[12] Casalecchio had been continuously occupied from early in the first millennium BC. In the sixth century it moved into an Etruscan phase without any violent break.

Casalecchio stood where the Reno valley finally opens out into the Po plain, on the road southwards to a place now known as Marzabotto. This stands on the Pian di Misano, and its ancient name was perhaps Misa.[13] Late in the sixth century BC a village market was established by Etruscans (or Etruscanized people of Bononia) at Marzabotto, and it became fully urbanized about a decade later. The architectural design of Marzabotto bears some resemblance to the grid pattern found at Greek cities, including those of southern Italy, from *c*. 500 onwards.[14] Nevertheless, in other respects the place has a more markedly Etruscan character than any other centre in the north. Situated in a narrow wooded valley overshadowed by harsh precipices, it stands at the point where the Reno, and the road from Etruria, begins to leave the Apennines for the northern plain; and in that significant location lies its importance. Like Bononia, Marzabotto was not founded or equipped for defence but for the working and exchange of the metals which were to be found in the immediate vicinity. Indeed, fragments of iron slag and remnants of a bronze foundry of the late sixth century BC have actually been discovered on the site.[15] Moreover, locally manufactured bronze statuettes of male and female votaries have come to light at a nearby sanctuary which fulfilled an important role in Trans-Apennine Etruscan religious life.[16]

As the Etruscan presence spread up the Reno valley to Bononia not far south of the Po, with outposts at Casalecchio and Marzabotto on the way, so, at some stage, this same presence was to be found across the Po – notably on one of its northern tributaries, the Mincio (Mincius), which flowed past Mantua (the Etruscan Manthva?). Mantua stood on rising ground in a zone of sluggish lakes formed by the waters of the Mincio, which were probably, for a certain stretch, extensive enough to be navigable. It was the native city of Virgil, whose *Aeneid* contains a remarkable passage describing the ethnic components of the place: 'Mantua, rich in ancestry, yet not all of one stock: three races are there, and under each race four peoples, and she herself the head of the peoples, her strength from Etruscan blood'.[18] Virgil is saying here that the place controlled twelve adjacent centres or villages,[19] or more probably that it was the product of their amalgamation, like so many other cities in Etruria and elsewhere. He adds that the populations of these villages were divided equally among three different races or nationalities.

Although this picture looks somewhat over-symmetrical,[20] the record of racial diversity which it displays seems highly probable. There must have been quite a number of displacements and movements of population to bring this situation about. Here the extremely varied components that were believed to exist in the various cities of Etruria itself, as well as on its fringes, for once receive detailed documentation.

The three strains of population to which Virgil refers – each evidently representing a comparatively small numerical total – presumably included not only the Etruscan element (which he specifically cites), but also Venetians and Umbrians, speakers of Indo-European Italic tongues. When he asserts that the Etruscan factor was dominant, his account may be correct, but it might also be coloured by the probability that he himself was partly of Etruscan origin. This is suggested by his name Publius Vergilius Maro: 'Maro' is almost certainly an Etruscan name connected with the title *maru*.[21] 'Vergilius', too, is commoner in Etruria than elsewhere; and the name of Virgil's mother, Magia, may be Etruscan as well. It is not surprising, therefore, that the *Aeneid* displays, in many passages, a profound and subtle preoccupation with the Etruscans and their destiny.

We cannot say when the union of Mantua's villages into a city, apparently under the inspiration of the Etruscans, took place. But presumably this happened at some stage during the gradual Etruscan-ization of Bononia; for Mantua fulfilled a vital function for Bononia as its advanced station across the Po. However, the tradition (preserved by Virgil's commentator Servius), that Mantua rather than Bononia was the leader of the Etruscan communities in northern Italy was of late origin and untrue,[22] despite the pretentious Mantuan foundation legends which allegedly supported such claims.[23] Such retrospective glorification of Mantua was due to the fact that this was probably the only city of the region in which the Etruscan element still survived in the first centuries BC and AD, when Romans were writing about such subjects.

The Etruscans may also have established a settlement north of Mantua, near Verona, where the existence of a community named the Arusnates recalls the Etruscan family-name Aruzinaie.[24] Other places in the north, too, take their names from Etruscan families, including Acerrae, near Cremona, which was linked to the Acerronii. As Strabo noted, the name of Acerrae turns up again in Etruscanized Cam-pania.[25] And the same link reappears in a more northerly Etruscan town, Melpum, perhaps the modern Melzo, near Milan, of which the name is echoed in the Campanian river Melpis – unless the influence was in the reverse direction. Mutina (Modena), Parma, and Placentia (Piacenza) north-west of Bononia likewise have Etruscan names, and

Etruscan influence is to be seen in local finds in these districts, especially in the neighbourhood of Mutina and around Regium Lepidum (Reggio Emilia).[26]

There was also a significant Etruscan presence in the south-eastern corner of the Trans-Apennine region on the confines of the modern province of Romagna. Ateste (Este) became partly Etruscanized. The name of Caesena (the Etruscan Ceisna (?) and modern Cesena), on the key transverse route later known as the Via Aemilia, probably provides yet another example of a link with the name of an Etruscan family – a family which is also found at Bononia.[27] And a very important settlement of strongly Etruscan character has now been found south-east of Caesena at Verucchio, near the Republic of San Marino. Verucchio evidently played an influential role from the eighth until the sixth century BC, and it has disclosed an exceptionally rich series of tombs. The series begins shortly after 700, employing the cylindrical form of a well, a type of burial which had been characteristic of the region in former times, and was now adapted and enlarged.[28] The earliest objects found at Verucchio include urns with helmet-shaped covers such as are also found in Etruria, together with shields of south Etruscan type.[29] Another discovery has provided the remains of a wooden throne of seventh- or sixth-century date with rich intaglio decoration after Etruscan models.[30] The throne also provides strong reminiscences of non-Etruscan and pre-Etruscan motifs – a constant feature of this region's art. Nevertheless, Etruscanization proceeded apace. The handles of bronze cups show highly stylized representations of female figures and animal shapes which recur in various parts of Etruria itself,[31] as well as on Bononian soil.

Verucchio owed these strong Etruscan links to its control of the adjacent River Marecchia (the Roman Ariminus), which had its source very close to that of the Tiber and thus provided one of the chief routes down into central Italy.[32] On its other side, the Marecchia only had nine miles to flow before it entered the Adriatic, and it was from this quarter that Verucchio received supplies of amber by sea.[33]

The East Coast

At the point where the Marecchia flowed into the Adriatic there was a harbour town, Ariminum (now Rimini), which gave the stream its ancient name. Although the place was not Etruscan but Umbrian, or partly Umbrian, in origin, its name was Etruscan, related to the family of the Arimna.[34] Imported bronzes from Etruria have been found

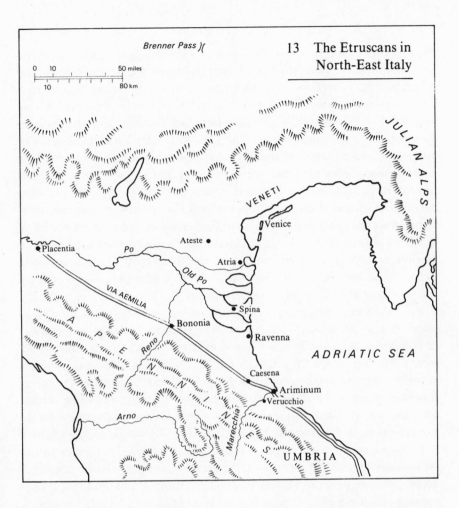

Brenner Pass)(

0   10   50 miles

10   80 km

JULIAN ALPS

VENETI

Venice

Ateste ●

Placentia   Po   Atria ●

Old Po

VIA AEMILIA

Spina

A   Bononia

P   Reno   Ravenna

E   ADRIATIC SEA

N   Caesena

N   Ariminum
                Verucchio

Arno   I   Marecchia

N   E   S   UMBRIA

nearby, and Strabo bears witness to the part played in local life by
Etruscans,[35] who probably possessed a trading-post or -quarter at this
highly strategic point – subsequently the terminal of the Via Flaminia
from Rome. North of Ariminum was Ravenna, which again has an
Etruscan name, although its dominant culture was provided by the
Umbrians.[36]

The principal centres of Etruscanization in this coastal region, however, lay just beyond the marshes that surrounded the site of Ravenna
and beside the mouths of the River Po itself, where a port of the earliest
years of the first millennium BC has now been discovered at Frat-
tesina.[37] But the place in this area where the Etruscans are most in
evidence is Spina, four miles west of the modern town of Comacchio,
where the mouth of one of the delta's branches formed a harbour in a
sea lagoon.[38] First of all, villages built on piles appeared on the site;

then, in the sixth century BC, the villages were amalgamated to form the port of Spina. It stood on a line of dunes between the sea lagoon and the coast, which lay farther to the west than it does now. Spina was centred on a long, wide canal – now detected by air photography – which was constructed to widen the channel between the sea and the lagoon. Nourished by an adjacent river mouth, this canal had a number of tributaries – a network of smaller canals or ditches crossed by bridges and adjoining a series of more or less rectangular houses. Spina covered an extent of over seven hundred acres, foreshadowing Venice, that greatest of all canal cities, which was not far away. Outside the main habitation area of Spina, its cemeteries lay along the ancient coastline on either side of the Old Po. The inhabitants enjoyed good fishing in the lagoon and possessed riverside grainlands. Their town was easily defensible from the mainland, with which it was only connected by narrow tongues of slightly higher ground.

Spina's name suggests an origin before either Etruscans or Greeks appeared on the scene;[39] but it was later inhabited jointly by members of both those peoples, as a rich blend of foundation legends confirm – a situation suggestive of much friendlier relations between the two peoples than sometimes prevailed on the west coast.[40] Even there, however, notable exceptions to this general hostility could be found, for example at Tarquinii and Caere, where Greek quarters evidently flourished under Etruscan rule. At Spina the abundance of Greek pottery, starting in the sixth century and reaching its climax in the second quarter of the fifth,[41] might seem to suggest Greek predominance, as might Spina's unusual distinction of possessing its own treasury at the quintessentially Greek sanctuary of Delphi; however, Caere, which had an unmistakably Etruscan government, also had a treasury at Delphi, and the balance of archaeological evidence suggests that Spina was primarily an Etruscan town with a subsidiary Greek element and quarter – at least, the Etruscans were apparently dominant for a brief period, at the very time when the influx of Greek material was at its height.[42]

Metalwork emanating from the Etruscans is found at points along this coast,[43] and Dionysius of Halicarnassus tells a strange story about how they got there in the first place. He says that they founded Spina after coming there by sea,[44] but since the next place he mentions on their itinerary, Cortona, is only introduced as a result of a demonstrable confusion with a town in Thrace,[45] his version must be regarded as extremely suspect. It seems much more probable that the Etruscan influences and traders, and Etruscan metals found on the adjacent coast, came to Spina by land from Bononia, which Spina served as its principal source of supplies from overseas (though probably remaining an autonomous entity). Spina continued to look towards Bononia and the west.[46] In particular, it was conscious of the potentialities of the upper reaches of the Po, whose mouth it commanded, utilizing that river as an avenue towards the western Alps, and a lifeline into the interior of Europe. On the other hand, direct links between Spina and Etruria by land cannot altogether be ruled out: it is significant that the place contains more bronze-work from Vulci than is to be found in any other northern city. Spina also possessed good communications up the coast to the north and maintained ties with the eastern Alpine regions, to which its version of the Etruscan alphabet travelled.[47] In particular, this line of communications gave it access to Baltic supplies of amber, which it subsequently passed on not only to Greece but also to Etruria, either through Bononia or directly.[48]

On the way to these Alpine regions lay the Venetians, who lived around the top of the Adriatic. They may have been at Spina before the Greeks and the Etruscans, and no doubt some still remained, for later on there were still people there who had Venetian names, yet did not speak the Indo-European Venetian language but Etruscan.[49] The Venetians not only played a part in the amber traffic and supplied Spina with horses for export, but also helped it to fulfil another of its principal roles, which was to collaborate with its fellow-traders from Greek maritime states in policing the Adriatic against rivals or 'pirates'.[50] This was a task that Spina shared with a second centre on the other, northern side of the Po delta, namely Atria (the modern Adria), which gave its name to the Adriatic Sea. After an original Venetian settlement,[51] Greeks and Etruscans lived together as the local population, at least from the second half of the sixth century BC.[52] As with Spina, the ancients were not agreed on whether the Greeks or the Etruscans were predominant among its settlers or traders. The Etruscans made a canal from an adjacent mouth of the Po to improve Atria's harbour.[53] Nevertheless, since the Attic vases found here often seem earlier than Spina's, whereas the graffiti which are the main evidence of the Etruscan presence seem relatively late, it may be concluded that, whereas Spina was the principal port of the Etruscans in the upper Adriatic, Atria probably played the same role for the Greeks – but in each case in co-operation with the other.

Spina and Atria achieved this co-operative enterprise precisely at the time when, in Campania, Greco-Etruscan exchanges were diminishing owing to hostile relations between the two communities in the area. In the north, a much more amicable relationship continued to develop despite these events. Nevertheless, the Etruscans in these Po delta centres, too, seem, on one occasion, to have intervened forcibly in the confrontation that prevailed in the south.

Dionysius of Halicarnassus, writing of the years 525–524 BC, tells, as we have seen, of a 'long march' of Etruscans and others in a southward direction, against the Greeks of Cumae in Campania. The march, he said, was undertaken by 'the Tyrrhenians [Etruscans] who had inhabited the country lying near the Ionian Gulf, but had been driven from thence in the course of time by the Gauls'. And these Etruscans, he adds, were joined by Umbrians, Daunians and 'many other barbarians'. The basic authenticity of this account need not be disputed.[54] Perhaps the 'Umbrians' came from Clusium in Etruria, while the 'Daunians', as was suggested, appear to have come from Ardea in Latium. As to the main body of Tyrrhenians, however, the ancients did not know our distinction between the Adriatic Sea to the north and the Ionian Sea to its south, but used the term 'Ionian Sea' (or Gulf) to refer to the Adriatic as well. Therefore, since Spina and Atria were the main Etruscan settlements along this coast, it would seem that it was the inhabitants of one or both of these places who participated in this expedition, perhaps as adventurers or mercenaries.[55]

Dionysius' suggestion that the march was prompted by pressure from invading Gauls, however, looks rather surprising, since the date he assigns to the expedition seems too early for their first, gradual infiltrations into north Italy, which other evidence does not place much, if at all, before 500.[56] Either Dionysius' date or the motive he puts forward may be wrong. Nevertheless, the incident gives a valuable flash of insight into the sort of population movement that probably characterized the whole period. The Cumaeans repelled the attack, but what happened to the attackers is unknown; there is no evidence that they ever returned to the north. By the middle of the fourth century the ports of Spina and Atria from which they may have come, like the rest of northern Italy, had fallen to the Gauls.

The West Coast

On the western (Tyrrhenian) coast of Italy there is also evidence for a chain of maritime markets or trading-posts containing Etruscan wares. They are less well known than those on the Adriatic, but were probably even more extensive, stretching from beyond the mouth of the Arno far

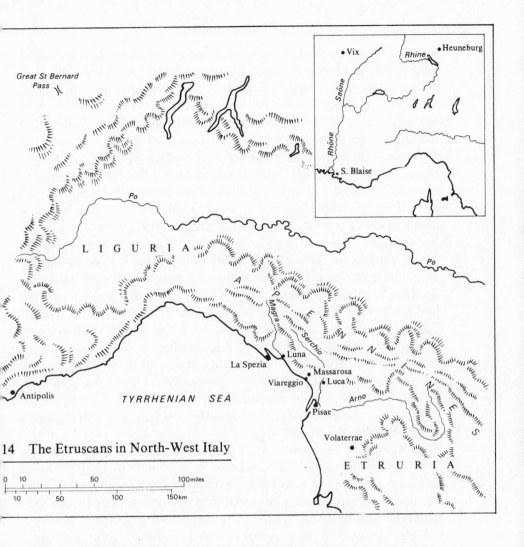

14   The Etruscans in North-West Italy

up into France – though it is by no means certain, in this region, to what extent trading was supplemented by settlement.

One probable but still somewhat mysterious link in this chain was Pisae (Pisa), on the north bank of the Arno estuary itself. It stood near the point where the river was joined in Etruscan times by the Serchio (the Roman Auser). Today the two rivers remain entirely separate, but at that epoch they apparently merged in a single huge basin from which their waters flowed together into the sea – a basin forming one of those large protected sea lagoons which were in ancient times a feature of the coastline of Etruria, providing splendid harbours, for example, at Orbetello, Vetulonia and Rusellae.[57] There is proof that Pisae had such a harbour, since the Emperor Augustus is on record as having developed its potentialities and expanded it southwards. But it had been a port at an earlier date, too, for we learn from Strabo that the Pisatans, a warlike people, had built ships from their own timber.[58]

The place seems to have been of very early origins, since its name appears in a list of the later second millennium BC from Pylos, one of the leading centres of the Mycenaean civilization in Greece. This may well signify that there was a Mycenaean market and trading-post at Pisae,[59] though archaeological evidence is still lacking, since the region cannot be fully explored owing to the enormous changes in its shore- and river-line. The antiquity of Pisae was hinted at in ancient times by its attribution to legendary Greek founders;[60] but there were also alternative traditions, recorded by Cato the Elder, that the port was founded by the Etruscans.[61] However, its position right beside a river-mouth is characteristic of an established settlement neither by Etruscans nor by Greeks but by the Ligurians, the people who pervaded north-west Italy and spoke a non-Indo-European language different from Etruscan and Greek. At the same time, excavations have confirmed that Pisae contained Etruscan or Etruscanized inhabitants, or at least objects, as early as the sixth or early fifth century BC,[62] and it may well be that future finds in this area will push the date earlier. These Etruscans must have possessed, and no doubt used, the skills needed to drain the extensive swamps round the river-mouth (which became marshy again in the Middle Ages).

The fact that Pisae was on the farther, non-Etruscan side of the river lagoon (a location which enjoyed better protection from the rear) would not have worried the men from the cities of Etruria who established themselves or spread their influence there, since they were prepared to go much farther afield than this, into the territory of the Ligurians (though as we saw these spoke another, quite different language) that lay beyond. For Etruscan pottery fragments have recently been discovered on a site nine miles farther north at Massarosa, where huts were built on piles in marshland near Lake Massaciuccoli – remnant of a northern offshoot or extension of Pisae's sea lagoon.[63] Their discovery further strengthens the likelihood of an Etruscan presence at Pisae. These finds go back to the eighth century BC. At that time the place was evidently still in Ligurian hands, but it became recognizably Etruscanized in c. 630–600, as the appearance of Etruscan lettering on pots of that date suggests.[64] Thereafter the place remained active, though perhaps only intermittently, for nearly two centuries.[65] The nearby town of Luca (Lucca), at a cross-roads on the River Serchio which carried much Etruscan traffic north from Pisae, likewise seems to have

ABOVE Painting in the Tomb of the Bulls, Tarquinii, *c.* 550–540 BC. Achilles lies in wait to kill the young rider Troilus. The earliest known Tarquinian wall-painting, infusing a scene from Greek mythology with many Italian, Etruscan touches.

ABOVE RIGHT Commemorative inscription of the Spurinna family at Tarquinii, perhaps mid-fourth century BC but referring to earlier events, unrecorded by Roman historians. Apparently Aulus Spurinna expelled Orgolnius, King of Caere, delivered Arretium from a slave war, and (according to another fragment) took nine Latin towns.

RIGHT Drawing of a tomb at Tuscania by Samuel Ainsley, 1842. On a cross-roads beside the Marta between Lake Bolsena and the sea, Tuscania became a major dependency of Tarquinii in about 600 BC.

ABOVE LEFT Gold brooch (*fibula*) from the Regolini-Galassi tomb in the Sorbo cemetery at Caere, mid-seventh century BC. The foot or catch-plate, with richly granulated decoration, is separated from the embossed bow by two transverse sections.

BELOW LEFT Black (thin-walled *bucchero*) pottery from Caere. *Left:* flask from Tomba Calabrese, late seventh century BC, in the form of a bird with two crowned horses' heads, and a standing male figure is part of the handle. *Right:* goblet from the Regolini-Galassi tomb; the figures are winged deities or demons, of near-eastern character.

ABOVE RIGHT The great, thickly clustering, magnificently furnished circular tombs of the Banditaccia cemetery at Caere, from the seventh century BC onwards, were covered with mounds of earth, like graves in various parts of Asia Minor and regions further east.

BELOW RIGHT The Tomb of the Shields and Seats, Caere. This chamber of the mid-sixth century BC is one of three in the tomb; the earliest is more than fifty years earlier. The design imitates a contemporary Etruscan house, with roof-beams. Above the seats, which have wide curved backs and foot-rests, are large round shields sculpted in relief on the walls.

ABOVE Part of a remarkable series of rock-cemeteries in the hilly hinterland of Caere's territory, adjoining the vanished town of Blera, which stood beside two important roads.

LEFT Water-pot (*hydria*) from Caere, *c*. 530–520 BC. These black-figured vases, a speciality of Caere, were probably made there, with due adaptation to Etruscan tastes, by Ionian immigrants. Despite Etruscan reverence for Herkle (Heracles, Hercules), the artist (the 'Busiris painter') presents a humorous picture of him disposing of his Egyptian enemies.

RIGHT Figures on a terracotta sarcophagus from Caere, *c*. 520 BC, displaying the Etruscan talent for utilizing Greek (Ionian) styles in order to produce something highly original. Husband and wife recline together on a banqueting couch, according to an Etruscan custom which was alien to the Greeks.

ABOVE The longer of two Etruscan inscriptions found, together with a Punic (Carthaginian) paraphrase, on sheets of gold foil at Pyrgi, one of the ports of Caere; end of the sixth century BC. The inscriptions refer to a dedication to Uni (Hera, Juno), identified with the Punic Astarte, by the Caeritan ruler Thefarie Velianas.

ABOVE Sculpture in stone (*nenfro*)
of a youth riding on a sea-monster,
c. 550–530 BC: probably the guardian
of a tomb. From Vulci, which was
the principal Etruscan centre
of sculpture in stone (in most
other places terracotta was
the usual medium).

ABOVE Painting from the
François tomb, Vulci, late fourth
to mid-third century BC. Marce
Camitlnas of Vulci is slaying
Cneve Tarchunies Rumach, i.e. a
Roman and a member of the
Tarquin family, presumably of
the sixth century BC. These
paintings open up vistas of
Etruscan history and legend
unknown from Latin or Greek
authors.

LEFT Bronze tripod from Vulci,
late sixth century BC. The figures
are made from moulds, which
were retouched and reworked
after each casting.

ABOVE The bank of the River Fiora. *Left*, on the hill-top: village of Final Bronze Age (early first millennium BC), with its cemetery in the valley. *Right*, above the road: site of Copper Age cemetery (second millennium BC). The Fiora provided Vulci with a vital valley route into its hinterland and had a port, Regae, near its mouth.

BELOW Terracotta revetment from a temple at Statonia (Poggio Buco), early sixth century BC, showing a chariot and infantry soldiers. Statonia overlooked the River Fiora and two of its tributaries, and controlled a strategic crossing.

An Etruscan road-cutting in the territory of Vulci,
near Suana (Sovana) and Pitigliano.

been Ligurian in origin but may have experienced alternating periods of Ligurian and Etruscan occupation, at least in the fifth century BC.[66]

One of the principal incentives that attracted Etruscan and other settlers or traders to these places was the presence of various metals, including copper and iron, in the coastal range of the Apuan Alps – a sort of northern extension or appendix of the previously described Catena Metallifera (Metal-Bearing Chain) that stretches up behind the coastal plain north of the Arno.[67] The Massarosa settlement is situated on the foothills of this range; other centres where Etruscan objects have come to light stood close to the seaside route that later became the Via Aurelia. Only two miles from Massarosa, beside this thoroughfare, is the modern port of Viareggio, near which recent discoveries have again disclosed a massive Etruscan presence, in spite of ancient forests and marshes.[68]

On the same Via Aurelia, towards the northern extremity of the plain, stood Luna (Luni), which was later to become a Roman river port and marble-quarrying centre, in the second century BC.[69] Livy recorded that its territory had earlier been under Etruscan occupation,[70] but until recently it has been customary to doubt this; the finds at Viareggio and Massarosa, almost half-way to the place from the Arno, now make it desirable to accept the account. Strabo also recorded a large Etruscan port a little farther north, in the Gulf of La Spezia.[71] Luna, which possessed a deep natural harbour, is probably the place to which he is referring – unless the La Spezia bay contained yet another port of which we so far know nothing.

These ports open up interesting vistas of Etruscan staging-points up the coast road to the north of the Arno,[72] and archaeologists are now able to add evidence much farther north still. A ship wrecked off Antipolis (Antibes) on the French Riviera was found to contain a great many Corinthian-style Etruscan amphoras and vases of the years around 575–550 BC,[73] while Etruscan objects have turned up in con-siderable quantities near the mouth of the Rhône, close to the adjacent Phocaean colony of Massalia, which was founded in c. 600, reached the climax of its commercial activity during the century that followed, and was never far from the minds of Greek and Etruscan traders operating up this coast. Moreover, abundant Etrusco-Corinthian pottery has come to light at the fortified centre of Saint Blaise (Bouches du Rhône), which seems to have been strongly Etruscanized and was evidently a redistribution centre for Etruscan goods. In addition Etruscan, as well as Greek, finds are dotted along the banks of the Rhône and Saône, half-way up into the eastern interior of France. There have also been

Etruscan discoveries at various sites far inland, for example Vix (Côte d'Or, Burgundy), a focal point near the great Celtic fortress of Mont Lassois, which reached the height of its power in the sixth century BC. Whether the Etruscan grave objects at Vix, such as a bronze wine-jug and basins and a bronze statuette of *c.* 500 BC,[74] came up the Rhône or across the Alps is uncertain – perhaps both routes were employed for these objects and for the magnificent Greek wares they accompanied. Etruscan artefacts are also found, not only in Spain and north Africa,[75] but particularly in Germany (as well as Belgium and Luxemburg),[76] dating for the most part from the fifth century onwards, when Etruscan outlets to the south were becoming more difficult to maintain. The influence of such imports on the Celtic art of those regions was varied and considerable.[77]

As we have seen, Dionysius of Halicarnassus had said that all western Italy was once described as Tyrrhenia, and Cato the Elder and Livy declared that the Etruscans had controlled the whole of the peninsula. This they did not quite do, though some southern and northern regions experienced a process of development very similar to that of Etruria, and there was also considerable expansive activity, at least in the commercial and cultural spheres, by one or another of the Etruscan city-states or by men emanating from them. Besides, in another sense, as is now clear, Cato and Livy claimed not too much but too little: the presence of the Etruscans not only extended almost from end to end of Italy but also far beyond its borders, until first the Greeks in the south and then the Gauls in the north finally made them retreat within their own homeland.

Part Two

THE INDEPENDENT CITY-STATES

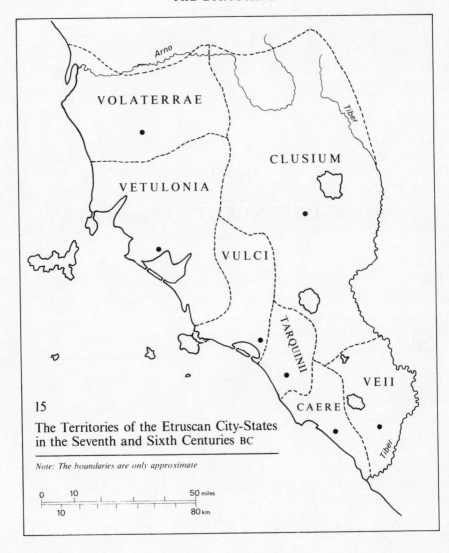

15

The Territories of the Etruscan City-States
in the Seventh and Sixth Centuries BC

Note: The boundaries are only approximate

CHAPTER 7

DISUNITY

Social Disunity

The massive Etruscan presences beyond the southern and northern boundaries of the Etruria, in so far as they involved the actual displacement of population, were probably intended to provide a safety-valve for the many frustrated and discontented persons whom the social system of their homeland was producing.[1] For the unity of the country, and the unity of each of the city-states that it contained, was rent by sharp social inequalities. With regard to these stresses and strains, more and more information is coming to light, but its total is still too insubstantial and fragmentary to throw any truly comprehensive light on the social development of the country. The time has not yet come to write a social history of Etruria, but Mauro Cristofani's recent books *The Etruscans* and *L'arte degli Etruschi* have shown how the task will one day be done. Here only a few things will be said. In the pre-urban period of the ninth century BC, the archaeological evidence suggests that the society of the villages in Etruria had been broadly uniform, egalitarian, and classless, with one exception: since this was a society which, from the beginning, was based on the traditional clan (and the families into which it was subdivided), the supremacy of the chiefs of these clans and families was generally recognized. In the following century, however, after the first important contacts with the Greeks and near-easterners, the appearance of enormously rich tombs indicates the emergence of a whole new wealthy class,[2] profiting from the foreigners' desire for local metals. Under the leadership of this class a strongly feudal society developed, in which there was a tendency for monarchies to be gradually replaced by oligarchic governments. The nobles were surrounded by artisans, clients, freedmen and slaves, some of whom became prosperous.[3] Dionysius of Halicarnassus tells of leading Etruscans bringing their own dependants on campaigns in 480 BC.[4] He uses a word elsewhere employed for serfs – underprivileged persons without

117

political rights – and it would seem that the armed infantrymen of Etruria were more closely bound to the ruling class, and to a less extent independent persons, than their counterparts in Greece.[5]

However, modest estates of peasant cultivators sometimes existed side by side with the huge properties cultivated by tenant and slave labour;[6] and the view, prevailing until recently, that the feudal situation remained static and unchanged throughout Etruscan history was exaggerated. On the contrary, a process of evolution is detectable: by the end of the seventh century, the class structure was already becoming less rigid. Tombs at Volsinii, for example, confirm the existence of mercantile and artisan elements,[7] and the same message is conveyed by the excavation of houses at Vetulonia, San Giovenale and Veii. Social mobility was on the increase, and great land-owning families were, of necessity, conceding some share of power to merchants and craftsmen. The great sanctuaries and temples and the diffusion of the alphabet provided such people with new power-bases which enabled them, to some extent at least, to counterbalance the authority of the nobles. And the appearance of 'tyrants' or unconstitutional dictators, towards the end of the sixth century BC – men such as Lars Porsenna of Clusium and perhaps Thefarie Velianas at Caere – may once again represent the supplanting of the aristocracies by this new economic class.

Nevertheless, it still remains true that this bridging of the social gaps never went very far: it may partly have replaced the hereditary nobility by a moneyed class and its hangers-on, but it never really gave Etruria an intermediate grade of society like that of the Greeks and Romans.[8] In the history of Rome, from the fifth to the third century BC, one of the great basic themes, as all its own later historians knew, was the prolonged power-struggle between patricians and plebeians. This struggle, though it never produced a democracy, at least led in the end (after considerable convulsions) to practical transformations and accommodations that enabled the Romans to move forward from a broad base to the vast tasks that lay ahead of them. However, the comparative social backwardness and imbalance which persisted in Etruria made it ill-prepared to confront the future.

In the last years of the fourth century BC, and throughout the period that followed, there were disastrous social conflicts within the populations of cities such as Volsinii and Arretium, conflicts that were duly recorded by Roman historians. It has been plausibly suggested that if the same historians had addressed themselves to Etruscan internal affairs during the two previous centuries as well, they would very probably have found similar situations existing already in the various city-states.[9] Such persistent internal disharmonies, of course, played right into the hands of the Romans, who exploited them – usually by supporting the ruling class, whether hereditary or mercantile – in order to make the various Etruscan governments dependent on themselves.

The Ineffective League

The whole Etruscan social community then was weakened by these internal inequalities, but it was also torn by a second major rift arising from the independent and indeed often mutually hostile policies adopted by one Etruscan city-state towards another. For this kind of disunity the evidence, though still patchy, is nevertheless considerably more extensive. It is true that the Etruscans regarded themselves as forming a homogeneous, distinct, ethnic or cultural entity, but they by no means formed a single political unit. On the contrary, they were a conglomeration of individual city-states; and at any given moment of their history it is necessary to pass on from the question of what 'the Etruscans' were doing to what was being done by these individual city-states – in so far as our information makes this possible.

Such an attempt has too rarely been made, largely because the existence of a so-called Etruscan 'league' has lulled enquirers into forgoing the endeavour. However, the 'league' was not much of a reality. True, at least in the relatively late times of the fifth and fourth centuries BC, the city-states of Etruria sent representatives to an annual meeting which was held at a holy place at some site, not yet located, in the neighbourhood of Lake Bolsena. This was the Fanum Voltumnae or shrine of Voltumna – the Etruscan Veltha or Veltune, who may have been a deity of the earth or seasons but is of uncertain sex, though if male he may be identifiable with a god described by the Romans at Vertumnus.[10] The annual meetings at the Fanum Voltumnae were for the most part of a religious nature, and they also included annual games on the Greek pattern. And another thing that happened on these occasions was that the assembled representatives of the city-states elected one of their number, just for a year, to their federal high priesthood, which has been described as the 'kingship' of Etruria.

The states that sent representatives to these meetings did come to be regarded as constituting a kind of league, although this development does not seem to have occurred until the middle or late years of the sixth century BC. The historian Livy even then – or rather in the period after

500 to which he is specifically referring – never actually describes the member states as comprising a 'league', preferring the vaguer and more non-committal and transitory-sounding terms *consilium* (council) or *foedus* (treaty).[11] Moreover, as has been more than once pointed out, his accounts of what actually transpired at these gatherings have a distinctly fictitious appearance. Like other historians, he indicates that the member states were twelve in number, and so they may have been – despite the difficulty of identifying the twelve at any given moment – during the comparatively late period to which these writers are referring. Twelve was a familiar number in groupings of Greek cities, and a particularly conspicuous example was the Ionian Federation. The Ionians influenced Etruria in many ways, and they surely influenced the development of its 'league'. But these Ionian influences only occurred in the latter years of the sixth century BC, so the Etruscan 'twelve' do not appear to be earlier than that.[12] By that time groupings of this kind were well known in the Greek world and did on occasion undertake political activity; no doubt Livy and others are right in attributing a certain amount of such activity to the Etruscan meetings at that epoch. But, as regards the earlier period, it would not be plausible to regard Etruria as more advanced than Greece, and in Greece, by that time, the idea of a primarily political league had hardly arisen. For example, the league centred on Delphi (the Amphictyony), though it dated back to about the eighth century BC, remained for the most part religious, devoted to purposes of common worship, until after 600. At any earlier date a political league would have been a remarkable anomaly,[13] and there is no reason to suppose that things would have been different in Etruria.[14]

Similarly, the notion that the expansions of the Etruscans into Campania in the north and the Po valley in the south were conducted by their city-states on a united, federal basis was no less misconceived. As for Campania, Strabo's idea of twelve Campanian colonies[15] founded on the model of (or created in unison by) the allegedly twelve cities of Etruria is far too neat, and is contrary to the archaeological facts, which indicate that it is to the individual Etruscan city-states or, sometimes, to groups of persons or single leading persons coming from them, that we must attribute the initiative – which may, in any case, not have involved *twelve* Campanian foundations at all. With regard to the Po valley in the north, a story of much the same kind, that there were twelve colonies sent out by the twelve in Etruria,[16] prompts precisely the same suspicions. And the rival ancient theory that the hero Tarchon founded the allegedly twelve northern cities shortly after establishing

Tarquinii itself is, once again, over-schematic: it is a product of Tarquinian pride, it refers these supposedly synchronized northern
'foundations' to much too remote a past.

To revert to the city-states of the Etruscan homeland, it is clear that
throughout the principal period of Etruscan power and prosperity their
'league' was not an effective body; it remained, practically speaking,
insignificant and inoperative as a political and military force. We have
no knowledge of the league ever entering upon a treaty or alliance with
an external power on its own account. Indeed, at least until the fourth
or even the third century BC (when it was already much too late for
Rome to be staved off), it failed conspicuously to produce unity or
united action among the city-states of Etruria. Livy and Dionysius of
Halicarnassus make it clear that such combined and co-ordinated
action was blatantly lacking – the failure of the other Etruscan cities to
save Veii in its fatal struggle against Rome is the classic example; and
no city lifted a finger to help Clusium against the Gauls. Moreover,
wall-paintings from Vulci and inscriptions from Tarquinii, to which we
shall come later, show that the people of one Etruscan city actually
fought battles and wars against the people of another – a situation
which Virgil's *Aeneid* reflects by pitting the Etruscan Mezentius against
other Etruscans.[17]

Whenever the common interests of Etruria clashed with those of
one of its city-states, the city's interests always took first place. There
is no reason why this should cause us surprise. Ancient Greek leagues,
too, were very far from being models of harmonious coherence, as are
the United Nations and smaller regional groupings today. As Luisa
Banti rightly asks, 'Are we then expected to believe that the Etruscans
were the sole exception, the only example of constancy?'[18] Yet it *is*
widely and unreasonably expected of the Etruscans that they must
somehow have varied from this norm and must have acted habitually in
collaboration with one another. This is, for the most part, the fault of
the ancient Greek and Latin authors. For they were only concerned
with the alien Etruscans when they happened to impinge on Greek or
Roman affairs; moreover, the Etruscans' alien language made it all too
easy to lump them together in an amorphous mass. These writers
therefore took no interest in distinguishing between one Etruscan city-
state and another but were content to describe them by the vague
generic term of 'the Etruscans', and so they failed to hand down the
evidence that would have given the individual city-states the distinctive
treatment that each merited. Luisa Banti is therefore right to conclude
that 'the Etruscan League has become a heavy chain attached to the

Etruscans throughout their history'. It is necessary to cast the chain off and to look at their city-states as separate entities.

It will be useful, whenever we can, to erase the term 'Etruscan' and replace it by the name of one of the Etruscan states. That will either have been acting as a corporate unit or through varying numbers of its citizens, sometimes behaving more or less independently of their government. On occasion, two or three of the city-states (or individuals from them) may have been acting in unison for the time being, in order to carry out some specific project or aim – or, perhaps more often, the ruling families of certain city-states may have formed shifting networks of collaboration with one another.[19] Thus, as Massimo Pallottino remarks, 'Rather than a history of the civilization of the Etruscans, what we ought to be considering is the history of Caere or Vulci or Tarquinii.'[20] This is the only proper course. Its desirability was already clear to D. H. Lawrence, as a flash of perceptiveness in his book *Etruscan Places* (1932) reveals: 'If you try to make a grand amalgam of [all the Etruscan cities], then you won't get the essential Etruscan as a result, but a cooked-up mess which has no life-meaning at all.'[21]

The Diversity of Etruria

To someone living in Tuscany today, or in northern Lazio which was southern Etruria in ancient times, the diversity of the country from a geographical point of view seems self-evident. First there are the enormous regional differences between the great volcanic, lake-studded plateau of the south, the wider landscape of sandstones, limestones and metalliferous hills in the centre and north-west, and the fertile valleys of the east and north-east. And even the most rapid tour of the principal museums containing Etruscan objects, and of the ancient cemeteries still to be seen at the Etruscan sites, shows that these differences were reflected in equally conspicuous regional variations in building materials, social customs, artistic themes and methods, and alphabetic forms of writing and dialects.[22]

Indeed, within the boundaries of each of those main regions, too, each smaller region – the sizeable piece of territory owned by each individual city-state – was quite remarkably different even from its nearest neighbours in all these respects (and sometimes, it would appear, in its system of government as well). How totally different, for example, was Clusium from everywhere else, and Vulci from Tarquinii, and Tarquinii from Caere – from which it was only a few miles distant.

Italy is still just as sharply divided up today, to an extent that the English, with their longer tradition of centralization, may find surprising, though the people of a strongly regionalized country such as Germany will understand it readily. Vernon Bartlett, the English writer and journalist who used to live near Lucca, illustrated the situation admirably by describing how two workers on his farm, one of whom came from Lucca and one from Pisa, were invariably determined to undertake each and every agricultural operation in different ways and on different days;[23] and yet Lucca and Pisa are only ten miles away from each other. That was about the distance between some of the ancient Etruscan cities also. And in ancient times, as each one of them independently grew and developed without the advantages of modern communications, it was inevitable that they should maintain their own distinctiveness very jealously indeed.

The remaining part of this book, then, will study each of the principal city-states of the Etruscans in turn as an individual and separate phenomenon. We have seen how their initial development was prompted by the external demand for metals, in which the Greek markets of Pithecusae and Cumae played such a prominent part. In response to this demand the groups of villages on the Etruscan hill-sites coalesced into a series of cities and city-states, each possessing the political, industrial and commercial organization needed in order to make the highly lucrative deals which brought them their power and prosperity. It must now be shown how they went on from there – how the various cities prospered and expanded and established their own peculiar, recognizable identities.

CHAPTER 8

TARQUINII

Wealth and Art

The first Etruscan centre to respond to an external desire for its metals by completing the process of urbanization, and thus organizing itself to form a manufacturing industry and drive bargains that would bring great riches, was, as we saw earlier, Tarquinii, on its defensible height beside the River Marta, which leads from Lake Bolsena (known as the Tarquinian Lake) down to the nearby Tyrrhenian Sea. Tarquinii rapidly attained power and a measure of local supremacy owing to the adjacent metals of Mount Tolfa.

Early Etruscan cities generally display a blend of old and new: while retaining cultural features going back to their own pre-urban past, they produce an outburst of novel developments arising out of their newly acquired wealth. Tarquinii is no exception. There is continuity with the local past in the unbroken series of artefacts found in its cemeteries, but at the same time the impact of the novel Greek commerce is vigorously felt. The people of the place formed immediate links with Pithecusae and Cumae, the markets established in the eighth century BC by Greek traders from Euboea; in particular, the pots with wiry 'Geometric' decoration imported by the Greeks to those markets and reproduced there reappear almost at once at Tarquinii, which promptly reproduces them in its turn. It was apparently the first place in Etruria to receive such goods and the first to make painted vases on its own account.[1]

Like the other cities of Etruria, Tarquinii, as far as the dwellings of the living are concerned, has virtually disappeared. The loss makes the task of understanding its civilization exceedingly hard. Yet not everything has gone: we can see from the walls that the place had a circumference of five miles, though it is unlikely that the whole area was built over at any one time. Inside those walls, upon the hill of La Civita, magnetic surveys comprising tens of thousands of computer-processed measurements have revealed the general plan the city eventually assumed, the design of its principal streets, and sometimes even the outlines of single buildings. The foundations and remains of a vividly decorated temple have also come to light.

For the rest, we are faced with our usual problem in Etruria: we can only reconstruct the lives of its people from what we see of the habitations they gave their dead. It is fortunate for us that, owing to their religious insistence on the afterlife, they lavished so much care on these tombs. Gradual changes in their character also occurred. Thus in the formative second half of the eighth century BC, at the time when all the new Greek influences were coming in from Campania, cremation graves at Tarquinii were at first supplemented and then largely superseded by inhumations in stone coffins laid in trenches, as in most other parts of Etruria. Then, soon after 700, burial places on an entirely different scale begin to appear – chamber tombs that are sometimes covered by a massive monumental mound of earth. These tombs were equipped with immense and increasing lavishness, testifying vividly to the new trade with Greek harbours.

This new economic and cultural phase is illustrated by the Bocchoris tomb. This is so called because the various imported objects from Greece and the near east that were found inside its chamber (together with a selection of local pottery) included a glass paste jar bearing the name of the Egyptian Pharaoh Bocchoris (Wohkerē), of the twenty-fourth dynasty. Bocchoris ruled from about 730 to about 715 BC, but the jar seems to be an imitation of an Egyptian original, made at a somewhat later date in Phoenicia,[2] the country which channelled so many near-eastern imports to Etruria via the Greek Campanian markets. Thus the date of the tomb may be assigned to c. 675. It was at this stage that the prosperity of Tarquinii entered a new and climactic phase.

From this time onwards the cemeteries of the Monterozzi plateau beside the city of Tarquinii reveal an extraordinary number of burials. Within the last twenty years alone, more than six thousand tombs have been found there by new geophysical techniques.[3] A hundred graves covered by mounds are still visible; a century and a half ago, there were more than six hundred. The continuing Greek influence at Tarquinii throughout this period is illustrated by the famous story of a certain Demaratus, who lived in the earlier part of the seventh century BC. According to this tale, Demaratus emigrated from his native city of Corinth with his whole family, an aristocratic refugee from political tyranny. Before taking this step, it was said, he had made large sums in the uniquely profitable Etruscan commercial market, and when he left Greece he settled in Tarquinii. The whole story has legendary overtones which gathered round Demaratus because he was believed to be the father of a King of Rome, Tarquinius Priscus. Nevertheless, the tale offers valid testimony to just the sort of population displacement that was characteristic of the times and made a great impact on Etruria in particular. Pliny the Elder adds that Demaratus brought with him to Etruria three artists or 'modellers' (*fictores*),[4] by which he probably means terracotta sculptors.[5] Their names, Eucheir, 'skilful-handed', Eugrammus, 'skilled draughtsman', and Diopus, 'a user of the *dioptra*' (an instrument for taking levels), have been dismissed by some modern authorities as fictitious, but they may be authentic – either real names, that is to say, or at least names which real people chose to assume – since 'Diopus' has also turned up on a fifth-century inscription from Sicily.[6]

In any case, whether these three men actually existed or not, they stand for a historically true situation, in which, at a time of major artistic developments in Etruria, a strong and continuing impact was made on the trade and art of that country by the rising mercantile power of Corinth and its colonies, partly effected by the presence of their immigrants and travelling traders and artisans. Thus a characteristic form of seventh-century Tarquinian ceramics echoes the Corinthian style. It may have been brought to Tarquinii by traders from Cumae, and is consequently known as Cumano Etruscan. Tarquinii is one of the prime leaders of the 'orientalizing' style which is so closely associated with the widely circulating Corinthian pottery and was probably the city which inaugurated its reproductions in Etruria.

Demaratus was said to have brought up one of his sons with an Etruscan and the other with a Greek education;[7] Tarquinii was clearly a place where a Greek could feel at home. Indeed, many of the people cremated in its imposing tombs had manifest Greek connections themselves. One of them, Lars Pulenas, known today as 'the magistrate', describes his great-grandfather as *Greices*, the Greek. Another whose ashes were interred in a Tarquinian grave was called Rutile Hipukrates;[8] his first name was Etruscan and his second Greek (Hippocrates), so he was apparently of mixed origin, the son of a Greek father and an Etruscan mother.

Rutile Hipukrates, like Demaratus, is attributable to the seventh century BC; but the outstanding manifestation of Greek artistic influence on Tarquinii did not occur until at least a century later.

This took the form of an extraordinary efflorescence of local tomb-paintings. About a hundred and fifty of the known tombs of Tarquinii contain paintings, of which twenty are reasonably well preserved. They are gay, brilliant, complex and energetic, executed in flowing and decisive lines and adorned with vivid splashes of green, blue, and red. They give the impression that, for the ruling class, life on earth has been enjoyable, and they offer the confident hope of an equally enjoyable life after death.

The first of these painted tombs appear in the mid-sixth century BC, when the city's burial places, though more numerous, had shrunk in size, since Tarquinii was no longer politically pre-eminent. In compensation, this was a time when many Ionian refugees were flocking into the region after the subjection of their country by the Persians. The paintings of Tarquinii surpass all others in Etruria; it is true that painters were also active elsewhere in the country, but in no other city is such a remarkable concentration and prolonged evolution of such masterpieces to be found. And this is not merely due to the fortuitous circumstances of survival, for these paintings constituted an art-form in which Tarquinii truly excelled – indeed, they were unique not only in Etruria, but in the entire ancient world. The Greeks themselves have nothing similar to show: their paintings on the walls of temples and houses have not survived, and in tombs they did not have any paintings (at least until many centuries later) since their burial places were not adapted to such methods of decoration. Nevertheless, the paintings of Tarquinii display the main characteristics of the successive Greek artistic styles which influenced Etruscan culture one after another – though with considerable modifications, owing to the peculiarities of Etruscan taste.

The oldest painted grave so far discovered at Tarquinii is probably the Tomb of the Bulls of about 550–540 BC. It is named after a picture of a horseman chased by a bull, but the main scene, painted on the central pillar which provides the most conspicuous wall-space, is from the mythological cycle of the Trojan War, showing Achilles lying in wait for the young Trojan Troilus, hiding behind a fountain to which his enemy is riding. This is the only known Tarquinian mythological painting. Its figures and decorative themes convey a spellbound and rather frightening atmosphere. The treatment, while showing certain Corinthian and other Greek and near-eastern analogies, has not yet fully assimilated these imported influences and accompanies them by themes and motifs derived from purely local sources. And nature – customarily played down by Greek artists so as not to distract attention from human beings

– is given a new emphasis, though, in Etruscan fashion, the approach shows a measure of stylization and is not wholly naturalistic. Three other chambers of the grave, including paintings of erotic scenes, show an emphasis on architectural features which was characteristic of this period.

As elsewhere, a period of strong Ionian influences followed almost at once,[9] and before long they became more fully integrated into the native traditions – although these still do not allow themselves to be forgotten. Colourful animal and plant motifs appear, such as were also employed to decorate temples and other large buildings. Sometimes the proto-types of the tomb-paintings can be traced back to the Phocaeans, who were particularly prominent in the western Mediterranean before their defeat off Alalia (Corsica) in c. 535 but still remained active thereafter. In this category is the Tomb of the Jugglers, particularly notable for the picture of a young girl performing a rhythmical dance, in contrast to an immobile form representing the dead man.[10] Of the same period and artistic style are the paintings in the Tomb of the Augurs, which launch a long series of Etruscan scenes depicting events in honour of the dead. The pictures in this tomb include a splendid representation of wrest-lers, with a referee signalling the start of the fight. There is also a representation of the demon-masked Phersu launching a savage black dog at another man. The victim of the attack, who wears an animal skin, holds a club to defend himself with, but is blindfolded, his head muffled in a bag. This scene may carry some esoteric mythological meaning,[11] but it has also been regarded, with some probability, as evidence of a cruel sort of Etruscan gladiatorial sport that fore-shadowed the beast-fights of the Romans. The style and iconography of these designs, though largely influenced by Ionia, display close analogies to wall-paintings in central and southern Asia Minor as well.[12]

Another less sinister masterpiece, again showing the hand or influ-ence of Ionian or other east Greek artists, is the Tomb of the Lionesses (c. 540–530). Its paintings are arranged in two major horizontal divisions instead of the three that had been customary hitherto, and the pictures reveal powers of vivid and luxuriant description. There has been a thematic shift from games to banquets; round the main scenes are friezes showing palms and lotus flowers and birds flying through the sky, while dolphins plunge among the waves. The Tomb of Hunting and Fishing (c. 530–520) again depicts birds and dolphins, stylized in form and abstract in colour, yet curiously evocative of nature. The main scene depicts a man fishing with a line from a boat, while another aims at a flying duck with his sling and a third is shown in the act of a graceful dive. Although Ionian influence is once again apparent, there is a frank exuberance in these fresh, dream-like seascapes that reflects a specifically Etruscan popular taste.

The Tomb of the Olympic Games (c. 520–510, or a little later) presents a chariot-race inspired by a vase of eastern Greek style, but given a livelier treatment; themes learnt from the Greeks and, through them, from the near east, are handled with imaginative originality. The figures painted in the Cardatelli tomb are shown posing and playing and parading by an artist notable for his fluency and vigorous humour. The Tomb of the Baron (c. 520–510) displays an exaggerated, colourful stylization of Ionic forms which includes curious echoes of the art of the Hittites who ruled the central regions of Asia Minor in the second Millennium BC.[13]

When we come to the fifth century, the Tomb of the Two-Horse Chariots provides the earliest attempts at naturalistic representations of the human figure, indicating that Ionian treatment has given place to Athenian, exercised through the widely circulating (though, as we have seen, not artistically very influential) 'red-figure' vases. This grave is unique not only for its selection of themes but for the scale and lavishness of the decoration and subtle employment of colours. The Tomb of the Hunter, displaying an unusual, richly ornate tent hung with trophies of the chase, offers a warning to those who might desire to fit Etruscan art into too close a chronological pattern, since a period of several decades elapsed between its first and last paintings were executed (c. 525–480). The Tomb of the Dining Room (c. 460–455) is painted in a fluent, refined Athenian style which displays an effort to achieve shading effects. But the Giustiniani tomb of c. 450 is more characteristic of the general attitude of Etruscan art of the period in its refusal to go all the way with the full, mature classicism of Athenian art of the period, preferring to retain features of previous archaic styles, executed floridly and not without suggestions of native Etruscan ideas. It has been customary to note a break or decline in good Tarquinian paintings after this date (until its resumption in the last three centuries BC), though recent discoveries suggest that this supposition may have to be modified or the gap narrowed.[14] But it remains largely true, as in other spheres of Etruscan art, that the spirit has lost much of its former vigour from about 500–450 onwards.

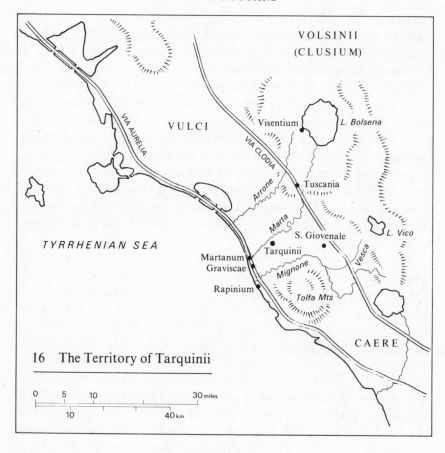

VOLSINII
(CLUSIUM)

VULCI

VIA AURELIA

VIA CLODIA

Visentium

L. Bolsena

Arrone

Tuscania

Marta

S. Giovenale

L. Vico

TYRRHENIAN SEA

Tarquinii

Vesca

Martanum
Graviscae

Mignone

Rapinium

Tolfa Mts

CAERE

16   The Territory of Tarquinii

0   5   10   30 miles

      10   40 km

Territory and Ports

When the villages of Tarquinii first united to form a city in the eighth
century BC, two of its dependencies, Luni on the River Mignone and
Visentium (Bisenzio) near the source of the Marta on Lake Bolsena,
seem to have been blotted out by the newly rising power. Visentium,
whose bronzes allocate it to the Tarquinian sphere of influence,[15] only
survived for a few years, long enough to produce certain 'Geometric'
jars under Pithecusan influence[16] and a wheeled incense-burner with
bronze figures inspired by the same style but including a deity of
monstrous pre-Greek appearance.

Nevertheless, Tarquinii retained a number of large settlements or
towns in various parts of its extensive territory. One was close by at
Tuscania (possibly the Etruscan Tusc(a)na), on the right bank of the
River Marta half-way to Lake Bolsena; standing at a cross-roads where
the valley road to the lake met a major trade-route running parallel to

the coast, the later Via Clodia, Tuscania began to become a major subsidiary centre of Tarquinii some time after the eclipse of Visentium, probably in about 600 BC.[17]

Looking towards the north-east, the Tarquinians had long been connected with Clusium by road, sending artists there and relying on the place as an intermediary for their exports beyond the Apennines. They also had close links with other Etruscan centres, since the central position of their city was convenient for undertaking commercial transactions along the land routes to all parts of Etruria – and for gathering lucrative tolls where those routes met. Thus even before the eighth century was over Tarquinii had begun exporting goods along the coast road to Vetulonia, and then or later a close connection was also formed with Vulci, which stood beside the same route. To the south, there are still traces of a road from Tarquinii to Veii – which may even have been, in origin, a colonial settlement founded by the Tarquinians.[18] Road communications in this direction were made possible because the Tarquinians actively opened up the forests in their extensive territory, which became popular and heavily cultivated. They also became well-known producers of spring-sown flax and thus of linen, and they were reputed to be the inventors of the hand-mill.[19]

But Tarquinii did not have to rely on its land routes alone for its flourishing commercial activity, for, as its coastal road to Vetulonia and Vulci reminds us, it was also very close to the Tyrrhenian Sea, and possessed fifteen miles of valuable coastline. At the height of its power, this extended from near the mouth of the River Arrone in the north (beside the modern Riva di Tarquinii) to beyond the Mignone to the south – thus including, for a time, the shore adjoining the metal-rich hills of Tolfa.

At that time the level of the sea was much higher and the coast showed considerably deeper and more useful indentations.[20] This made it possible for Tarquinii to develop no less than three ports. Each was only a few miles from the city, the distance of Piraeus from Athens, or of Lechaeum and Cenchreae from Corinth. We do not know the Etruscan names of any of Tarquinii's ports but we know where they were. One was at the place the Romans later called Martanum, at the mouth of the Marta; another was Graviscae (Porto San Clementino), a little farther south, again very near to Tarquinii itself; and a third was Rapinium, farther on beside the mouth of the Mignone.

From the beginnings of the history of urbanized Tarquinii in the eighth century BC, some at least of these ports must already have been very busy, for by that time a sea-route was already in use from

Tarquinii to Etruscan Campania (which used the Tarquinian form of the Etruscan alphabet).[21] Moreover – and this was especially notice-able from 650 onwards – Tarquinian exports found their way not only to Campania but also to the Aegean basin, and subsequently even to north Africa.[22] And 'the Etruscans' – thus vaguely defined by the ancient writers – already possessed a seapower as early as the eighth century, and the first navy to wield that power must have been a navy belonging to the earliest maritime city to achieve power and prosperity, namely Tarquinii.

Which of its ports the Tarquinian fleet chiefly used we cannot tell – perhaps Martanum, which was the closest, although today the harbour only shows sparse remains, and they are of later, Roman, date. But recent excavations have shown that Graviscae was active as a port of Tarquinii before the end of the seventh century BC. It occupied a large, roughly rectangular site, with elaborate rock-cut tombs on the neigh-bouring slopes that led up to the plateau of Tarquinii. But the significant feature of Graviscae, it now proves, is that the place housed a community of Greek traders; their presence is confirmed from c. 600 BC.[23] Two of their wells have been found, a few post-holes of wattle-and-daub huts, and a small shrine dedicated to Aphrodite (the Etrus-can Turan and Roman Venus). This seems to have been the first permanent religious construction on the site; but about forty years later new cults of Hera (Uni, Juno) and Demeter (Ceres) were added. More than half the fifty Greek inscriptions that have been found at Graviscae are dedications to Hera. Other discoveries include more than five thousand lamps, which comprised an important feature of the cult of Demeter. One lamp in the shape of a boat had been brought from Sardinia, and indicates contact with that island.[24]

Most of the Greeks who appeared at Graviscae seem to have come from the coastline of Asia Minor, at the time of Persian pressure on that region in the latter part of the sixth century BC; perhaps a majority originated from the island of Samos. Tarquinii gave them permission to establish a trading-post at Graviscae, in the same way as Egyptian pharaohs allowed other Greeks marketing bases at Naucratis (Nabira) and elsewhere.[25] These harbours in Egypt were reminiscent of other Greek (Euboean) commercial centres that had earlier been established at Al Mina and Tell Sukas on the Syrian coast, though, unlike those outposts, places such as Naucratis appear to have been granted a specific juridical status by the host state; the same may well have been true of Graviscae. At an earlier date, perhaps, the social structure of Tarquinii had been more open and thus more willing to absorb alien elements as part of its own community – such as the Corinthian immigrant Demaratus. Graviscae bears witness to a new and more closed Tarquinian society which preferred foreign populations to be concentrated in separate trading areas.

Later on, at the end of the sixth century, other Greek maritime powers besides the Ionians made their appearance at Graviscae. One was Athens, of which the vases are to be seen at the port. Another was one of Athens's rivals, the island state of Aegina. Its presence is recorded by an inscription found just outside the sanctuary of Hera (the only Greek stone inscription so far to have been discovered on Etruscan soil), declaring: 'I belong to Apollo of Aegina. Sostratus had me made.' The island of Aegina was an important maritime power at the end of the sixth century, when its long and eventually unsuccessful struggle against the Athenians began. The Aeginetans may have had a formal share of Graviscae along with the Ionians, just as they (and others) shared the main sanctuary of Naucratis. The incription clearly refers to a statue of Apollo, dedicated by a trader named Sostratus who is perhaps identifiable with a rich Aeginetan merchant named by Herodotus, a successful trader with Tartessus in southern Spain. Alternatively the visitor at Graviscae may have been one of this man's relations.[26]

After 480, when relations between the Etruscan homeland and Greek southern Italy were sharply deteriorating, the Greek presence at Graviscae seems to have come to an abrupt end, and the sanctuary was transformed into an Etruscan shrine of only modest pretensions.

Monarchs from Tarquinii at Rome

Tarquinii pursued ambitious commercial policies, facilitated by communications both on land and on the seas, and it was inevitable that its people should reach out beyond the borders of Etruria to north and south alike. Their pretensions in the north are illustrated by the fraudulent chauvinistic story that Tarchon, the legendary founder of Tarquinii, also established all the Etruscan centres in the Po valley. In the south, they may well have given their name to Tarracina (Terracina) in Latium. And, much more important, they seem to have provided a dynasty to Rome – the dynasty that presided over its Etruscanization.

The successful businessman Demaratus, who migrated to Tarquinii from Corinth as a political refugee shortly before the middle of the seventh century BC, married a noblewoman of Tarquinii – we are told by Emperor Claudius[27] – and had two sons, one of whom, Lucumo, survived him. But then Lucumo (the story continues) moved on with a number of followers to Rome, where he won the favour of many, including the king, Ancus Marcius, whom in due and peaceful course, traditionally in 616 BC, he succeeded on the Roman throne, with the assistance of his masterful wife Tanaquil. Thereafter he was known by the name of Lucius Tarquinius Priscus, 'the original' (or 'elder') Tarquinius'. He and his son or grandson, Lucius Tarquinius Superbus 'the proud' (together with another ruler, Servius Tullius, between them, of whom more will be said later), were believed to have reigned over Rome for just over a hundred years, at the end of which Superbus was deposed in favour of a newly declared Republic.

The form in which the story has come down to us contains legendary and unacceptable details. For instance, Demaratus is unlikely to have been the father of a Roman king: the well-balanced pattern of his migration to Tarquinii and his son's migration to Rome looks altogether too symmetrical. Secondly, Tarquinius Priscus's former Etruscan name 'Lucumo' merely means 'chief', and this seems to have been chosen by the saga-writers to provide colour for his royal pretensions and a motive for his move to Rome.[28] Besides, the change of name to 'Lucius' looks a feeble fabrication, based on a characteristically false etymological analogy with 'Lucumo'.[29] The duplication of the royal Tarquins is suspect, too. The presentation of one of them as 'good' and the other as 'bad' is designed to explain how it was that (1) Rome quite obviously owed highly important developments to its Etruscan dynasty, but (2) the dynasty nevertheless had to be condemned as wicked, because it was overthrown by the glorious Republic. Nor is it at all certain that Tarquinius Priscus' accession was as peaceful as tradition emphasized; this is the sort of story that was told in order to avoid the suggestion that Rome had been forcefully conquered by a foreigner.

Nevertheless, the main features of Rome's Etruscan dynasty still remain convincing. The approximate date of 616 BC for its beginnings fits in very well with the archaeological evidence concerning Rome, which was becoming Etruscanized and urbanized at just about this time. And Tarquinii is a very plausible place for the first of the Romans' Etruscan rulers to come from – not least because of another tradition that their regalia came from there as well.[30] Some have maintained that the tradition is wrong and that he came from Caere instead, where a tomb (of later date) identified by inscriptions as belonging to the family of the Tarchna or Tarquinii has come to light[31] (and it was at Caere that

Tarquinius Superbus and his sons were supposed to have taken refuge after his deposition). Yet the Tarchna were a large clan known not only at Caere but at a number of other Etruscan towns also – including, emphatically, Tarquinii itself. So the Caeritan tomb is insufficient reason for tampering with the tradition attributing the origin of the Tarquins to Tarquinii – which, even after encroachments from Caere and Vulci, still remained a very important place, as its wall-paintings are quite enough to show.

Livy and Dionysius of Halicarnassus say that Tarquinius Priscus had decided to emigrate from Tarquinii because its people, regarding him as an outsider, despised him and excluded him from citizenship; he chose Rome as his destination because it was a young and rising place that was receptive to foreigners.[32] Both these reasons are plausible enough, and throw some light on the obscure population movements of the period; Tarquinius Priscus comes under the heading of the stray Etruscan adventurers who established themselves as settlers and rulers of cities other than their own. As for Queen Tanaquil's notorious masterfulness, we may discount the obvious legendary components – intended by Greek and Roman writers to stress the excessive emancipation of Etruscan women – but still conclude that she may have fulfilled a leading role, since leading Etruscan women *were* more masterful than their early Roman counterparts.

Later History

The later history of Tarquinii is strangely and fitfully revealed by a group of Latin inscriptions of the first century AD which have been found there.[33] Like analogous documents that have come to light in other cities, they are *elogia*, brief statements of the careers of officials or commanders inscribed on the bases of statues or monuments erected in their honour. Such *elogia* probably, for the most part, incorporate material from family histories and archives.

The Tarquinian group of *elogia* honours the local family of the Spurinnas. Allowing for a little complimentary exaggeration, there is no need to deny these inscriptions a good measure of historical reliability – though to reconstruct the genealogies of these men with any exactitude, or to identify the activities that they are describing, remains a considerable problem. We are told that the 'praetor' Velthur Spurinna I led an army to Sicily, thus becoming the first of all Etruscan leaders to take troops across the sea, and that he received a shield and gold crown for his victory. Various attempts to identify this occasion have been offered, of which the most profitable suggestions include *c.* 474 BC, when there was an Etruscan presence in the southern Tyrrhenian Sea, *c.* 413 BC, when Etruscan fleets helped the Athenians in their expedition against Syracuse, and *c.* 307 BC, when eighteen Etruscan ships and a thousand men gave help to Syracuse against Carthage. The choice between these occasions remains disputed.

What is important to our present discussion, however, is not so much the exact determination of the dates that are referred to but the fact that this is an inscription recounting a tradition of the city-state of Tarquinii and of its citizens. There is no reason to suppose that whatever expedition is being described was 'Etruscan' in any general sense. It was the expedition of a fleet sent by Tarquinii (possibly with allies, though they are not mentioned), not by the Etruscan 'League', which was too weak and amorphous to undertake such enterprises. The 'praetorship' of Velthur Spurinna was once again an office, not of the League, but of the city-state of Tarquinii.

The same official seems to assert, though the text is incomplete, that he also led an army against Caere, while another and equally difficult inscription appears to record that Aulus Spurinna, the son of Velthur, expelled Orgolnius, the King of Caere, and intervened forcibly at another Etruscan town, Arretium (Arezzo). Whether these events belong to the fifth or fourth century BC is once again not certain. If the latter is the case they may refer to social disturbances that took place within the cities in question in *c.* 358–351 BC.[34] But the significant fact that emerges, once again, is this demonstration that the Etruscan city-states or their citizens, far from always acting together as 'the Etruscans' and harmonious members of a league, were perfectly capable of warlike interventions in one another's territory. The same inscription goes on to say that Aulus Spurinna also captured nine 'Latin towns' – either towns in Latium itself, or communities in the more or less Etruscanized borderlands.[35]

During Rome's decisive war with Veii, Tarquinii raided Roman territory on at least one occasion. However, like the other Etruscan cities, it made what proved to be the fatal mistake of not helping its Veientine compatriots effectively enough. After Veii's total, catastrophic defeat (*c.* 396 BC), it was towards Tarquinii in its turn that Rome cast unfriendly eyes, for it was the Tarquinians who were now Etruria's only potential leaders. War flared up in 358 and lasted for seven years[36] (during which time Rome accused its Etruscan enemies of living up to their reputation by maltreating prisoners of war). Then, after a pause of nearly forty years, hostilities broke out again in 314.

Three years later, Rome emerged victorious and imposed stern conditions on the Tarquinians. The Roman formula was to make unequal 'treaties', or perhaps truces, with such Etruscan cities;[37] but Tarquinii, like the rest, had by this time ceased to have any real existence as an independent power.

CHAPTER 9

CAERE

Wealth and Art

Strategically located at the junction of the coastal plain and the hills, Caere seems to have become urbanized, by the usual amalgamation of a group of adjacent villages, only a little later than its north-western neighbour Tarquinii. The fact that Caere was able to achieve this transformation at so early a date suggests that it must already have had some share in the rich metals of Mount Tolfa that lay between the two places. At first the mines seem to have belonged primarily to Tarquinii (see Chapter 2). But before very long, perhaps near the end of the seventh century BC, the greater part of their metals seem to have passed into the hands of Caere, which thereafter – owing to the foreign demand for these resources – became one of the most sumptuous centres of the Mediterranean world. There is continuity between the artefacts of the pre-urban and urban ages of Caere, and this particularly applies to its pottery. Nevertheless, after the successful encroachment on Tolfa, radical and sensational new developments occurred, owing to the enormously increased wealth that was now available to the governing class.

As at Tarquinii, comparatively little information about the course of events can be derived from the actual habitation area, since not very much of it has survived. Still, a beginning has been made. It can be stated that the city eventually reached a size of about 375 acres, with an estimated population of about twenty-five thousand. Little is known about the plan of the place, but the remains of at least eight temples and sacred areas have been identified, and the excavation of some of them has begun. One of the sanctuaries was connected with the cult of medicinal waters that spring from the hillside nearby and provided a specialized feature of Caere's excellent water-supply.

However, as is so often the case in Etruria, it is necessary to look at burial places, rather than residences of the living, to gain some insight into what urbanization meant in terms of wealth. The Sorbo necropolis, west of the city, had already been employed as a cemetery in pre-urban times. It had, in those days, mainly been used for cremations, which, as we have seen, in the urban age gave place to inhumation. One of the most startlingly rich graves of the new epoch is the Regolini-Galassi tomb (named after the men who discovered it), dating back to the mid-seventh century. A long entrance-corridor flanked by two chambers of elliptical shape leads into the tomb itself, which consists of two rectangular rooms with false vaults – that is to say, vaults consisting of progressively overhanging and converging blocks laid in horizontal courses up to an apex. In addition to these false vaults the Regolini-Galassi tomb provides examples of their equivalent on a square or round base, the false dome constructed on similar principles, such as had appeared already in the pre-urban period at Populonia farther to the north. The false vaults, like the 'false' domes, are ultimately of Mycenaean origin; those in the Regolini-Galassi tomb are reminiscent of structures at the Mycenaean fortress of Tiryns. False domes and vaults alike had probably been transmitted to northern Etruria by way of Sardinia, and then from northern to southern Etruria.

But the most noteworthy feature of the Regolini-Galassi tomb is its burial furniture, for the grave escaped the attention of subsequent plunderers, since the original mound had been enclosed, almost at once, in a larger one which hid it out of sight. As a result, the contents have survived and are to be seen at the Museo Gregoriano Etrusco at the Vatican. They include gold jewels of unparalleled lavishness which belonged, in part, to a woman buried in the inner chamber of the tomb and described as the wife or daughter of Larth. It was the Caeritans' possession of saleable copper and iron that made it possible for them to afford these massive quantities of gold from the Greek markets of Pithecusae and Cumae. Moreover, they commissioned Greek gold-workers to fashion some of it for them, at those places, though they themselves also no doubt had their own local metal-workers operating in styles indistinguishable from those of the Greeks.

The details of these gold bracelets and brooches and corsages and earrings were Greek, borrowed from a variety of near-eastern sources, but the forms and overall patterns (as well as the large dimensions) were Etruscan, or at least adjusted to suit Etruscan tastes; so was the extensive use of granulation and embossing techniques. They were not, it is true, unknown in Greece and the near east, but were refined to an extraordinary degree for this Etruscan market. The objects from the

Regolini-Galassi tomb reveal clearly that Etruscan gold jewellery achieved unsurpassable heights of skill. Indeed some of its secrets have still not been wholly solved today – the question, for example, of how the minute grains of gold were attached to the gold plate is not as fully answered as was thought.[1]

There is also a strong possibility that the Etruscan alphabet was introduced to the country by way of Caere. It was an adaptation of the Greek letters in use at the Greek market, and later colony, of Cumae in Campania, and it was from Cumae that this alphabet originated. The Etruscans initially needed and adopted it for purposes of trade, and then made great use of it for writings connected with their religion. It was thanks to Etruria that central and northern Italy, and through them western Europe, became literate. Opinions change at frequent intervals about what may be the earliest Etruscan inscriptions and where they came from – new discoveries are constantly being made. At present, inscriptions on silver vessels found in the Regolini-Galassi tomb, together with another from Tarquinii – all of the earliest years of the seventh century BC – share the claim to priority, while alphabets (of slightly different character) from Veii and Marsiliana, belong to the same century.

Among these centres, either Caere or Veii (even if their first hitherto-known examples may prove a trifle later than their Tarquinian counterpart) is most likely to have acted as the initial recipient and adapter of the alphabet from the Greeks, owing to their geographical proximity to Cumae. But between Caere and Veii, the former still seems the best candidate for the major intermediary role: at the time when the alphabet first appeared in Etruria, Caere was in far closer touch with Greek Campania than inward-looking Veii and was a far more important centre. It takes its place naturally as one of the Etruscan cities credited with founders from Greece, since it had powerful Greek connections. Greeks or part-Greeks appear frequently on Caeritan inscriptions; some of them, such as Lars Telecles towards the end of the seventh century BC, may well have been among the teachers who imparted to native scribes the knowledge of the Cumaean alphabet and conveyed suggestions as to how it could be adapted to local Etruscan needs.

Greek imports to Caere increased rapidly at about this time, and so did Greek visitors. One Greek who was there was a distinguished potter and ceramic artist, Aristonothus, who signed his name on his vases, which he almost certainly made at Caere and did not import from outside. His name or *nom de plume*, meaning 'Aris [*aristos*, 'the best'] son of a bastard (non-citizen)', shows an immigrant's touch of self-irony.[2] A fine mixing-bowl by his hand found at Caere depicts a naval battle in which the contestants seem to be Greeks and Caeritans.[3] To judge from the styles and shapes of his wares, it looks as though Aristonothus came from the island of Euboea which had provided the traders and then colonists at Pithecusae and Cumae. It has also been deduced from his techniques that after leaving Euboea he had subsequently worked at Athens and in Greek southern Italy – perhaps at Cumae – before moving on to Caere. In the last quarter of the seventh century Caere also made fine pottery in the Corinthian style; some of the men with mixed Greco-Etruscan names who continue to appear at Caere in these years are probably Corinthians and may have been potters. But Etruscans soon took over this sort of work and produced the same styles.

A similar shift from Greek immigrants to their local Etruscan adapters characterized one of Caere's and Etruria's major inventions in this field, namely black *bucchero* pottery (from *c.* 650). The misleading modern name *bucchero* comes from the Spanish term *bucaro*, applied to central and south American pots belonging to periods previous to Columbus. Etruscan *bucchero*, made of unusually fine clay – preferably with a manganese content – was turned on the wheel and then baked in a slow-burning fire, in such a fashion that the oxygen reached the clay in insufficient quantities to turn its iron content red, but turned it black instead. These wares seem to have been designed in the first place for funerary use, but were then extended to household employment as well, and, as we shall see, were exported on an enormous scale. They owed something to Greek and near-eastern wares, and particularly to earlier unglazed (*impasto*) Caeritan pottery. But the new artists adapted and transformed these models into something remarkably original.[4] Once again the first designers were evidently Greek visitors or settlers, followed soon afterwards by Etruscan successors. Caere specialized in the fine or thin-walled variety of *bucchero*, as opposed to a heavier type that became popular in northern Etruria, especially at Clusium. The best Caeritan pieces are noteworthy for their smoothly harmonious contours. They are elegant, cheaper substitutes for vases and cups in bronze, and indeed their shapes sometimes echo these metal vessels, which were readily available for copying.[5] Caere was probably the point of entry into Etruria of large bronze receptacles in eastern styles from Pithecusae and Cumae; their local imitation was easy, since metal from Tolfa was now at Caere's disposal.

The vast prosperity conferred upon the Caeritan upper class by the availability of these metals becomes conspicuously apparent in the Banditaccia necropolis north-west of the city, which is best-known, most impressive, and largest, of the local cemeteries. It had already been in use before urban times, but in the years just before 600 it was specially selected for maximum expansion, superseding the Sorbo and other large burial places of previous times which lay nearer the city; the change may have been made partly because of the availability of suitable volcanic stone. George Dennis described the Banditaccia as 'a singular place – a Brobdignag warren, studded with molehills'.

But this is not Dennis at his best; in fact, the site is a unique memorial of the Etruscan civilization. It comprises a great assemblage of earth mounds heaped up on plinths of rock or stone, some of which attain a diameter of a hundred feet. Beneath the mounds are groups of chamber tombs carved out of the rock. Here at Caere, the old tombs in cylindrical pits and in trenches continued for a time, side by side with the new type, until, in the seventh century, graves topped by mounds began to dominate the scene. Mound tombs had already been seen in southern Etruria in pre-urban times, but the Caere monuments are of much greater size and complexity than anything that had appeared hitherto.

One very large grave, the Tomb of the Shields and Thrones, contains three chambers of different periods from the late seventh to the early sixth century BC, and the Giuseppe Moretti tomb comprises no less than ten chambers. These Caeritan graves mirror the arrangement of a city in their relation to one another, with smaller tombs geometrically assembled round a larger one. There must originally have been an impressive central avenue, along which the cemetery was systematically planned. Moreover, architectural principles are once again always apparent in the designs of the individual graves as well. Their proportions and spatial qualities, which display remarkable taste and skill, reflect a religious determination that the dead must be given habitations that will ensure them a life after death worthy of their way of life before they died.

While the designs of the graves do not exactly copy the houses of the living, they nevertheless deliberately echo various kinds of domestic interiors, at a time when these were evidently beginning to be more elegant. For example, the Tomb of the Thatched Roof – the first to be cut out of the volcanic rock, in the mid-seventh century BC – reproduces a straw-roofed hut of pre-urban type. In *c.* 600, the ceiling of the Tomb of the Ship and then of the Tomb of the Painted Lions as well – one of the earliest Etruscan graves to contain paintings – imitate the woodwork and beam-construction of private houses. Next, in the early years of the sixth century, the Tomb of the Capitals displays capitals adorned with flowered volutes (spiral scrolls) of a type traditionally related to the vigorously artistic Aeolian Greeks (north of the Ionians) on the west coast of Asia Minor.[6] The Tomb of the Cornice (*c.* 550) has an engraved cornice round its walls. It also contains two large stone seats with foot-rests, along with a stone back-rest inspired by metalwork. The sixth century also witnessed the inauguration of a new square or rectangular type of grave, the cube tomb, of which we shall encounter other examples in the countryside behind the city. Prefigurations of the enclosed *atria* or courtyards that later became familiar features of domestic design at Pompeii and elsewhere are also to be found in early Caere.

These architectural features displayed in the tombs of Caere provide us with our chief source of knowledge about the Etruscan houses from which they are reproduced – buildings that have wholly disappeared. And from about 500 BC, too, a poorer type of tomb takes its place alongside those of the very rich, thus making a valuable contribution to our sparse evidence for Etruscan social history.

From the middle of the sixth century onwards Caere was advancing to fresh artistic achievements in other fields as well. Supplied with metal from Tolfa, it continued its career as a centre for bronze-workers, becoming prominent, in particular, in the working of hammered sheet-bronze with *repoussé* decorations. When Virgil, in the *Aeneid*, brings Aeneas to the vale of Caere to receive the divine armour,[7] he does so because of the city's reputation for this craft.

From about 540 onwards the Caeritans, following up the earlier successes of Aristonothus and others in this field, also developed a particularly impressive new school of ceramics. Their initial guides in this activity were the Ionian artists who were flooding into Etruria at the time because their own country was menaced and overrun by Persia. One particularly notable and individual Ionian workshop at Caere produced a series of stocky and handsome water-jars (*hydriae*) displaying rich polychrome paintings of Greek mythological scenes. These were executed for the local market by at least two talented painters, who displayed racy and humorous styles.[8] Evidently an Ionian Greek could set up his business in sixth-century Caere in a liberal and welcoming atmosphere, and he could, and did, worship the Greek Hera, the city-goddess of Samos in his own country, under her own name (rather than its Etruscan equivalent Uni), at a shrine in one of Caere's ports.

Prompted by these same pervasive Ionian influences, Caere also produced a remarkable school of terracotta sculpture, reaching its climax in the later years of the same century. Sculpture was not new in the area, since brilliantly individual terracotta seated figures of women date from *c.* 600–570 BC.[9] Then come a series of equally remarkable sarcophagi. One group of about 520 BC shows life-size figures, a husband and wife, reclining together on a banqueting couch.[10] The most famous of these receptacles is in the Museo della Villa Giulia at Rome: the husband, whose torso is nude, has his right arm round his wife's shoulders, and the couple are gesturing in animated conversation. The manner in which they are depicted illustrates the capacity of Etruscan art to be very Greek and very un-Greek at the same time. The egg-shaped heads, oval faces, smooth unmuscular bodies and softly folded drapery built up in rounded ridges are redolent of Ionian refinement, and the motif of figures reclining at a banquet is Greek as well. But, as was remarked earlier, the Greeks never showed husband and wife reclining together in an equality that they would have found shocking. The woman's long tunic and cloak, too, and her shoes with curved points, are peculiarly Etruscan. So is the large mattress falling heavily on either side of the couch. There is also something very Etruscan about the intentionally unbalanced angularity of the design, and its abrupt changes of direction. Although the artist had learnt much of his technique from Ionians, he is also an original master in his own right, distributing masses and volumes, and organizing movements from one plane to another, in a way that deviates from Greek taste and practice, and deliberately creates a disturbing, enigmatic disharmony.

Territory

Caere's hinterland stretched as far as Lake Bracciano, where rich early tomb equipment has been found at Trevignano Romano. Soon, too, Caeritan territory was extended farther north. The wild and picturesque zone north of the River Mignone looks, on the map, as though it ought to belong to Tarquinii, and so at first it no doubt did. But when Caere gained much of the Tolfa metal at Tarquinii's expense, archaeological evidence suggests that the Caeritans pushed farther on as well, cutting off an additional large slice of Tarquinian territory for their own commercial (and probably political) exploitation. One centre which probably passed into the hands of Caere at this time was the ancient settlement of San Giovenale. Originally a dependency of Tarquinii, it had imported Corinthian and other Greek ceram-

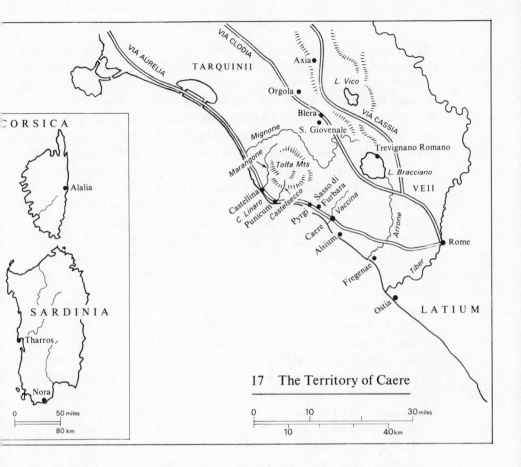

17   The Territory of Caere

ics from the seventh century BC onwards; but it became a large and important settlement in about 600 when its mound tombs began to display artistic links with Caere. The town's remains include, somewhat unusually, a number of one-storey houses of people who were not particularly rich. In addition, the Caeritans exercised a strong influence in a wide area west of Lake Vico, as can be seen from a number of centres they established there from the early sixth century BC onwards, flanked by cemeteries containing funerary furnishings like those found at Caere. This is a tortuous, seamed landscape of sheer rock walls towering over deep gorges scored by erosion; within the cliffs and slopes are graves cut out of the rock. These picturesque monuments testify to the existence of quite important Etruscan residential areas in the vicinity, which have now disappeared without a trace. When they existed, they were apparently outlying dependencies of Caere.

One of these places was Blera (the Etruscan Phleva [?], later Bieda).

The key-point of a complex road network, it stood on the old major north–south thoroughfare that later became the Roman Via Clodia. Passing near Caere, this was the most important route traversing Etruria, until the Romans built the Via Cassia farther inland in 171 BC. But the Via Cassia, again, was only the replacement of another Etruscan route likewise passing beside Blera, which thus benefited from a double traffic.[12] The lost habitation site of Blera stood at the end of a mile-long ridge that dropped at the other extremity to a point where four glens meet. The ridge also contained Blera's Etruscan necropolis, which dates back to the seventh century BC and displays the cube tombs characteristic of Caere early in the century that followed.

North-west of Blera, on the same Via Clodia, is another remarkable assemblage of tombs at Orgola (the Etruscan Orcle and modern Norchia), but its cemetery does not seem to have developed until the fourth century BC. In the vicinity, however, is the much earlier centre of Axia (Castel d'Asso), which likewise appears to have belonged to Caere at the height of that city's power. Tombs with façades like the fronts of houses are carved in the sides of Axia's precipices. 'Tomb after tomb', wrote George Dennis, 'hewn out of the cliffs, on either hand – a street of sepulchres hewn into square architectural façades, with bold cornices and mouldings in high relief, and many inscriptions graven on their fronts in the striking characters and mysterious language of Etruria.'[13]

Dennis also comments on the solemnity of the site, the loneliness and utter stillness of the scene. Yet despite the seclusion of Axia's valley in his day, the place was, in ancient times, within easy reach of the two major land routes, the Via Clodia on one side and the Via Cassia on the other.

The Seapower of Caere

In its links with the outside world, Caere relied heavily on its maritime communications, for having once taken a large part of the Tolfa metals from the Tarquinians, it also succeeded them as the leading Etruscan naval and sea-trading power. It was probably by sea that the Cumaean Greeks brought their alphabet to Caere in the seventh century BC, and it was by sea that the enormous wealth of gold found its way into the Regolini-Galassi tomb. Imports continued to flow into the city in increasing quantities thereafter. Moreover, the Caeritans did not only have the copper and iron of Tolfa to offer in return for this wealth: they also had their *bucchero* pottery and whatever products of their land and industry it might contain. This pottery passed in huge quantities along the sea-routes;[14] shortly after its inception in the seventh century, it developed a massive external distribution throughout the Mediterranean and Aegean regions. And if it is true that the Aegean island of Lemnos was an Etruscan commercial station, it was probably Caeritans, the principal Etruscan maritime people, who manned it, until the base fell to the Athenians in about 500 BC.

Caere's geographical position explains these extensive Greek contacts, for it was the southernmost of the Etruscan maritime cities and the nearest to the Greek markets and colonies of Campania: that is to say, it was the first Etruscan state reached by traders from Pithecusae and Cumae, and that is why it lay uniquely open to successive Greek influences. When the geographer Strabo paid Caere the rare compliment of saying that its people were the only Etruscans who were not pirates,[15] what he meant was not only that they were good friends of the Romans but also that their sea trade was on a uniquely well-organized basis. Not that their trading with the Greeks, of course, was without violent moments: Aristonothus was not the only, or the last, Caeritan vase-painter to depict a sea-battle between Greeks and Etruscans; and the latter were Caeritan soldiers travelling and fighting on Caeritan ships. The timber needed to build these powerful fleets was also readily available to Caere, both on the Tolfa hills, when it gained possession of their resources, and beside its own stream, the Vaccina. That is why Virgil singles out for special mention, among all the numerous, varied timber supplies of Etruria, these particular notable pine-woods.[16]

Caeritan vessels ranged far to the south. It is true that when *bucchero* from Caere is found (and was imitated) in northern Campania, for example at Capua,[17] it might have come there by land, but the numerous Caeritan objects excavated in the southern part of Campania are much more likely to have arrived by sea. This applies, for example, to a seventh-century dish that has come to light at Picentia and is very similar to those discovered at Caere,[18] while an inscription from nearby Fratte di Salerno shows the Caeritan alphabet.

The existence of the important Caeritan navy, which must have assisted in such operations, involved complex relationships with other powers active in the Italian seas. One of the most important of these states was Carthage in North Africa, the western successor of Phoenician Sidon and Tyre. By the late seventh century, Carthage was receiving not only Etruscan metals and imitations of Corinthian pottery made in Etruria, but also Caeritan *bucchero*. Yet this connection between Carthage and Caere was not only commercial and peaceful but also involved a strong and perilous element of competition, which could easily lead to conflict. The danger of such a clash became particularly acute from 600 onwards, when the Carthaginians were stepping up their expansionist endeavours.[19] However, the rivalry was a triangular affair, for a third and very powerful element of competition was provided by the Greeks. In particular, it was just at the turn of the century that Ionian Greeks from Phocaea established themselves at the strategic site of Massalia (the Roman Massilia, now Marseille). And then, among the many other Phocaean centres which were established in the western Mediterranean, a particularly prominent part was played by Alalia (the Roman and modern Aleria) in the eastern part of the island of Corsica, a harbour town which fulfilled a key role on the trade-route to Spain. Alalia commanded access to the interior of the island and to lakes rich in fish and salt. It looked out over the alluvial plain of the River Tavignano, one of the few stretches of level shore on the island, situated beside a large bay (now filled in) which enjoyed protection from the north-east wind. From this strategic location the Alalians dominated the approaches to Caere and other ports of mainland Etruria, which lay directly across only eighty miles of sea.[20] So the Etruscans, Carthaginians and Phocaeans were locked in an uneasy balance in central Mediterranean waters.

In about 550, a brusque attempt was made to adjust this balance in favour of Carthage when one of its commanders, Malchus, embarked on a double *coup*. First he consolidated the Carthaginian position in western Sicily, using existing colonies as springboards, and then he made a forcible endeavour to repeat the same process in Sardinia. There was strong resistance from the native Sardinian city-states and communities, and they claimed some success.[21] Malchus probably achieved something, all the same. But if so, he paid a high price, for the result of his enterprise was to bring the Carthaginians onto a collision course with the Phocaeans, for whom Sardinia was a highly sensitive area.

What, then, was the third interested seapower, that of Etruscan Caere, to do? Its leaders considered the matter and decided that the most pressing peril to themselves came not from the Carthaginians, in spite of their expansion, but from the Phocaeans, whose colony in Corsica was so close and menacing a neighbour. In consequence, Caere decided to throw in its lot with Carthage.[22] Thus began the important, perhaps fluctuating, but on the whole durable alliance (emphasized later by Aristotle) between the Carthaginians and 'the Etruscans'.[23]

The clash between the new pair of allies and the Phocaeans was not long in coming. It took the form of the historic naval engagement somewhere off the coast of Corsica (or perhaps nearer Sardinia) in *c.* 535, known as the battle of Alalia. Herodotus, writing in the following century, tells how the Phocaeans – whom, although they were fellow Greeks, he blames as plunderers and looters – mustered sixty ships against a hundred and twenty of the enemy, comprising sixty each of the Carthaginians and 'Tyrrhenians' (Etruscans), or rather Caeritans. The Phocaeans won the battle but suffered so much damage that the survivors decided to evacuate Alalia altogether and establish a colony in the far south-west of Italy instead.

'As for the crews of the destroyed [Phocaean] ships,' Herodotus continues, 'the Carthaginians and Etruscans drew lots for them, and by far the greater share of them fell to . . .' Here a few words have dropped out; they have been plausibly restored as 'the Etruscan city of Agylla', the Greek name for Caere, for we are immediately told that 'the Agyllaeans led the prisoners out and stoned them to death; and in expiation of this offence they sent to the Delphic oracle which told them what rites and Games to perform'. The story is revealing on several counts. In the first place, the way in which Herodotus tells the story confirms the view, already stated, that it was not 'the Etruscans' as a whole who took part in this action, but the Caeritans. It was Caere that had allied itself with the Carthaginians, had fought as their allies in the battle of Alalia, and had ill-treated the Phocaean prisoners – an action, incidentally, which did much to encourage the Greek, and later Roman, view that the Etruscans were cruel. But the tale is significant for another reason also – because of Caere's application to the Delphic oracle. Apparently the Caeritans possessed their own 'treasury' at Delphi – a frequent practice among Greeks, but Caere was the only city-state of the Etruscan homeland to follow the custom. This testifies to the uniquely close relations with Greece that are displayed by the whole cultural history of the place,[25] notwithstanding the war against the Phocaeans.

As to that war and its results, there is archaeological evidence that, during the next four decades or so after the battle, the Phocaeans, despite their evacuation of Alalia, were not so completely excluded from Corsica as a whole as Herodotus' moralizing account might suggest (for he is eager to show that their previous piratical behaviour was punished). Yet there had been a shift in the balance of power in favour of the Carthaginians and Etruscans. The position of the Carthaginians in Corsica was now strengthened; but Diodorus Siculus, the historian of the first century BC, adds the curious information that the Etruscans (Caeritans) founded a colony on the same island – probably at some date after the battle. It was in the north-east, perhaps at or near

Alalia itself.[26] Diodorus adds that the original settlers gave the place the Greek name of Nicaea, or Victory-Town, which has caused some to suppose that the colony must have been Greek and not Etruscan. But the Caeritans, deeply Hellenized as they were, might well have given their colony a Greek name and, for all we know, Greek settlers; there is no reason to doubt Diodorus' story. He adds that the Etruscans exacted tribute from Corsica in the form of resin, wax and honey.

By the turn of the century, there was also an Etruscan workshop and Etruscan graffiti at Alalia, and chamber tombs of Etruscan form and contents make their appearance there. Alalia had connections with all the Etruscan ports, perhaps with Caere most of all. There may also have been groups of Caeritans in Sardinia, whose inhabitants Strabo describes, loosely, but none the less revealingly, as 'Etruscans'.[27]

In order to see how Caere was able to operate as a maritime and naval power, we must have a look at its ports. Caere's coastline, longer than that of its neighbour Tarquinii, extended, at the height of Caeritan power, from near the estuary of the River Mignone in the north down to only a mile or two short of the Tiber in the south. Recent discoveries suggest that the coastal installations of Caere, and the settlements on which they were based, were spread along almost the entire length of this substantial waterfront. The picture that emerges is of five more or less consecutive port areas – two in the north, two in the south, and the most important in the middle.

In the north, the two ports were at Castellina (near the Roman Castrum Novum) and Santa Marinella (the Roman Punicum). At Castellina, a fortified hill-top site commanded a harbour near Torre Marangone. The harbour lay at the mouth of the River Marangone, which provided the shortest and easiest communication with the Tolfa hills, the source of Caere's mineral wealth and the timbers needed for the construction of its ships. It seems that this port below Castellina's hill was used by early Greek traders and prospectors, since fragments of seventh-century pots that have been found there resemble discoveries at Pithecusae.[28]

Just to the south of Castellina was another small harbour town at Punicum. Remains of its ancient port-works are still to be seen, or are in process of excavation, beneath the low rocky promontory of Cape Linaro, and the site of a sanctuary of Menrva (Minerva) has been found on the other side of the bay.[29] The name 'Punicum' is best regarded as derived from the Roman word for 'Carthaginian', and indicates that the place was, or contained, a settlement of Carthaginian merchants and traders, no doubt operating there in accordance with the treaty between Carthage and Caere. Like Castellina, Punicum commanded a stream (the Castelsecco), linking it with metal-bearing Tolfa.

The two southern ports of the Caeritans which balanced those in the north were Alsium (Palo, near Ladispoli) and Fregenae (Fregene). Alsium was of importance because it was much the nearest of all Caere's harbours to the city itself, from which it was only four miles distant, along the course of the River Vaccina. Tombs of the late seventh or early sixth century have been found in the place. The tradition that it was named after a Greek, though based on a false etymological analogy,[30] may well mean that there had once been Greek traders or settlers at Alsium, as there were also at Tarquinii's harbour town of Graviscae. To the south of Alsium, the small harbour at Fregenae was located at the mouth of the River Arrone, which came down from Lake Bracciano (and has to be distinguished from a stream of the same name north of Tarquinii). Fregenae was about thirteen miles from Caere and Veii, but none the less probably belonged to Caere rather than to Veii. It is true that this left Veii only a very short coastline, but it was a city without maritime pretensions.

Pyrgi

Between the Caeritans' northern and southern ports – Castellina and Punicum on the one hand and Alsium and apparently Fregenae on the other – was yet another harbour, already mentioned, at Pyrgi (Santa Severa).[31] This seems to have been a port area of some antiquity: a little to the south, three hundred yards from the sea, in a cemetery belonging to a settlement of the early first millennium BC at Sasso di Furbara, an oak boat has been found in a tomb.[32]

Coastal currents have now largely eaten away the harbour of Pyrgi, but it is clear from excavations that it became Caere's principal port. It is a little difficult to see why. It is true that, like the other harbour towns just to its north, Pyrgi was connected by valley communications with Tolfa. Moreover, traders must have been attracted by the small bay, which provided its anchorage and was sheltered to the north-west by a promontory. Pyrgi was as much as eight miles away from Caere, twice the distance of Alsium. However, it was linked to the city by a fine wide road, flanked by graves surmounted by massive mounds: one of them is the monumental Monte Tosto tomb of the mid-sixth century BC, close to the platform of an exceptionally large Etruscan temple. The thoroughfare that ran from Pyrgi to Caere may have been a Sacred Way, for, in addition to Monte Tosto's holy place, Pyrgi itself was a major religious centre, and that, in addition to its harbour facilities, was presumably the reason why it became so important.

In 1964 three thin rectangular sheets of gold leaf were found at Pyrgi. Each of them displays inscriptions – one in the Punic (Carthaginian) language, the other two in Etruscan.[33] The sheets are pierced with holes for the insertion of nails, so that they could be set up on wooden tablets for public inspection. They appear to belong to the years just before, or possibly just after, 500 BC. Although the Punic inscription presents textual difficulties, it can be translated. At first there were hopes that the Etruscan plaques might turn out to be exact versions of it – for, if so, we might have been able to crack the secrets of the Etruscan language, just as the Rosetta stone, now in the British Museum, has made it possible to understand ancient Egyptian. Tantalizingly enough, however, neither of the two Etruscan inscriptions has proved an exact counterpart of the Punic version. The smaller Etruscan text appears to differ from it sufficiently to defy exact comparison, and the larger version evidently differs more markedly still, so that it is scarcely a translation at all, but a free paraphrase.

Nevertheless, these tablets remain of first-class importance. The Punic inscription is the first ever to have been found on the soil of continental Italy. The other two comprise our first contemporary, official Etruscan sources of information about Etruscan history. And the contents of all three inscriptions, though somewhat obscure at certain points, are of considerable interest. The Punic original and the smaller of its Etruscan adaptations refer to the dedication by Thefarie Velianas, Lord of Caere, in the third year of his power, of offerings and a holy place (or annual religious ceremony) to the Carthaginian (Phoenician) goddess Astarte or Ashtart (the Etruscan Uni, Greek Hera and Roman Juno).[34] The other, more extended Etruscan inscription adds instructions regarding procedures commemorating Thefarie Velianas' act.

Thefarie Velianas was the earliest Etruscan ruler of any city of whose name we have knowledge derived from his lifetime. However, although the Punic text describes him as 'King of' or 'reigning over' Caere, the title *zilath* ('supreme magistrate') in the Etruscan versions has been held to suggest that he was not a hereditary monarch. Indeed, there is some reason to suppose that at Caere, as at many other Etruscan city-states, the original monarchy had been abolished before this time. It is therefore likely, instead, that he was a strong man or 'tyrant' who had seized power at the city, like others at just about the same date – not only Greeks, such as Aristodemus of Cumae, but fellow-Etruscans such as Lars Porsenna at Clusium and its dependent territories including Rome. Such dictatorial figures, disguising their illegality under the respectable title of supreme magistrate, were often the products of social disturbances in which a new rising economic class displaced the traditional aristocracies and oligarchies.

Moreover, Thefarie Velianas' obeisance to the Carthaginian goddess Astarte – to whom Uni is specifically assimilated (*Uniel Astres*) – seems to comprise not only a religious dedication but a reference to the external politics of the city, and in particular to its continuing alliance with Carthage. Despite all Caere's historic connections with Greece, the general hostile situation reflected in the battle of Alalia, in which the Caeritans and Carthaginians together had fought against the Phocaeans, was still in existence some three or four decades later. Indeed, it is possible that the inscriptions display a certain subservience of the Caeritan ruler to the Carthaginians, who seem to have been his backers. Perhaps they even put him on the throne – or kept him there in the face of a possible pro-Greek *coup*.

Be that as it may, the years around 500 were a period when the Greek threat to both Caere and Carthage alike, far from diminishing, was on the increase. Both faced implacable Greek hostility in Sicily, and the Etruscans, in addition, were receiving severe blows from Cumae in Campania and its Latin allies. These were blows which Caere must have felt more than any other Etruscan city, owing to its geographical position at Etruria's southern extremity and the maritime responsibilities that this position involved. So there was every reason for the alliance between Caere and Carthage to continue.

The gold plaques were found in a sanctuary area of Pyrgi, within a rectangular enclosure constructed to house precious objects at a subsequent date, when buildings in the zone were being dismantled.[35] The sanctuary may have been very ancient indeed, since the name of Pyrgi, which is Greek and means 'towers', seems to go back to Mycenaean times.[36] In due course, the shrine seems to have become the most important sacred complex in the whole of non-Greek Italy, of a type not hitherto known in such territories. The sacred zone in the middle of the precinct included an altar and a well in which the bones of an ox, a badger, a young pig and a cock have come to light.

The Greeks, referring to the Pyrgi sanctuary in inscriptions in their own language, indicated its dedication to a divine personage named variously as Leucothea and Eileithyia; the former was a goddess of the sea, and the latter of child-birth, whose worship went back far beyond the first millennium BC But it is virtually certain that the Etruscan name of the deity worshipped at the holy place was Uni (Hera, Juno, Astarte), the goddess to whom Thefarie Velianas offered his dedication; for the Greeks often identified Eileithyia with Hera, and indeed used the former name as one of her titles. Moreover, a further tablet of bronze found on the site is concerned with Uni's cult, perhaps at a slightly earlier date, and other votive inscriptions on clay from the same place are dedicated to her worship.[37]

On either side of the sacred central zone are the remains of two temples, built parallel to one another and facing the sea. One ('Temple B') dates from about 500 BC, and the other ('Temple A'), it is now believed, from about 460–450. The earlier of the two buildings contains a single shrine (*cella*) preceded by a broad portico with columns all round, an arrangement that has been variously described as a purely Greek formula or a compromise between Greek and Etruscan traditions. The later temple shows the characteristically Etruscan pattern of three shrines and exhibits a frontal portico enclosed by extensions of the side walls. Fragments have also come to light of a high relief from a plaque on the front gable, depicting a battle of the giants. This is the earliest survival of this sculptural genre in Etruria, and reveals debts to the pediment of the Temple of Zeus at Olympia in Greece which was consecrated in 456 BC.

Endeavours have been made to link these two temples at Pyrgi with contemporary political developments relating to Caere. This would be easier, in the case of the earlier of the two shrines ('Temple B') if we knew whether it was the building that Thefarie Velianas had announced, on his gold tablets, that he was dedicating. This remains perfectly possible, and if so, the shrine is a monument to the alliance between Caere and Carthage; indeed, some scholars, maintaining this view, have detected Punic influence in its construction.

The later temple at Pyrgi ('Temple A'), however, is wholly Greek in character. Moreover, an enormous number of Greek votive deposits have been found here, including no less than fifteen hundred lamps from the Greek mainland and eastern Greek cities. This is sufficient evidence to show that there was a considerable Greek settlement or commercial post at Pyrgi – traders and craftsmen, perhaps captives, perhaps friends of the local Etruscan nobility. It has therefore been suggested that the government of Caere had by this time performed a complete *volte-face* and had adopted a pro-Hellenic stance and reaction against the anti-Hellenic, pro-Carthaginian policies of Thefarie Velianas. This is possible, since in 480 a very large Carthaginian force had suffered a shattering defeat at the hands of the Greeks (Syracusans) at Himera (Imera) in northern Sicily. As a result, the Carthaginian position in the central Mediterranean was greatly weakened, and it is likely enough that Pyrgi's later temple reflects the desire of the Caeritans to adapt and adjust themselves to this new situation by attempting a pro-Greek gesture.

Indeed, it may well have been at this time that Caere openly clashed with its former ally Carthage – as far away as the Atlantic Ocean. By its settlement at Gades (Cadiz), Carthage had successfully established a dominant influence over Tartessus, the great port for metals at the mouth of the Guadalquivir, outside the Pillars of Heracles (Straits of Gibraltar).[38] These advances by the Carthaginians brought them into direct conflict with the Greeks. But some Etruscans, too, entertained ambitions in this part of the Atlantic, for they also had a Spanish trade, and it must have been largely in the hands of their principal maritime power, Caere. It is interesting, therefore, to learn from the historian Diodorus Siculus (writing in the first century BC but deriving his information from Timaeus, three centuries earlier) that 'Etruscans', again identifiable as Caeritans, wanted to found a colony on an island out in the Atlantic Ocean – an island which has been tentatively identified as Madeira – but were stopped from doing so by Carthage.[39] Caere's purpose in making this exceptional thrust to the distant west was probably to break the Carthaginians' monopoly of the tin supply from Gaul, Spain and Cornwall. This could only be done by commanding the sea-route, for the Phocaean colony at Massalia, although they traded with it and through it, prevented them from controlling the land-route up through southern Gaul to the tin-mines that lay beyond. The date of the Atlantic conflict between Caere and Carthage is uncertain, but it seems plausible to relate the incident to the years around 460–450, when the younger of the two temples at Pyrgi may bear witness to a worsening of the relations between the two powers.

Relations with the South

Caere's links with the outside world were not exclusively by sea; it also had land-links with other Etruscan city-states, as one might expect. Up the Via Cassia, for example, it enjoyed economic connections with Clusium and influenced its art. Fine bronze-work found at Perusia also seems to come from Caere, and its styles are even echoed north of the Alps at Etruscanized Bononia (Felsina).[40]

Nearer home, the Caeritans' relations with their northern neighbour Tarquinii continued to be poor, as the reference to hostilities in a

Tarquinian inscription suggests. Veii, the southern neighbour of Caere, also presented it with problems. Although the Caeritans (or possibly the Tarquinians) may actually have founded the place, Veii was far too close a neighbour and rival to Caere for their relations to remain harmonious; it is one of the basic facts of the history of Etruria that they became strained. The result of this uneasy relationship was to throw the Caeritans into the arms of Veii's other neighbour across the Tiber, Rome, with which, over the years, they maintained an exceptionally close friendship.[41] Tombs at Rome (Sant'Omobono) of c. 600 or shortly after already seem to show Caeritan influence.

One vital aspect of the relationship between Caere and Rome was provided by the former's ports and ships. The Romans, at this stage, had none of either; their first settlement at Ostia had been intended to guard the salt-pans, not as a harbour. So Rome, under its Etruscan monarchy and early Republic, used Caere's harbours and fleets for its overseas trade. When Strabo declares that the Caeritans were 'the only Etruscan who were not pirates', he is not merely praising their excellent organization but also complimenting them on their Roman policies.

It would probably not be true to say that Rome's Etruscan royal house, the Tarquins, actually came from Caere, as has sometimes been supposed; yet so close were the dynasty's relations with that city that Tarquinius Superbus and two of his sons took refuge there after they had been expelled from Rome in the last years of the sixth century BC.[42] Moreover, it is recorded that, just before their expulsion, the Romans had sent a delegation to the Delphic oracle. In doing this their intermediary must have been Caere, which as we have seen was the only non-Greek city of the Italian peninsula to have its own treasury at Delphi. Early in the following century, the Caeritans furnished terracotta temple decorations to Rome, and Greek pottery of the same period found on Roman soil probably came from the same source. It is true that Mezentius – the brutal villain of Virgil's *Aeneid*, portrayed as an arch-enemy of Aeneas – is described as a king of Caere; yet Virgil also emphasizes that the Caeritans had rejected Mezentius and thrown him out, so that the city-state of Caere itself could still be presented as the friend of Aeneas and Rome.[43]

In making the Romans free of its ports and fleets, Caere remained for a long time Rome's leading partner – and expected something in return. What it expected, and got, was ready access to Latium beyond. Cato the Elder, in the second century BC, tells a story of how the same Mezentius imposed a tribute of wine on all the Latins,[44] and both Cato and Virgil use his story to symbolize the control of Latium by the

Etruscans. They were probably correct. What lies behind these tales is a period of strong Caeritan influence over parts of Latin territory, aided and abetted by Rome.

The most manifest sign of this Caeritan dominance in Latium is the extreme similarity between the jewellery and *bucchero* pottery in the wealthy seventh-century tombs of Caere and objects of the same date in graves at Praeneste (Palestrina) in Latium. Indeed, the two sets of finds are indistinguishable. It is true that this can be partly explained by the exposure of the two cities to the same influences, emanating, in both cases, from Pithecusae and Cumae in Greek Campania (where many of these luxury goods were made for export to Etruria and Latium). But the similarities are too striking for this explanation to be altogether sufficient. Caere and Caeritan immigrants to Praeneste must, presumably, have acted as guides and intermediaries. 'Vetusia' (an inflection of a masculine or feminine name) on a silver cup of the seventh century BC found in the Bernardini tomb at Praeneste may have been one of these Caeritans. Whether such influences went as far as outright political control cannot be said for certain, but they were strong enough for this to be quite probable. At all events, in spreading their influence in this way, the Caeritans found Rome extremely useful, since it lay directly on the easiest thoroughfare to Praeneste,[45] and Praeneste in its turn stood near the course of the later Via Latina to the east and south.

Caere also seems to have opened another route into the westerly and southerly areas of Latium. Between Rome and the sea there are testimonies to a Caeritan presence in new excavations at Politorium (Castel di Decima), where brooches of amber and gold are identical with others found at Caere.[46] Indeed, Politorium was virtually an Etruscan city in its own right, and may have owed no political allegiance to Caere – which may account for its destruction, probably at the hands of the Romans, in *c.* 630–620. But Latium also contained other thoroughly Etruscanized towns, in which the Caeritan impact was strongly felt. These included a group forming a triangle – Velitrae (Velletri) near the later Via Appia, Satricum (Conca) further south on the other side of the same route, and Ardea to their west. At Velitrae, friezes of pairs of armed riders and of a banquet are replicas of Caeritan reliefs,[47] and terracotta Gorgons' heads assume exactly the same forms at Satricum and Caere. At Satricum, too, there was an important sanctuary containing *bucchero* cups given by a certain Laris Velchainas, whose name recurs in a Caere tomb; indeed, it has been suggested with some plausibility that the Satricum shrine was a sort of offshoot or branch of Caere's holy place at Pyrgi.[48]

Another sanctuary of a similar kind, to which people came from many towns in the region, was at the Fosso di Pratica, beside a small port belonging to Ardea; close analogies have been pointed out between the topographical relationship of Ardea to Fosso di Pratica on the one hand, and that of Caere to Pyrgi on the other.[49] Ardea had particularly close links with the Caeritans: it was named by Livy as an ally of Mezentius of Caere[50] and regarded as one of the Latin peoples that paid him tribute. Ardea was the capital of the Rutulians (Daunians), whose leader in the *Aeneid*, Turnus, has an Etruscan name related to Tyr-rhenus; it was apparently these Daunians who, as we have seen, joined an 'Etruscan' force in invading Campania in 525–524 BC. The Etruscan contingent seems to have come from Spina and Clusium in the north, and the Caeritans may have played a part vicariously through their Ardean allies; for Caere, by virtue of its geographical position and convenient communications, predictably had very close connections with Etruscan Campania. Excavations show that it exported consider-able quantities of *bucchero* to Capua and other centres in the region. Being a maritime power, it could use the sea-route; but the existence of its connections with so many Latin cities shows that it may well, in due course, have employed the major land-routes as well.[51] However, the interests of Caere in Campania must have been severely threatened by the strong opposition of Greek Cumae under Aristodemus, who defeated the Etruscan expedition of 525–524. Caeritan power was further damaged by the vigorous enterprises of Sicilian Syracuse, not-ably a foray of sixty Syracusan warships which not only overran Elba and Corsica but successfully plundered many harbours on the main-land in about 453 BC.

Throughout these years, the key-note of Caere's policy still seems to have been its continued friendship with Rome. This received striking expression towards the end of the fourth century BC, when the Romans became locked in a life-and-death struggle against Veii, the Etruscan neighbour of Rome and Caere alike. The Caeritans failed to help their Veientine compatriots, and by this omission played a large part in Veii's subsequent fall and disappearance from among the major powers of the area.[52] Caere had judged (wrongly, as hindsight would suggest) that it had more to gain from its Roman than from its Etruscan neighbour; and so it did not cease to persevere in its pro-Roman policy. When the Roman general Camillus, in honour of the victory over Veii, dedicated a golden bowl in Apollo's sanctuary at Delphi, it was no doubt Caere, the possessor of a treasury there, which acted, not for the first time, as an intermediary in Rome's approach to the Delphians.

And when, in about 387, an invasion of Gauls from the north under King Brennus attacked and temporarily occupied the city of Rome, Caere offered positive and invaluable help to the Romans once again; it not only gave refuge to the sacred objects from the Roman shrines but exerted military pressure to hasten Brennus' evacuation of the city – an initiative that may have been decisive in securing his departure. The Caeritans were still glad to help Rome, for Greek threats and raids were menacing their sea-coast, and they hoped for Roman assistance in their turn.

Responding to this friendly attitude, the Romans granted Caere special legal privileges. They also combined with Caere to send joint settlements of colonists first to Sardinia (c. 378–377) and then to Corsica (c. 357–354). The sources refer only to Roman settlers, but the expeditions can only have taken place in association with Caere, which must have provided the ships.[53] By such means, Caere fought back against the Syracusans, who had continued their raids by making a serious attack on Caeritan territory in 384 and plundering a huge amount of gold from Pyrgi.

Finally, however, there came a time when the Caeritans began to have second thoughts about their association with Rome, whose annexation of Veii had made it unbearably powerful in southern Etruria. Restless as a result, Caere had the temerity to reverse its friendly policy towards the Romans (c. 353), joining Tarquinii in objecting forcibly to this painful inferiority. The rising or protest, however, was soon brought to order, and Caere was forgivingly accorded a hundred-year treaty or truce. Roman nobles, in the fourth century BC, still sent their sons to this great cosmopolitan city to study the Etruscan language and literature, and perhaps to learn Greek as well;[54] and Caere became a prolific producer of 'red-figure' pottery. But its days as an independent power were over.

CHAPTER 10

VULCI

Wealth and Art

On the south side of Tarquinii was Caere: on the north side was Vulci. Although now surrounded by cultivated land for the first time since antiquity, the hill of Vulci rises above a strangely deserted countryside which offers no indication of its ancient might. Moreover, apart from a bare record in the catalogues of the geographers, there is absolutely no account of the ancient city and its history in the works of any Greek or Roman writer. These are gaps which stand in strange contrast to the immense wealth of jewellery, metalwork, pottery and other ancient objects that have come out of Vulci's cemeteries since the 1820s – when Napoleon's brother Lucien Bonaparte, Prince of Canino, after accidental discoveries by a ploughman on his estate, first brought out of the soil thousands of artefacts (and his wife appeared at the British ambassador's parties loaded with Etruscan jewels).[1] In 1842 it was remarked that the yield from this site already exceeded even the riches of Pompeii and Herculaneum.

In ancient times, Vulci had evidently been one of the places which took the lead in urbanization, contact with Greek markets and colonies, and the explosion of wealth that went with these developments. Though its major role did not come quite so quickly as the similar evolution of Tarquinii and Caere, it shared this process with them as an equal; when Caere began to encroach upon Tarquinii from the south, Vulci was getting ready to do the same from the north.

As at Tarquinii and Caere, the inspiration was apparently a local supply of metal, but the source of this supply was not Tolfa, but the more northerly Catena Metallifera (Metal-Bearing Chain). This extends almost as far as the lower reaches of the River Fiora, beside which the city lay,[2] and the Vulcentines were able to secure metals down the valley. In addition, there were valuable metallurgical resources on

Mount Amiata, which lay very close to the head-waters of the same river; and the metals of Amiata (until Clusium later took over a large part of them) seem also to have belonged to Vulci, which developed them through a chain of settlements on the way. As usual, it was this wealth in metals that attracted the Greek traders and settlers from Campania; once again it was this process that offered Vulci enormous opportunities to get rich and thus prompted the villages on its plateau to amalgamate at about the end of the eighth century BC. There had already been cultural advances in the area, and now they gained strength.

Vulci's evolution is displayed not by the habitation site itself, which has so far proved unproductive, but by the ruins of almost endless cemeteries along a very extensive area in the neighbourhood. Already by 1856 more than fifteen thousand tombs had been opened, and that was only a beginning. The link of the early great tombs with the Greek (Euboean) markets of Cumae and Pithecusae, which were so eager for Etruscan metals, is clear. Vases in 'Geometric' style found at Vulci, dating from the last quarter of the eighth century, confirm the presence of traders or potters from those markets, since the pots are made by local imitators of their wares.[3] Impressive gold objects, too, that may have been worked at the Campanian centres (if not at Vulci itself), have been found in the Polledrara tomb (c. 600) and other local graves.[4] They include a late-seventh-century necklace covered with fine granulation, and incised ostrich eggs with decorations in ivory and gold displaying Greek and oriental motifs. Diadems of various kinds, too, go back to a variety of near-eastern models. There are also various types of earrings, including a pair in the form of chiselled open-work discs (originally adorned with a central inlay that has now disappeared), a type of object traceable back to contemporary Syria, from which the Euboean trading-post of Al Mina may have secured it, or its model, for transmission to the west. A bronze bust from Vulci shows a female figure holding a horned bird;[5] her hair-style is very close to that of north Syrian ivories, though echoing various Greek artistic schools as well. The school of the island of Rhodes, lying between Syria and Greece, particularly comes to mind. Indeed, it has been suggested that the object was actually imported from that island, though it is perhaps more likely to be a local adaptation made at Vulci itself.[6] The statuette has been conjecturally identified with the Egyptian goddess Isis, after whom the tomb in which it was discovered has been named. It also contained a scarab of the Egyptian pharaoh Psammetichus (Psamtik) I (c. 663–610 BC), though it has been deduced from other contents of the grave that this object, and so the burial itself, may rather belong to the early years of the following century.

Vulci's cemeteries have their own characteristic type of chamber tomb with an antechamber open to the sky.[7] Only three tombs crowned with earth mounds have survived on these sites, but one of them is the largest of its kind in the whole of Etruria. This is the inappropriately named Cucumella ('little coffee-pot') of c. 560–550 BC. Its huge mound rose in isolation, topping a perimeter wall no less than seventy yards in diameter.[8] Inside this monument, at the lowest level, is a tortuous honeycomb of labyrinthine passages. The tomb was originally surmounted by two thirty- or forty-foot-high towers of uncemented masonry, one cylindrical and one conical.[9] This enormous structure could be a grave of one of the great rulers of Vulci, or it might have been erected as a shrine and memorial in honour of one of the legendary Vulcentine heroes, of whom more will be said later. At all events, it vividly reflects the pretentious grandeur of Vulci at the height of its power.

By this time the city had evidently become one of the most prosperous centres in Etruria. Corinthian vases had begun to arrive there in considerable quantities, and the Vulcentines themselves soon became the principal Etruscan mass-imitators of these wares. By embarking on this activity, they created the first major school of what is known as the 'Etrusco-Corinthian' style of polychrome vase-painting. These pots were intended for the export of oil; wine, too, was sent to France and other countries in vessels made at Vulci.[10] This process seems, at first sight, to exhibit a new economic formula, for Vulci apparently did not, like other cities of southern Etruria, depend almost exclusively on metals for its very great wealth. True, like the other cities, it owed its original urbanization and wealth to metals. But it also became a significant exporter of agricultural produce.

As elsewhere, the Corinthian vases found and imitated at Vulci were followed by pottery of Ionian origin or style. When Greek craftsmen in the latter half of the sixth century BC fled from the Persian threat to their Ionian homes and came to Etruria, some of them set up pottery centres at Vulci. In particular, persistent finds have identified an extremely important Vulcentine workshop of bright 'black-figure' vases known misleadingly as 'Pontic' wares.[11] The painters of these pots – sometimes Ionians and sometimes no doubt their Etruscan pupils as well – covered them with paintings of gay and cheerful scenes, which can be traced throughout a considerable number of interrelated but separate schools. In the first phase, a very distinctive artist can be recognized in the 'Paris painter' (*c.* 550–540). While duly displaying influences, he is an original and entertaining mythological narrator on his own account, with a preference for the use of white colouring. We do not know his real name, or whether he was a Greek or an Etruscan. But more visibly Etruscanized versions of this 'Pontic' painting soon followed, with other hands at work, and achieved an increasingly vigorous approach.[12]

In pursuance of the usual Etruscan evolution, according to which towards the end of the sixth century Ionian influences were gradually replaced by Attic (Athenian) trends, the 'Pontic' painters increasingly Atticized the shapes, stylistic features and subject-matter of the vases. For Attic 'black-figure' pottery was now pouring into Vulci – indeed, the unparalleled quantity of such vases is the most remarkable of all the features of this site. The series, illustrated by thousands of local discoveries, continued and expanded for more than a century. No less than 40 per cent of all Attic 'black-figure' pots that have come to light in Etruria are from Vulci. In the fifth century, when the 'red-figure' technique took over, the proportion rises to 50 per cent. Out of all the centres, not only of Etruria, but of the whole ancient world including Greece itself, Vulci provides us with our greatest wealth of evidence for the study of Greek vases. Moreover, although the Vulcentine artists, like other Etruscans, show no great taste for the full, mature Athenian classicism, 'black-figure' and 'red-figure' alike were extensively imitated and adapted on the spot – considerable liberties being taken with the iconography of the Greek myths.

This local activity is what one would expect at Vulci, which was not only an importer and consumer on an exceptionally large scale, but also one of the principal artistic centres of Etruria. One remarkable development was the establishment of a tradition of stone statuary – something unusual in this country, where suitable stone was not readily available. Though examples of this art had already appeared at Vetulonia, Vulci was the main centre of Etruscan stone sculpture.[13] Its sculptors were able to use a locally quarried volcanic stone, hard grey or greyish-pink *nenfro*. Required to provide sculptures for the entrances of burial chambers or tombs, they followed their Vetulonian colleagues in drawing on the Greek school of sculpture in the round. This school had developed in the mid-seventh century on the islands of Rhodes and Crete and in the Peloponnese, where sculptors had freely adapted north Syrian models, moulding what they learnt into an original achievement. Vulci, too, added further twists of its own. Thus a sixth-century statue of a centaur parades a notable native touch of energy and aliveness. A rider on a sea-horse, perhaps of *c*. 550–530, is another vivid work, deriving additional inspiration from Ionian models. Female Vulcentine statuettes of about the same period are loosely adapted from prototypes of Greek southern Italy. Stylized lions are another characteristic feature of the sculpture of Vulci in the later sixth century, showing a time-lag of twenty or twenty-five years in comparison with similar products of Tarquinii. A *nenfro* lion from Vulci displays a curious technique by which the body and mane are drawn rather than sculpted, with little or no modelling to indicate muscle.

But Vulci's principal claim to contemporary artistic fame was its bronze-work. The bronze statue of *c*. 600 found in the Tomb of Isis may or may not have been made locally; but from *c*. 540 onwards the place was the centre of a flourishing bronze industry which became, like its stone statuary, the most important in all Etruria.[14] These bronzes were cast, and thus present a very different appearance from the hammered bronze-work of Caere. They include fine pieces intended for religious (votive) dedication as well as an extensive range of domestic objects, including tripods, censers, candelabra, amphorae with figure handles, and dancing maenads.

This metalwork, though exhibiting the usual series of Greek and especially Ionian influences, was by no means inferior to that of Greece; indeed, when Etruscan bronzes were singled out for praise by Greeks, it was very often Vulcentine work that they had in mind. A fragment of a bronze tripod which was probably made at Vulci has been discovered on the Acropolis of Athens,[15] and that is just one of innumerable places to which this type of bronze-work was exported. It is found, for example, not only in other parts of Etruria but in Corsica and Latium, too, including Rome itself, while many examples also appear in southern Italy,[16] and in the north as well, where Vulci played its part in the exploitation of the Po valley. At Spina such finds are particularly frequent.[17]

Moreover, Vulci's bronzes, or local copies indistinguishable from the originals, even turn up in north Africa at Carthage. This suggests that Vulci, in the sixth century BC, managed to have some share in Caere's Carthaginian trade. In rivalry with the Phocaean Greeks, it probably conducted these commercial operations, in part at least, through the Carthaginian settlements in Sardinia, for Sardinian objects have recently been found in Vulci's tombs. Bronzes of Vulcentine types also make their appearance as far afield as central Europe.[18]

Even though it is not always possible to distinguish between bronzes made at Vulci and copies made elsewhere, the actual production of

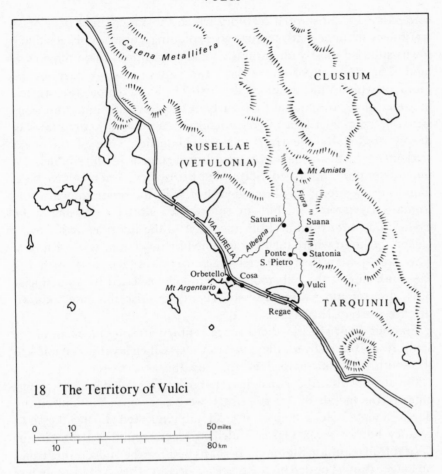

18   The Territory of Vulci

Vulci itself must have been on an enormous scale. Its territory produced copper, but did it produce enough to make all this bronze-work? If not, Vulci must have augmented its own local supplies by importation. This would not have been beyond its powers, since the Vulcentines had products of their land to offer in exchange: they sent wine, as has been noted, as far as Sicily and southern France, and their city evidently owed much of its success to its position as a centre of this commerce[19] – as will be seen more clearly from a brief survey of the territory and harbours they controlled.

Territory and Ports

The two bases of Vulci's hinterland were the valleys of the Fiora (the Roman Armenta or Arnine) and Albegna (Albinia).[20] These rivers commanded a substantial territory which the Vulcentines developed vigorously in the seventh century BC, exploiting a number of subsidiary towns situated mostly on naturally fortified positions upon tongues of land. The more important of these two valleys was the basin of the Fiora, on which Vulci itself was situated. The Fiora region, already rich in archaeological material from early in the first millennium BC, consisted of a series of hills of volcanic origin, including many plateaux deeply eroded by the river and its tributaries. One of the main settlements in this zone was Poggio Buco; since lead sling-bullets (of much later date) inscribed 'Statnes' in Etruscan characters have been found on the site, it has been identified with the town known to the Romans as Statonia. Its hill-site controlled a strategic crossing of the Fiora on a route running from the coast to the interior, and it over-looked the point where the river is joined by two minor water-courses. The three streams thus protected the place to west, east and north. On the south side of the hill stood the acropolis, isolated by an artificial ditch and mound which are believed to comprise the oldest known defence work in Etruria.

Statonia flourished in the seventh century and the first half of the sixth. It was linked by a valley road to Vulci, which lay thirteen miles to the south. Statonia helped to open up the area to serve the city's political and cultural expansion, but above all it served it as a staging-point to the metals of Amiata which were so essential to Vulcentine development.[21] Nevertheless, it gradually vanished during the sixth century BC; for some reason Vulci no longer found it necessary or desirable to maintain Statonia – perhaps because the Vulcentines could no longer control or defend the place, or because they had lost much of the Amiata metals to Clusium.

Farther up the Fiora from Vulci was Suana (the Etruscan Sveama[?] and modern Sovana), on a spur of volcanic rock just off the river, between two of its tributaries. Although the habitation of Suana has not come to light, its existence is demonstrated by many tombs of the seventh and sixth centuries BC[22] containing objects from Vulci, of which it was evidently another dependant. These objects resemble finds from Statonia nearby, and Suana, like its neighbour, subsequently dis-appeared. Before doing so, it had already passed out of Vulcentine hands, since a painting in the François tomb of that city shows warriors of Vulci and Suana fighting against one another.

Two ancient roads out of Suana have been identified. One of them leads to Saturnia (the Etruscan Urina and Roman Aurinia),[23] a little to the west. The site overlooks the rich plain of the Albegna, of which the upper valley provided Vulci's second northward lifeline, leading to Clusium and regions beyond. Saturnia stood on an outcrop of porous rock (travertine) at the juncture of the Albegna with one of its tributaries, at the centre of a communications network. There is no concrete proof that the place belonged to Vulci – settlements lower down the Albegna probably did not – but for Saturnia this seems, on geographical and archaeological grounds, the most probable solution. However, in the early fifth century BC, in the wake of other Vulcentine dependencies, it disappeared for a long period, perhaps, once again, owing to frontier adjustments.

As for Vulci's coastal situation, it must be assumed that the state possessed a fleet of its own, for its enormous overseas trading operations could scarcely have been conducted entirely on vessels belonging to other powers. Indeed, Vulci itself was perhaps strong enough at sea to provide shipping space for other Etruscan city-states, notably Clusium. Moreover, in Etruscan times parts of the maritime plain of Vulci were probably covered with pine that could be used as ships' timber. Vulci's coastline was longer and more complex than that of its southern neighbours, extending from beyond the mouth of the Albegna down beyond the estuary of the Fiora, along the route of the later Roman Via Aurelia which connected the coastal cities of Etruria.

Vulci itself stood back from the sea in a protected position, like Tarquinii and Caere, and needed a port or ports to serve it. Twenty-two miles west of the city lies one of Italy's most peculiar geographical features, the protruding promontory and peninsula of Mount Argentarius, now Argentario.[24] Today, after a long process of the large-scale erosion characteristic of this coast, the Argentario is joined to the mainland at either side by sand-bars – isthmuses of silt thrown up by centuries of waves. The sand-bars form the sides of an enclosed lagoon upon which lies the mainland town of Orbetello, situated on a spit (a third sand-bar which never fully developed[25]). In antiquity the more westerly of the two isthmuses was scarcely emerging, and the lagoon was open to the Tyrrhenian Sea at that side.[26] It was also open on the other side, since the eastern isthmus, too, was penetrated by two exit channels.

Orbetello, in ancient times, thus enjoyed a harbour of striking potentialities, comprising a sea lagoon which was partially enclosed and well protected, and yet which at the same time opened out at both ends into the sea. It is by no means surprising, then, to find that an Etruscan settlement existed there as early as the eighth century BC and that it was continually inhabited thereafter. No trace of the ancient town has yet been discovered, but its existence and prosperity are demonstrated by discoveries at an Etruscan cemetery on the spit.

The place may have borne the name of Cusa in Etruscan times.[27] Under the Romans, this name, in the form of Cosa or Cosae, was applied to a place four-and-a-half miles to the south-east, now called Ansedonia. It used to be thought that this, too, had been an Etruscan harbour town, but excavations have proved pretty conclusively that it was not: on the contrary, Ansedonia only started life as a Roman colony in the third century BC, and the canals leading into its inner basin, although one of them is erroneously known as the 'Etruscan Cutting' (Tagliata Etrusca), are likewise not Etruscan but Roman.[28] The Etruscan Argentario port was not Cosa but Orbetello.

A sphinx of volcanic stone that has been found at Orbetello shows the clear influence of Vulci,[29] and a glance at the map confirms that it was Vulci's territory to which the place presumably belonged.[30] Yet, in considering the Etruscan ports in general, we must divide them into two categories. There are those which stand very close to their mother-city and served it directly, like Piraeus in relation to Athens, and Cenchreae and Lechaeum in respect of Corinth. To this category belonged Graviscae and Pyrgi, ports of Tarquinii and Caere respectively. There are also other Etruscan harbour towns which belonged to the territory of a city-state (not being independent city-states themselves), but were too far away from the city itself to be regarded as its own ports in the same sense; such was the relation of Thoricus and Crommyon to Athens and Corinth respectively, and of Dicaearchia (Puteoli) and Palaeopolis (Neapolis, Naples) to early Cumae. And this, it will be argued, was also the original relationship of Populonia to Vetulonia, and of Telamon to Rusellae: although dependent on major city-states, they were also prominent markets and harbours and townships on their own account. This, evidently, was the position of Orbetello as well.

Vulci, however, must also have had a nearby port of its own, in the same sense that Graviscae and Pyrgi were ports of their respective cities. The almost inevitable place for Vulci's port was not far from the mouth of its river, the Fiora. This estuary was scarcely more than six miles from the city, and, as early maps show, led into a large sea lagoon of its own; indeed, an ancient guide-book, the *Itinerarium Maritimum*, specifically indicates that a harbour existed beside this river mouth. Moreover, Vulci's most important cemeteries lie along this same lower stretch of the Fiora, beside which there ran a route going back to the second millennium BC. And so it is not surprising that only three miles south of the Fiora mouth there is known to have been a harbour town of legendary origins named Regae, from a Greek word meaning 'clefts' – the Roman Regisvilla (now Le Murelle).[31] Here, then, at Regae, was Vulci's principal port, which still remains to be discovered and excavated. Just inland, the Romans later built Forum Aurelii on their coastal road, the Via Aurelia.[32]

The Heroes of Vulci

The relations of Vulci, or its citizens, with other powers in and around Etruria receive an isolated flash of illumination from remarkable paintings found in the nearby François tomb, which is named after the man who discovered it. The tomb is cut from the rock high above the banks of the Fiora, approached by a ninety-foot corridor penetrating into the depths of the hillside. The paintings are now in the Torlonia Museum (Villa Albani) at Rome;[33] they were commissioned by the proprietor of the grave, a certain Vel Saties, who is portrayed in a triumphal dark-blue mantle decorated with dancing warriors. Accompanied by a deformed dwarf, Arnza, who is launching a bird for the processes of divination to which the Etruscans attached such great importance,[34] Vel Saties seems to appear in the guise of a magistrate or priest about to take the auspices in order to determine whether the omens for some course of action are favourable.

The other paintings in this François tomb include a whole cycle celebrating the triumphs of Vulcentine warriors over combatants from other Etruscan or Etruscanized states. The paintings comprise our most important documents for the attitudes of the Etruscans to their own historical or legendary past. Other such Etruscan paintings no doubt existed and may well have been used by Livy for some of the scenes he describes in his history, but if so they have vanished. On grounds of stylistic and technical analogies, the paintings of the François tomb are datable between the late fourth and mid-third centuries BC – that is to say, they are earlier than Roman historical writings. They represent a native Etruscan, Vulcentine tradition. But are the scenes that they show history or legend? They are so circumstantially depicted that they look like attempts to represent historical happenings, even though an element of legend may also have crept in.

The scenes are described as follows by labels which appear on the paintings themselves. Larth Ulthese kills Laris Papathnas Velznach. Rasce kills Pesna Arcmsnas Sveamach. Avle Vipinas kills Venthi Cau[les?] ... Plsachs(?). Marce Camitlnas kills Cneve Tarchunies

169

Rumach. Macstrna frees Caile Vipinas from bondage. In each pair, the first person named is that of a warrior of Vulci. 'Laris' and 'Larth' may mean warrior or champion, or perhaps constitute an official title. Ulthese is perhaps the name Latin-speaking peoples later adapted as 'Volteius'. The man he slays, Papathnas (the Latin Fabatius?), is described as 'Velznach', meaning probably that he comes from the Etruscan city of Volsinii. Rasce, perhaps the Latin Ruscius, kills a man whose name Arcmsnas is analogous to the Etruscan name Arcumenna (Arcumnius). His title 'Sveamach' suggests that he came from Suana, evidently now no longer Vulci's dependant but its enemy, or the enemy of this Vulcentine at least. The two men named Vipinas (related to the Latin Vibius) are better known under their Roman names of Aulus and Caelius (or Caeles) Vibenna (or Vivenna). 'Macstrna', who is freed by Caile Vipinas, corresponds with the known name Mastarna. The name and place of origin of Avle Vipinas' victim are uncertain, but the last letters may represent the name of Salpinium or Sapienum, an Etruscan town of uncertain location which Livy describes as an ally of Volsinii in the fourth century BC.

Macstrna, unlike the other Vulcentines depicted in these paintings, is freeing a man instead of killing him, a scene unique in Etruscan art as we know it.[34] The man he is freeing is evidently a compatriot of his own who had been taken prisoner by an enemy. The other men of Vulci who are portrayed in the adjacent pictures may well have been prisoners too, rising against their captors; the men they are killing all seem to have been just aroused from sleep, unprepared, though Venthi is wearing some uniform, comprising armour and a red robe, which suggests that he may have been a bodyguard looking after the prisoners. The scene of Marce Camitlnas and Cneve Tarchunies Rumach, a cringing figure whom the naked, bearded, armed warrior springs forward to seize by the hair, is a separate picture, but seems to form part of the same composition and story.

That Cneve Tarchunies Rumach is 'Cnaeus Tarquinius of Rome' seems certain; but who was this Tarquin slain by a man of Vulci? The Roman king-list of the sixth century shows two Tarquins only, Lucius Tarquinius Priscus – the immigrant from Tarquinii who had formerly been described as Lucumo – and his son or grandson Lucius Tarquinius Superbus, whose downfall in the last years of the century was accompanied by the inauguration of the Roman Republic. Was the victim of Camitlnas one of these two? The fact that the two kings are named in the historical tradition as Lucius, whereas he is Cneve (Cnaeus), need not be a decisive argument to the contrary, since this

'Lucius' is suspect, having been derived, it would appear, from a false analogy with the Etruscan name or title Lucumo. Bearing this in mind, some modern scholars have identified Cneve Tarchunies Rumach with Tarquinius Priscus. According to Roman tradition the latter was murdered by the sons of his predecessor Ancus Marcius – not by the personage Marce Camitlnas depicted here. But that, too, is not a wholly decisive argument against the identification, since Etruscan and Roman traditions must often have been markedly divergent, especially if the former reported a victory by an Etruscan over a Roman.

However, there still remains no cogent reason for identifying Cneve with Tarquinius Priscus. Cneve might, instead, be a third Tarquin on the Roman throne, of whom we know nothing; or we could point to that variant form of the tradition that makes Superbus the grandson instead of the son of Priscus and suggest that the further Tarquin who came in between (Priscus' son, who predeceased him) could have been the Cneve of this picture.[35] But there were numerous other Tarquins who were not kings, as literature and archaeology alike confirm. So unfortunately, in the present state of our knowledge, we cannot say who Cneve Tarchunies Rumach was, except that he was a Tarquin and a Roman.

The bare fact that he was a Roman, however, throws light on the curious significance of this Vulcentine tradition. At some time or other, it records – presumably in the sixth century BC, when the Tarquins were prominent – a Roman prince or leader or warrior of that name was killed by an enemy from Vulci; that is to say, there was intervention by Vulci, or by one or more of its citizens, in the affairs of Rome.

Moreover, other personages who figure in the inscriptions of the François tomb confirm that this belief existed. These are Caile Vipinas (Caelius Vibenna or Vivenna) and Macstrna (Mastarna). A commentary on their affairs was later provided by the Emperor Claudius (AD 41–54). He wrote a huge book on Etruscan history that would have added enormously to our knowledge of the subject had it survived;[36] he also had the habit of inserting formidable pieces of erudition into his public speeches on other themes. On one occasion, he imparted an observation of this kind (perhaps derived from Dionysius of Halicarnassus) to the Roman senate while advocating a more liberal admission of foreigners into the senatorial order. Claudius first tells the familiar story of the emigration of Tarquinius Priscus, the son of Demaratus, from Tarquinii to Rome. Then he goes on:

Between him and his son or grandson – the authorities differ on this point – was inserted Servius Tullius, who was, if we follow our historians, son of the captive Ocresia, if we follow the Etruscans, a former faithful companion of Caelius Vivenna and the companion of all his fortunes; who, when after various turns of fortune he had been expelled with all the survivors of Caelius's army and left Etruria, occupied the Caelian hill, so-called from his leader Caelius, and changing his name (for he had been called Mastarna in Etruscan) took the name by which I have spoken of him [Servius Tullius], and obtained the kingship, to the great advantage of the state.[37]

So Claudius declares that Servius Tullius, traditionally the penultimate King of Rome who reigned between Tarquinius Priscus and Tarquinius Superbus, had originally borne the Etruscan name of Mastarna – which was also the name (in the form Macstrna) of the warrior shown rescuing Caile Vipinas (Caelius or Caeles Vibenna or Vivenna) in the painting of the François Tomb. The origins of Tullius, thus inserted between the traditional pair of Tarquins, were always a mystery, even in ancient times, and the complex and varied legends on the subject came to be moulded in various ways by the political considerations of Rome five centuries later.[38]

Servius Tullius himself had a real historical existence.[39] The basic Roman view was that he had been of Latin origin, interrupting the sequence of Etruscan monarchs. However, there were also certain persistent Etruscan elements in the traditions that grew up around him. For one thing, although he was said, in one version, to be the son of a slave – his name Servius was believed to have come from the Latin servus, which means this – that derivation appears to be incorrect, and both 'Servius' and 'Tullius' are probably Latinizations of Etruscan names.[40] Secondly, an alternative report that he was of divine paternity, expressed by Livy in the phrase that he 'had no father', is associated by Dionysius of Halicarnassus with Etruscan divination.[41] The Romans, before the development of the story repeated by Claudius, did not favour the opinion that Servius Tullius had been a third Etruscan monarch, because he was, in some circles, a Roman national hero. But there is, in fact, no historical objection to believing that he was an Etruscan, since the measures ascribed to his reign show a general continuity with the developments characteristic of the Etruscanizing age which had been initiated by Tarquinius Priscus.

We can therefore approach with some sympathy Claudius' assertion that an Etruscan is just what Servius Tullius was, that his name had been Mastarna and his home-town was Vulci. After all, the emperor had not only been married to a woman of Etruscan origin but was the leading Etruscan expert of his day; besides, pottery from Vulci that is found in Rome dates from just about the time when Servius Tullius was believed to have reigned. Moreover, in view of the fame of this Mastarna to whom Claudius refers, it is only natural to identify him with the Macstrna of the same city, who appears on the painting of the François tomb.[42]

This Vulcentine connection with Rome can also be clothed in a little further detail. Claudius remarks that Mastarna underwent 'various turns of fortune' (*varia fortuna*) including expulsion from Etruria, or from some Etruscan centre, together 'with the survivors of Caeles Vibenna's army', followed by their occupation of the Caelian Hill of Rome. This piece of information is probably false, since it relies on an etymological link with the name Caelius (Caile), a link which is fictitious.[43] But that does not mean that the Vulcentines never arrived at Rome at all, since an independent tradition preserved by Verrius Flaccus (an antiquarian of the time of Augustus who was well-informed about Etruscan affairs) likewise records the arrival at Rome, in the company of the 'Vulcentine Vibenna brothers', of a certain 'Max . . .' – the rest of the word is missing, but it probably represents a variant form of the name Mastarna.[44] Indeed, even if the Caelian connection is illusory, Etruscan settlers at Rome were independently recorded, as the name of the street, Vicus Tuscus, evidently testifies. When, therefore, the ancient writers ascribe Roman settlement to Mastarna and the Vibennas, they are offering a theory which, in its general lines, is plausible enough.

The name of Aulus Vibenna, in the form of Avile Vipiiennas, also appears in an Etruscan votive inscription upon a black *bucchero* vase of the mid-sixth century BC. The vase, although dedicated at Veii, was probably made at Vulci,[45] and Vipiiennas may be regarded as the same man as the Vibenna recorded by the Roman writers. Then again, when the foundations of Rome's Capitoline temple were laid not much later, the severed head of a certain Olus was said to have been discovered intact on the site by the diggers; this scene is represented on Etruscan gems. Olus (Aulus), described by the north African writer Arnobius as a Vulcentine who had been cast out of his city and murdered by a slave,[46] appears to be the same as Aulus Vibenna. Evidently he, and his brother Caelius as well, passed quite quickly into legend. A number of Etruscan towns, for example, produced artistic representations of the two Vibennas launching an attack on a famous divine seer, Cacus, in a sacred wood.[47] The name Aulus Vibenna appears again, in the form Avles V(i)pinas, on an Etruscan 'red-figure' cup of about 450 BC: the painter wanted to increase the cup's value by pretending it had once been the property of this traditional hero.

The compiler of the *Chronographia Urbis Romae* in the fourth century
AD, evidently drawing upon a much earlier authority, describes Olus
(Aulus Vibenna) as a 'king'.[48] Now, we cannot immediately rule out the
possibility that he became one of the monarchs of Rome, since it is
notorious that the traditional list of the Seven Kings need not be
regarded as complete or sacrosanct. If a Vibenna did attain the Roman
throne this might have happened during the confused events that
followed the ejection of the Etruscan monarchy of the Tarquins at the
end of the sixth century BC, when Lars Porsenna of Clusium (and
perhaps others too) seized the city for a time. If, however, we accept
Claudius' identification of Mastarna with Servius Tullius, whose reign
is traditionally assigned to an earlier period (578–535), then, if one of
the Vibennas ever became King of Rome, he must have reigned shortly
before or after Servius Tullius (Mastarna), well before Rome's
monarchic period came to an end. But perhaps, despite the *Chronographia*, neither of the Vibennas ever did become Kings of Rome.

What remains significant is the light this group of stories throws on
the general way in which Etruscan expansions and movements of
population took place. What seems to have happened at Rome is that a
gang of Vulcentine leaders 'expelled' from their home-town (or from
somewhere else), led an expedition on their own account – either with
peaceful or, more probably, predatory intentions – at a time when the
distinction between national and private campaigns was often still
somewhat vague. Some of the men these adventurers had brought to
Rome in their company then settled and stayed in the city to add to the
blend of different ethnic and cultural elements that were already there.
It is hardly surprising, then, in view of this special impact of Vulci on
Rome, that Pliny the Elder preserves a tradition regarding the Vulcentines as synonymous with the Etruscans, or as Etruscans *par excellence*.[49]

But the paintings in the François tomb comprise a second series also;
this goes back to the mythological cycle of the Trojan Wars and shows
the sacrifice of the Trojan prisoners by Achilles. The gruesome scene
was a particularly favourite theme of Etruscan artists, who presumably
drew it from some common original.[50] The thought behind such representations is that the deceased, in whose honour the paintings are
dedicated, is compared to famous mythological victims who have likewise succumbed to mortality. However, the appearance of this particular subject at the François tomb, in direct confrontation with the
pictures of the successful Vulcentine duellists, cannot merely be
explained by that general idea alone: some more specific relationship
and connection between the two themes must also be intended.[51]

The relationship lies in the sympathy of the painters, and the Etruscans in general, with the Trojan cause. That is the point of the juxtaposition of the two sets of paintings in the Vulcentine tomb. The Trojans had succumbed to their enemies, whereas the warriors of Vulci, in dramatic contrast, are triumphant over theirs; the Vulcentines thus saw themselves not only as the spiritual heirs of the Trojans but as their avengers as well.

This sympathy was focused on the mythical Trojan personage Aeneas. The Virgilian tradition made Aeneas the ancestor of the Roman nation; but long before the Romans, it was the Etruscans who revered him. By the sixth century his cult was greatly honoured in Etruria, as many artistic representations confirm. When this cult began, we cannot say: a sudden and strong interest evidently arose in about 525 BC, but the Etruscan reverence for Aeneas may have existed at an earlier – perhaps much earlier – date. It was the Greeks who transmitted his saga to the Etruscans,[54] just as they transmitted the legend of that other western explorer, his enemy Odysseus. In addition, the Etruscans soon became attracted by the erroneous tradition of their own ethnic origins from Asia Minor, for which Aeneas, from Troy in that peninsula, could serve as an appropriate link. The legendary Aeneas had two qualities, resourceful bravery and exemplary dutifulness, which he displayed in his behaviour both to the gods and his own family. He and his family were even said to have been of Etruscan origin, and the story is embodied in myths indicating how, after his arrival in Italy, he allied himself with the Etruscans Tyrrhenus and Tarchon or married Tarchon's sister.[55]

The reverence for Aeneas was outstandingly strong at Vulci; out of seventeen Athenian vases displaying aspects of his myth that have been discovered in Etruria, no less than ten come from finds at Vulci. Veii, too, was another important centre of Aeneas' worship, but its statuettes showing the standard theme of the hero carrying his father Anchises out of the ruins of Troy are now shown to be considerably later than the earliest representations at Vulci.[56] Vulci had taken the initiative; and Vulci too, owing to its powerful Roman connections, is likely enough to have been the transmitter of the story (directly or through Veii) to Rome. The Romans were glad to have the cult, because it gave them international status. Virgil, himself partly Etruscan and deeply versed in Etruscan traditions, cannot have failed to be aware that Rome had taken Aeneas from Etruria, but he removed the disagreeable implications of his hero's foreign (and even hostile) origins by making the Etruscans who appear in the *Aeneid* into allies and even subordinates of

Aeneas. They were useful to his story, to strengthen Aeneas' tiny Trojan force against its numerous enemies.[57]

Relations with the South

Rome was of great importance to the Vulcentine leaders not only for its own sake and because of the sagas that bound them together but also as a staging-point on their main line of communications towards the south. Indeed, it is indicated by the archaeological evidence that people from Vulci, in addition to their exploits at Rome itself, were principal agents and pioneers in the Etruscan expansion into Campania.[58]

In the first place, they played a part, or even took the initiative, in Etruscanizing Capua itself, the centre of Etruscan power in the area. They had easy access to the place by land by way of Rome, from which they moved on southwards along the course of the later Via Latina and river valleys.[59] They may at some stage have used the sea-route as well, for this seems to be the implication behind Virgil's statement that the leader of the Etruscan fleet helping Aeneas was called Massicus and that he commanded men coming from Cosa.[60] For Cosa (regarded by the poet as an Etruscan foundation) was in Vulcentine territory, and Massicus is also the name of a mountain near the north Campanian coast, not far from Capua; thus the legend reflects a sea link between Vulci and Campania.

There are also further indications of a Vulcentine presence on Campanian territory. The town of Urina in that country, mentioned on coins, seems to have an etymological connection with Aurinia (Saturnia) in Etruria, which was under the control of Vulci.[61] Urina was in the north of Campania, but there are also various additional pieces of evidence linking Vulci with the Etruscanization of the southern parts of the country: discoveries at the Etruscan sites near Salerno include objects from Vulci.[62] And secondly, a town thirty-five miles farther east – the modern Buccino – was known by the Romans as Volcei or Vulcei, which is an Etruscan name and suggests that the place was originally founded by Etruscan Vulci or some of its citizens.[63] Coins inscribed 'Velecha', which were issued in Campania in the later third century BC, may well belong to this same place.[64]

By what means, peaceful or warlike, the Vulcentines conducted these expansive activities, must remain undetermined. Perhaps their government itself took the lead by military expeditions or piracy; or perhaps individual adventurers, men like Mastarna and the Vibennas at Rome, were to the fore; or it may be that the major initiative

View from Vetulonia towards Rusellae,
overlooking the plain of the River Bruna.
In ancient times the plain was a sea-lagoon,
Lake Prilius, providing both cities
with their ports.

ABOVE The island of Elba: the Gulf of Portoferraio, the Roman Fabricia, renamed Feraia in the Middle Ages because of its iron mines, for which it provided a harbour. Remains of Etruscan smelting furnaces are found along its shores.

ABOVE LEFT Tomb in the form of a shrine (the Tomba del Bronzetto di Offerente) in the San Cerbone cemetery at Populonia, second half of sixth century BC. Robbed in the third century BC, it was subsequently hidden under heaps of iron-slag, and rediscovered in 1957. It is unique because of the preservation of its roof.

Etruscan silver coins, probably fifth century BC.
Above: a boar (the reverse is blank): issued at Populonia.
Below: a sea-monster and a bull's head, inscribed 'Thezle': issued at a port, perhaps serving Rusellae (or Vulci).

BELOW LEFT A smelting furnace at Populonia, where the iron of the neighbouring Campigliese region succeeded copper as the principal industry and attraction to the outside world.

The city wall of Rusellae.
It dates from the sixth century BC, but
was constructed, at least in certain sections,
over a wall of the previous century,
the earliest known in Etruria. It may
have been intended as a defence against
Vetulonia, which Rusellae superseded
and may have temporarily eliminated.

Air view of Telamon (Talamone),
a port which probably depended on Rusellae.
Telamon was characteristic of a series of
Etruscan harbour-towns which, while not
immediately adjacent to a principal
city, formed part of its territory.

ABOVE Gravestone of Avle Tite at
Volaterrae, second quarter of sixth century
BC. The earliest known example of this kind
of sculptured tombstone, which was also
new in Greece at the time. Avle Tite wears a
layer-wig and short tunic, and carries a
spear and bow (or machete-like sword).
RIGHT Bronze statuette, fourth century BC,
from Volaterrae. These elongated figures, of
which Perusia has also provided a rich crop,
carry the Etruscan love of fantastic
exaggeration to extremes.

ABOVE Le Balze, scene of a series of enormous landslides which carried away parts of the western slopes of the hill of Volaterrae, including its Etruscan cemeteries.

LEFT Ash-urn from Montescudaio, south of Volaterrae's River Cecina, late seventh or early sixth century BC, decorated with geometrical and swastika reliefs. On the lid sits a bearded man beside a table laden with food; a woman stands facing him, and there is a mixing-bowl nearby.

Tomb from Casale Marittimo (Casalmarittimo), south of the River Cecina, early sixth century BC. It has a 'false dome' (*tholus*), i.e. a dome built of rows of overlapping stones gradually closing up to form a conical summit. These structures were customarily supported by central columns.

was conducted by traders. Originally, relations with the Greeks in Campania, though competitive, seem to have been fairly friendly; after all, Pithecusae and Cumae had been founded in order to trade with the Etruscan homeland. But when Cumae and then Syracuse became enemies of the Etruscan homeland from the later sixth century BC onwards, hostile attitudes between those cities and the Etruscan communities in Campania also developed, for instance on the occasion of the Etruscan 'long march' of 525–524 BC. However, these conflicts subsequently became irrelevant, because before the next century had come to an end, both Etruscans and Greeks in Campania had been superseded by the invasions of an Italic people, the Samnites, who played a major part in forming a new Campanian nation.

The eclipse of Etruscan interests in Campania must have been a major blow to Vulci. Nevertheless, this collapse did not affect the Vulcentines as gravely as might have been supposed, since they transferred their commercial relations with Greece to the north. In particular, they were present in considerable strength at the market-town of Spina at the mouth of the Po, where Etruscans and Greeks lived and traded together. Some of the best bronze-work and jewellery found at Spina came from Vulci or borrowed its techniques,[65] and, conversely, many of the 'red-figure' Greek vases that continued to arrive at Vulci may well have come from Spina, at least until the middle of the fifth century BC. Moreover, the Vulcentines were active in the interior of northern Italy as well, using the route which passed through Clusium and then across the Arno and the Apennines to Bononia (Felsina, Bologna).[66] However, we cannot reconstruct the process in any detail.

When we come to the later history of Vulci, our information remains insubstantial. Like other Etruscan cities, it failed to help Veii in its war against the Romans, and thus connived in that city's destruction in about 396. Nevertheless, to judge from the paintings of the François tomb, grandiose traditions about the city's past were still held in great honour towards the end of the same century or later. In 281 BC, however, a Roman general fought against both Volsinii and Vulci, and celebrated a triumph.[67] Part of Vulci's territory was taken away to provide land for the new Roman strategic colony at Cosa. But, by this time, Vulci, as a power in its own right, was no more.

CHAPTER 11

VETULONIA

Wealth and Art

The history of all the Etruscan states is lost, but nowhere is the loss more complete than at Vetulonia. Yet the place was very important: the decisive factor was its close proximity to the uniquely prolific mines of the Massetano (Massa Marittima).[1] The exploitation of these metals seems to have begun in the eighth century BC, when the Greek markets of Pithecusae and Cumae in Campania were founded in order to acquire them.

Under the impact of this stimulus, the two villages on the site of the later city of Vetulonia became wealthy even before their amalgamation into a single urban unit. Thus the last decades before 700 BC already witnessed the beginning of 'interrupted circle' tombs, peculiar to the region. These took the form of cylindrical pits (or less often trenches) dug into the rock and grouped together within rings of stones about three feet apart.[2] The contents of these tombs show links both with the pre-urban past and with the rich, urban, fully Etruscan future. In the century that followed, these 'interrupted circle' tombs were succeeded by 'white-stone' circle tombs in which the circles have become continuous; they consist of a series of rough stone blocks marking off circular spaces ranging from forty-five to nearly a hundred feet in diameter. Inside each circle was a trench, or more than one, often lined with stone slabs. When there were two trenches in a tomb, one was used for the burial and the other served as a receptacle for the rich objects that were interred at the same time.

While still dependent on earlier cultures of the region, the two successive series of circle tombs show the breakthrough into the new, wealthy mode of life which was made possible by the imports from Greek Campania and elsewhere, and was to result, in due course, in the amalgamation of the adjacent villages into a single unit. Thus the

Circle of the Cauldrons (Circolo dei Lebeti), of the early seventh century BC, contained large bronze cauldrons of types that are found extensively not only in the near east but at Pithecusae and Cumae, where they were copied. Particularly impressive are the bronze objects – including an embossed and silver-plated cremation urn – and black *bucchero* vases discovered in the Tomb of the Leader (Tomba del Duce), where no less than five successive deposits have come to light. The cremation urn may have been imported from Caere. Yet although the tomb furnishings at Vetulonia are rich, they are less extravagantly showy than those of Caere and other southern centres.

From about 700 BC the Vetulonian tombs begin to be covered by great mounds, a formula which was derived, directly or indirectly, from Asia Minor and is found, as we have seen, to a particularly notable extent at Caere, though the first mound tombs at Vetulonia may be earlier. The largest of them reach a height of nearly fifty feet and a diameter of nearly two hundred and fifty. This, for example, was the size of the Tomba della Pietrera (meaning 'heap of stones'), c. 650–625. It contained two chambers, one on top of the other. When the roof of the lower chamber collapsed – soon after its original construction – it was replaced by a 'false dome' of the type that had already been seen at Populonia nearby, and was apparently borrowed from Sardinia. The stonework of the Tomba della Pietrera, under eastern influences, is already very skilful. To support the dome, however, a central pillar was necessary; the resulting effect can be seen at a grave that has been moved and reconstructed in the garden of the Archaeological Museum at Florence.[3]

The contents of the Vetulonian tombs reveal certain remarkable local specialities. The Tomba della Pietrera provides the first examples of large Etruscan stone statues, earlier in date than those of Vulci and not much later than the first Greek statuary, which consisted of adaptations from north Syrian originals. The statues at Vetulonia show both male and female figures. The costume and hair-style of a female bust, less badly preserved than the rest, displays strong near-eastern connections, particularly with Cyprus.[4] But direct contact with this and other eastern Mediterranean countries need not necessarily be assumed, for it may well be that these influences came rather through the more usual channels of Greek Campania.[5] Another outstanding element in Vetulonia's early production was its bronze-work, the abundance of which need cause no surprise, considering the immediate proximity of so much copper. At first, a wiry style of decoration develops, depicting human limbs bent in curving forms as if fashioned from malleable metal.[6] There are fine representations of animals, including heads of lions. These appear, for example, on bronze horse-buckles (*c.* 700), which testify to the horse-traffic that enabled the ruling class to exploit the local copper production. There are also horses' bits ornamented with small human figures, and horses and horsemen appear on the feet of tripods.

In direct relation with Vetulonia's bronzes was its abundant gold-work, since it was in exchange for its own copper that Vetulonia received its gold from abroad. Some may have come from Carthaginian Tharros in Sardinia,[7] but most was no doubt brought from Greek Campania. On occasion, the gold arrived already made up into splen-did jewellery, though these Campanian models were no doubt copied at Vetulonia as well. Its products in this field comprise the earliest important Etruscan jewel-work, extending from the early years of the seventh century BC onwards. One of the favourite techniques was granulation, already mentioned, the process by which tiny grains of gold were applied to surfaces of the metal. Other examples of this art-form have been seen in more southerly centres of Etruria, but the Vetulonian and north Etruscan use of the method is distinctive: whereas the south preferred a plastic, three-dimensional style of decora-tion (the 'outline' style), the northern school favoured a linear, geometric design, employing a special kind of granulation (*pulviscolo*) so minute that it looks like a solid mass of gold dust, and creates an opaque area which contrasts with the shiny smoothness of the remaining gold surface. The northern technique is neither the forerunner nor the sequel of the southern type of gold-work; it is simply different.[8] Its centre seems to have been Vetulonia, where this jewellery perhaps came from a single workshop. In the latter part of the seventh century (as in Greece) granulation started to become less popular than the simpler process of filigree. This is displayed by bracelets made of thin strips of sheet gold joined together by plaited gold wire, of which specimens are found in a number of Vetulonian tombs.[9]

It was not until after this cultural efflorescence had got well under way that the two villages on the site seem to have completed their amalgamation into a single city, shortly before 600 BC. Vetulonia seems to have reached the climax of its political power during the century that followed; at its conclusion, awareness of perils ahead may be shown by the erection of a city wall of large six-faced stones built round a perimeter of nearly two miles. Inside the wall there is little enough of the residential area to be seen today, but a winding ten-foot-wide main thoroughfare has been identified, together with traces of two irregular crooked streets crossing it at an oblique angle. Remains of square buildings have also come to light; they include a number of one-storey houses for poor people.[10]

The general impression of the early years of the Vetulonian city-state, however, is a scene of rapidly rising wealth. The city's pretensions are illustrated by a gravestone of the late seventh or early sixth century BC from the Tomb of the Warriors, bearing an incised figure of Avle Feluske; it was apparently erected by a companion-at-arms, Hirumina, from Perusia.[11] Avle Feluske strides menacingly in his crested helmet, carrying a round shield and brandishing in front of him a double axe, the symbol of political and religious power in the Aegean region since the second millennium before our era.

Territory and Ports

Like other Etruscan city-states, Vetulonia possessed quite a considerable hinterland. It is true that we cannot draw the frontiers of the Etruscan states with any certainty, and to derive political borders from the cultural affinities of objects found in cemeteries can be perilous. Nevertheless, it is a practice we have to continue to adopt (with due caution) owing to the scarcity of other methods.

To the south-east, Vetulonian territory reached, at one time, to the neighbourhood of the River Albegna, which was then navigable.[12] But the settlements overlooking its stream present a delicate problem. Saturnia, on its upper reaches, looks as though it belongs to Vulci; but Marsiliana (the medieval Castrum Marsiliani), situated between Vulci and Saturnia, is a more curious case.[13] Its habitation centre, near the junction of the Albegna and Elsa, remains unexplored, while its cemeteries carry a specific message about local allegiances. It might well have been expected that a place in this geographical position would be associated, like Saturnia, with Vulci, especially as Marsiliana was rich in copper from the mines of Amiata, of which Vulci at one time exercised at least partial control. Yet Marsiliana unmistakably displays closer links with Vetulonia instead, directly reproducing its peculiar circle tombs and the character of their bronze contents as well.[14] Moreover, its communications with Vetulonia were a good deal better than its links with Vulci. So Marsiliana, at least in its most important period, seems likely to have been under Vetulonian rule.[15] The cemeteries show a high and indeed spectacular degree of prosperity from before 700 until about 600 or soon after; but then, just at the time

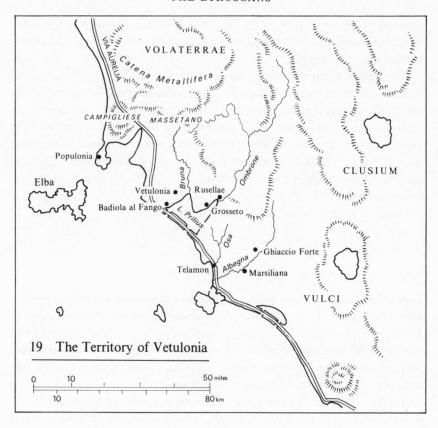

19   The Territory of Vetulonia

when its wealth was at its height, the town went into eclipse. This may have been during the beginnings of the decline of Vetulonia which, as we shall see later, was soon to follow in earnest.

A little to the east of Marsiliana, along the same Albenga valley and road, was an Etruscan hill town on a site now known as Ghiaccio Forte. Occupying an area of about eight and a half acres, Ghiaccio Forte was prosperous by the second quarter of the sixth century BC,[16] partly because it possessed an important healing cult. But then in about 550, like Marsiliana somewhat earlier, the settlement came to an abrupt end. Once again, its collapse may have been a nail in Vetulonia's coffin. All that survived of Ghiaccio Forte was its sanctuary.

The next important valley to the north of the Albegna was the Ombrone (Latin Umbro). Tuscany's second river in length, it was the centre, in antiquity, of a very fertile valley before silting reduced the riverside acres to marshland. Moreover, the Ombrone, like the

Albegna, was navigable for quite a distance.[17] It therefore afforded
Vetulonia important contacts with its north-eastern neighbour,
Clusium (Chiusi), via the valley of a tributary (the Orcia) and the roads
that ran beside that stream and beyond it. By this route numerous
Vetulonian objects reached Clusium. Moreover, Vetulonia opened up
relations with the upper Tiber valley beyond;[18] they are confirmed by
the gravestone of Avle Feluske at Vetulonia, which seems to have been
set up by a man of Perusia (Perugia), a foundation and, at this time,
dependency of Clusium near the upper Tiber. Does the relief signify
that Vetulonia and Perusia (Clusium) were acting as allies? Or does it
merely mean that two individual adventurers, from these different
Etruscan centres, were collaborating on some enterprise, probably of a
violent nature? The latter seems the more likely. In any case, we are far
removed indeed from the mirage of an Etruscan league acting in
unison.

The communications of the Vetulonians up the River Ombrone, and
their relations with Clusium, also gave them commercial openings
across the Arno and the Apennines to the north, and they were making
use of these opportunities even before their villages amalgamated into a
city. Vetulonia sent filigree jewellery to Bononia (Felsina, Bologna),
while Bononia, apparently at an earlier date still, sent buckets (*situlae*)
to Vetulonia. Amber of Baltic origin, too, arrived at Vetulonia from
across the Apennines, and a stylized bird on a bronze urn found at the
same place is reminiscent of central Europe.[19] Indeed, objects from
Vetulonia are found over a very large central and northern region of the
continent of Europe, from the Baltic to the Danube and south-eastern
France.[20]

These various contacts, in which the Ombrone and the other streams
it controlled played such a significant part, prompt the question of what
was happening at the rivers' mouths, for the wealth of Vetulonia's
cemeteries proves that it possessed not only important landlinks but
strong overseas connections as well – that is to say (contrary to former
opinions) a large maritime trade. The bronze coins of Vetulonia, when
it began to issue them in the third century BC, showed nautical types
(anchors and dolphins), and a monument of the time of Claudius (AD
41–54) at Caere displayed a personified Vetulonia with a steering
wheel on her shoulder.[21] This is evidence, of course, dating from long
after the age of Vetulonian prosperity; yet it still may be relevant to far
more ancient times, for this coast had enjoyed an overseas commerce
since the first centuries after 1000 BC.

In the first place, there had been early links with Sardinia. They are illustrated by the false-domed tombs that came to nearby Populonia from Sardinia in about 800 and are found in Vetulonia not long afterwards. Bronze model boats of Sardinian fabrication, or copied from Sardinian imports, have also turned up in no less than three Vetulonian tombs of the seventh century BC, together with a whole 'Noah's ark' of bronze animals from the same island.[22] Conversely, excavations at Sardinian ports such as Tharros have yielded many Etruscan products, so that Strabo could even describe the inhabitants of the island as Tyrrhenians,[23] and, as mentioned earlier, one of their communities, the Aesaronenses, seem to have possessed an Etruscan name. There is no good reason to assume that this traffic was exclusively carried on Sardinian transport; there must have been ships from Vetulonia as well. After all, it had timber to make them with from its adjacent hillsides, and the bark of local cork-oaks was used to seal bronze receptacles in its tombs.

If Vetulonia had ships, it also had ports in its neighbourhood, like other Etruscan cities which were only a few miles from the sea. But the location and identification of these Vetulonian harbours presents difficulties. Whether there was a port at the mouth of the Ombrone (if any – see below) is hard to say, since the estuary has been transformed by a fall of the sea-level along the whole coast, accompanied by silting.[24] But if such a port existed, it could only have been loosely dependent on Vetulonia, as Orbetello was loosely dependent on Vulci. It was not an adjacent, closely dependent city harbour like Regae beside the same city (or Graviscae and Pyrgi adjacent to Tarquinii and Caere); the Ombrone mouth was too far from Vetulonia, which lay thirteen miles to its north.

In any case, however, there is evidence of at least one port much nearer to Vetulonia – though one has once again to bear in mind the astonishing changes of the coastline to locate it. Vetulonia's hill lies just to the west of the stream or torrent of the Bruna; east of the Bruna today – on the seaward side of the modern city of Grosseto – there are five miles of flat land before we come to the nearest reach of the Ombrone. In ancient times, however, when the sea-level was so much higher, this flat land, as we have seen, was an extensive lagoon named Lake Prilius. The lagoon was fed by the Bruna and Ombrone alike (just as Pisae's lagoon, which has likewise disappeared, took the inflow of both the Arno and the Serchio) – or canals may have linked it to the two rivers. Lake Prilius was also open to the sea through deep and navigable entrances, apparently augmented by a man-made channel.

Traces of the buildings that stood along the shores of the lagoon in ancient times can be seen today. They date from the third and second centuries BC, showing that Lake Prilius still existed at that time; and Cicero mentioned an island in the middle of its waters in 52 BC.[25] Indeed, maps of the Renaissance and even later times continue to depict this lagoon and its outlet to the sea, though by then, like other Etruscan sea lakes, it had become an almost landlocked, lethally malarial swamp. We have noted how another similar lake, in front of Orbetello, was gradually cut off from the sea by sand-bars that were the products of silting. At Prilius the silting eventually destroyed the lagoon altogether and obliterated all trace of its ports – leaving the sort of harbourless tract that makes it so hard to understand today that the ancient Etruscans were a seafaring nation. They themselves, keenly interested in hydraulics, were surely aware of the perils of silting, and they must have learnt from the Phoenicians, from whom they learnt so much else, something about how to circumvent them. With hindsight, it is easy to point out that neither they nor the Romans who followed them did enough to keep the problem away. Nevertheless, Lake Prilius outlasted the Etruscan age, and it provided Vetulonia with its harbours.

At least one of them can still be identified: it was at Badiola al Fango, now half-way between the city and the sea, a place where the road from Vetulonia meets an east–west route.[26] Moreover, other hamlets on either side of the lagoon's shores, though once again wholly landlocked today, have or had Italian names that are suggestive of earlier maritime activity – Casa Galera (boat-house), Porto a Colle (hillside port), Porto alle Cavalle (mares' port), Piscara a Mare (sea-fishing). It seems likely, therefore, that Vetulonia had a whole series of adjacent harbour installations on Lake Prilius. They served its trade with Sardinia, and no doubt with Corsica as well, and other countries farther afield. Moreover, either by sea or land or both, the Vetulonians had close trading-connections with Tarquinii and Caere and Vulci. In these exchanges, Vetulonia, whose jewel-work and other cultural achievements were so distinctive, sometimes figured as an exporter, but more often as an importer and receiver of influences.

As for contacts across the Tiber, the Latin poet Silius Italicus claims that the Romans borrowed their official insignia from Vetulonia.[27] This is a more surprising assertion, at first sight, than Strabo's statement that these emblems came from Tarquinii; yet Vetulonia undoubtedly had contacts with Latium, as recent excavations at Politorium, south of Rome, have confirmed. Indeed, curiously enough, Politorium seems to have had stronger connections with Vetulonia than with cities of southern Etruria – presumably because of the greater importance of

Vetulonian metals. There are also certain close resemblances between objects discovered at Vetulonia and another Latin city, Praeneste (Palestrina). Some of these similarities, it is true, may be merely indicative of a common source from which both cities acquired the same sort of material; but vase-handles found at Praeneste had probably been brought from Vetulonia, where identical objects have come to light.[28]

Populonia and Elba

Twenty-five miles up the coast from Vetulonia were the two villages that eventually joined up to become Populonia (Etruscan Pupluna or Fufluna). Their inhabitants became prosperous owing to the enormously rich supplies of metal in the hills of the Campigliese nearby and on the island of Elba, which was likewise within easy reach.[29] Populonia was situated on an almost impregnable promontory which was at that time a peninsula and virtually an island; it overlooked a harbour which, although somewhat vulnerable to westerly winds, enjoyed a spacious site on an extensive bay. This, as ancient writers noted, was the only Etruscan centre to be situated on the sea coast, by which they must have meant the only such centre among those that achieved city-state rank.[30]

Behind the port were extensive cemeteries, at first in the same locations as those of earlier periods and then in the areas round about. The false-domed chamber tomb appears to have been imported to Populonia and then the rest of Etruria from Sardinia as early as 800 BC; and then come chamber tombs of two larger types covered by earth mounds, one with a plinth or drum beneath the mound and the other lacking a plinth but displaying rows of limestone slabs round the periphery of the grave, like its counterparts at Vetulonia. Tombs of the former category in the San Cerbone area are datable to the mid-seventh century BC. The Tomb of the Chariots (Tomba dei Carri) disclosed the relics of two two-wheeled chariots covered by thin sheets of embossed hunting scenes with inlays of imported amber. The Tomb of the Funeral Couches (Tomba dei Letti Funebri) contains the remains of six stone couches. Discoveries in the Tomb of the Fans (Tomba dei Flabelli) included four fans and four helmets of bronze, as well as gold-work and pottery. The Tomb of the Jewellery (Tomba delle Oreficerie), named after the lavish gold objects found inside it, still retains its original 'false dome', dating from the years immediately before 600.

The villages of Populonia had probably presided over, or been associated with, a maritime market or *emporion* since earlier times, but this outburst of wealth first began to appear after the Greek markets and colonies of south Italy began to take an interest in the place. They were drawn by Populonia's metal wealth, already confirmed by the presence of smelting furnaces of *c.* 750. In return for these metals, the traders supplied the Greek and near-eastern objects seen in the local tombs – indeed, Populonia was the largest importer of Greek artefacts in the whole of northern Etruria.[31] For example, it was probably from Pithecusae and Cumae that the Populonians obtained two-handled cups of Phoenician style and learnt of the god Sethlos of Sidon in Phoenicia, whom they incorporated into their own divine hierarchy as Sethlans[32] (equated by the Greeks and Romans with Hephaestus and Vulcan). But it also remains possible that the cult came to them direct from Phoenician sources; and the same applies to the worship of the god Fufluns – from which Populonia took its own name – since 'Fufluns' may be derived from the name of the Phoenician city Byblos. However, the Greek relationship remained persistent, and in Populonia, as elsewhere in Etruria, Corinth and then the cities of Ionia subsequently took over as the principal traders.[33]

In the later seventh century BC, as wealth mounted up from their growing Greek and near-eastern connections, the two constituent villages and *emporion* of Populonia joined together to form a single unit, and the period that followed witnessed a great growth of prosperity. This was also the course of events at Vetulonia; yet, unlike that centre, Populonia did not at once become an independent city-state. In this respect, it was a much later starter. Indeed Servius, the commentator on Virgil in the fourth century AD, quotes a report that it was only 'after the twelve peoples of Etruria had been constituted' that Populonia came into existence at all.[34] Servius seems to have intended to date this development to the years after Rome's destruction of Veii (*c.* 396 BC), which he probably believed Populonia to have replaced as a member of the (somewhat hypothetical) twelve.[35] His assertion that Populonia only began to exist at that time is of course misleading, as excavations show. But the statement makes sense if understood as a reference to its belated establishment as an independent entity and city-state.

Before that time it must have been dependent on another Etruscan centre; it is not easy, however, to decide which one. Servius declared that Populonia was a 'colony of its northern Etruscan neighbour Volaterrae', though he also quoted a variant tradition which maintained that the Volaterrans had not been there first, but had seized the place from Corsicans, who were thus the original colonists of Populonia. Both these assertions are puzzling. It would appear, however, that the statement about the Corsicans does not refer to early times, but to the events of the fifth century BC, when Alalia in Corsica contained an Etruscan workshop and displayed, in particular, notable links with Populonia[36] – which may even have included a trading-settlement or quarter of Greeks or others from Alalia.

Equally enigmatic is Servius' reference to the 'colonization' of Populonia by Volaterrae, which lay to its north. For one thing, although there is evidence of contacts along the coast-road,[37] Volaterrae is a long way away: no less than thirty-eight miles separate the two places. But, in any case, Volaterran colonization of Populonia seems extremely unlikely for another reason: the tomb furnishings in the two centres display entirely different characteristics, and the furnishings at Populonia are far more advanced and wealthy than those of Volaterrae. These two considerations make it almost impossible to conceive of the Volaterran priority and initiative which Servius claims.[38] What he was probably referring to, without knowing it, was the movement of some small group of Volaterrans to Populonia, not necessarily at an initial stage – migrants or visitors attracted by Populonian metals.

Yet it must be insisted once again that Populonia, in the days of its seventh- and sixth-century prosperity, can scarcely have been independent. The days when it was a more or less autonomous *emporion* or marketing-post were ended. So, on the whole, despite what Servius says, it seems they are much more likely to have been dependent on Vetulonia than on Volaterrae.[39] For one thing, Vetulonia is only twenty-five miles away and it is separated from Populonia by only a single broad bay. Moreover, there is a distinct affinity between the early objects found in the two centres, including urns, weapons and cauldrons, which apparently came to Populonia from Vetulonia;[40] and the two places traded with the same towns – for example Bononia (Bologna), and Politorium (Castel di Decima) in Latium. That does not mean that Populonia was one of Vetulonia's own private ports after the manner of its ports on Lake Prilius; for Vetulonia, although so much closer than Volaterrae, was still too far from Populonia for such a close relationship to have existed. But the latter seems to have been a harbour town in the territory of Vetulonia, and more or less loosely controlled by it, in the same way as Orbetello was a harbour town in the territory of Vulci.

In view of Populonia's exceptional commercial importance, it may have been one of the very first Etruscan centres to issue coinage. It had long been customary for Etruscan centres to employ bronze ingots in a quasi-monetary fashion by valuing them according to weight, and, satisfied by this practice, they did without coins for centuries – far longer than many Greek cities, although those in southern Italy (including Cumae) were equally slow. Thus it was probably not until the fifth century that the Etruscans first minted coins at all – and even then they may at first have been simply private issues, affixed with the producer's own seal.[41] In due course, Vetulonia and Volaterrae were among the centres that produced them. But the coinage attributed, with considerable probability, to Populonia is a good deal earlier in date; such a harbour town was clearly well suited for this innovation.

The issues comprise poorly designed silver coins with types of a seal, a lion (sometimes with a serpent's tail), a boar, and the frontal head of a Gorgon, which seems to have been the badge of Populonia or of its coining agent;[42] also, though this attribution is rather less certain, gold pieces with the head of a lion.[43] The chronology of these series is disputed; dates between the late sixth and early fourth century have been suggested, with some preference for a compromise solution in favour of the fifth. It is not until later that coins actually bear the name of Populonia, as of other Etruscan centres. The silver for the coinage was no doubt obtained nearby.[44] Its metrology may perhaps have been derived from Euboean and other colonies in Sicily, notably Rhegium on the Straits of Messina,[45] and an attempt has also been made to derive types and stylistic features of this series from the same sources – or there may be links with Phocaea and some of its eastern colonies.[46] As for the gold used in the second series of mintages tentatively ascribed to Populonia, it presumably formed part of the very extensive Etruscan imports of that metal from Greek Campania or Carthaginian Sardinia.

Populonia's accession to the rank of a city-state, apparently at the beginning of the fourth century BC, recalls that, during the previous years, it had managed to escape the economic recession which at that time afflicted most of declining Etruria. Populonia, at this time, was still receiving (and copying) Athenian ceramics – unknown at this late period in most of the other Etruscan coastal towns. As massive traces still show, the people of the place had long been accustomed to working the iron of the neighbouring Campigliese, which was becoming an immensely lucrative monopoly. Many of the older tombs of Populonia were subsequently covered over by the slag from these foundries, but new cemeteries continued to emerge, bearing witness to a town that was still flourishing.

Much of the prosperity of Populonia was derived from the adjacent island of Elba. Already before there were any cities in Etruria there had probably been a harbour market on the island, as there was at Populonia itself. In Etruscan times Elba, perhaps called Vetalu or Eitale after its Greek name Aethalia,[47] continued to produce and supply metals, presumably under the control of Vetulonia which seems to have ruled over Populonia as well.

It had at first been the copper of Elba that attracted the interest of the Populonians and others from farther afield. But the island, especially on its east side, also possessed huge quantities of iron, which its various Etruscan settlements worked in open-cast mines (except for one short covered gallery). It was in order to plunder this source of wealth that a Syracusan force attacked Elba, as well as Corsica, in 454–453 BC.[48] When the Populonians, not long after, took over a great deal of the smelting of this metal from the Elbans, it was because the wood-coal on Elba itself was no longer sufficient – though it was not entirely exhausted, since a certain amount of smelting still continued on the island. In due course, as elsewhere, Rome gained increasing control, but Elba continued to be very active and prosperous as late as the third century BC.[49]

Rusellae

During the sixth century BC, Vetulonia, with the aid of its lake ports and Populonia and Elba, still seemed to be at the height of its prosperity and power; yet before the century was over its life was suddenly and almost completely suspended for more than two hundred years. When similar fates befell other, less important towns in Etruria during the same period, notably Vetulonia's own dependents Marsiliana and Ghiaccio Forte in this very region, their downfalls have conjecturally been ascribed to aggression by other Etruscan powers. The same fate may be attributed to Vetulonia, for it had an embarrassingly near and increasingly strong neighbour – a neighbour the Vetulonians may have founded themselves. This was Rusellae (an Etruscan name, now Roselle), only nine miles away on the other side of the broad sea lagoon, Lake Prilius. Overlooking the agriculturally rich valley of the River Ombrone, near the point where its waters merged into the lagoon, the original villages on the plateau of Rusellae amalgamated with one another on a new site in the seventh century BC.[50]

Already before 600, the new town had, at least in one sector, a wall with stone foundations and upper portions of unfired brick – one of the oldest urban fortifications to have come to light in Etruria, apparently earlier in date than those of its rival Vetulonia. This wall at Rusellae was subsequently replaced by another, made entirely of stone, reaching a height at some points of over twenty feet and a breadth of eight or nine. The nineteenth-century traveller George Dennis commented on the 'stupendous massiveness, and the rude shapelessness' of this imposing masonry, which set a pioneer pattern for other Etruscan centres and was subsequently reconstructed and strengthened at various epochs.

The wall enclosed a perimeter of almost two miles, but the enclosed area was never completely filled by buildings. On this site, we have the reverse of the Etruscan situation that usually confronts students of the country today. For here at Rusellae the usual cemeteries have not yet been found, whereas the traces of the habitation centre inside the city have come to light on a sufficient scale to provide a unique and, to some extent, detailed picture of what such a place was like. Up to 550 BC, structures wholly made of crude unfired brick were still being erected, but by then baked bricks, too, were coming into use. Subsequently, stone foundations are also found, and sometimes the construction was entirely of stone.[51] Both public and private buildings have been identified. The former, of which the exact purpose cannot generally be determined, were placed side by side in a central valley separating the two main portions of the city area. The residential quarters lay above the valley on either side. Some of these private houses are small, consisting of two rooms and a single storey, affording an unusual insight into the lives of the less rich members of an Etruscan community.

Rusellae, as we have seen, was only just across the waters of Lake Prilius from Vetulonia, which was linked to it by a lake-side road. The two cities, rising on twin hills, were clearly visible to one another across the lake which both had to use, and they were far too close for comfort – like Veii and Rome. Even if the foundation of Rusellae had originally been due to Vetulonia, one can see why the Rusellans felt the need to build such enormous, fortified walls to keep their neighbour out. Indeed, as excavations of fifth- and fourth-century buildings clearly demonstrate, it was Rusellae that proved the more important survivor, while Vetulonia seems to have gone into eclipse at least until about the third century BC (from which date a building was found in 1979).

The suggestion that Vetulonia declined because its harbours, or the lake, silted up is not very plausible, because Rusellae, beside its opposite shore, continued to flourish; and indeed, as can be shown, the lake still remained in existence in Roman times. In spite, therefore, of dissentient views, it seems reasonable to assume that in the years between 550 and 500 Vetulonia flagged and then succumbed to Rusellae and was partly destroyed, or at least eliminated from power politics.[52] Perhaps it had already lost Marsiliana and Ghiaccio Forte to Rusellae at an earlier stage. Even more important, however, was the presumable loss of its sources of metals in the Campigliese and on Elba – and, it seems likely, the loss of Populonia at much the same time or not much later. Rusellae may already, at an earlier date, have had partial access to the great mining resources of the Massetano; the elimination of Vetulonia gave it full control of the area. A heap of selected tin has been found at Rusellae, and charcoal for smelting was available from the firs beside the Ombrone basin.

Rusellae also obtained ships' timber from the same source (in 205 BC,[53] and no doubt much earlier as well), and conducted its own trading operations: excavations reveal traces of commercial contact with Carthage, in which Sardinian harbours perhaps acted as intermediaries. Like Vetulonia, Rusellae had its own port or ports on Lake Prilius, perhaps at or near the Terme di Roselle. It is not impossible that one of these ports was called Thezi or Thezle, and was the issuer of silver coins inscribed with those words.[54] These seem to have been among the very first monetary issues ever to be made in Etruria, probably during the fifth century BC. In this respect they are to be bracketed with the coins attributed to Populonia. That was a harbour town (to which such an innovation was particularly appropriate), and the Thezi–Thezle coins seem to have been issued at a port, since the various types that appear on them include a sea-monster. Other designs accompanied by the same inscriptions are derived from Greek coinages of southern Italy and Sicily, and there may be metrological links with Rhegium on the Straits of Messina,[55] with which the Populonia coins were likewise connected. The evidence for the locality in which the Thezi–Thezle issues were minted is not entirely conclusive, but seems to suggest this general coastal area; Vulci has also been suggested, but the special availability of silver from the Massetano makes it tempting to attribute the mint instead to one of the ports of Rusellae, which now controlled these mines.[56]

Near the River Albegna, which apparently served as its southern frontier with Vulci, Rusellae seems to have established or developed another harbour town as its outpost. This was Telamon, now Talamone.[57] Situated on a steep hill upon a promontory a little south of the modern town, Telamon overlooked a bay which was bordered by the River Osa on the other side. The bay formed a good harbour and evidently served as such in ancient times, when the coastline was more deeply indented, following the route of the later Roman road from north to south, the Via Aurelia. Traditions of a foundation of Telamon going back to a legendary Argonaut of the same name show that the place had certain pretensions, but they are not confirmed by any important archaeological evidence going back to very early times. On the other hand Telamon evidently flourished during the late sixth and early fifth centuries BC, from which impressive architectural terracottas have survived. Telamon was not *the* port of Rusellae in the sense that Graviscae and Pyrgi were ports of Tarquinii and Caere, because it was too far away from the city. It was, rather, an out-lying port and market under Rusellan control,[58] in the same way as Orbetello and Populonia were ports and markets of Vulci and Vetulonia respectively.

Operating through centres of this kind, Rusellae continued to play an increasingly important part as a link between northern and southern Etruria and between the interior and the coast. There is also evidence that it enjoyed a flourishing agricultural economy.[59] During the years when Rome was only just emerging, Rusellae long retained an unusual degree of self-confidence which even the fall of Veii did not impair. For the Rusellans, unlike their neighbours, declined to enter peacefully into a subordinate relationship with the Romans; instead, perhaps from 302 onwards, they fought a prolonged war against them. Finally, in 294, a Roman consul, after devastating the territory of Rusellae, besieged and captured the city; it is the first major Etruscan town after Veii of which Livy records the fall to Rome.[60] The ancient fortunes of Rusellae have been inherited by the modern Grosseto nearby.

CHAPTER 12

VOLATERRAE

Wealth and Art

Vetulonia's northern neighbour was Volaterrae. From its formidable height it overlooked the River Cecina, which runs into the Tyrrhenian Sea, and the Era, a tributary of the Arno. Objects in the styles of the earlier centuries of the last millennium BC, persisted at Volaterrae for an unusually long time,[1] and the union of its lofty villages took place rather late, towards the end of the sixth century BC. The first stone buildings of the habitation zone date from that period,[2] and so does the earliest stretch of a massive, uncemented city wall, this was subsequently enlarged to form a circuit of four-and-a-half miles, one of the most extensive in Etruria (and twice the size of the modern Volterra), although, as so often, the area within the walls was not everywhere inhabited.

Since our knowledge of Etruscan cities (except at Rusellae) depends so largely on their cemeteries rather than on the residences of the living, it is a severe disadvantage that a part of the early burial places of Volaterrae have disappeared, owing to the enormous landslide of the Le Balze at the north-western extremity of the plateau.[3] But George Dennis, in 1831, saw vestiges of two mound tombs with 'false domes', not unlike those of Vetulonia farther south; several burials between the seventh and fifth centuries have also yielded fragmentary discoveries. They show that, even before the process of urbanization had been completed, Volaterrae was quite an important manufacturing centre, notably for the fabrication of small bronzes.

Later finds include the gravestone of the warrior Avle Tite, not unlike that of Avle Feluske at Vetulonia, but in low relief and round-topped; he displays an elaborate hair-style in the near-eastern manner and carries a long spear and bow or short sword. Vetulonian relief of Avle Feluske is datable to the late seventh or early sixth century BC, but a more northerly centre such as Volaterrae could have experienced a cultural time-lag, and Avle Tite may not have died before 500. At about that epoch, too, sculptors of Volaterrae (like those of Vetulonia and Vulci) were producing stone statuary in the round. One example is a male head which shows Greek influences, perhaps coming from Massalia, but which also echoes the native techniques of Etruscan bronzes.[4] The head is made of marble, but that is exceptional: the usual sculptural materials of Volaterrae, down to the fourth century BC, was volcanic stone. This was the material, for example, employed for the earliest in the great series of burial urns which were the special peculiarity of Volaterrae, where no less than six hundred are to be seen in the local museum: they are receptacles for ashes, since cremation persisted in this northern part of the country. The sarcophagi are decorated with animated reliefs and surmounted by reclining figures;[5] reliefs and figures alike originally displayed polychrome colourings and gildings.

However, these monuments are a comparatively late development, starting in about 400 but mostly datable to the Hellenistic period when Volaterrae reached the height of its prosperity[6] and its sculptors began to use the local material of alabaster, a granular form of gypsum. The reliefs mainly depict episodes from Greek mythology, often portrayed with an Etruscan twist; indeed, some myths and figures are purely Etruscan – and in certain instances impossible to interpret. Such, for example, is a scene of a monstrous chained wolf coming out of a well in the presence of a gathering of demons and human beings. In the last quarter of the fourth century BC, Volaterran 'red-figure' pottery, of a characteristic local type, became popular.[7]

If Avle Tite is one of the few Volaterran leaders of whom we have personal knowledge, the leading family of the place throughout most of its history seems to have been the Ceicna (Caecina) clan, which owned extensive lands including clay-pits, kilns and salt-pans. Four tombs inscribed with their names have come to light at Volaterrae, one containing no less than forty cremation urns.[8] The Caecina clan also gave its name to the adjoining river, now the Cecina (or vice versa). Along the river valley ran the road that gave Volaterrae its access to the sea-coast, twenty miles away. It seems likely that Volaterrae, being not only rich but also an important centre of bronze-work, paid early attention to the exploitation of the metal resources of the slopes beside the valley. On either side of it, Etruscan burial places have come to light: to the south they include Casale Marittimo, where a large false-domed tomb was found, and Montescudaio, the site of the discovery of an extraordinary ash-urn of the late seventh or early sixth century BC surmounted by a group of figures taking part in a banquet.[9] A second road from Volaterrae crossed the River Cecina at Saline (named after its salt-works) and led southward to the greater metal resources of the Massetano, though the Volaterrans presumably had to negotiate for a share of these with Vetulonia.

Ports

Consideration of the River Cecina brings us to the question of Volaterrae's harbour facilities. The city is a good deal farther away from the sea than the other major Etruscan centres that have been discussed, so there was no question of a port as close as Graviscae was to Tarquinii, or Pyrgi to Caere. Nevertheless, one would have expected a place of such importance to have a port or ports of its own, though the greater distance of such a port from Volaterrae would make it more comparable to harbour towns loosely attached to their mother-cities, such as Orbetello and Telamon in the territories of Vulci and Rusellae respectively. In 205 BC we find Volaterrae providing ships' rigging, as well as grain, to the Roman fleet – a contribution indicative of a nautical role, which presumably existed earlier as well. The prominence of the theme of Odysseus (the Etruscan Uturze and Roman Ulysses) and the sirens among the mythological reliefs on its funerary urns is equally suggestive of a maritime tradition.

Three miles north of the Cecina estuary, the Romans later had a port, Vada Volaterrana (the 'shallows [or ford] of Volaterrae', not far from the present Vada), a posting-station on the Via Aurelia leading from north to south. Rutilius Namatianus, in the fifth century AD, described it as a harbour reached through a hazardous channel, as today.[10] Various remains have been found at Vada both on land and under the sea; it is not impossible (the coastline having greatly changed) that in ancient times the mouth of the Cecina was nearer to the place than it is now – and that the Volaterrans, in the time of their prosperity, had a port, still undiscovered, at Vada. Alternatively, or in addition, they may have had harbours a little farther to the north (beside the mouth of the Fine stream, where ancient objects have been found underwater, and at Castiglioncello, which seems to have been a minor Etruscan harbour town), or to the south, beside the present Cecina estuary (Marina di Cecina).[11]

It should not, therefore, be concluded that early Volaterrae was a city-state which had no outlet to the sea, or deliberately avoided it. Moreover, the place must be considered in relation to the whole line of

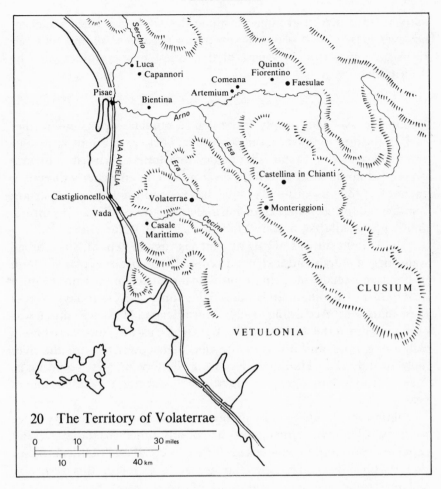

20   The Territory of Volaterrae

Etruscan maritime trading-posts or markets beyond the Arno, extending far to the north. At the outset, they seem to have included Pisae, an
Etruscan or Etruscanized port on the mouth of the Arno itself, where in
ancient times it was joined by the Serchio. In those days, a sea lagoon
came right up to Pisae, providing it with a magnificent harbour.
Farther up the same coast were other places where Etruscan objects are
found: Viareggio, fronting a settlement on the foothills of the metal-
bearing Apuan Alps, and then Luni (Luna). For geographical reasons
the only city-state of the Etruscan homeland which could easily have
sponsored this expansion was Volaterrae; it seems therefore that this
city must have exercised some measure of control or influence over a
greater part of the coastline of north-west Italy. But whether the

outposts thus placed at intervals along this shore remained attached, however loosely, to Volaterrae, or after a time were shared by other Etruscan city-states, or even acted autonomously, cannot now be determined.

The Northern Interior

Volaterrae was also deeply interested in similar expansions farther east, in the interior parts of the peninsula. These expansions were once again geared to the Arno. The theory that initial Etruscan influence proceeded up its waters from the river mouth, in an easterly direction, cannot be proved; yet the river must have constituted a very important commercial route for the expansion and unification of Etruscan culture, and it was available, first and foremost, to the Volaterrans.

The Arno basin was not by any means easy to exploit, since broad waterlogged marshlands extended across the almost level plain on both its banks, especially in spring-time after the floods: in the third century BC it took the Carthaginian Hannibal, invading Italy, four days to cross these marshes.[12] According to a Florentine legend Heracles himself was needed to drain the Arno swamps, but the Etruscans, too, were highly skilful irrigators, and it was not beyond their power to cross the river more quickly than Hannibal. Knowing the terrain, they could make such crossings into a regular practice by choosing a suitable time of year.

Volaterrae, to whom this opportunity fell, possessed a very large territory of its own, larger than that of any other coastal state, and capable of providing springboards for commercial and political expansion that would reach much farther still. Through this territory, Volaterran pioneers advanced up to the Arno along a broad front. In doing so, they made use, in particular, of the routes beside that river's southern tributaries. The nearest of these streams was the Era; Volaterrae itself overlooked its headwaters, and the earliest of the Volaterran cemeteries extends in that direction. Discoveries of Etruscan objects up and along this Era valley route mark the direction of the Volaterrans' northward drive. It led them right across the Arno, where they established a settlement at Bientina on the other side. This settlement, which already had a past going right back to remote Palaeolithic times, stood on a lake beside a northern Arno tributary (both lake and tributary are now drained). Iron from Elba has been found on the site, and is rightly recognized to have reached it by way of Volaterrae.[13] Ten miles north of Bientina is Capannori, where Etruscan jewellery of 475–450 BC has been discovered.[14] Capannori, close to Luca (Lucca), which alternated in the fifth century BC between occupation by the Etruscans and the natives of Liguria to the north-west, is very close to the River Serchio. That river, descending from a region of Apennine passes, came right down as far as Pisae in ancient times, and this Serchio thoroughfare has been identified as a route that carried Etruscan traffic, much of which was no doubt of Volaterran origin.[15] The only Etruscan inscription so far discovered in Piedmont (north-western Italy) is on a limestone gravestone rounded at the top like the gravestones of Volaterrae.[16] This single object is too isolated, perhaps, to demonstrate direct penetration by Volaterrans to as remote a region as that; yet they undoubtedly played an important part in distributing Etruscan artefacts, and particularly the metals found in their territory, throughout the north.[17]

Returning to that territory itself, we find that the next tributary east of the Era to flow into the Arno is the Elsa. Near its sources, close to the modern Siena, was Monteriggioni. Its cemetery displays urns like those of Volaterrae, but chamber tombs like those of Clusium; a similar picture appears in the region of Castellina in Chianti, a little to the east of the river, where a remarkable narrative bronze relief has been found.[18] These examples of the dual influence of Volaterrae and Clusium, which also occur quite frequently farther to the north, show some process of competition or collaboration. It has been concluded that Volaterrae's early control over the Elsa valley, whether by infiltration or conquest, is by no means proven.[19] Nevertheless, it still seems likely that the area was controlled by Volaterrae rather than, or prior to, Clusium,[20] although parts of the area may have changed hands on more than one occasion. Across the Elsa there was little possibility of moving farther north, owing to extensive stretches of water and marshy wasteland.[21]

A little farther to the east, substantial Etruscan centres have now been identified just on the other side of the Arno, at a point near the modern city of Florence. A great many Etruscan finds have now come to light in this region.[22]

The capital of the zone appears to have been at Artimino (which was probably Artemium in Latin). This stands just beside the juncture of the Arno with one of its northern tributaries, the River Ombrone Pistoiese.[23] The strategic significance of Artemium lay in its command of the valley of this river, which opened up large regions lying to the north; its inhabitants also controlled an adjoining ford across the Arno. Finds on the lofty, defensible hill of this settlement include Greek 'black-figure' vases and Etruscan black *bucchero* ranging from the seventh to fifth centuries BC. Moreover, just below Artemium, at Comeana in the direction of the river, the discovery has been made of a large false-domed tomb of princely grandeur surmounted by an earth mound, dating from the later seventh or early sixth century. Artemium seems to have been a key point on the route of Etruscan explorers and traders to the north, and to judge from the finds, the initial impulse behind its foundation and development came from Volaterrae.[24] According to a recent emendation of a passage in Cicero's letters, Artemium was still in existence in his time.[25]

This was not the only prosperous Etruscan centre just beyond the Arno in this region; for a little to the east, beside the small stream of the Zambra – in what are now the outskirts of Florence – enormous Etruscan mound tombs (circular structures built of limestone blocks) have been found at Quinto Fiorentino, dating from the seventh and sixth centuries BC.[26] The rich tomb of La Montagnola which has survived almost intact contained numerous imported objects, including vessels made out of Egyptian ostrich eggs. The approach corridor (*dromos*), flanked by two lateral chambers, is surmounted by an imposing false vault. The main chamber to which the corridor leads is crowned by a 'false dome', supported by the usual central pillar. No such pillar is to be seen (though it probably once existed) in an even larger grave nearby, La Mula, which is eighteen feet high and twenty-seven in diameter; this tomb, unfortunately, was later transformed out of all recognition. There are also remains of a third princely tomb in the area.

These burial places at Quinto Fiorentino are so like their counterparts in Volaterran territory that we must regard the Etruscan settlement to which they belonged as a cultural and perhaps political dependency of Volaterrae[27] – and a very important one, too, to judge by the massive size and grandeur of the graves. The settlement in question was probably on a hill overlooking the tombs, the Poggio del Giro. The hill has now been gutted by a quarry, and only a fragment of an ancient wall of uncertain date survives. But the site is well adapted to the defence requirements which, in this outlying area, must have been paramount.[28] It has been suggested that Poggio del Giro and Artemium owed their prosperity either to agriculture or to plunder. No doubt both activities played a part, but only the latter, perhaps dignified by the name of trading, could account for the wealth of the local tombs.

A little to the east of these centres was the hill-top settlement of Faesulae, the Etruscan Visul (now Fiesole, a northern extension of Florence). Fiesole became the centre of a rich agricultural zone extending to the south-east along the curve of the middle Arno towards Clusine territory, with which the Volaterran state maintained such close connections. But above all Faesulae stood on a major route from the Arno to the north across a main Apennine pass. Faesulae eventually became a fully fledged Etruscan city, but this did not happen before the sixth or fifth century BC,[29] when it became the headquarters of an important quarrying and stone-carving industry. Once again, the founders apparently came from Volaterrae, with which Faesulae was connected by a direct cross-country route, so that its gravestones partially imitated those of the Volaterrans[30] (although lesser influences from Clusium and its dependency Volsinii are also apparent). One such stone, in memory of Larth Ninie (c. 520–510), is not unlike the monument of Avle Tite at Volaterrae.[31] Faesulae eventually became the central point of Etruscan and Volaterran influence in what is now the Florentine area, succeeding Artemium and Poggio del Giro in this role.

After expanding as far as Faesulae, the Volaterrans used it as a springboard for a further northern movement, employing a route leading up into the intensely cultivated Mugello valley, where there was an Etruscan settlement at Poggio di Colla.[32] Finds in the area include objects of the later seventh century BC, followed by gravestones of Faesulan type.[33] Furthermore, Volaterrae's influence extended much farther northwards still into the valley of the Po, where its explorers and businessmen played a leading part. At Marzabotto and Bononia (Felsina, Bologna), bases of statues are similar to Volaterran figures. Moreover, the gravestones in the shape of horseshoes (from c. 510 BC) that are found at Bononia not only resemble those of Faesulae[34] but, on occasion, commemorate the Caecina family, who were so prominent at Volaterrae.[35] From the beginning of the fourth century BC, too, fine Volaterran pottery began to arrive in the north, at the time when Volaterrae was flourishing as never before. Yet, even at this much later period, the detailed history of the place is still a closed book. All that can be said is that, like other Etruscan cities, it gradually lost its independence to the Romans; in 298, a Roman consul claimed victory over its forces.[36]

CHAPTER 13

CLUSIUM

Wealth and Art

Volaterrae's inland neighbour was Clusium, sixty miles to the south-east, situated on a hill overlooking the now vanished River Chiana (Clanis), a tributary of the Tiber. The villages on the site had originally been occupied by the Camertes Umbri, a branch of the Indo-European-speaking Umbrians, whose territory in ancient times only started on the other side of the Tiber. The villages coalesced into a city in about 700 BC, and it may have been at about the same time that the place, while remaining bi-racial, became Etruscanized.

A few portions of Clusium's stone walls have been discovered; their small circumference, comprising an area of only sixty-four acres, indicates that its population did not, like those of many other Etruscan cities, farm inside the perimeter. Of the ancient city, as so often, little enough has survived, but the cemeteries have left something to be seen; they make it clear that by the seventh century Clusium had become the most important city in north-eastern Etruria and was growing richer and increasing its exports all the time.

An ivory box from the Pania tomb, of the later seventh century BC, is carved out of the hollow section of an elephant's tusk which had been imported from the near east; the designs incised on the object likewise show strong near-eastern associations,[1] though in this region, so far from the coast, there is always likely to be a certain time-lag in the diffusion of such influences. They reappeared strongly, in the forms of hair-styles and clothing, on a handled silver vase (now lost) from Clusine territory, which bore the name of its owner Plikasna. Indeed, the 'oriental' styles imported by way of the Greek markets and colonies of southern Italy could even have been introduced to the northern part of the country by this very vase.[2] However, the cultural picture presented by its reliefs are complex, for they depict warriors whose arms and armour are of Corinthian type.[3] There is a further complication too, since the shape of the vase is very much that of the buckets (*situlae*) characteristic of trans-Apennine Etruscan settlements. Where the Plikasna vase was made is uncertain: both Caere and Phoenicia have been suggested, but its northern *situla* form suggests its place of origin may be Clusium, where it was found.

The principal Clusine cemetery, to the north-east of the habitation centre, remained in continuous use from pre-urban times and makes it clear that the place, in its comparatively remote geographical situation, resisted the general Etruscan tendency to adopt the inhumation of the dead; like its northern neighbour Volaterrae, it retained cremation for centuries instead.[4] The form of cremation receptacle favoured by Clusium was a large unglazed terracotta jar (of pre-urban shape) containing the ash-urn and funerary furnishings. But the most peculiar feature of these jars was their lids, which were fashioned into the shape and features of a human head.[5] Primitive precedents for these human-headed urns, just before and after 700 BC, can be noted at various centres and towns of middle (and occasionally southern) Etruria, as well as in the territory of Clusium itself. But the custom soon became almost exclusively characteristic of Clusium and its immediate surroundings. There, after an initial stage in which bronze and then terracotta face-masks were set on top of the urns, the most ancient group of jars with human-headed lids is datable to the second quarter of the seventh century BC. Therefore the design rapidly evolved, and production increased substantially from 600 onwards. The jars were sometimes set on high-backed bronze or terracotta thrones (the latter copying the former) and placed in front of tables. Their human appearance was intended to restore and perpetuate the physical integrity that the cremation process had obliterated. Yet despite this emphasis on personal survival – and the increasing expressiveness of these hauntingly vivid faces – their features are only portrayed in general terms: the low foreheads, strongly stressed eyes and mouths, and full-face poses reminiscent of the old detached masks are repeated without much variation and do not represent lifelike portraits.[6] Sometimes the bodies of the jars shows hands clasped in intercession, reminiscent of the art of northern Syria and Asia Minor. Moreover, right from the beginning of the series, there had also been more fundamental varieties of design. Thus some jars, instead of possessing human-headed lids, are surmounted by entire separate female figures clothed in network dresses; lower down, further small figures appear, or heads of griffins imitated from the bronze cauldrons of near-eastern origin that had become known through Greek Campania.

The Clusines also developed two other schools of sculpture. One worked in the medium of bronze, presumably deriving its copper from Mount Amiata. In addition to producing fine candlesticks and cauldrons, these, operating from *c.* 580–560 onwards, enabled Clusium – alone among Etruscan cities – to offer an uninterrupted series of statues for nearly two centuries. In their execution, once again, the usual successive Greek influences became apparent, with time-lags due to the geographical remoteness of the place.[7]

Clusium's other school of sculpture in the round employed stone. The use of this medium seems to have spread inland to the Clusium region from Vetulonia in the early sixth century BC.[8] An early bust of a woman is a bizarre version of Syrian-influenced Greek models and a sphinx of *c.* 550–520 seems to go back to Assyrian prototypes. A Clusine ash-urn in the form of a male bearded figure seated in a chair (like those on which some of the human-headed jars were placed) dates from between ten and thirty years later. The pose of the figure, with both hands on his knees – one hand open and the other clenched – is taken from an eastern stereotype.

Clusine artists also created a different type of stone funerary sculpture in the form of reliefs. These appear on circular and then rectangular bases made to support the spherical or bulbous markers (*cippi*) of tombs.[9] The sculptors offer animated versions of scenes such as banquets, dances and funeral games, anticipating the joyful festivals awaiting the dead in the after-life. Those happenings are carved in an immediately recognizable style that cleverly combines archaic formality with lively and elaborate rhythmical effects. The reliefs, employing a local soft limestone (*pietra fetida*), begin towards the end of the sixth century BC and display Ionian and then archaic Athenian artistic influences,[10] duly modified, as usual, in accordance with the Etruscan tastes and purposes of the artists themselves and their clients.

Clusium also evolved an entirely distinctive school of *bucchero* pottery. In southern Etruria, this glossy black ware was chiefly produced at Caere; in the north, after being initially shared among a number of centres, its production was mainly in the hands of Clusine craftsmen.[11] Their wares diverged sharply in appearance from those of Caere, which were thin-walled and light, whereas Clusium's were thick-walled and heavy. They also displayed a special kind of relief decoration, impressed by a cylinder onto a band round the vessel. 'Heavy' *bucchero* is not found with Clusium's human-headed urns and only seems to have begun as a serious industry in the sixth century BC, probably during its latter half. These pots were too porous to contain liquids, and must have been intended for funerary and ornamental purposes.[12]

Clusium's sixth-century King Lars Porsenna was regarded as the most powerful Etruscan of all time. His grandeur was illustrated by traditions of his enormous tomb beside the city. Varro, the Roman antiquarian of the first century BC, has left us what purports to be an account of the monument. He described it as a stone construction three hundred feet square, towering above a fifty-foot-high pedestal containing a tangled labyrinth of chambers. On the pedestal, he added, stood five pyramids, four at the corners and one at the centre, each seventy-five feet broad at the base and a hundred and fifty feet high; they supported a bronze disc which formed the base of a conical cupola hung with bells fastened with chains. Around the cupola were five further pyramids, and these in their turn supported another platform above which four additional pyramids towered.[13]

Pliny the Elder, who quoted the passage, rightly dismissed much of its contents as fantastic – especially the dimensions assigned to the structure. Yet conical and square towers crowned the Cucumella tomb at Vulci, and other pyramidal or conical elements or obelisks appear on graves in the district of Faesulae and outside Rome.[14] Bells had cult associations,[15] and coins show two suspended from the capital of a column at Rome.[16] Such analogies, however, belonged to epochs subsequent to Porsenna and it has accordingly been conjectured that Varro's account was really a record, garnished with exaggerations, not of Lars Porsenna's sixth-century tomb at all, but of a building of the fourth century or later.[17]

Nevertheless, the account is correct insofar as it testifies that Lars Porsenna was buried in a mighty tomb; and the glory of Clusium and its leaders receives independent testimony from the actual survival of a stupendous grave three miles from the walls. This is the Poggio Gaiella, a whole hill converted into a city of the dead. Three hundred feet in diameter – five times the size of the largest single mound tomb – it is hollowed out, like the 'labyrinth' to which Varro referred, into no less than forty underground sepulchral chambers at three levels, interconnected by a bewildering system of dark winding passages. Within this complex interior, rich funerary furniture has been found.[18] Here, then, was evidently the grave of some great dignitary of Clusium. The Poggio Gaiella can hardly have given rise to the tradition of Lars Porsenna's tomb, since, despite its labyrinthine hugeness, it corresponds too little with the details of the story. But its existence makes it easy to believe that Porsenna did have a very magnificent tomb somewhere in the neighbourhood, although it still remains to be discovered. It is rumoured to be under the present cathedral of Chiusi. Like most north Etruscan centres, the same site has been continuously inhabited down to modern times – which is one important reason why remains of the ancient city are so sparse.

Already in Porsenna's time, at the end of the sixth century BC, there had been a few painted tombs at Clusium, quite early in the history of this type of Etruscan monument.[19] But the most notable Clusine examples, carved into the natural rock, do not occur until after 500. The Tomb of the Monkey (c. 480–470) is like the Tomb of the Chariots at Tarquinii, except that here the ceiling is in the form of a diminishing three-stepped series of sunken painted panels – the earliest known example of this feature. The paintings represent the traditional games in honour of the dead, presided over by a seated woman in Etruscan costume. Near the door of one of the chambers is a picture of a monkey chained to a tree. The cross-shaped Tomb of the Hill (c. 460), in which various painters once again display funeral games as well as a banquet with dancers and musicians, has a ceiling which copies a pitched roof supported by a wide ridge-pole.

The Development of Inland Etruria

Clusium possessed metals on Mount Cetona, and in the course of time gradually took over from Vulci the bulk of the metals on Mount Amiata as well. Two rivers, the Paglia and Orcia, rise in the Cetona range, and communications with Amiata, too, were easy for the Clusines; excavations on its slopes have produced female heads that were the work of their sculptors. Yet the wealth of the city came not only from metals but also from agriculture. This had, to some extent, been the position at other Etruscan towns, notably Vulci and Tarquinii; but for them metals appear to have been the primary cause of urbanization and prosperity, with agriculture coming second, while at Clusium, the reverse seems to have been the case. There were many ancient testimonials to the extraordinary fertility of the Chiana valley, and its grain was carefully cultivated and highly praised.[20] Vast irrigation was necessary to limit the flood-waters of the river, but this the Etruscans of Clusium were well able to provide; an elaborate system of trenches, tunnels and conduits is the evidence of their success. Moreover, the shores of Lake Trasimene, a little to the north-east, added fish, fowl and reeds, and provided fine pasture land and easy communications by water. As a result of this unique blend of natural advantages, the area ruled by Clusium was densely populated by flourishing rural settlements.

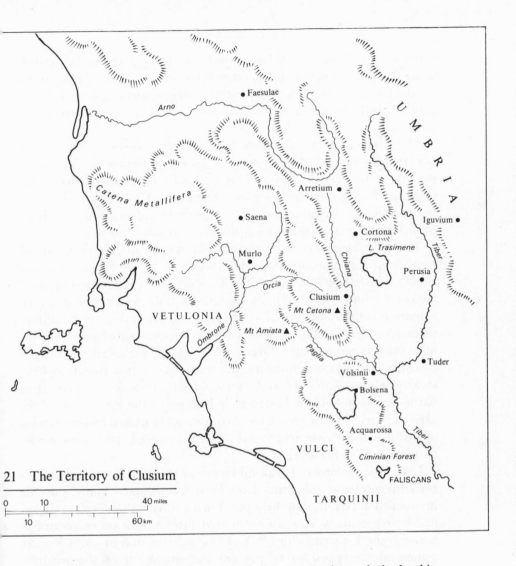

21 The Territory of Clusium

The Clusines, more than any other Etruscan people, took the lead in establishing major centres in their territory – centres which later became prosperous on their own account and subsequently achieved independence. One of the most important of these places was Arretium (Arezzo), thirty miles away. The place stood on a plateau which overlooked the northern extremity of the Chiana valley and was close, on the other side, to the southward curve of the Arno.[21] This was potentially the best pasture and arable land in Italy, and Arretium was superbly sited to exploit this situation. Yet its people had to work hard to gain its full benefits, because the watershed between the Chiana and the Arno is almost dead-level: both streams, when they were in flood,

207

covered it with their overflow, which had to be elaborately drained away. In contrast with so many other Etruscan cities, Arretium was not perched high on an almost impregnable height but lay sprawled on a gentle hillside. Strabo described it as the farthest inland of all the towns of Etruria.[22]

The villages previously on the site of Arretium seem to have amalgamated in the sixth century BC, and an acropolis was established on the site of the modern town. This was done on the initiative of the Clusines,[23] whose artefacts are found along the Chiana route between the two places; Arretium evidently remained a dependency of theirs until their power waned during the years around 500 BC.

The Arretines were probably already specializing in bronze-work right from the time of their urbanization or earlier.[24] The industry developed because Arretium (like Clusium) developed important trading connections with the Gauls of northern Italy, to whom it provided extensive supplies of arms[25] in the hope of mitigating their military threat. Arretine bronze-work includes superb miniature figures, but the most famous piece of all is larger, depicting the wounded two-headed monster known as the chimaera; this masterpiece probably dates from shortly before or after 400 BC.[26] A temple with terracottas representing battle scenes in belated Ionian style belongs to the early years of the same century.[27] Somewhat later, Arretium was fortified by the erection of walls, of which stretches have been discovered; they were made, unusually, of unfired brick.

Latin inscriptions at Tarquinii known as the *elogia Tarquiniensia* have been interpreted as indicating that a Tarquinian named Aulus Spurinna intervened at Arretium to help put down a slave rising, perhaps in the mid-fourth century BC – an event that throws light on relationships between the Etruscan cities.[28] And Livy tells us that in 302 a Roman commander stepped in to prevent the expulsion of the wealthy, powerful, and originally royal family of the Cilnii, from whom subsequently Augustus' adviser Maecenas derived his origins.[29] Evidently the Arretine leaders suffered particularly severely from social discontents. And it was for this reason, ignoring any pan-Etruscan considerations, that they turned willingly to Rome, into whose hands their city passed peacefully and permanently by treaty or truce in the third century BC. In later Roman times Arretium became the best-known of all Etruscan cities because of its mass-production of the red pottery known as 'Arretine', often stamped with graceful decorations in low relief.

Between Clusium and Arretium stood Cortona (the Etruscan

Curtun). Situated on a hill that presides over the plain between the Chiana and Lake Trasimene, it offers what, even for Tuscany, is an exceptional view.[29] Cortona is especially rich in foundation myths, but they are all of late origin and based on false etymological analogies.[30] They are only relevant to the history of the place because they show that its later inhabitants, before and after the city became subordinated to Rome, were by then grand enough to claim venerable origins. Thus when George Dennis wrote, 'Ere the days of Hector and Achilles, ere Troy itself arose, Cortona was,' he is subscribing not to fact but to legend.

In reality the first signs of Cortona's future greatness had appeared in the seventh century BC, when great monumental mound tombs (known locally as *meloni*) first appeared in the area. They were no doubt related to villages that must have existed at that time on the hill of Cortona[31] before their amalgamation into a single city in the fifth century BC.[32] This amalgamation must have been taken on the initiative of Clusium (which had already performed the same function at Arretium farther up the road), and the imposing two-mile-long wall that was round the new city shows that the Clusines regarded the place as a military bastion.

Like Arretium, Cortona was a centre of bronze-work; a lamp of the middle or late fifth century BC, now in the local museum, is one of the most complicated and richly decorated of all Etruscan objects.[33] And the people of Cortona like their neighbours at Arretium and Clusium enjoyed rich agricultural resources as well. Cortona was also strategically placed at the centre of a network of routes: two of them made their way to the Tiber not far off, another ran east-north-east beside a tributary of that river, and another extended in a south-easterly direction along the shore of Lake Trasimene.

This last road led to Perusia, which was another relatively late starter among the cities of Etruria; and once again it was apparently Clusium that united its villages into a city. Perusia was promisingly located very close to the fertile valley of the upper Tiber, which was navigable, in antiquity, for a considerable distance.[34] In early times, there were villages dotted along the hill slopes between the Tiber and Lake Trasimene, each with its own burial ground. Before the Etruscans established control over the area, it seems that, like Clusium, it had been inhabited by Umbrians, from whom Pliny the Elder records that Etruscan aggressors seized three hundred towns.[35] In due course of what must have been a long and complex struggle, extensive racial assimilations gradually came about.[36] Perusia was also largely responsible for the spread of Etruscan cultural influence across the Tiber into

Umbria itself, to which, for example, it transmitted the alphabet in the fourth century BC. An important intermediary role in this expansion was played by the Umbrian town of Tuder (Todi), which became a centre for the diffusion of Etruscan culture.[37]

As at neighbouring Cortona, the pretentious local foundation legends of the Perusians do not accurately reflect the origins of their city (it was not a very early foundation) but bear witness, instead, to its importance at the later date when these stories were devised. In particular, they boast of the part Perusia had allegedly played, at a mythical epoch, in expansion to the north – the tales being apparently invented in order to eclipse the authentic feats performed in that area by Clusium, whose suzerainty Perusia had thrown off by the time the legends were invented. Perusia's own existence seems to receive its first mention in the late seventh or early sixth century on the gravestone of Avle Feluske of Vetulonia, which was, according to a plausible interpretation, set up by a Perusian comrade-at-arms, Hirumina. This does not necessarily mean that Perusia was already an independent city-state at that time, but a century later perhaps it was – though the influence of Clusium still remained dominant in various examples of its artistic production,[38] including a sarcophagus of c. 475–450 BC (the Sarcofago dello Sperandio), depicting banqueting scenes and the return of a party of soldiers. Moreover, like its neighbours, Perusia was a centre of bronze-work, reflecting the influence of Ionian models in its piquant little figures, and then, from the mid-fifth century, subjecting these statuettes to a strange process of exaggerated elongation (attractive to modern sculptors and painters) which reflects the native Etruscan taste for the fantastic and bizarre.

After asserting its independence from Clusium, Perusia was destined to become, after 400, the most powerful Etruscan centre in the upper Tiber valley; its grandeur is still to be seen today in stone walls and impressive city gates, though these have been much reconstructed in subsequent epochs.[39] By the turn of the century, like their neighbours, the Perusians became officially bound by treaty or truce to Rome, but under Roman sway they still continued to build magnificent tombs.[40]

After much modern debate, Volsinii can be safely located at Orvieto, south-west of Perusia.[41] The modern name of the town comes from the Latin Urbs Vetus (Old City); its Etruscan name, to judge from later coins and inscriptions, seems to have been Velsu or Velzna. It stood upon a cliff-protected and reputedly impregnable volcanic plateau overlooking the junction of the Chiana and Paglia, another tributary of the Tiber. The Chiana valley provided a direct road link with Clusium, of which Volsinii should be regarded as yet another offshoot – the heavy bucchero pottery of Volsinii is a provincial branch of the Clusine industry, and the two places have a distinct version of the Etruscan alphabet in common. Clusium amalgamated the villages on the site, in the late seventh or early sixth century BC; when, in the latter part of the sixth century, the great ruler of Clusium, Lars Porsenna, is also described as 'King of Volsinii',[42] this is probably because, as King of Clusium, he ruled Volsinii as its dependency.

In Porsenna's time, Volsinii already enjoyed considerable prosperity. Beneath its hillside is to be seen a network of irrigation and drainage channels testifying to agricultural activity. The control of Volsinii also gave Clusium access to the rich valley of the navigable Tiber. Moreover, another and very special reason why the Clusines were interested in Volsinii was that the greatest of the Etruscan religious centres and sanctuaries, the Shrine of Voltumna (Fanum Voltumnae), lay in its neighbourhood. We do not know exactly where it was situated, but the reverence attached to the shrine gave Volsinii special religious importance. As excavations show, it possessed an unusually large number of temples, acquiring a sort of Delphic status (combined with the usual claims to civic antiquity)[43] which Clusium, as its suzerain, was very glad to exploit.

The most striking features of Volsinii today are the cemeteries round the base of its plateau. The rectangular tombs of volcanic stone in the Crocifisso del Tufo cemetery, datable before and after 500, are disposed in blocks designed to reproduce, in miniature form, the arrangement of a city, fronting long streets intersecting at right angles. Most of the tombs have a small entrance-hall and a burial chamber containing two seats. The structures are generally of modest dimensions, indicating that these Etruscans, at least, were far removed from the splendours to be seen elsewhere in Etruria. Furthermore, the names of the dead inscribed on the tombs, which add up to a total of ninety families between 550 and 500,[44] show a high proportion of non-Etruscan Italians and Greeks, thus indicating the cosmopolitan character of the community.

Volsinii also showed its interest in the outside world in other ways. It maintained close communications with other cities of Etruria, and it also made itself known north of the Apennines, where Volsinian elements and objects are found.[45] And the influence of Volsinii was manifest in the south too, as far afield as Campania, to which its traders penetrated by the land route. There, the Etruscan nomenclature of Capua shows unmistakable signs of Volsinian connections.[46]

Moreover, coins of Campanian appearance display the inscription 'Velzu,' which is closely reminiscent of the 'Velsu' on coins of Volsinii itself.[47] It seems, therefore, that the Campanian town, hitherto unidentifiable, which issued this coinage must have taken on the name of Volsinii and received its traders or settlers; indeed, it may even have been founded by Volsinian emigrants or adventurers. Probably Volsinii, when it engaged in such enterprises, enjoyed or claimed special prestige, owing to its connection with the shrine of Voltumna.

After the eclipse of Clusine power in about 500, Volsinii became an independent city-state; it is from this period, during the second half of the fifth century, that the architectural terracottas of one of its principal temples are to be dated. They are Greek-inspired, but show traces of native artistic tastes as well. The series of terracottas continued until the third century BC, when the Romans, unable to tolerate Volsinii's potential control of the route to the north, put an end to its independence. The Volsinians had lost their natural defences when the supposedly impregnable Ciminian Forest to the south was penetrated by a Roman consul in 310. Thereafter, it was not long before other Roman consuls were able to celebrate triumphs over Volsinii (294, 281); and then in 265 the Romans intervened to suppress a rebellion of the lower orders, bolstering up the members of the local ruling class, whom as usual they had kept on or installed as their puppets.[48] However, as a result of the revolt, the Romans evidently decided that the place had no future, and they ordered its evacuation.

In the course of this heavy-handed action, the Romans removed the population to New Volsinii (Volsinii Novi), which is still called Bolsena, on the productive shores of the lake of that name. But Bolsena had long been in existence; indeed, it had already been an important centre in the pre-urban epoch. Thereafter, tombs of Etruscan type appear from the seventh century BC. Subsequently, after the villages on the site had been unified into a single town, a strong wall was built round it, constructed, as time went on, upon five separate terraces at different levels. No doubt Etruscan Bolsena was at first under Clusium, and then, after Volsinii had asserted its autonomy, changed hands and came under Volsinian control instead.

Other major settlements in the region lay to the south-east of Lake Bolsena, an area which was extensively opened up by the Etruscans in the 600s; these too may have been outposts of Clusium, though such an assumption implies a wide extension of Clusine territory.[49] One such centre was Acquarossa. This place, standing on a plateau of volcanic stone descending steeply on all sides, had already, like Bolsena, been inhabited in pre-urban times, and it, too, embarked on a major expansion in the late seventh century BC. Its town plan at that time can be largely reconstructed. One important discovery, comprising numerous fine architectural terracottas, go back to the years around 550 BC – before such objects multiplied elsewhere in Etruria.[50]

The terracottas seem to have belonged not to a sanctuary, as has been sometimes supposed, but to a residential building, and numerous lesser private houses have also come to light. Their foundations were cut deep into the rock, but the buildings themselves were constructed of wood or made of reeds and poles daubed with clay.[51] These houses often consisted of a vestibule in front of three parallel rooms, resembling the plans of Etruscan temples and tombs elsewhere. Acquarossa was one of the places that suffered sudden destruction in about 500 BC, perhaps when Clusium was asserting its power.

In a westerly direction, the territory of Clusium extended as far as the River Ombrone and beyond. One of its farthest outposts in this direction seems to have been Murlo (Poggio Civitate). The ancient name of the place is unknown. It is just on the other side of the river, upon a wooded ridge between two of its tributaries, a little to the south of Saena (Siena). This ridge forms an eastern extension of the Catena Metallifera, from which metals were available to Murlo.[52] Although the place shows cultural links with various parts of Etruria, its terracottas and artefacts are very similar to those of Clusium, which was linked to it by a route running along the Ombrone, and was probably its master.[53]

The most important discovery at Murlo is a large stone building. It has sometimes been regarded as a sanctuary or holy place, like the partially comparable structure discovered at Acquarossa; but once again it seems more likely to have been a residential building, perhaps the official residence of the leading citizen, who may have been a governor sent from Clusium.[54] This Murlo palace appears to have been constructed in two phases, dating from c. 650 and c. 575 respectively, the second stage following the destruction of the original building by fire. This later structure comprised four wings round a colonnaded central court measuring a hundred and eighty feet across. On the west side is a small rectangular construction that may represent a sacred area.[55] The whole precinct may perhaps be regarded as an ancestor of the Fora of Roman times, and makes a novel contribution to our knowledge of the life and architecture of ancient Etruria.

Another remarkable feature of the discoveries at Murlo comprises a group of terracotta statues that belonged to the second stage of the palace and came from the apex and lateral extremities (*acroteria*) of its pediment. There are so far thirteen of these male and female seated figures, nearly life-sized and wearing broad hats.[56] These sculptures possess a number of peculiar stylistic features, including reminiscences of pre-urban times, but in general their affinities are Clusine. The faces are like the metal masks attached to jars from Clusium, and the costumes resemble those of the figures surmounting other receptacles from the same place. Moreover, the wide-brimmed hats show contacts with northern Italy that were surely obtained through Clusium.[57]

The excavations at Murlo have also disclosed friezes (revetments or wall-facings) of approximately the same date, which is unusually early for this form of architectural decoration. On their reliefs the local leader himself is seen seated, holding in his hand a curved horn (the Roman *lituus*) which is the emblem of his religious authority. A slave is in attendance, carrying his sword and lance, and behind the chief sits his wife on an imposing throne, beside which stands a serving girl bearing a fan and pail.[58] A further relief shows a banqueting scene which synthesizes Greek and native elements.[59] Another displays the earliest known formal portrayal of a horse-race, thus recalling Livy's statement that, when the Etruscan King Tarquinius Priscus celebrated the first Games at Rome, most of the horses came from Etruria.[60] These friezes and the pointed hats of charioteers and jockeys are reminiscent of north Italian models.[61]

In about 530, Etruscan Murlo abruptly ceased to exist. This was also what was to happen a little later at Acquarossa, on the opposite periphery of Clusine territory, and the same explanation may apply – the ruthless assertion of power by rising Clusium, to which the population of these destroyed centres may even have been transferred.[62]

The picture of Clusium's development of internal Etruria, then, in and around the sixth century BC, is a curiously contradictory one, presenting on the one hand the probable obliteration of some widely separated settlements such as Murlo and Acquarossa, and on the other, the vigorous development of further centres extending from end to end of the eastern border of Clusine territory, namely Volsinii, Perusia, Cortona and Arretium.

The Drives to the North and South

The three northernmost foundations, Perusia, Cortona and Arretium, fulfilled a role in another of Clusium's remarkable enterprises, which was an extensive drive outside Etruria beyond the Arno and the Apennines. One of them, Perusia, claimed to have played a particularly large part, even asserting that its founder was the brother or father of a mythical personage to whom the foundation of Bononia and Mantua was sometimes attributed.[63] It is not impossible that Perusians took part in the northern expansion, but their prominence in the story only dates retrospectively from the later time when Perusia had become important and Clusium had waned. In fact, Clusium had assumed the lead in these contacts at a time when Perusia had not yet been important enough to do so: the very name of Bononia in Etruscan, Felsina, is linked with a Clusine family, the Felsnal. Clusium took the lead in the north from Volaterrae at about the beginning of the sixth century BC, and although Volaterrae's activity in this area did not cease, Clusium appears to have been henceforward the more active of the two. As a result, it incorporated northern Italian features into its own art, and, conversely, the Clusines were the principal source of Etruscan influences north of the Apennines.[64] When the oldest Etruscan inscriptions in this northern region appear in about 530, they are seen to employ the form of alphabet that prevailed at Clusium, and by the beginning of the following century this had spread right up to Venetia in the north-east, becoming the foundation of the Venetic, Illyrian and Raetian alphabets, and the basis, too, of German and Scandinavian runes.[65]

The route the Clusines mainly followed ran up through Arretium and crossed the Arno near Faesulae, where the gravestones, that had hitherto been of Volaterran type, became influenced by decorative motifs from Clusium.[66] Marzabotto, too, is linked more intimately with Clusium than anywhere else, producing, for example, sculptured heads of Clusine type.[67] Clusium likewise seems to have provided the middle-men for the trade of other Etruscan cities north of the Arno,[68] and exported wine and agricultural products in their direction.[69]

As usual, however, we are left completely in the dark about the extent to which these trading operations were accompanied by the use of force, and whether the initiative was taken by Lars Porsenna or some other ruler of the city-state of Clusium, or by individual adventurers like those who made their way from other Etruscan centres to Rome, such as Tarquinius Priscus from Tarquinii and the Vibennas and Mastarna from Vulci.

When we turn to the south, Clusium is recognized to have been one of the leaders of the drive by the Etruscans into Campania, including their settlement of Capua.[70] This raises the Clusines to a unique historical position: they expanded extensively in northern and southern Italy alike. Once again, one of the towns dependent on Clusium took a share in this expansion, though this time not Perusia, as perhaps in the north, but the more southerly centre of Volsinii. When Cato the Elder referred to a 'foundation' of Capua at a date not far from 500 BC,[71] he may be alluding to a refoundation in which Clusium and Volsinii played a part.

We can reconstruct the land route by which Clusines travelled to the south: they went down through the Tiber valley and then through the valley routes of the Sacco (Trerus) and Liri (Liris), roughly along the course of the later Via Latina. They have left their traces in the names of two Campanian rivers, the Clanis (the former designation of the Liri) and the Clanius or Clanis or Glanis (now the Regi Lagni canal);[72] both these seem to take their names from Clusium's river, the Clanis (Chiana). Moreover, it is very likely to have been Clusines who joined their compatriots from Spina and others in the 'long march' into Campania in 525–524 against Greek Cumae, since the associates of 'the Etruscans' in this enterprise were specifically stated to include Umbrians, and Clusium ruled over a population of those people (Camertes Umbri) – the previous occupants of its site. Once again, it can be conjectured that Lars Porsenna may have played a part in the expedition.

Virgil presents a more surprising picture in the *Aeneid*, for he names a King of Clusium, Osinius, among Aeneas' *naval* allies on board ship. He also explicitly related this Clusine activity to Campania by stating that another of these Etruscan shipboard commanders was called Massicus,[73] which is the name of a mountain north-west of Capua. The poet adds that Massicus' thousand soldiers came from 'the walls of Clusium and the city of Cosae'. The association of Clusium with distant, maritime Cosae is curious. The Roman colony of Cosae (Cosa) had not existed in Etruscan times, but there was an Etruscan port at Orbetello very nearby – probably bearing the name of Cusa at that time – and it is to this that Virgil refers. However, his repeated assertion that Clusium, which was far inland, provided a naval contingent has caused surprise. To suppose that the poet is referring to a second, unknown, maritime Clusium seems too desperate a way out, since there is no evidence whatever for the existence of such a place from any other source.[74] Virgil must be referring to the authentic inland city.

If Clusium really sent men by sea to Campania, it could only have done so by agreement with a maritime Etruscan state. Cusa (Orbetello), with which Virgil associates it, was in the territory of Vulci, and at first sight Vulci does not seem a very obvious candidate for an alliance with Clusium, owing to the rivalry of the two places for the metals of Mount Amiata. On the other hand, we need not suppose that such hostility lasted all the time; indeed there was a road-link between the two places, and Vulci exported objects to Clusium and influenced its sculpture. It may well be, therefore, that at times Vulci provided Clusium with shipping space as well. Of course it is also possible that the Clusine association with the sea was pure invention on Virgil's part, in total disregard of geographical probabilities, and that the reason why he perpetrated this fiction of the alliance with Aeneas, the forerunner of Rome, was in order to honour the memory of Clusium's good relations with Rome in early Republican times.[75]

Clusium and Rome

These relations were preceded, however, by the aggressive phenom-enon of Lars Porsenna, King of Clusium during the sixth century BC. The stories associated with his Clusine tomb show that the formidable ascent of Clusium during the latter part of that century is indissolubly linked with his career. We do not even know his name for certain, since both 'Lars' and 'Porsenna' may be titles of rank or glory.[76] But what-ever he was originally called, he attained an influence in Italy that no Etruscan had achieved before; in the words of Macaulay's *Lays of Ancient Rome*, under him 'the banner of proud Clusium was highest of them all'.[77]

Lars Porsenna was described, not merely as King of Clusium and King of Volsinii, but actually as King of Etruria;[78] but this is a loose or misleading description. It does not mean that he ruled all the city-states of the country, for they possessed no corporate, federal political entity, and he did not create one. Yet the place where their representatives were accustomed to meet one another for annual religious ceremonies was, as we have seen, the Shrine of Voltumna, which, being in the region of Volsinii, was probably within Clusine territory. And it was entirely natural that the presidents whom the cities elected for these annual ceremonies, officials who had in former times been described in complimentary fashion as 'kings', should have included at least on one occasion, if not more, Lars Porsenna, King of Clusium.

It has been surmised in the foregoing discussion that Lars Porsenna may have played a leading part in Clusium's unique double expansion both to the north beyond the Apennines, and to the south into Campania. Indeed, on the way to Campania, it is specifically possible, despite legendary accretions, to identify his presence at Rome. After the Etruscan Tarquinius Superbus had been expelled by the Romans towards the end of the sixth century BC, and the monarchy had been superseded by the Republic, it was said that Lars Porsenna endeavoured to restore the fallen monarch, who had fled to him for refuge. Now, it is true that Porsenna certainly attacked Rome; but his attempt, according to the accepted Roman canon, failed because of the heroic defence of the Tiber's Sublician Bridge by Horatius Cocles, an event commemorated by the most exciting of Macaulay's *Lays of Ancient Rome*. However, from a strictly historical point of view, there are two things wrong with this story. In the first place, as the historian Tacitus knew, there was a markedly different, contradictory tradition, indicating that Porsenna, instead of reeling away in defeat, actually conquered Rome and held it for a time; Pliny the Elder adds that he granted the Romans a treaty, and Dionysius of Halicarnassus even tells how the senate offered him the emblems of kingship.[79] This version, so much less flattering to the Romans, should probably be accepted as accurate, since the alternative tale looks so very like a patriotic Roman attempt to explain away a defeat at Etruscan hands.[80] But there is also another objection to the Roman canonical legend: it seems more than doubtful that Lars Porsenna's intervention was on behalf of Tarquinius Superbus at all.[81] If that had been his purpose, why then, since his attempt to capture the city, as we now know, proved successful, was Tarquinius not restored?[82] Furthermore, it is recorded that the expelled Tarquins (after first fleeing to Caere) took refuge with Aristodemus of the Greek colony of Cumae, the enemy of the Etruscans and of Lars Porsenna himself. Probably the truth is that Porsenna, taking advantage of the growing weakness or ejection of the Tarquinian dynasty at Rome, was acting on his own account; it is even possible that it was he, and not the native Republican revolutionaries of Rome, who actually overthrew the house of the Tarquins – in which case the first 'republican' consuls may have been his dependants or prefects.[83]

At all events, Porsenna himself became the ruler of Rome. What is more, despite later chauvinistic Roman attempts to forget the interlude, we learn from Plutarch that his rule was even remembered by a statue near the senate-house.[84] Here we have something different from the earlier arrivals of Tarquinius Priscus from Tarquinii and Mastarna and the Vibennas from Vulci. They had been proceeding on their own account as individual adventurers, without the backing of the Etruscan city-states from which they came. But Lars Porsenna was acting as King of Clusium, to whose greatly extended territory he added Rome for a while – and perhaps quite a long while, too, because there were stories about how he became lastingly reconciled with the Romans. Moreover, using their city as a base, he extended his power deep into Latium until Aristodemus apparently came up from Cumae in a successful attempt to protect the Latin town of Aricia against him (*c.* 506–504 BC).[85]

At this juncture the success of Clusium began to recede. In due course, its rulers lost control of the towns its ancestors had founded, Volsinii, Arretium, Perusia and Cortona, and each of these became an independent city-state. Nevertheless, the Clusines remained a power to be reckoned with, and their relations with the Romans, who occupied such a key position upon their commercial route to the south, remained particularly important. In spite of Porsenna's earlier Roman connection – or because of it – Clusium continued to enjoy and cherish good relations with the Romans. When, in the course of the fifth century BC, they suffered from famine and purchased wheat from 'the Etruscans', no doubt some of it came from Clusium, which was particularly rich in grain and could ship it straight down the Tiber. And when, at the end of the century, Rome became locked in mortal combat with its Etruscan neighbour Veii, the Clusines took the lead among Etruscan cities in withholding help from their own compatriots, thus becoming responsible for the piecemeal subjection of Etruria to the Romans that gradually followed.[86]

Clusium's close connections with Rome continued thereafter. Livy tells an anecdote relating how a Clusine nobleman Arruns exported wine to sell among the Senonian Gauls (*c.* 400).[87] This was the time when the Gauls were infiltrating into northern Italy. In the process, they were coming under strong Etruscan influences, and many of these no doubt emanated from Clusium, which enjoyed such strong links with the north. This being so, despite certain legendary intrusions, the basic features of Livy's account of Arruns' transaction are reasonable enough. The story goes on to tell how the Gauls increasingly wanted more and more of the agricultural wealth of Clusium, particularly its wine, and even began to covet the land that produced these good things so lavishly. Finally Arruns (who was at odds with his ward the Clusine ruler) arranged for Gallic migrants to be invited into Etruria by 'treaty' to settle on his city's territory – a plausible enough scenario of an internal factional conflict resulting in external intervention.[88]

Very soon, however, the story continues, a dispute broke out between the Clusines and their Gallic visitors, and Clusium was now in the gravest danger. The tradition went on to tell how its leaders appealed to the Romans for help, and how the Romans in response sent 'mediators' belonging to the Fabian clan – which is independently recorded at Clusium.[89] One of these Fabii, not content with mediating, fought a duel with the Gallic chief and killed him, whereupon the Gauls moved onwards against Rome itself, overwhelmingly defeated its troops on the River Allia, and put the city to fire and sword (in 390 or 387). The Clusines' appeal for the assistance of Rome has sometimes been dismissed as a romantic fiction invented by Romans in order to 'explain' the Gallic invasion[90] – and it is true that some features of the narrative look legendary. Yet its main lines remain possible, since Clusium and Rome were friends and, despite their geographical distance, possessed excellent river and road communications with one another. Moreover Clusium, like Veii before it, got no help from its fellow Etruscans when the crisis struck, so it was natural that its rulers should look a little farther afield. It was lucky for the Clusines that the Gallic army marched off to Rome instead – indeed, this was a development which some of their leaders may have encouraged.

Clusium was little affected by the subsequent decline of western Etruria, and continued to flourish; but its defences were threatened when the Romans penetrated the Ciminian forest into Volsinian territory in 310, and in 295 they and the Clusines were involved in a clash. On the whole, however, their absorption into the Roman sphere during this century was peaceful. During the early Romano-Etruscan period, a large area round Clusium seems to have been in the hands of only about twenty families, and one can be sure that the Romans, in accordance with their usual policy, bound them carefully by ties of friendship to their own ruling class.

CHAPTER 14

VEII

Wealth and Art

While Clusium was the greatest centre of north-eastern Etruria during the sixth century BC, its counterpart in the south-east, although possessing a far smaller territory, was Veii. The villages on the hill of Veii coalesced to become a city between 750 and 700 BC. This event can be associated with the impact of the Greek (Euboean) markets established at Pithecusae and Cumae at this time. Even earlier than the creation of these markets, in about 800, Veii had already shown signs of Euboean contacts, and recent excavations have brought to light Greek vases of *c.* 750 which point to links with Pithecusae almost immediately after it was founded. As we have seen the Greek markets wanted metals, which Veii did not possess in any substantial quantity; but owing to its geographical position at the south-eastern extremity of Etruria it was seen by the Greek traders and then colonists in southern Italy as a natural intermediary with other Etruscan cities which did possess them.

The imports of Veii itself were at first not very extensive, and the place began its urban existence on a comparatively unpretentious scale. However, it was populous enough to possess a number of early cemeteries. Some of them were new; others, however, were just continuing their existence from the pre-urban epoch, and these can be seen descending in chronological succession from the top to the bottom of the hills on which they were lodged.[1]

The early tombs of Veii's urban period include a type peculiar to this place, comprising a room-like trench reached by a staircase with niches cut into the walls. Two graves, however, show precocious artistic achievement. The Tomb of the Ducks (Tomba delle Anatre, of the late seventh century BC) is the oldest painted grave that has hitherto come to light anywhere in Etruria. It is named after a frieze of five ducks on the end walls. The walls of the tomb display paintings in two bands

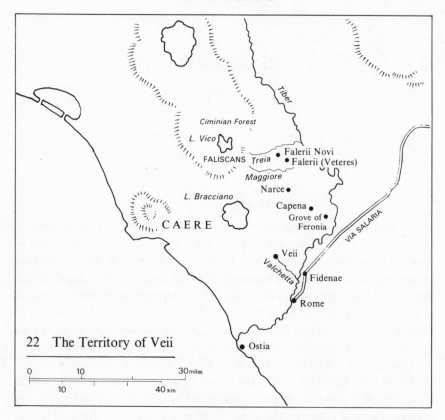

22   The Territory of Veii

applied directly to the face of the rock, red above and yellow below, colours which reappear on the ceiling. A second early painted grave, the Campana tomb (named after its discoverer), also appears to belong to the end of the seventh century.[2] The tomb contains two burial chambers reached through a long entrance corridor flanked by two lateral rooms. One of the chambers, which contained the bodies of a man and a woman, has a gabled roof. Its wall-paintings, reminiscent of eastern rather than Greek models, consist of a series of closed compositions beside the door. The pictures are arranged in bands and depict, from top to bottom, a pattern of lotus flowers; figures on horseback preceded and followed by people on foot and by animals; and a further frieze of real and imaginary animals. The figures on horseback may be hunters departing for the chase, a new theme in Etruscan art.[3]

Such tombs were apparently rare at Veii, and the early 'political power' of the place is a false retrospective projection devised by the Romans in the fifth and fourth centuries BC to show that their great rival of that time had always been formidable in the past as well. In fact, however, Veii had only begun to be prosperous after 600 BC, much later than its coastal neighbours.[4] In those later years it did indeed become a great city-state, the most powerful in Etruria and second to Rome in the whole of non-Greek Italy. When ancient writers ascribed Veii a population of a hundred thousand, they were probably exaggerating; nevertheless, Dionysius of Halicarnassus felt it was entitled to comparison with Athens.[5]

Excavations have revealed main streets intersecting at right angles according to Greek models, but also narrow crooked streets containing the variously sized houses of people of modest means, made of sun-dried brick and timber on stone foundations. The acropolis (Piazza d'Armi) was not at the highest point of the plateau, but upon its southern extremity above a crevasse; on the other side it was separated from the remaining parts of the city by an artificially deepened ditch. The Piazza d' Armi also contains the remnants of one of the five temples so far identified at Veii. It is the earliest of these buildings, dating from the mid-sixth century BC, and it is thus one of the earliest temples in all Etruria of which anything much has survived, illustrating the first tentative efforts at Etruscan temple-building.[6] It was a plain, rectangular, timber-framed structure, with no porch or pedestal (podium), displaying a crude frieze and ornamental blocks (antefixes) to cover the ends of the tiles along the lower edge of the roof – among the oldest of their kind. A more imposing temple has been excavated in the Portonaccio sanctuary area outside the city. Dedicated to Menvra (Athena, Minerva) in c. 520–500 BC, its triple shrine was fronted by a porch. This was enclosed within projections of the side walls, according to a plan described by the Roman architect Vitruvius as typical of Etruscan temples.

Terracotta statues, larger than life-size, were placed on the massive central beam of this Portonaccio shrine, forming the top of its roof from front to back. A substantial part of the group has survived, and its artistry and workmanship are superb. The most famous of these statues depicts Apulu (Apollo) contending with Herkle (Heracles, Hercules) for the body of a hind. There are also equally vivid heads of Turms (Hermes, Mercury) and of a goddess carrying a child. Overcoming the difficulty of terracotta as a medium for the creation of large figures, this masterly sculptor has produced works as good as the statues of Caere, but in a different and distinctive style. The relationship to Greek art displayed in these figures, at its moment of transition from the Ionian to the Athenian manner, shows the characteristic Etruscan method at its zenith, utilizing its models as a general guide but injecting an element that is alien to Hellenism. Apollo, caught frozen in a moment of fierce emotion as he tenses himself and begins to thrust forward upon his opponent, bulges and almost bursts with vital energy,[7] expressing a dramatic and near-brutal sense of strength and movement that is purely Etruscan and a tense roughness that is the artist's own – a roughness that is paradoxically and almost perversely accentuated by the drapery that clings delicately to his massive form and is rendered in waywardly elaborate detail.

At this time, Veii was the leading artistic centre of southern Etruria. It was so famous that, uniquely, even the name of one of its sculptors has survived. He was called Vulca,[8] and his work was in demand beyond the Veientine borders, notably at Rome, where he may have had a workshop. It is tempting to regard these exceptional statues from the Veii shrine as his personal achievement – or preferably as the achievement of his school, since the literary tradition assigns him a date that seems slightly in advance of the sculptures.[9] But some would instead prefer to assign to him, or his workshop, a series of friezes exhibiting a style that seems to be a decade or two earlier.[10]

Agriculture and Salt

Unlike nearly every other Etruscan city, Veii did not owe its urbanization and development to a local supply of metals, sought after by foreigners; its evolution came about through other kinds of production. Only Clusium and perhaps to a lesser extent Vulci were in a similar position, and they enjoyed secondary sources of revenue from local metals as well. Apart from a small amount of iron ore from the slopes of the lower Tiber valley, Veii had no supplies of metal – that was why its development was at first slow – but then, like Clusium, it became rich and finally very rich indeed.

The primary reason for this prosperity was the wealth of Veii's agricultural resources. Their potentialities were exploited by extremely skilful irrigation, so characteristic of the Etruscans who in their turn became the mentors of Rome. Veii conserved its water in cisterns replenished by shafts leading through the rock. In the Piazza d'Armi, an elliptical pool lined with blocks of volcanic stone has survived almost intact. So has the remarkable Ponte Sodo, a tunnel which channelled the Tiber's tributary, the Fosso Valchetta (Cremera).[11] Partly natural but enlarged and deepened by human enterprise, the Ponte Sodo extended for a length of over two hundred feet, cutting through a rocky outcrop which protruded into the ring of water flowing round the city, and thus gave rise to frequent flooding.

Veii extended its system of water control for miles around the town. Through the whole of this low-lying, waterlogged, eroded area, many streams were carried underground in artificial, rock-cut, arched drainage channels, some nearly two miles long. They follow the lines of the valleys, with vertical shafts every hundred feet or so to facilitate the extraction of the excavated soil and make subsequent maintenance possible. These channels, which must have been carefully planned by the city's central authority, can be traced back as far as the fifth century BC,[12] but it is reasonable to suppose that they were in fact earlier, and that they had already made a vital contribution to the initial rise of Veii's prosperity.

In the hinterland of Veii there were no satellite towns like those attached to other Etruscan cities, but a thick network of farms instead. The territory of Veii extended to Lake Bracciano in the north-west, to the borders of Falerii and Capena to the north, and to the Tiber in the east and south. On the east side, the Veientines had excellent water communications with that river because its tributary, the Valchetta (Cremera), on which the city stood, had not appreciably silted at that time and was still navigable.

The situation at the Tiber's mouth is enigmatic. Although Veii was only fourteen miles from the Tyrrhenian Sea, the coastline it possessed just north of the estuary extended for only five miles at most, and on that small stretch of coast no signs of a Veientine port can be found. It is conceivable that there was one and that the extensive silting in the area has subsequently obliterated every trace of it; but even if so, it could only have been an uncomfortable and perilous little anchorage. It is more probable that no such port existed.[13] Veii, despite its closeness to the sea, was not primarily a maritime city like its neighbours.

Even if the Veientines scarcely used the seashore as a harbour, however, they relied on this coastal zone for another source of enormous wealth. This was salt, which was abundantly present at the mouth of the Tiber and did not appear in comparable quantities anywhere else in Etruria.[14] Salt was the very symbol of the progress from nomadic to agricultural life. Its indispensable preservative qualities gave it an enormous economic (and political) significance, which was reflected in numerous ancient proverbs and ceremonial procedures.[15] The Carthaginians were extremely well aware of its advantages, and many of their markets and settlements in North Africa, Sardinia and Spain were situated within reach of natural salt-pans. Salt was also essential to all Etruscan cities, and most of them could only obtain it from here; moreover the Greek markets at Pithecusae and Cumae were no doubt interested as well. And as Dionysius of Halicarnassus confirmed, it was Veii which controlled these vital salt-beds at the mouth of the Tiber.[16]

Not metals, then, as in neighbouring Caere and other Etruscan centres, but these two resources – grain and salt – were what brought the Veientines their wealth. They could send this produce up the Tiber on river-boats by way of Rome, at such times – frequent enough in earlier days – as their relations with the Romans were good enough to do so (and one of Rome's principal routes into the interior was known as the salt road, the Via Salaria). But the Veientines had access to their salt-works not only by the river route but also by a direct land route of their own, through the Fosso La Galeria, which bypassed Rome. This thoroughfare was part of an elaborate network of roads, for they were fine road-builders, and taught this science, like irrigation, to Rome. Veii had no less than seven main gates, from which an elaborate system of routes radiated outwards, routes capable of carrying heavy-wheeled traffic in every direction.

The Faliscans

Veii enjoyed important commercial and probably political links with a territory in its hinterland. This was the Faliscan region, which extended as far as Lakes Bracciano and Vico and the Ciminian Forest to the east, and to a bend of the River Tiber to the west. The cities, towns and villages of the Faliscans were perched on platforms of volcanic rock rising steeply among the deeply scored valleys of the Tiber's tributaries.

Although situated on the Etruscan right bank of the river, these Faliscan settlements were only partly Etruscanized. Their inhabitants do not seem to have been Etruscan by race or to have admitted substantial numbers of Etruscan immigrants: their language was not Etruscan[17] but Faliscan, an Indo-European tongue related to Latin, of which it gradually came to resemble a local dialect. Moreover, as recent research has increasingly revealed, the Faliscans of the eighth and seventh centuries BC already had a rich and original culture of their own, containing a good many internal diversities yet well-defined all the same and going back to pre-Etruscan origins.[18]

This Faliscan culture became subject, from shortly after 700 BC if not earlier, to extremely powerful influences from Etruria, with which they possessed such strong geographical ties, and the links grew stronger in the sixth and fifth centuries. Indeed, as Livy and Pliny the Elder record, the Faliscans considered themselves, or were considered by others, to be Etruscan.[19] Their political affinities, too, were with Etruria, and they also formed early links with the Greek markets and colonies in Campania which had contributed so enormously to early Etruscan civilization.[20]

The destiny of the Faliscans thus resembles and foreshadows that of Rome, some thirty miles away to the south. There, too, the population spoke an Indo-European tongue but were strongly subject to Etruscan cultural influences, emanating in part from Greek Campania. Indeed, the Romans, from the later seventh century BC onwards, were under Etruscan rulers for a considerable period. But whether the same was true of the Faliscan territory we do not know. Nor is it even certain whether it ever formed a single political unit, though at the height of its prosperity this is possible.

It is at least clear that the Faliscan leadership often acted in collaboration with the Veientines. At times, indeed, the Faliscans may be regarded as a kind of extension of Veii, though perhaps remaining formally autonomous. In the sixth century they also enjoyed close relations with Rome and played a part, along with Veii, in furnishing its artistic models. But later the Faliscans opted politically for Veii against Rome, which they had evidently come to regard as the greater danger to their Tiber trade. This decision eventually cost them their independence, since, unlike the cities of Etruria proper, they actively supported Veii in its decisive war against Rome, a development obliquely echoed by Virgil, who singles them out as the allies of Rome's Etruscan enemy Mezentius.[21]

In the centre of the Faliscan territory stood its principal town Falerii, later known to the Romans as Old Falerii (Falerii Veteres) and now Civita Castellana. Like so many towns of neighbouring Etruria, it stands on an easily defensible plateau bounded by ravines, which mark the course of two tributaries of the Tiber, the fast-flowing River Treia and the Maggiore. Falerii, at its height, was in some respects as important a city and state (or state capital) as the purely Etruscan centres, or Rome itself at the same period.

Falerii also had an exceptionally rich religious background. The remains of a number of temples are to be seen, both inside and outside the walls, showing a variety of Greek influences;[22] and one of the local foundation legends even claimed a Greek origin for the city.[23] That, as so often, was merely a boastful assertion of its alleged antiquity and independence; a more significant and accurate foundation story stressed the connection with the Veientines instead. It was noted by Servius, the commentator on Virgil, who also recorded that Halaesus, the founder of Falerii, was an ancestor of the kings of Veii.[24]

After the Faliscans had supported Veii in its fatal struggle against Rome, the Romans seized a number of their outposts; but Falerii successfully resisted a Roman siege for a whole year (394) and continued to prosper, producing an extensive series of 'red-figure' vases and architectural terracottas. Moreover, it continued to follow a policy hostile to Rome, supporting Tarquinii in its first Roman war in 358 BC. The Romans defeated them both and forced them to sign treaties or truces involving political subjection. Falerii attempted to revolt on two separate occasions, and in 241 was destroyed; its surviving inhabitants were resettled at Falerii Nova (Santa Maria di Falleri), which was chosen for this purpose by the Romans because it was situated on a plain and could never, if its loyalty waned, be defended against them.

Ten miles south of Falerii was an older Faliscan centre at Narce (the modern Calcata) in the valley of the Treia, which enters a broad, flat-bottomed gorge a little farther on.[25]

It has now been determined that Narce was much more ancient than had previously been supposed, for it was already occupied soon after the middle of the second millennium BC. In the seventh century, Narce was importing amber and gold brooches resembling finds at Caere, Marsiliana and Politorium. Other imports of the period include a series of bronze vases, all apparently from a single Caeritan workshop. On the strength of this evidence, it might have seemed that Narce's closest Etruscan contacts were with Caere, which was not far from Faliscan territory. But in common with other Faliscan towns its most intimate link was probably with Veii instead. Other discoveries at Narce include vases showing representations of a youthful god between two horses;[26] this 'horse-tamer' motif had appeared in Greece in the earlier, pre-urban period, and also occurs on Italy's Adriatic coast, from which a number of Balkan influences filtered through to Narce and other Faliscan centres. But the main importance of the excavations at Narce is the light that they throw on the life led by ordinary people in a rural village or small town.

Near Narce is Capena, perched on a precipitous hill surrounded by the ravines of Tiber tributaries, with a small plain not far off. Its cemeteries date from the eighth century BC, but Capena gained greatly in importance from the years before 500 because of its proximity to the sanctuary of the Italian goddess Feronia, whose name may be

Etruscan, though her functions and character are uncertain. Her holy place, which has recently been discovered near Mount Soratte (the ancient Soracte) beside the Tiber, stood in a favourable position to attract visitors from many parts of Italy, since it was situated on a cross-roads between the territories east and west of the river. People flocked to the shrine therefore, from many directions.

Capena was related to Veii by a curious foundation legend, quoted by Servius from Cato the Elder.[27] According to this story, a King of Veii named Propertius was induced by local overpopulation to compel all the young men of his kingdom who were born in a certain year to emigrate and found a new settlement at Capena. This procedure was known as the 'Sacred Spring rite'. Examples are recorded from a number of regions, but the practice was especially common among the Italic hill-tribes of Italy. Lacking a sufficiency of land for their growing populations, they would from time to time dispatch a whole generation of their people to found a new colony, dedicating the enterprise to the deity Mamers (the Etruscan Maris and Roman Mars), who was the Italian god of agriculture as well as war.[28]

Cato's account has been doubted on the grounds, first, that Propertius was not an Etruscan but an Umbrian name, and, secondly, that Capena's language and material remains show that it had closer links with Falerii than with Veii.[29] As to the former point, the story may have got the name of the Veientine king wrong, but it is also perfectly possible that Capena was founded by Veii and subsequently developed a largely Faliscan culture.[30] Many Greek parallels could be sited for such a transfer,[31] and Populonia may provide an Etruscan parallel. That, then, is what is likely to have happened at Capena: it was probably, in origin, a Veientine foundation. Etruscan names occur on inscriptions found at its site, and Livy, writing of the late fifth century BC, regards it as a member of the Etruscan league.[32] Capena's closest Etruscan connections as Cato evidently knew, were with Veii, which was only ten miles away by a direct road. Like Falerii, it was one of the Faliscan centres that sided with Veii against Rome, to which it succumbed in the very year after the conquest of the Veientines.

Veii and Rome

Veii's proximity to the Tiber involved close contact not only with the Faliscan region, but with Latium across the river. Indeed, it even had a left-bank outpost of its own on Latian soil, only five miles north of Rome. This was Fidenae (Castel Giubileo), upon a hill overlooking a ford of the Tiber just opposite the point where the river is joined by the Valchetta (Cremera). Fidenae was in a position to control the Tiber traffic; moreover, it gave Veii a link with the south by way of Praeneste (Palestrina), where the Bernardini tomb produced an inscription recording a form of an ancient Veientine royal name, Vetusia. And a little to the south of Praeneste, on another part of what later became the Via Appia, the antique city of Alba Longa likewise had a curious link with Veii: a fragment of Naevius, the Roman poet of the third century BC, tells how a King of Veii named Viba or Vibe paid a visit to a King of Alba Longa named Amulius. When that was supposed to have taken place we cannot tell, yet this isolated piece of information hints at a whole possible network of diplomatic, as well as trading, relationships between Veii, at the height of its power, and Latin cities.

A little farther down the Via Appia was Velitrae (Velletri), where the temples had terracotta friezes and decorative tile ends (antefixes) identical with those of Veii; it was there that the Velitran objects or their matrices were evidently made.[33] Employing this land route through Latium, the Veientines also took a particularly keen interest in Campania. Being the southernmost state in Etruria they may also have been leading intermediaries for Etruscan trade with Sicily, where numerous seventh-century pots, believed to originate from Veii, have come to light.

In the times of the Etruscan Kings of Rome, Veii's relations with that city, to which it was linked by an early road,[34] were generally good, and it was in the interests of both parties' trade that this should be so. It was recorded that in very early times Rome adopted one of its religious institutions, the priesthood of Mars known as the Salian order, from the Veientine King Morrius or Mamurius Veturius (whose name is related to Vetusia, mentioned above). Moreover, the Romans of the regal period, although governed by kings from Tarquinii and then connected with Vulci and Clusium as well, relied on their neighbour Veii as their chief cultural model. Not only are Veientine *bucchero* pottery and metal work found at Rome from *c.* 625 BC onwards but a century later terracotta friezes that appear at the two places are identical. Besides, the Romans invited the great sculptor Vulca of Veii to make the statue of Jupiter for the huge temple that their Etruscan monarchs constructed for Jupiter, Juno and Minerva.[35]

However, soon after the fall of Rome's Etruscan monarchy, the potential perils in its relationship with Veii rapidly became apparent. The course of events is obscured by a mass of tendentious Roman legend, but the salient factor is clear: the two places were preposterously close – only twelve miles apart – and in this situation it was inevitable that they should clash. The Tiber was as much a river of Veii as of Rome; the Veientines claimed it had been named 'Tiber' after one of their kings,[36] and in addition it had another unmistakably Etruscan name, Velthurna or Volturnus, like a river in Campania. Along the Tiber and in the south as well, Rome and Veii were rivals for all the same commercial markets. Moreover, the Romans were a constant threat to Veii's salt-beds at the Tiber mouth, and when they established a colony at Ostia and built a bridge over the river in the seventh century BC, part of their motive, perhaps a substantial part, was to stand a better chance of seizing the Veientine beds.[37] At the same epoch, too, they occupied and fortified at least a portion of the Janiculum Hill just opposite their own city on the Veientine bank of the Tiber. However, the Romans still smarted, because at all other points the land controlled by Veii came all the way down to the river, directly overlooking the city of Rome on the other side.[38] Worse still, the extension of this Veientine territory to Fidenae seemed an intolerable provocation to the Romans, since this place, which commanded the Tiber and its tributary the Valchetta (Cremera), was actually on their own side of the stream.

Given such extreme proximity, the competing demands and mutual jealousies of the two states were bound to lead to open war. Indeed, intermittent clashes were recorded as early as the seventh century BC, but the most ancient of these conflicts should largely be discounted since they were often invented by later Roman historians who, as we have seen, wanted to pretend that Veii had always been a bitter and formidable adversary. In fact, it was not until shortly before 500, at the time of the fall of the Roman monarchy, that relations decisively deteriorated. According to one report, Lars Porsenna, while ruling over Rome, won it another foothold on the right bank near the estuary of the Tiber.[39] That is not certain, but in any case serious tension developed not long afterwards, in the 480s. At this time the government of the recently established Roman Republic was mainly under the control of the clan of the Fabii. They possessed particular links with Etruria, and may have owned land in the direction of Veii.[40] In consequence they were entrusted by their government with the defence of the Veientine frontier, which they protected with a private semi-feudal army of their own, such as were also to be found in Etruria and Greece at this time.

As was to be expected, Fidenae became the bone of contention and may even have changed hands more than once. It still seems to have belonged to the Veientines in c. 477–475, when the Fabian leader, after a series of cattle raids, set up a frontier fort near the offending outpost. In the battle of the Cremera that followed, the Veientines won a considerable victory, killing most of the Fabian expeditionary force and totally destroying the Roman block-house. The whole right bank was now firmly in the hands of the Veientines, and they were even able to camp once again on the Janiculum Hill, as in the past.

In 474 BC the prospect for Rome improved, for the Etruscan city-states were greatly daunted by the defeat of their leading seapower, Caere, and its Carthaginian allies by Hiero I of Syracuse off Cumae. In consequence, Veii felt it advisable to make a truce with the Romans, undertaking to provide them with grain and financial assistance. From the middle of the century onwards, the balance of strength continued to shift in the Romans' favour. In 442 they improved their position along the Tiber, and soon afterwards they began to prepare for the final showdown, all the more readily because they were suffering from famine and pestilence, and stood in urgent need of additional land.

In about 437 – predictably claiming intolerable provocation at Fidenae – the Romans moved into aggressive action, and King Tolumnius of Veii was slain by a Roman general.[41] Next, in 435 or perhaps 425, a Roman force seized possession of Fidenae. Appeals directed by the Veientines to the feeble and mainly religious Etruscan 'league' succeeded in persuading a few individual cities such as Tarquinii to allow volunteers to go to their help, but the pleas were otherwise entirely fruitless.

Excuses allegedly offered by the Etruscan cities to justify their failure to provide assistance included Veii's regrettable constitution, since its monarchy, abolished twenty years after the death of Tolumnius, had recently been reinstated, contrary to the practice of all (or some) of the other Etruscan cities. And the new King of Veii was said to have behaved arrogantly and violently at the annual gathering of the league.[42] It was also claimed by the other states that the reason why they could not send help was that they were preoccupied by Gallic pressures in the north. But the fact was that they were happy to get a city that was a commercial rival out of the way, quite regardless of the fact that it was Etruscan.

Having failed to secure the support of their compatriots against Rome, the Veientines set about strengthening the natural defences of their city. Where possible, the cliffs on which it stood were cut back to make them more precipitous, and elsewhere along the periphery an earthen rampart with a stone breastwork was erected. Meanwhile, however, the Romans retained the initiative, and, in the last decade of

the fifth century BC, they placed Veii under siege. The fighting, conducted with forces of a size that had never been seen before, may not
have continued for the whole decade recorded by historians – a duration which they evidently borrowed from the mythical Trojan War.
Nevertheless, the war lasted for at least six or seven years. In the end,
the Roman general Camillus, who emerges, however legend-encrusted,
as the first authentic figure in the history of the Roman Republic,
succeeded in occupying the only neck of land that offered level access to
Veii, located on the northern side of the city. Then follows the story
(which has been doubted but may well be true) of how a party of
Roman soldiers managed to pass beneath the city walls through one of
the famous drainage tunnels and emerged in the middle of Veii itself,
which thus fell into their hands.

It was afterwards believed that the Romans wholly destroyed the
captured city and expelled all its surviving population; the theme was
turned into a poignant contrast with the past glories of Veii. Excavations have shown that this tradition was not entirely true, for some
buildings and inhabitants remained; yet the conquerors inflicted
extremely severe damage. Above all, they terminated the very existence
of Veii as an independent city-state – even taking over its patron
goddess, Uni, under the name of Juno Regina. This total obliteration of
an independent neighbouring power was a sinister historical landmark.
It was not, perhaps, an entirely new experience for the Etruscans, who
had blotted out their own subordinate towns before now, and those of
their neighbours; and it is even possible that one of their city-states,
Vetulonia, had been more or less eliminated by its neighbour Rusellae.
But no city of Etruria up to now had been destroyed by a foreign power
– which is what Rome, now that its Etruscan monarchs were removed,
had by this time become.

The sack of Veii was a turning-point that virtually marks the end of
Etruscan preponderance in central Italy. A first result was the annexation of the entire Veientine territory by the Romans, whose own posses-
sions thus became considerably larger than those of any other state in
Latium, controlling the traffic up the Tiber and the salt-mines at its
mouth. Before long, the other Etruscan states were able to see how
short-sighted their failure to help Veii had been; for within little more
than a hundred years every one of them had been obliged to sign a
treaty or 'truce' with Rome – arrangements which, in effect, reduced
them to subject status.

23 The Etruscan World

CISALPINE

GAUL

Po

Atria

APENNINES

Reno

Spina

Massalia

Bononia

Arno

Volaterrae

ETRURIA

ADRIATIC SEA

Vetulonia

Elba

Clusium

CORSICA

Tiber

Vulci

Tarquinii

Falerii

Veii

Caere

Rome

Praeneste

LATIUM

SARDINIA

Capua

Cumae

CAMPANIA

Pithecusae

Pontecagnano

TYRRHENIAN SEA

Sybaris

IONIAN

SEA

Carthage

SICILY

Syracuse

0   50   100 miles

50   150 km

CHAPTER 15

SUMMING-UP

The Homeland

It should now be possible to draw all the strands of the Etruscans' activity together, and to attempt an overall view of their history. Perhaps the most important time in all its course was a period of a few decades that reached its climax in the eighth century BC; for it was then that groups of adjacent villages – each group on its own defensible plateau – became amalgamated to constitute larger entities which before long became recognizable as the Etruscan cities and city-states. This is a process of urbanization which can also be identified, at much the same period, at the principal habitation centres of Greece, and at Rome as well. The motives that prompted such a development in those countries were various, but in Etruria there was a single predominant cause and motive almost everywhere. We have seen that this was the accessibility of the main urbanizing centres to substantial sources of metals, particularly copper and iron. There was an enormous foreign demand for the metallic resources of Etruria, and its people could only meet this demand in a satisfactory manner by merging each of their groups of little villages into cities containing specialized industrial sections and obeying a single authority with decision-making powers. The full story of the Etruscan exploitation of all these resources is still difficult to tell; excavations have not yet revealed anything like the whole of the picture. But it was assuredly these metals, and the foreign desire for them, that brought into existence the rich and cultured Etruscan society, which the archaeologists have revealed to us, by prompting the local inhabitants to transform their groups of villages into cities and city-states.

The foreigners who sought so eagerly to acquire Etruscan metals had a great deal to give in return. Etruscan arts and crafts reveal two sets of foreign influences at work: one comes from the near east, beyond Greece – mainly from Phoenicia and Syria, but also from Cyprus,

235

Babylonia, Assyria and Asia Minor – and the other set of influences comes from Greece itself. The near-eastern impact was exerted on a considerable scale by the Phoenicians, who had themselves become great imitators and adapters of the arts and cultures of their various neighbours. In the latter half of the second millennium BC the greatest seafaring people of the region, who penetrated as far as the western Mediterranean, had been the so-called Mycenaeans, centred upon the mainland of Greece. When the Mycenaean civilization declined in c. 1250–1200 BC, its mariners and traders were eventually succeeded by Phoenicians based upon Sidon and Tyre. Then, in the years around 800, Tyre founded its famous colony of Carthage in north Africa, which soon became an independent power on its own account. The Phoenicians, followed by the Carthaginians, also established commercial posts or quarters on the coasts of France, Spain and its islands, Sardinia, and Sicily.

These traders, in east and west alike, were prominent among the people who were determined to possess Etruscan metals. That is why enormous quantities of objects closely resembling theirs have come to light from Etruscan soil. Sometimes these objects are imports to Etruria from the near east, sometimes imports from Greek trading centres in the western Mediterranean which had imitated such wares, and sometimes copies or adaptations made in Etruscan lands.

Some of the imports to Etruria were no doubt brought directly from Phoenicia or its western outposts; but most came indirectly through Greek intermediaries. The first group of such intermediaries, during the eighth century BC, were traders in Campania, first on the island of Pithecusae (Ischia) off the northern end of the Bay of Naples, and then at Cumae on the mainland opposite. The Mycenaeans had already possessed an outpost on Pithecusae (and a neighbouring island) many centuries before, and the Phoenicians, too, may have had traders there much more recently, just before the Greeks came. But it was the Greeks of the eighth century who made their mark at Pithecusae and Cumae, and the reason why they came this very long distance from their homeland was to get as close as they could to the metals of Etruria; lumps of iron discovered at Pithecusae have been proved by metallurgical analysis to come from Etruscan Elba. Moreover, other recent discoveries at Pithecusae and Cumae include a varied array of artefacts which recur in finds made in Etruria itself.

Particularly abundant at Pithecusae and Cumae is material strongly reminiscent of Phoenicia and other near-eastern countries. Why they appear at these Campanian trading-posts is now known. The Greeks who sent their traders there in the eighth century BC originated for the most part, as their pottery shows, from two cities of the Greek island of Euboea, Chalcis and Eretria. These were ports which, in these early days of Greek history, took the lead in the expansion of Hellenic goods and influences to the western Mediterranean area. But the reason why they filled that region with near-eastern objects was that, in rivalry with the Phoenicians, they had already expanded vigorously to the eastern Mediterranean as well – notably to Al Mina at the mouth of the Orontes; it was from there that they sent many of those Phoenician and other near-eastern wares to their fellow-Euboeans at Pithecusae and Cumae, in order to be sent on to Etruria as part of the deal for Etruscan metals.

The tombs of Etruria make it abundantly clear what the new rich Etruscans wanted, above all, in exchange for their copper and iron. This was gold, which appealed to their luxurious tastes but could not be found in their own country. So the Euboeans furnished them with near-eastern gold from Al Mina, via Pithecusae and Cumae, and the gold, after it had been brought from the near east to those Campanian centres in unworked bars, was sometimes worked in those centres. Strabo refers to gold-workings on Pithecusae, and finds of gold jewellery at Pithecusae and Cumae are making it more and more evident that many objects of this kind that we regard as characteristically Etruscan were in fact designed and worked in Campania for subsequent export to Etruria. Cumae also gave the Etruscans their alphabet and the names of some of their gods, and it may well also have taught them the cultivation of the vine and the olive.

Before long, the Euboeans who came to Italy started to found not just marketing outposts but regular, institutionalized colonies, including one such foundation at Cumae itself and others at places in strategic positions beside the Strait of Messana (Messina). Then the Euboean traders and colonists were eclipsed by other Greeks: especially by the Corinthians, who in their turn, and in pursuance of the same desire for metals, made an enormous impact (directly and through their colonies) on Etruria, as the profound and far-reaching influence of their 'orientalizing' vases on Etruscan art confirms. Subsequently, the influence of the immensely active Ionians became dominant – particularly the men from seafaring Phocaea and its western colonies, including Massalia (Marseille, c. 600) and before long Alalia (Aleria) in eastern Corsica (c. 560), which stood just across the water from Etruria and was expressly located to obtain its metals. The Etruscans may have had a trading-post of their own in the Aegean, on the island of Lemnos, until

Athens seized it in *c*. 500. By that time, Athenian styles were super-seding Ionian as the dominant art of the Greek world, and the change is duly reflected in Etruria. But its art and prosperity alike would soon be on the wane, and despite abundant Athenian imports, Etruscan artists only had a limited sympathy with mature Attic classicism and hum-anism; the preceding, more archaic and stylized Corinthian and Ionian styles remain more characteristic of Etruscan art at its greatest.

Yet, as I have argued, it is misleading to insist too strongly on the Greekness of Etruscan art. The near-eastern component complicates the matter. As we have seen, it was apparently introduced in two ways: first, through the mediation of the Greeks at a time when this 'orien-talizing' tendency formed an important element in their own art, and, secondly, to some extent, by direct contacts with the Phoenicians and their outposts and offshoots. Whatever the relative proportions of goods and motifs that reached the Etruscans through these two chan-nels, it remains indisputable that the Etruscans, partly because of this near-eastern element and partly because of their own temperaments and tastes, transformed the Greek influences to which they were subject into something coarse and vigorous and gay, sometimes eerie and grisly, but always un-Greek and un-classical.

Considerably un-Greek, also, was the architecture of the Etruscans, including the temples and tombs they constructed for their un-Greek religion. They possessed widely recognized, distinctive gifts of their own, notably for medicine and music. Their way of life, too, was different. This was at once noticeable in their personal appearance; the upper class dressed and wore their hair differently from the Greeks. The position of their women was also far freer. Nor did the vertical pattern of the society of the Etruscans follow Greek or Roman norms. They never developed, to anything like the same extent, social groups spanning the gulf between aristocracy and serfs; that was one of the main reasons why they were liable to paralytic internal strife, which meant that they eventually failed to compete with Rome.

The most famous of their differences from Greece and Rome was in the character of their language, which does not seem to have possessed an Indo-European structure. Its peculiarity astonished the Greeks and Romans, though the populations of no less than half of Italy spoke non-Indo-European languages, and had spoken them, in some cases, before the others arrived. So the language of the Etruscans does not help us to answer the old question, 'Where did they come from?' This question may be an unreasonable one to ask – the answer to a similar enquiry about the British or Americans, for example, would be very long and complicated. Nor were the ancient Greek and Roman writers very well informed on the subject: Herodotus quoted a story from Lydia in western Asia Minor indicating that the Etruscans originally came from that country; but the story is based on etymological analogies which are fictitious and demand its rejection. Besides, archaeological evidence confirms that the cultural links of the Etruscans with the Lydians were comparatively sparse and unimpressive. The emphasis in Etruscan art and customs is far more on features emanating from Phoenicia and Syria than from Lydia or other zones of internal Asia Minor. Accordingly, when Dionysius of Halicarnassus, in the first century BC, flatly denied that the original Etruscans had come from Lydia, pointing out that their laws and religious and other institutions were entirely different, he was right.

Herodotus' account also presents a chronological difficulty: whereas the Etruscan civilization, in the form in which we first encounter it, began in the eighth century BC, he attributed the supposed migration from Lydia to a period some five centuries earlier in the supposed epoch and aftermath of the Trojan War. But even if external corroboration of this view was convincing this would by no means explain why the cities of Etruria only took shape and rose to prosperity so many hundreds of years later. Furthermore, efforts to find apocalyptic cultural breaks in the life of Etruria – breaks so complete that they must have been caused by large-scale immigration – have been unsuccessful in relation to the later second millennium BC, and no more successful in relation to the eighth century either, especially when we bear in mind that the logistics of such an operation, involving both movement and settlement *en masse*, would have been beyond the powers of peoples at those times.

When Dionysius, therefore, went on to conclude that the Etruscans had come from nowhere at all – that they were indigenous – his assertion is acceptable in the limited sense that no single large-scale mass immigration (much less two such immigrations) can be regarded as probable. On the other hand, during the course of all these centuries full of convulsions of every kind, there must have been almost innumerable relatively small displacements of population, not only from one part of Etruria to another, but also from outside to inside the country and the reverse. Such fragments of information as have come down to us reveal a few of such movements at many different epochs, conducted by traders, refugees, colonists, artists, mercenaries, princes, noblemen and adventurers.

Some of these persons were Etruscans fighting against their compatriots from other Etruscan centres, for the country suffered from deep divisions between the governments of its various, wholly independent city-states. The mainly religious Etruscan 'league', like comparable Greek associations, only assumed political functions of any significance at a relatively late date, in the fifth or fourth century BC. Even then, it was conspicuously unsuccessful in securing unified political or military activity by the Etruscan city-states as a whole. At an earlier date, in the time of maximum Etruscan prosperity, the 'league' had likewise produced no unity whatever. On the contrary, these city-states had operated separately, without any consideration for the interests of their neighbours. Indeed, they even fought against one another, or did not prevent their individual citizens from doing so. The classic and fatal example of their disunity was their failure to help the Veientines in their disastrous struggle against Rome – a decision which not only resulted in the immediate destruction of Veii itself but had the longer-term effect of enabling Rome to destroy all the other Etruscan communities in piecemeal fashion as well.

The continual failure of the various Etruscan cities to collaborate with one another is partly explicable by the great physical diversity of the country itself, which is reflected in marked divergences between the customs, cultures and arts of its different regions. The resulting powerful individuality which each city-state developed suggests that we should refer as rarely as possible to the 'Etruscans', and should instead name the specific state or states to which we are alluding.

The earliest Etruscan locality to become a unified, highly prosperous centre profiting from the foreign demand for its metals was Tarquinii. The villages on its site had begun to flourish in pre-urban times, during the tenth and ninth centuries BC, when they were already exploiting the adjacent metals on the Tolfa hills. In the eighth century these villages coalesced into the new city of Tarquinii. The date is significant, because it was in this period that the Greek markets at Pithecusae and Cumae were founded with the specific intention of acquiring Etruscan metals. As a result – although continuity with the past is always apparent – important tombs begin to appear at Tarquinii in the early seventh century BC. They were covered by mounds of earth according to a formula which was well known in the near east, and the furnishings of the graves were of great and increasing lavishness. But what makes these cemeteries particularly noteworthy is the unique series of painted tombs which appear from the middle of the sixth century onwards. Greece itself has nothing comparable to show to them. These paintings faithfully reflect the successive Greek influences on Etruscan art, and yet they display many a characteristic native twist.

ABOVE Drinking-horn of *bucchero* pottery, late sixth century BC. The spade-bearded head terminates in a leg shod in a high (leather) boot with a pointed toe. Clusium was the chief centre of this 'heavy' (thick-walled) *bucchero*.

ABOVE Incense-holder (?) of black (*bucchero*) pottery, late seventh century BC. It was found at Artimino (west of Florence; probably the ancient Artemium), one of a group of important Etruscan centres under the influence of Volaterrae. The stem bears the potter's signature: 'I was made by Larthuza Kulenie.'

BELOW LEFT Ash-urn from Clusium (the Gualandi urn), late seventh century BC. The female figure, wearing a network or plaid robe and cloak, is surrounded by small dancing figures and the heads of griffins (imitating those on bronze cauldrons of near-eastern types) which menacingly protect the dead woman.

BELOW Terracotta jar for ashes, with lid shaped as a human head: one of the so-called 'Canopic urns' that were a speciality of Clusium, early sixth century BC. The heads and faces were intended to revive and give permanence to the physical entity destroyed by cremation.

BELOW Alabaster sarcophagus from Clusium, third century BC. The dead man carries a sacrificial bowl. This is the *obesus Etruscus*, the over-weight citizen who gave the Etruscans a bad name among Greeks and Romans.

ABOVE Rectangular base of a tomb-marker from Clusium in local limestone (*pietra fetida*), *c.* 500 BC. The low relief shows a group of dancers, characteristic of a series of such Clusine scenes depicting the festivities the dead person will enjoy in the after-life.

BELOW The cemetery of the Crocifisso del Tufo at Orvieto, now convincingly identified as Volsinii, sixth and fifth centuries BC. Arranged to imitate a town, the tombs of volcanic stone (tufa) are of modest size, comprising a small vestibule and a burial chamber with two benches. The lintels are inscribed with the name of the first person whose ashes were placed there.

ABOVE Bronze Chimaera from
Arretium, *c.* 400 BC or later. The
two-headed monster is wounded in the
foot (Cellini's sixteenth-century
restoration of the snake biting the goat's
head is wrong). Founded by Clusium,
Arretium was now independent and the
centre of a major bronze industry.
BELOW Lamp of cast bronze from
Cortona, mid-fifth century BC. Round the
central head of Medusa is an inner frieze
of wild animals fighting and an outer
circle of winged sirens alternating with
crouching, flute-playing Sileni. Like
Arretium, Cortona was a Clusine
foundation which became an
independent centre of bronze-work.

BELOW Bronze side-panel of chariot
from Monteleone di Spoleto, *c.* 550 BC.
Two heroes are duelling over the body of
a third; the victor receives miraculous aid
from a bird deflecting his enemy's spear.
This Umbrian territory was intensively
Etruscanized by the Clusine foundations
Perusia, Arretium and Cortona.

LEFT One of a group of thirteen recently discovered terracotta seated statues from Murlo (Poggio Civitate), *c.* 550 BC. These nearly life-size male and female figures, wearing broad-brimmed hats, stood on the pediment of a substantial building which may have been the residence of a governor appointed from Clusium.

ABOVE Braces for the teeth of Etruscans: an example of their dental skill, which formed part of their general medical learning.

ABOVE Mixing-bowl of the later seventh century BC, probably from the Faliscan territory (centred on Falerii) which, although Latin-speaking, was largely Etruscanized and closely linked with Veii. This theme of the young god between two horses is found particularly often at the Faliscan town of Narce.

LEFT The head of a terracotta statue of Apulu (Apollo) from the roof of the Portonaccio temple at Veii, *c.* 520–500 BC. Wearing the fixed smile of Greek archaic (Ionian) art – which is here endowed with a formidable Etruscan vigour – he is moving against Herkle (Heracles, Hercules) in a dispute over a hind.

RIGHT The Ponte Sodo at Veii. This artificially enlarged tunnel, a characteristic masterpiece of Etruscan hydraulic engineering, channelled the Fosso Valchetta (River Cremera) through a rocky outcrop so as to prevent flooding and assist irrigation.

BELOW Coin of an Etruscan-founded city in Campania, third century BC: the head of the sun and an elephant. The inscription 'Velecha' seems to indicate mintage at Volcei (Buccino), which takes its name from Vulci.

RIGHT Amazon from the rim of a cauldron from Capua (S. Maria Capua Vetere) in Campania, fifth century BC.

ABOVE LEFT Ash-urn of pottery in the form of a hut; Rome, eighth century BC. This was made before the villages on the Roman hills united and came under Etruscan rule, but urns of this type, though they may have originated in Latium, are also found extensively in southern Etruria. They imitated contemporary huts of plaited twigs and mud, with wooden poles.

ABOVE Reconstruction of an Etruscan temple as described by the Roman architectural writer Vitruvius (first century BC). The great Etruscan shrine of Tinia, Uni and Menrva (Jupiter, Juno, Minerva) on Rome's Capitoline Hill (end of sixth century BC) was of this type but larger, having a six-column, three-deep front porch and side-porches extending to the back.

LEFT Gold bracelet from Etruscanized Praeneste (Palestrina), seventh century BC. The rectangular strips are decorated with embossed figures and granulation.

RIGHT Bronze head of a siren (a bird with a human head and arms) from the rim of a cauldron from the Bernardini tomb, Praeneste. These cauldrons, which are found in various countries, seem to be ultimately of north Syrian origin.

BELOW Gravestone from the Certosa cemetery near Bononia, c. 380 BC. *From top:* sea-monsters; journey of a dead man to the underworld; athletes; women. The horseshoe shape, traditional to the region, may have come from a fusion of ancient local (menhir) forms with round-topped Etruscan gravestones.

ABOVE Bronze bucket (*situla*), used as an ash-urn, from the Certosa cemetery near Bononia (Etruscan Felsina, now Bologna), c. 475 BC. *From top:* cavalry and infantry soldiers; a religious procession; country scenes; animals. These buckets, which also occur in Slovenia and neighbouring regions, may have come to Etruscanized Bononia via the Adriatic.

LEFT Silver-gilt bowl from the Bernardini tomb at Praeneste, mid-seventh century BC. This style, containing Egyptian, Cypriot and other near-eastern features, might have reached Italy direct from the near east, but more probably via Phoenicia and then Greek markets in Campania. *Centre:* a triumphant Egyptian Pharaoh.

LEFT Foundations of grid-planned houses at the Etruscan town of Marzabotto (perhaps the ancient Misa), *c.* 500 BC. Marzabotto stood at the point where the River Reno, and the road from Etruria, begin to leave the Apennines for the northern plain of the Po.

BELOW Air view of Spina, a north Adriatic port at the mouth of the Po where Etruscans and Greeks lived and traded together. Beneath the white lines (modern drainage) are dark lines showing the ancient canals, which flowed between the blocks of houses in the town.

Despite the disappearance of some of its satellite centres, Tarquinii retained a number of large settlements and towns in various parts of its territory. It also possessed three ports, from which it operated a fleet representing the beginnings of Etruscan seapower. From at least *c*. 600–580 BC one of these harbour towns, Graviscae, included a community of Greek traders who established a shrine dedicated to Aphrodite (Turan, Venus) and then, about four decades later, sanctuaries of Hera (Uni, Juno) and Demeter (Ceres). Other events in the history of Tarquinii are reflected in a series of inscriptions honouring the family of the Spurinnas. After the fall of Veii (*c*. 396 BC), Tarquinii became the chief Etruscan enemy of the Romans, to whom it became virtually subject before the end of the same century.

Tarquinii's virtually unchallenged primacy had only lasted, perhaps, for less than a hundred years, after which the control of the Tolfa metals, the source of its rise to power, passed in large degree to Caere (Cerveteri), urbanized very shortly after its neighbour. Caere, too, displays seventh-century tombs with extremely magnificent contents, including much jewellery imported from Pithecusae and Cumae or made of gold that had come from those markets. It is also probable that the Etruscan alphabet made its first appearance at Caere through the agency of the Cumaeans. Fine pottery, too, was made there by Greek immigrants and their local pupils, and Caere also became the main production centre of the distinctive Etruscan type of ceramics, black *bucchero*, in its fine or thin-walled form. Another remarkable speciality of the Caeritans was their construction of huge mound tombs, which reveal a wide range of architectural features including a series of imitations of various kinds of domestic interior. In the sixth century, under Ionian influence, an original school of terracotta sculpture also made its appearance.

When Caere embarked on the seizure of Tolfa metals at Tarquinii's expense, it also appears to have annexed a substantial wedge of Tarquinian hinterland, including the hilly, picturesque area of the rock tombs. Most important of all, however, was its supersession of Tarquinii as a seapower. In taking over this role, it was the Caeritans (not 'the Etruscans' in general) who allied themselves with Carthage to stop the encroachments of the Phocaean Greeks and their colonists at Massalia (Marseille) and Alalia (Aleria in Corsica). In *c*. 540–535 the two sides clashed in a naval engagement known as the battle of Alalia, as a result of which the Phocaeans, though victorious, were too greatly weakened to retain their grip over Corsica for much longer.

Caere's coastline displayed an almost continuous series of ports.

One, Punicum, bore that name because it housed a settlement of Punic (Carthaginian) traders. Another of these harbour towns, Pyrgi, has yielded three sheets of gold leaf with Punic and Etruscan inscriptions. They refer to a dedication by Thefarie Velianas, Lord of Caere, to the Carthaginian (Phoenician) goddess Astarte (Hera, Uni, Juno). The plaques were found in a sanctuary area which was apparently dedicated to the same goddess and has revealed the remains of two temples of *c.* 500 and *c.* 460–450 BC.

Caere's policy towards the Romans was traditionally friendly – in particular, it gave signal assistance when Rome was invaded by the Gauls. But a momentary reversal of this policy in the mid-fourth century led to its virtual subordination to the Roman government.

When Caere had encroached on the territory of Tarquinii from the south, Vulci embarked on a similar process from the north. The territory round Vulci had seen human habitation since the second millennium BC, and cemeteries of the early eighth century or earlier bear witness to flourishing villages. These united to form a single city in about 700, shortly after the first links had been established with the Greek markets of Pithecusae and Cumae. One of the three mound tombs surviving round Vulci, the Cucumella of *c.* 560–550 BC, is the largest grave of its kind in all Etruria.

The city overlooked the valley of the River Fiora, which provided a route to the metals of Mount Amiata. These formed the principal source of the Vulcentines' early wealth, though it also owed a good deal to agricultural development. The commercial importance that Vulci derived from these assets is shown by a unique, astonishing influx of Greek vases over a considerable period, supplemented, in the later sixth century BC, by the development of a considerable local ('Pontic') school set up by Ionian Greek refugees from the Persians. At about the same period, Vulci developed two further artistic activities of its own: one consisted of the production of statuary in stone (the local *nenfro*), and Vulci also utilized the metals of Amiata to create the most flourishing bronze-working industry in Etruria.

During their early expansion in the seventh century BC the Vulcentines exploited the valleys of the Fiora and Albegna. However, a number of prosperous towns in the hinterland proved short-lived. On its complex coastline, Vulci evidently controlled the market or trading-station Orbetello (probably the Etruscan Cusa) with its excellently protected harbour, though it was too far away to be regarded as the city's port in the sense that Graviscae and Pyrgi were the ports of Tarquinii and Caere. Vulci's port, in that more particular sense, was probably at Regae, not far from the mouth of the Fiora beside which Vulci itself stood.

The lost history of Vulci and a whole lost heroic tradition are illustrated by paintings from the François tomb, now in the Torlonia Museum (Villa Albani) at Rome. These paintings, datable between the late fourth and mid-third century BC, tell of wars fought by long-dead Vulcentines against men of other Etruscan and Etruscanized cities – handing down traditions that put paid to any belief in the political unity of the Etruscan 'league'. Vulci also appears to have been the centre of the cult of Aeneas, which later passed, directly or through intermediaries, to Rome.

To the north-west of Vulci was Vetulonia, which grew rich because of its close proximity to the metals of the Massetano. Two considerable villages established early in the first millennium BC became united to form a city before 700. Soon afterwards, when imports from the Greek markets of Campania had begun to arrive, Vetulonia developed its special feature of circle graves grouped within rings of stones. When mound tombs developed, the chambers beneath them were roofed by 'false domes' supported by a central pillar. Like Vulci, Vetulonia had its own stone sculpture. But its most remarkable art was gold jewellery, partly perhaps imported from Pithecusae and Cumae and partly of local fabrication; the special form of granulation which was in favour at Vetulonia displays a technique different from that employed at Caere and elsewhere in southern Etruria.

The territory of Vetulonia may have extended as far south as Marsiliana, which exhibits similar circle graves and tomb furniture and was very prosperous from the late eighth century to about the beginning of the sixth. Ghiaccio Forte, too, flourished after 700, abruptly disappearing in about 550. In addition to its possession of these inland centres, Vetulonia also enjoyed a maritime life, possessing contacts with Sardinia, for example, from an early date. There may have been a market under Vetulonian control at the mouth of the River Ombrone, but if so it was too far from the city to be its particular, closely associated port. This, or these, lay rather on Lake Prilius, which Vetulonia directly overlooked. The lake has now completely disappeared, but in ancient times it was an extensive lagoon opening out to the sea.

Populonia, north-west of Vetulonia, was the only major Etruscan centre to be directly situated on the sea. After already presiding over a market harbour (*emporion*) in much earlier times, its two component villages joined up with one another in about the seventh century BC. Populonia owed its position and its prosperity to the adjacent metals of the Campigliese and the island of Elba. Following upon the appearance of a false-domed tomb dating before 800, apparently based on Sardinian models, large mound-covered chamber tombs begin to appear in about 650. Despite these relatively early phenomena, Populonia only became a fully-fledged Etruscan city-state at a much later period. Until then, it remained under the control of one of the others, probably Vetulonia.

Across Lake Prilius from Vetulonia, Rusellae (Roselle) likewise had a port or ports on the lakeside with access to the sea. Its villages were amalgamated into an urban centre on a new site in the seventh century BC, and very soon afterwards the city was surrounded by a wall, one of the oldest fortifications so far known in Etruria. Rusellae has also provided unusual insight into the design and housing of an Etruscan town. The city may originally have been founded by Vetulonia, but the two places proved uncomfortably close to one another; when Vetulonia ceased to prosper in about 550–500, this was probably because Rusellae superseded its authority. At all events, the Rusellans then established a dominant position in the area. Reaching down to the borders of Vulci, they probably controlled the market town of Telamon (Talamone), which possessed an excellent harbour.

Volaterrae (Volterra), north-west of Vetulonia and Rusellae, stood on a lofty hill overlooking the valley of the River Cecina. The valley was rich in metals, which Volaterrae is likely to have exploited from an early date. Although an enormous landslide has made it difficult to generalize about the early history of the site, the amalgamation of its villages to form a city probably did not take place until shortly before 500 BC. Unlike southern Etruscans, the people of this northern region long continued to cremate the dead. The Volaterrans' principal artistic speciality was the production of cremation urns surmounted by reclining figures, but they mostly date from the fourth century BC onwards. Soon afterwards, locally found alabaster became the favourite material for their manufacture.

Volaterrae probably had a port at or near the mouth of the River Cecina. More than most Etruscan cities, however, it tended to look inland, expanding up the valleys of the Arno's tributaries. One of these streams was the Era, beside which the city itself stood; to its east was the Elsa, which flowed close to two Etruscan settlements at Monteriggioni and Castellina in Chianti. These have cemeteries that show the influence both of Volaterrae and of its great eastern inland neighbour, Clusium.

In pre-urban times there were already villages on the site of Clusium as well as at a number of other substantial centres in the area, containing a population that was mainly Umbrian in race and language. But in about 700 the Clusine settlements, which were now mainly Etruscan-speaking, destroyed or absorbed the others and united to form a city. To a greater extent than most other Etruscan city-states Clusium depended for its prosperity on agriculture, in which the valley of the Clanis (Chiana) was extraordinarily productive. Nevertheless, Clusium also derived metals from Mount Cetona, and in the course of the sixth century BC it gained access to a substantial share of the metallic resources of Mount Amiata, which had hitherto, perhaps, been monopolized by Vulci.

Like the inhabitants of Volaterrae, the Clusines resisted the southern Etruscan innovation of burying their dead and continued to cremate them instead. From early in the seventh century BC onwards, and increasingly after 600, they produced terracotta cremation jars of a highly individual type, the so-called *canopi* which are surmounted by sculptured human heads. Moreover, towards the end of the next century a distinctive series of funeral reliefs made its appearance, adapting Ionian and then Attic artistic styles in an original fashion. Clusium also developed its own school of black *bucchero* pottery, thick-walled ('heavy') in contrast to the thin-walled ('light') ware of Caere.

The grandeur of the city in the sixth century is reflected by the massive hill of the Poggio Gaiella, honeycombed with tombs, and by garbled stories of the enormous mausoleum of King Lars Porsenna, of which the remains may be hidden under Chiusi's modern cathedral.

Arretium (Arezzo), Cortona, Perusia (Perugia) and Volsinii (Orvieto) all seem to have been Clusine foundations before becoming independent city-states. Arretium, the product of a union of villages in the sixth century BC, benefited from the fertility of the Chiana valley and looked to the north. Cortona stood at a communications centre, within easy reach of the Tiber. Perusia was concerned with Etruscan expansion into the territory of the Umbrians, to whose race its original population, like that of Clusium, had belonged. Lars Porsenna was described as 'King of Clusium and Volsinii', with the implication that the latter was yet another Clusine foundation. It flourished especially during the sixth and fifth centuries BC, deriving special prestige from its proximity to the Shrine of Voltumna, where the representatives of the Etruscan states attended a meeting of their 'league' every year. Bolsena was probably at first under Clusium and then became a dependency of Volsinii when the latter became self-governing.

Clusine territory may also have extended to Acquarossa and Murlo;

these places have disclosed the remains of important buildings, apparently of a residential character. But both centres were demolished in the third quarter of the sixth century BC, perhaps as an outcome of Clusine imperialism – for at this time the Clusines under Lars Porsenna were expanding in unprecedented fashion to north and south alike. When he vanished from the scene the tide began to turn, and it was in the years which followed that the empire of Clusium was carved up into several independent city-states.

In the south-eastern corner of Etruria was Veii, on a broad two-ridged plateau where permanent settlements were first established early in the first millennium BC. They joined up to form a city in the second half of the eighth century. In Etruscan dealings with the new Greek markets at Pithecusae and Cumae, the Veientines, owing to their geographical situation, were natural intermediaries. At first, however, the material prosperity of the place was not very great: the town plan revealed by excavations is notable for houses of modest dimensions. Nevertheless, a tomb of 700–650 is the oldest painted grave that has so far been discovered in Etruria, and in the two centuries that followed, Veii became the greatest of the Etruscan cities. Moreover, it was conspicuous for artistic brilliance, as displayed by the terracotta sculptures of its temples.

Like Vulci and Clusium, the Veintines owed a large part of their wealth to agriculture. In contrast to those cities, they were not in a position to supplement this revenue from resources in metals; instead, however, they possessed a unique source of riches in their salt-pans at the mouth of the Tiber. Whether the city owned a small beach harbour there or not is uncertain. But in any case, apart from its exploitation of coastal salt, Veii was primarily an inward-looking state, relying on the communications provided by the Tiber, which formed the boundary of its territory.

During the seventh and sixth centuries Veii's relations with Rome, just across the Tiber, were good, but the nearness of the two cities meant that a clash was bound to come. Finally, after several renewals of hostilities, the Veientines, left almost alone by their fellow-Etruscans, succumbed to Rome in *c.* 396.

The Expansion

The nucleus of Etruscan expansion in fertile Campuania was Capua (the Etruscan Volturnum, now Santa Maria Capua Vetere), strategically located at a crossing of the River Volturnus on an important route from north to south. Excavations in recent years have confirmed that from before 800 BC there was uninterrupted development of the site. At first it comprised several villages, but contacts with the adjoining Greek markets at Pithecusae and Cumae stimulated them to amalgamate by 700 or soon afterwards. In the same period, too, the Etruscanization of the new city began, reaching completion about a hundred years later. Capua soon acquired enormous commercial and industrial significance, achieving special fame for its bronze-work.

In the area of the Bay of Naples there were additional Etruscan settlements, and recent excavations have revealed that a further major focus of Etruscan activity existed farther to the south-east as well, near the Gulf of Salernum (Salerno), notably at Fratte di Salerno and Picentia. From the end of the sixth century BC the relations of these Etruscan foundations with Greek Cumae, and then with the great Sicilian city of Syracuse also, gravely deteriorated, and the Etruscans were more than once defeated. In the years following c. 430, however, not only the Etruscan but also the Greek settlements in Campania came to an end, invaded and conquered by Italic (Samnite) tribes from the hills in the centre of the peninsula.

The formation of Etruscan Campania is virtually part of the same process as the formation of Etruscan Etruria. The former process, it is true, must have involved the arrival of some Etruscans from the homeland, but it is clear that there was no federal colonization by the Etruscans as a whole, which their 'league' would have been too ineffective to undertake. Just as the Etruscan city-states, in their own country, proceeded independently of one another, so their expansion into Campania was never a collaborative affair. Instead, each city-state in Etruria struck out on its own – or, alternatively, individuals or groups of individuals took the initiative.

Some of the principal leaders in the Campanian drive unmistakably came from Vulci, employing both the land route and the sea route. Vulcentine products, or their imitations, had appeared in Capuan cemeteries even in pre-urban times, and a town east of Salernum that the Romans knew as Volcei (now Buccino) evidently owed its name to the same source. Indeed, there are also reasons for supposing that the foundation or refoundation of Capua itself as the Etruscan centre of the country was the work of Vulci. If so, however, Etruscan names found on Capuan inscriptions suggest that Volsinii shared this role, perhaps on the basis of the prestige that it derived from the Shrine of Voltumna in its territory. Since Volsinii was at first an offshoot and client of Clusium, the Clusines too may well have had a share in the foundation of Capua (which gave one local stream the name of their river, the Clanius). Dionysius of Halicarnassus seems to confirm this supposition when he refers to 'Etruscans and Umbrians' invading Campania in 525–524 BC, for these probably included, among others, the people of Clusium, who were the successors and overlords of the Camertes Umbri. This 'long march' may be associated with the aggressive activities of Lars Porsenna, who is known to have been involved in warfare against the Campanian Greeks.

Expansion into Campania had required the Etruscans to maintain an active presence in Latium, which lay between that territory and their own. Names at the ancient Latian city of Alba Longa are demonstrably Etruscan, and indeed a wide variety of Latian sites show material remains that are identical with the artefacts of Etruria. Outstanding in this respect is Praeneste (Palestrina), whose initial burst of wealth before 700 was followed by tombs of the next century that are indistinguishable from those of Etruria.

Among the various Etruscan cities which demonstrably maintained links with Latium, the leading part seems to have been played by Caere. Not only are many objects discovered at Praeneste astonishingly similar to Caeritan finds, but the same applies to half a dozen other Latian centres, including some that are still being excavated. There appears to be a germ of truth in the legend that Mezentius, King of Caere, reduced the peoples of Latium to tributary status. In the seventh century, the Caeritan sphere of influence, cultural and possibly political as well, seems to have extended over large parts of Latin territory. At the end of the following century the aggressive armies of Lars Porsenna of Clusium overran Latium, but his son Arruns was killed at Aricia by a coalition of Latins and Campanian Greeks.

The bridge between Etruria and Latium was provided by Rome; for some years of the seventh century BC, and almost the whole of the sixth, it came under the rule of Etruscans and was Etruscanized to a considerable extent. Tarquinius Priscus, who reigned at Rome between dates traditionally recorded as 616–579 BC, seems to have come from Tarquinii, where his father had arrived from Corinth as a political refugee. Priscus then moved on to Rome which he apparently governed, as an independent state, not as a satellite of Tarquinii. His son or grandson Tarquinius Superbus was enshrined in story and legend as the ruler whose fall inaugurated the Roman Republic (c. 507 BC). Whether the Roman monarchs of this dynasty from Tarquinii were really only two in number we cannot say; but one of the paintings from the François tomb at Vulci shows the death of a certain Cneve

Tarchunies Rumach (Cnaeus Tarquinius Romanus) at the hands of a warrior from Vulci; Cneve might be a third Roman monarch of the house of the Tarquins, hitherto unknown, or he might be a Tarquin who never came to the throne.

The same paintings depict three further heroes of Vulci – Caeles (Caelius) Vibenna, his brother Aulus Vibenna, and Mastarna. All these men are variously described by ancient literary traditions as having emigrated from Vulci and settled with their followers at Rome, and at least one of them may have ruled over it for a time.

Not long afterwards, Rome had a ruler from Clusium as well. It emerges from the literary tradition relating to the years after the fall of Tarquinius Superbus that the chauvinistic Roman stories proclaiming that Lars Porsenna was rebuffed before the city were untrue. On the contrary, he occupied Rome for a time, and ruled over it. Furthermore, the connection between the two cities remained, for there was a story that when, at the beginning of the fourth century BC, Gauls from the north threatened Clusium, its leaders appealed to the Romans.

Rome, in the course of receiving these influences from Tarquinii, Vulci and Clusium, underwent a considerable process of Etruscanization; but the process was not total. The Romans continued to speak their own Italic (Latin) tongue, which survived as their only language after the Etruscans had gone. This same interesting type of partially Etruscanized but largely non-Etruscan-speaking community was also to be found among the Faliscans, whose principal city was Falerii. They, like the Romans, continued to speak their own Italic language or dialect, although they were under the strong cultural influence of Veii, which was even believed, probably correctly, to have founded the second in importance of the Faliscan towns, Capena.

In northern Italy, later known to the Romans as 'Gaul this side of the Alps' (Cisalpine Gaul), there was also an extensive Etruscan presence. The nucleus of this development was Bononia (Felsina, Bologna), where a group of villages already existed in about 900 BC. They prospered owing to their proximity to metals, and Etruscan influences were already apparent before 700, becoming predominant in the fully urbanized society that subsequently developed on the site. Bononia controlled the Reno valley, and its dependency Casalecchio stood where the valley opens out into the plain. On their route to Etruria was another market at Marzabotto, a purely Etruscan centre established late in the sixth century to control the trade passing through the Apennine passes. Another town in which the Etruscans were strongly represented was

Mantua; Virgil, who came from the place, illuminatingly described the mixed character of its population.

Other wholly or partly Etruscanized places were to be found on the confines of the modern Romagna, where Caesena (Cesena) and Ariminum (Rimini) had Etruscan names. Ariminum was on the Adriatic, at the mouth of the River Marecchia. Beside the same river, a short distance inland, was another centre, Verucchio; it contains impressive tombs from the eighth to the sixth centuries BC in which Etruscan objects abound. A little higher up the Adriatic coast, near the mouths of the Po, the Etruscans shared two important commercial harbour towns with the Greeks. These were Spina and Atria, which developed very substantial trading operations with Greece and northern Europe from the sixth and fifth centuries onwards – operations in which the two constituent communities appear to have collaborated, regardless of the deterioration of Greco-Etruscan relations in southern Italy.

The Etruscans possessed influential trading-posts not only on the east but also on the west coast of northern Italy. At the mouth of the Arno and Serchio, which at that time merged their waters to form a joint estuary, was Pisae (Pisa), which had a protected harbour on a sea lagoon that has now vanished. Pisae seems to have been an Etruscan or Etruscanized port, or at least possessed an Etruscan maritime quarter. A line of similar ports extended northwards along the coast, including Viareggio (the harbour of Massarosa) and Luna (Luni); by this coastal route Etruscan objects travelled onwards to harbour-towns of southern France, from which they made their way up the Rhône and Saône valleys into the interior of the country and onwards into central Europe.

The middle reaches of the Arno also possessed two major Etruscan centres. These were at Artemium(?) (Artimino, commanding the northward route along the Arno's tributary, the Ombrone Pistoiese), and Quinto Fiorentino (now a suburb of Florence), where massive mound-tombs have been found. Later, an Etruscan city was established at Faesulae in the same region.

In these areas of Etruscan influence – as geographical considerations would suggest – it seems that Volaterrae played a very large part. At about the beginning of the sixth century BC, however, the people of Clusium appear to have largely superseded the Volaterrans in these northern regions, employing its dependency Arretium as a springboard and then moving across the Arno to Bononia and the Apennines. The Etruscan name of Bononia, which was Felsina, appears to be derived from a Clusine family, the Felsnal; the closest links of Marzabotto, too,

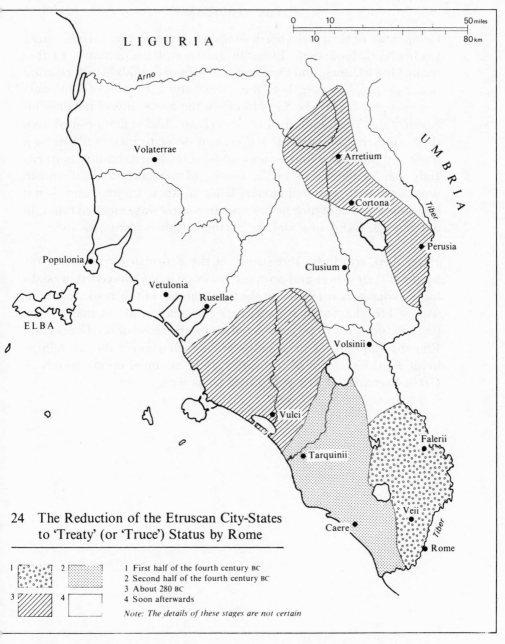

Arno

Volaterrae

UMBRIA

Arretium

Cortona

Tiber

Perusia

Populonia

Vetulonia

Rusellae

Clusium

ELBA

Volsinii

Vulci

Falerii

Tarquinii

Veii

Caere

Rome

Tiber

24   The Reduction of the Etruscan City-States
     to 'Treaty' (or 'Truce') Status by Rome

1   2

3   4

1 First half of the fourth century BC
2 Second half of the fourth century BC
3 About 280 BC
4 Soon afterwards

Note: The details of these stages are not certain

are with Clusium. Although private initiatives can never be excluded, a considerable amount of Clusium's expansionist activities may have been organized by its outstanding leader, Lars Porsenna.

Between the last years of the fifth century BC and the third quarter of the fourth, the Etruscan city-states lost their power, first in Latium and

Campania and then in the north. Within Latium, Rome and other cities gradually shelved their Etruscan rulers and connections. Farther south, Greek Cumae and then Syracuse proved formidable adversaries; in *c.* 430–423, however, both the Greeks and Etruscans of Campania were swept away by the Samnites from the mountains of the interior. North of the Apennines, the Etruscan centres had at first profited from their southern compatriots' setbacks in order to increase their own trade and prosperity, but by the middle of the fourth century northern Italy was in the hands of the Gauls. Meanwhile, in the Etruscan homeland itself, Veii had already fallen to Rome (*c.* 396); and then it was only a matter of time before Roman control was extended throughout Etruria, Campania and the northern Italian territories alike.

Here, then, concludes this survey of the Etruscan city-states at the height of their power and prosperity. I hope it has succeeded in establishing what was suggested in the first sentence of this book: that their way of life, despite our inadequate information about many of its features, deserves to be considered alongside those of the Greeks and Romans – so that the principal western civilization of the last millennium BC, the ancestor of our own, may be summed up not merely as Greco-Roman, but as partly Etruscan as well.

CHRONOLOGICAL TABLE

CHRONOLOGICAL TABLE

ETRURIA	SOUTH ITALY AND THE GREEK WEST	LATIUM AND ROME
1400–1000 BC. 'Apennine Culture' ('Bronze Age'). 1300–1200. Mycenaean imports.	1300 BC. Mycenaean contacts with Pithecusae, Vivara, Lipara.	
10th–9th cent. Groups of villages ('Iron Age'). 9th–8th cent. Bronzes arrive from Sardinia (and then 'false dome' at Populonia). 750–700. Urbanization and new wealth of Tarquinii, Caere, Vulci, and then Veii and Clusium. Seapower of Tarquinii. 7th cent. Urbanization of Vetulonia and then Rusellae. 700–650. Chamber tombs with mounds at Vetulonia and Caere; also jewellery. c. 650. Caeritan *bucchero* pottery. Seapower of Caere: Greek alphabet comes there from Cumae. c. 650 and 575. Palace at Murlo. c. 650–625. Stone statuary at Vetulonia. 7th cent. City wall at Rusellae. 7th cent. Falerii under influence of Veii. c. 640. Demaratus at Tarquinii. c. 625–600. Human-headed jars at Clusium. 6th cent. Heavy *bucchero* at Clusium. c. 550–540. Earliest painted grave at Tarquinii.	c. 775. Euboean market at Pithecusae. c. 750. Euboean market at Cumae. c. 734–720. Colonies at Cumae, Naxos, Zancle (Messana), Rhegium, Syracuse and Sybaris. c. 600. Phocaean colony at Massalia. c. 600. Cumaean colony at Neapolis. c. 560. Phocaean colony at Alalia in Corsica.	10th cent. BC. Alba Longa centre of association of Latin villages. 10th–8th cent. Settlements at Rome. 8th–7th cent. Urbanization and Etruscanization of Praeneste. 753. Traditional date of foundation of Rome. Late 8th cent. Prosperity of Politorium. Late 7th cent. Memorial (subsequently shrine) at Lavinium. c. 625. Roman Forum drained; first amalgamation of villages. 616–579. Tarquinius Priscus founds Etruscan dynasty. c. 600. Alba Longa conquered by Rome. 578–535. Servius Tullius, Mastarna (= Servius Tullius?) and the two Vibennas of Vulci at Rome.

NORTH ITALY	GREECE	PHOENICIAN AND CARTHAGINIAN CENTRES
	1700–1200 BC. Mycenaean civilization.	
	1250. Traditional date of Trojan War.	
900 BC. Villages at Bononia (Felsina) and port at Frattesina.		10th cent. BC. Sidon and then Tyre take the lead.
Early 8th cent. Urbanization of Bononia.	825–800. Euboean market at Al Mina.	Late 9th or early 8th cent. Foundation of Carthage.
8th–6th cent. Prosperity of Verucchio.	8th cent. Urbanization of Athens, Corinth, Ionian cities completed.	Early 8th cent. (?) Foundation of Nora.
8th–7th cent. Etruscanization of Massarosa.	Early 8th cent. Euboean (Eretrian) colony at Corcyra (c. 733 Corinthian).	8th or 7th cent. Foundation or refoundation of Gades.
	Late 8th cent. Lelantine (Euboean) War.	Early 7th cent. Foundation of Motya.
	Late 8th cent. Traditional date of Homer.	c. 654–653. Foundation of Ebusus.
	7th cent. Commercial supremacy of Corinth.	7th cent. Foundation of Melita.
	625–520. Athenian 'black-figure' vases.	
c. 600. Bronze buckets (situlae) at Bononia.		
c. 600. Prosperity of Artemium and Quinto Fiorentino.		
6th cent. Casalecchio Etruscanized.	594–593. Solon lawgiver at Athens.	
6th cent. Spina and Atria jointly settled by Greeks and Etruscans.		

CHRONOLOGICAL TABLE

ETRURIA	SOUTH ITALY AND THE GREEK WEST	LATIUM AND ROME
c. 540. Bronze industry at Vulci.		
Middle or late 6th cent. Loose Etruscan 'league'.		
550–500. Decline of Vetulonia, rise cf Rusellae.	c. 535. Battle of Alalia.	
Late 6th cent. Urbaniza-tion of Volaterrae.	525–524. 'Long March' of Etruscans and others against Cumae.	
Late 6th cent. Greek quarter at Graviscae (port of Tarquinii).	524–492. Aristodemus ruler of Cumae.	535–507. Tarquinius Superbus.
Late 6th cent. Lars Porsenna of Clusium.	Late 6th cent. Caeritan colony at Nicaea in Corsica.	507. End of Roman monarchy, beginning of Republic.
Late 6th cent. Thefarie Velianas of Caere.	510. Destruction of Sybaris by Croton.	506–504. Cumaeans and Latins defeat Etruscans at Aricia.
500–450. Arretium, Perusia, Cortona, Volsinii independent.	480. Syracusans defeat Carthaginians at Himera.	
500, 460–450. Temples at Pyrgi (port of Caere).	474. Syracusans (Hiero I) defeat Carthaginians and Etruscans off Cumae.	
477–475. Veii defeats Romans at R. Cremera.	454–453. Syracusan expedition against Etruria.	
435. Fidenae taken by Romans from Veii.	c. 430–423. Campania overrun by Samnites.	See Etruria.
5th cent. First Etruscan coins at Populonia and a port of Vetulonia (?).	413. Etruscan force with Athenian expedition against Syracuse.	
396. Veii destroyed by Romans.	378–377. Joint Caeritan and Roman colonists in Sardinia.	See Etruria, S. Italy and Greek West.
Early 4th cent. Populonia becomes city-state.	357–354. Joint Caeritan and Roman colonists in Corsica.	387. Romans defeated by Gauls at Allia. City sacked.
4th–3rd cent. Social disturbances in Etruria and gradual absorption by Rome.		
Late 4th or 3rd cent. François tomb at Vulci.		See Etruria.

NORTH ITALY	GREECE	PHOENICIAN AND CARTHAGINIAN CENTRES
	560–546. Ionia subjected to Croesus of Lydia.	c. 550. Malchus in Sicily and Sardinia.
	546–527. Pisistratus ruler of Athens.	
	530–4th cent. Athenian 'red-figure' vases'.	
	549–529. Ionia subjected to Cyrus of Persia.	
6th or 5th cent. Faesulae urbanized.		
5th cent. Gradual migrations of Gauls into N. Italy.	490, 480–479. Persian Wars.	See S. Italy.
	431–404. Peloponnesian War. Athens defeated by Sparta.	
Mid-4th cent. N. Italy in hands of Gauls.	336–323. Alexander III the Great of Macedonia.	
3rd–early 2nd cent. Romans take over N. Italy from Gauls.		264–241, 218–201 BC. Carthage defeated by Rome in First and Second Punic Wars.

257

ABBREVIATIONS IN THE NOTES

AJA	*American Journal of Archaeology*
AR	*Archaeological Reports* (Society for the Promotion of Hellenic Studies and British School at Athens)
Aspetti	*Aspetti e problemi dell'Etruria interna* (Atti dell'VIII Convegno di Studi Etruschi e Italici, Orvieto–Perugia, 1972) (Florence 1974)
Assimilation	*Assimilation et résistance à la culture gréco-romaine dans le monde ancien* (Travaux du VIe Congres International d'études classiques) (Madrid 1974)
Aufstieg	H. Temporini (ed.), *Aufstieg und Niedergang der Antiken Welt* (Berlin 1972–)
Banti	L. Banti, *The Etruscan Cities and their Culture* (London 1973)
Brendel	O. J. Brendel, *Etruscan Art* (ed. E. H. Richardson) (Harmondsworth 1978)
CISME	*Contributi introduttivi allo studio del monetazione etrusca* (Atti del V Convegno del Centro Internationale di Studi Numismatici, 1975) (Naples 1976)
CR	*Classical Review*
Cristofani, *AE*	M. Cristofani, *L'arte degli Etruschi: produzione e consumo* (Turin 1978)
Cristofani, *Etr*	M. Cristofani, *The Etruscans* (London 1979)
DA	*Dialoghi di Archeologia*
Dennis	G. Dennis, *Cities and Cemeteries of Etruria*, 2nd ed. (London 1878)
DH	Dionysius of Halicarnassus, *Roman Antiquities*
EC	F. Boitani, M. Cataldi, M. Pasquinucci, M. Torelli, *Etruscan Cities* (London 1975)

XI Int. Congr.	*Programme of XI International Congress of Classical Archaeology* (London 1978)
EM	*L'Etruria mineraria* (Atti del XII Convegno di Studi Etruschi e Italici, Florence–Populonia–Piombino, 1979) (in press)
GCR	C. F. C. Hawkes (ed.), *Greeks, Celts and Romans* (London 1973)
GICW	*Greece and Italy in the Classical World* (Acta of the XIth International Congress of Classical Archaeology, 1978) (London 1979)
Heurgon	J. Heurgon, *The Rise of Rome* (London 1973)
Hus, *SO*	A. Hus, *Les siècles d'or de l'histoire étrusque (675–475 avant J-C)* (Brussels 1976)
IBR	D. and F. Ridgway (ed.), *Italy Before the Romans* (London and New York 1979)
JHS	*Journal of Hellenic Studies*
JRS	*Journal of Roman Studies*
Mansuelli	G. A. Mansuelli, *Etruria and Early Rome* (London 1966)
ME	*Le monde étrusque (Musée Borely)* (Marseille 1977)
Mél. Heurgon	*L'Italie préromaine et la Rome républicaine* (Mélanges offerts à Jacques Heurgon) (Paris 1976)
Pallottino, *Etr*	M. Pallottino (ed. D. Ridgway), *The Etruscans*, rev. ed. (London 1974)
Pfiffig	A. J. Pfiffig, *Einführung in die Etruskologie* (Darmstadt 1972)
Pliny, *NH*	Pliny the Elder, *Natural History*
Potter	T. W. Potter, *The Changing Landscape of South Etruria* (London 1979)
PP	*La Parola del Passato*
RE	A. Pauly, G. Wissowa and W. Kroll, *Realencyclopädie der klassischen Altertumswissenschaft* (Stuttgart 1894–)
Richardson	E. H. Richardson, *The Etruscans: Their Art and Their Civilization* (Chicago 1964)
Röm. Mitt.	*Mitteilungen des deutschen archäologischen Instituts, Römische Abteilung*
Scullard	H. H. Scullard, *The Etruscan Cities and Rome* (London 1967)
SE	*Studi etruschi*
Strong	D. E. Strong, *The Early Etruscans* (London 1968)

Studi Banti	*Studi in onore di L. Banti* (Rome 1965)
Torelli, *ET*	M. Torelli, *Elogia Tarquiniensia* (Rome 1975)
Trump	D. Trump, *Central and Southern Italy before Rome* (London 1966)
Vacano	O.–W. Von Vacano, *The Etruscans in the Ancient World*, 2nd ed. (Bloomington 1965)

NOTES

INTRODUCTION

1 D. Ridgway in Pallottino, *Etr*, pp. 20f.
2 M. Grant, *Proceedings of the Classical Association*, LXXV (1978), p. 10.
3 M. Pallottino, *Mél. Heurgon*, II, pp. 784f.; D. Ridgway, *Antiquity*, XLVIII (1974), p. 192.
4 The Etruscan city-states are here described by their Latin names (when known), since the original Etruscan names (when known) are too unfamiliar, and their modern Italian names, too, are either less familiar to readers of English than their Etruscan equivalents (e.g. Veio than Veii), or seem anachronistic (e.g. San Maria Capua Vetere for the ancient Capua). The problem is discussed by Mansuelli, p. 7. Ischia, however, is given its Greek name Pithecusae, not its Latin name Aenaria, which belonged to a different site on the other side of the island.
5 These maps, incidentally, try to remedy a particular strain generally imposed on the non-specialist reader: as many as a dozen (modern) place-names appear in identical form at two different sites in Etruria and Etruscan territory, but explicit attempts to point this out, or differentiate between them, are rare.
6 Cf. Hus, *SO*, p. 6; Strong, p. 10.

CHAPTER I
Etruria and its Metals

1 For the transitional 'sub-' or, 'late Apennine' and 'Pre-' or 'Proto-Villanovan' epochs (the latter covering the tenth and ninth centuries, when cremation became normal), see Trump, p. 137, Pallottino, *Etr*, pp. 42f., Cristofani, *AE*, p. 30, A. Talocchini, *L' età di ferro nell' Etruria marittima* (1968), p. 15, R. Peroni, *IBR*, pp. 7–30, M. A. Fugazzola Delpino, ibid., pp. 31–51. For the original Italian

Note: Secondary sources are often quoted here in preference to excavation reports, especially when they are more accessible or provide valuable comments.

THE ETRUSCANS

character of the
'Proto-Villanovan' culture, see
M. Pallottino, *GICW*, p. 62. The
mature 'Villanovan' Iron Age
that followed owed this gravely
misleading name to the village of
Villanova near Bononia
(Bologna), where the first of its
characteristic cemeteries was
found in 1853.

2 H. Hencken, *Tarquinia and
Etruscan Origins* (1968), p. 116;
Banti, p. 22.

3 Diodorus V, 316.

4 From *c.* 900 to 300 BC the
climate was comparatively cold.

5 Pallottino, *Etr*, p. 87; Heurgon,
p. 43, Richardson, pp. 29f.,
A. Alföldi, *Römische Fruhgeschichte*
(1976), p. 144; Mansuelli, p. 20;
cf. many contributors to *EM*, in
press. Maps of the mineral
resources of Etruria are shown in
Cristofani, *Etr*, p. 54, and M.
Boni and F. Ippolito, *CISME*,
Map II.

6 Banti, p. 39 – but 'minerals' not
'metals' because of modern oil.

7 Potter, pp. 36, 47.

8 M. Boni and F. Ippolito,
CISME, p. 51.

9 Museo del Lazio, E.U.R., Rome.
On metals of Etruria in Copper
and Bronze Age, see A. M.
Vigliani, A. M. B. Sestieri, *EM*,
in press.

10 Mostra del Minerale, Massa
Marittima.

11 G. d'Achiardi, *SE*, I (1927), pp.
412f.

12 G. P. Carratelli, *PP*, XVII
(1962), p. 9; A. Rathje, *IBR*, p.
179 (also zinc).

13 R. J. Forbes, *Studies in Ancient*

Technology, III (1955), pp. 180ff.;
Cristofani, *Etr*, p. 59.

14 G. P. Carratelli, *PP*, XVII
(1962), p. 7.

15 In the late Roman Republic, and
perhaps earlier, molluscs were
cultivated at points along the coast
including Mount Argentario;
Cristofani, *Etr*, p. 59.

16 Pliny, *NH*, XXXV, pp. 52, 183;
M. Zecchini, *Gli Etruschi all' isola
d'Elba* (1978), pp. 65ff.

17 The workings of Elban iron at
Follonica may also go back to
Etruscan times; A. Mori,
*Bollettino della Reale Società
Geografica Italiana*, Ser. 6, VIII
(1931), p. 555.

18 Strabo, V, pp. 2, 7, 225; R. C.
Raspi, *Storia della Sardegna*, 3rd
ed. (1977), pp. 93, 100; S. von
Reden, *Die Etrusker* (1978), pp.
240f.

19 G. D' Archiardi, *SE*, I (1927), p.
414; M. Boni and F. Ippolito,
CISME, pp. 51f. Doubted by
Cristofani, *Etr*, p. 10, who points
instead to copper at
Camporbiano and Montaione
north of Volaterrae (p. 54).

20 Potter, p. 19; Hus, *SO*, p. 44;
Trump, p. 106 (copper in second
millennium BC).

21 Pliny, *NH*, XXXV, pp. 36, 111;
G. Carobbi and F. Rodolico,
I minerali della Toscana (1976),
pp. 2, 136; Cristofani, *Etr*,
p. 10.

22 Trump, p. 131.

23 Cristofani, *Etr*, p. 10;
F. Bulgarelli, D. Maestri and
V. Petrizzi, *Tolfa etrusca e la
necropoli di Pian Conserva* (1977).

24 Potter, p. 21.

CHAPTER 2
The Creation of the Etruscan Cities

1 W. D. Blawatsky, *GICW*, p. 196.
2 Cristofani, *Etr*, p. 54; Brendel, p. 18. For the metallurgical leap forward, see R. Peroni, *IBR*, pp. 9, 15.
3 Potter, pp. 28, 72, 32; Trump, p. 170.
4 A. M. Snodgrass, *Archaeology and the Rise of the Greek State* (1977), pp. 11–16, 25.
5 Aristotle, *Politics*, I, 2, 1252b, 28.
6 J. G. Evans, *Introduction to Environmental Archaeology* (1978), pp. 68, 92; M. Grant, *The Ancient Mediterranean* (1969), pp. 233f.
7 Potter, p. 79. For Etruscan horse-transport, see E. Rawson, *JRS*, LXVIII (1978), p. 138.
8 Potter, p. 72.
9 *Poleis*: 'Complex social and economic agglomerations resting on conscious intellectual outlooks and on specialization of functions.' C. G. Starr, *The Origins of Greek Civilization* (1962), p. 27.
10 Banti, p. 40 (Potter, p. 29, is doubtful).
11 Cf. H. Hencken, *Tarquinia and Etruscan Origins* (1962), pp. 17f.
12 Perhaps the hut-urn originated in Latium (though this is disputed); Heurgon, p. 23.
13 Strabo, V, 2, 2, 219.
14 Pallottino, *Etr*, p. 94; Scullard, p. 84.
15 E. Peruzzi, *Assimilation*, p. 175.
16 M. Cataldi and F. Boitani, *EC*, p. 251.
17 Ibid, p. 254; Potter, p. 47. For the similarity of Italian and

Greek bronze knives and swords in the late twelfth and eleventh centuries cf. A. M. Bietti-Sestieri, *Proceedings of the Prehistoric Society*, XXXIX (1973), pp. 383–424. Some Cretan motifs passed into Etruscan art through Mycenaean channels, though there was a second such wave in the seventh century BC.
18 Cristofani, *AE*, p. 31.
19 Material from Luni and Tolfa is similar: M. Cataldi and F. Boitani, *EC*, p. 255.
20 A settlement has been found under the lake, which was thirty feet deeper in antiquity, R. F. Paget, *Central Italy: An Archaeological Guide* (1973), p. 144.
21 Banti, p. 105. For the site, see F. Delpino, *La prima età di ferro a Bisenzio* (1977).
22 From a family name, Ceizra. C. de Simone, *SE*, XLIV (1976), pp. 163–84.
23 Strabo, V, 2, 3, 220. The water supply of Cerveteri was restored in the 1920s.
24 Potter, p. 55.
25 Servius on Virgil, *Aeneid*, X, 183. One of the early hill-top sites overlooking Caere's rivers was Castellina sul Marangone.
26 Scullard, p. 120; V. d'Ercole and M. Penacchioni, *Vulci: rinvenimenti di superficie d'epoca preistorica* (Rome 1977); G. Riccioni, *IBR*, pp. 241ff.
27 Ponte San Pietro; now in Museo del Lazio, E.U.R., Rome. For Crostoletto di Lamone, see F. Rittatore-Vonwiller etc., *La*

civiltà arcaica di Vulci e la sua espansione (1977), pp. 99ff.; Cristofani, *AE*, p. 31; M. Pallottino, *GICW*, pp. 62, 67.

28 Hus, *SO*, p. 41; G. Colonna, *CISME*, pp. 4f.; L. K. Poppi, *ME*, p. 24.

29 There was also an important site at Sticciano Scalo, north-east of Vetulonia, from the earliest first millennium BC. A. Talocchini, *L'età di ferro nell'Etruria marittima* (1965), pp. 15f.

30 M. Pasquinucci, *EC*, p. 93.

31 G. Colonna, *CISME*, pp. 5, 46; L. K. Poppi, *ME*, p. 24.

32 E. S. Vetulonia, Lake Accesa. A. Talocchini, *L'età del ferro nell'Etruria marittima* (1965), pp. 16, 66. A model pottery boar from Accesa, which may be about the same period (or a little later), resembles seventh-century bronze boats from Sardinia found at Populonia and Vetulonia.

33 Pallottino, *Etr*, p. 85; G. Colonna, *CISME*, p. 5; Vacano, p. 89. For early Etruscan relations with Sardinia, see F. Lo Schiavo, *SE*, XLVI (1978), p. 45, and for the Etruscan *Tholos* see G. Caputo, *EM* (in press).

34 Pallottino, *Etr*, p. 85; G. Kahl-Furthmann, *Die Frage nach dem Ursprung der Etrusker* (1976), p. 26. For the date of the decline of the Mycenaean world, see S. Iakovidis, *Antiquaries Journal*, VIII (1978), p. 27; C. Souvinou-Inwood in R. A. Crossland (ed.), *The Sea Peoples (Proceedings of the Third International Colloquium on Aegean Prehistory)*, Sheffield 1973.

35 Hus, *SO*, p. 65; C. F. C. Hawkes, *SE*, XXXVI (1968), p. 372.

36 G. Pugliese Carratelli, *SE*, XVII (1962), pp. 7f.; XXI (1966), pp. 155f.; Pallottino, *Etr*, p. 247 n. 26; Raspi, p. 92.

37 A. M. McCann, *Muse*, V (1971), pp. 208; D. Ridgway, *AR* (1973–4), p. 55.

38 Strabo, V, 2, 6, 233.

39 Servius on Virgil, *Aeneid*, X, 172.

40 S. C. Humphreys, *Rivista storica italiana*, CXXVII (1965), pp. 421–3; D. Ridgway, *GCR*, p. 19.

41 Richardson, p. 233. For his identification with Bacchus (Pachies), see M. Cristofani and M. Cristofani Martelli, *SE*, XLVI (1978), pp. 132f.

42 G. Buchner, *DA*, III (1969), (1970), pp. 97f; D. Ridgway, *GCR*, p. 18.

43 M. Zecchini, *Gli Etruschi all' isola di Elba* (1978), p. 8; Heurgon, p. 55; cf. p. 43.

44 Strabo, V, 2, 6, 223.

45 E. Fiumi, *Volterra* (1977), pp. 19, 20, 21.

46 Banti, p. 148.

47 Trump, pp. 118–20

48 Pliny, *NH*, III, 9, 1.

49 R. F. Paget, *Central Italy: An Archaeological Guide* (1973), p. 144 (La Capriola, etc.).

50 J. Close-Brooks, *NS* (1965), pp. 53–64; *SE*, XXXV (1967), pp. 323–9; D. Ridgway, *GCR*, pp. 25f; J. Close-Brooks and D. Ridgway, *IBR*, pp. 113ff; Cristofani, *AE*, p. 33.

CHAPTER 3
Decisive Influences from the East

1 H. Schubart and V. Tusa, *L'espansione fenicia nel Mediterraneo* (1971); S. Moscati, *Problematica della civiltà fenicia* (1974).

2 M. Grant, *The Ancient Mediterranean* (1969), p. 120.

3 S.-E. Tlatli, *La Carthage punique* (1978). 'Phoenician' settlements may be regarded as 'Punic' (Carthaginian) when the north African element from Carthage becomes predominant; M. Guido, *Sardinia* (1963), p. 192. For a map of Phoenician (and Greek) settlements see A. Rathje, *IBR*, p. 146.

4 A. M. Bisi Ingrassia, *GICW*, p. 203.

5 M. Tarradell, *Assimilation*, pp. 343–55.

6 G. Pesce, *Nora* (1977); S. Moscati, *I Cartaginesi in Italia* (1977), pp. 183ff.

7 Pallottino, *Etr*, p. 186; cf. *Aesar* (*aisar*), an Etruscan name for a god, Suetonius, *Augustus*, 97.

8 S. Moscati, op. cit., pp. 253ff., R. C. Raspi, *Storia della Sardegna*, 3rd ed. (1977), pp. 119, 163, 167. Tharros adjoins the Gulf of Orestano. For the background of the gold industry, see G. Camps and H. Fabier (ed.), *L'industrie de l'or dans la préhistoire* (1975).

9 Conversely, an Etruscan amphora has been found at Tripoli in Syria. M. Chollot, *Cahiers d'archéologie subaquatique*, II (1973), p. 52.

10 A. Rathje, *IBR*, p. 181 (traders or even settlers); S. Moscati, op.

cit., pp. 300f.; doubted by J. N. Coldstream, *Greek Geometric Pottery* (1968), p. 388.

11 For a Greek seeking copper there, see Homer, *Odyssey*, I, 184. But does Temese refer to Tamassus in Cyprus (as the scholiast) or Temesa (Tempsa) in Bruttium, south-western Italy (Strabo, VI, 1, 5, 255)? G. P. Carratelli, *PP*, XVII (1962), p. 13.

12 For early tin sources, see N. K. Sandars, *The Sea Peoples* (1978), pp. 74, 89; P. S. de Jesus, *Anatolian Studies*, XXVIII (1978), p. 101.

13 For the Etruscan need to import tin, see M. Boni and F. Ippolito, *CISME*, p. 53.

14 Heurgon, p. 73.

15 M. Guido, *Sardinia* (1963), p. 151.

16 Mansuelli, p. 47; Richardson, p. 51; A. Boethius and J. B. Ward-Perkins, *Greek and Roman Architecture* (1970), p. 56.

17 M. Gras, *Mél. Heurgon*, I, p. 364. For the lion motif, see W. Brown, *The Etruscan Lion* (1960); P. Müller, *Löwen und Mischwesen in der archäischen griechischen Kunst* (1978).

18 E. Akurgal, *Die Kunst Anatoliens* (1961), pp. 56–69; Brendel, p. 55; L. Vlad Borrelli, *GICW*, p. 190.

19 E. F. Macnamara, *GICW*, p. 192.

20 For eastern influences on Greek textiles, see E. Kjellberg and G. Säflund, *Greek and Roman Art* (1968), p. 60.

21 Only fragments of the Greek

counterparts of these fabrics have survived. G. M. A. Richter, *Greek Art*, 6th ed. (1969), p. 380.

22 Y. Takeo, *Social Change and the City in Japan* (1968, pp. 358f., 361ff.

23 D. Ridgway, *GCR*, p. 19; for the soil, see Strabo, V, 4, 9, 247.

24 M. Manazzi and S. Tusa, *PP* (1976), p. 473. Vivara was at one time joined to the island of Prochyta (now Procida).

25 G. Vallet, *CISME*, p. 75 (unpublished excavations of G. Voza).

26 Brendel, pp. 38f., 41, 47, 83.

27 D. Ridgway, *GCR*, pp. 8ff.; J. Boardman, *Annual of the British School at Athens* (1957), pp. 9, 24f.; Cristofani, *AE*, pp. 35f. For the copies, see A. M. Small, *GICW*, p. 191. For the Cyclades, see J. Thimme (ed.), *Art and Culture of the Cyclades* (Berlin 1980).

28 Evidence in D. Ridgway, *GCR*, pp. 19, 37; J. Boardman, op. cit. On a suggested identification of Posidium with Ras el Bassit, see P. L. C. Courbin, *GICW*, p. 198. Another trading-post was Tell Sukas (the Greek Paltos, New Balda or Bulda), a little farther south, also a Mycenaean and Phoenician site; see P. J. Riis, *Sukas*, I (1970).

29 'Chalcis' comes from *chalke* (purple shell, murex), thus providing a link with Phoenicia, which specialized in this industry. S. K. Bakhuizen, *Chalcis in Euboea* (1976), pp. 7–13, 78–82.

30 W. Johannowsky, *DA*, I (1967), p. 162, n. 35; Von Geisau, *RE*, XI, p. 2474; M. Frederiksen, *IBR*, p. 282. Cyme was later suppressed by Chalcis.

31 On early Pithecusae see G. Buchner, *AR* (1970–1), pp. 63–7; D. Ridgway, *AR* (1976–7), p. 44 and *GCR*, pp. 5–28; E. Kirsten, *GICW*, p. 230.

32 Pliny, *NH*, III, 6, 82; D. Ridgway, *GCR*, p. 22. There were, however, various explanations of this name, as also of Aenaria, the Roman name of the island and of a town at its eastern end (Porto d'Ischia).

33 G. Buchner and C. F. Russo, *Rendiconti dell'Accademia dei Lincei*, Ser. 8, X (1955), pp. 215–34; Hus, *SO*, p. 150; D. L. Page, *CR*, LXX (1956), pp. 95f.

34 F. de Salvia in *Contribution à l'étude de la société et de la colonisation eubéennes* (1975), p. 97.

35 M. Frederiksen, *AR* (1976–7), p. 44.

36 G. Buchner, *IBR*, p. 133. Geometric vases: Tarquinii, Veii, Vulci, Castellina sul Marangone. Scarabs: Tarquinii, Veii. P. Zazoff, *Etruskische Skarabäen* (1968).

37 Strabo, V, 4, 9, 247. G. Buchner, *IBR*, pp. 136, 138. D. Ridgway, *GCR*, p. 22.

38 W. Johannowsky, *Contribution*, op. cit., p. 102; R. F. Paget, *JRS*, VIII (1968), pp. 152–9; against R. M. Cook, *Historia*, XI (1962), pp. 113f.

39 G. Buchner, *IBR*, pp. 130f.; R. A. Higgins, *Greek and Roman*

Jewellery (1961), pp. 134, 139.

40 *Homeric Hymns*, VII, 8. Etruscan pirates were also reported off Sicilian Naxos (Ephorus). Lipara: settlers from Cnidus (south-western Asia Minor), *c.* 580 BC; Hus, *SO*, p. 245 (sources); M. I. Finley, *Ancient Sicily* (1968), p. 37.

41 The Etruscans had previously imported wine from Phoenicia and the Ionian island of Chios and probably olive oil from Phoenicia. Cristofani, *Etr*, pp. 51f. Olive stones have been found inside a vessel in a tomb at Caere of *c.* 580 BC; ibid, p. 52.

42 The colonies at Naxos and Zancle might slightly precede the colony at Cumae. M. Guido, *Southern Italy* (1972), p. 35. For their strategic intention, see J. B. Ward-Perkins, *The Cities of Ancient Greece and Italy* (1974), p. 23. Cumae founded Neapolis (Naples) on the site of an earlier town ('Palaeopolis'); M. Frederiksen, *AR* (1976–7), p. 45, *IBR*, p. 297; and established a harbour at Dicaearchia (Puteoli); *IBR*, loc. cit.

43 F. Jacoby, *Fragmente der griechischen Historiker*, 566F.50.

44 Aristoxenus in Athenaeus, XIV, 632a. Paintings at Posidonia are identical with those of a south-Etruscan group; Pallottino, *Etr*, pp. 100, 122.

45 Heurgon, p. 86.

46 Taras (Tarentum, Taranto), a colony of Sparta, in the gulf named after it – in which Sybaris was also located –

likewise exercised a considerable influence over the Etruscans, to whom it taught gold-working techniques. Taras came to be regarded as representative and symbolic of the Hellenistic civilization of southern Italy.

47 W. G. Forrest, *Historia*, VI (1957), pp. 160ff. (the war for the Lelantine plain).

48 W. Johannowsky, *DA*, I (1967), p. 175; J. N. Coldstream, *Greek Geometric Pottery* (1968), pp. 369f.

49 Hus, *SO*, p. 78; J. G. Szilagyi, *Wissenschaftliche Zeitschrift der Universität Rostock*, XVI (1967), pp. 543, 553; I. Strøm, *Problems Concerning the Origin and Early Development of the Etruscan Orientalizing Style* (1971), p. 11 (various theories).

50 Pliny, *NH*, XXXV, 43, 152.

51 Plato, *Phaedo*, 109B.

52 Pliny, *NH*, VII, 56, 209.

53 A. M. Snodgrass, *Arms and Armour of the Greeks* (1967), pp. 66f. Later, in the north, the small round shields of the Etruscans proved no match for the massed onslaughts of the Gauls. B. Cunliffe, *The Celtic World* (1979), p. 132.

54. M. Torelli, *DA*, VIII, 1 (1974–5), p. 14. Date doubted by Banti, pp. 26f. For Corinthian armour on 'Plikasna' vase from Clusium see Cristofani, *AE*, p. 46; for Corinthian-type soldiers on vase from Tragliatella (east of Caere) see Brendel, p. 441, n. 19.

55 Especially Rhodes (whose three city-states were still independent

of one another until the late fifth century BC) and Crete. For the role of Rhodian ships in the Adriatic in the ninth and eighth centuries BC, see L. Braccesi, *Grecità adriatica*, 2nd ed. (1977), p. 56. For Rhodian influence in Etruria, see Pallottino, *Etr*, pp. 71, 77; Brendel, p. 53. Influence was also exerted through Rhodes' Sicilian colony Gela. Strong artistic impulses from Crete also reached Etruria in the second half of the seventeenth century, see L. Bonfante, *Studi Banti*, pp. 81ff., Vacano, p. 119.

56 For the Hittites, see Å. Åkerstrom, *GICW*, p. 194. The capitals of Phrygia and Lydia were Gordium and Sardis respectively.

57 Cristofani, *AE*, pp. 61, 81; cf. sculpture in Latium, p. 96.

58 M. Gras, *Mél. Heurgon*, I, p. 364.

59 Herodotus, IV, 152; accepted by R. Carpenter, *Beyond the Pillars of Hercules* (1966), p. 57.

60 Herodotus, I, 163; L. Casson, *The Ancient Mariners* (1960), p. 81; Brendel, p. 435, n. 1.

61 E. Langlotz, *Die kulturelle und künstlerische Hellenisierung der künsten des Mittelmeers durch die Stadt Phokaia* (1966); recent evidence in *Bulletin de correspondance hellénique*, XCIX (1975), pp. 853ff.

62 H. A. Ormerod, *Piracy in the Ancient World* (1924, reprint 1979). Cf. above, pp. 47 and 57.

63 For Massalia's rise, see M.

Euzennat, *GICW*, pp. 264f. Its harbour was Lacydon (Vieux Port).

64 G. P. Carratelli, *PP*, XXI (1966), p. 157.

65 Heurgon, p. 101.

66 G. Colonna, *CISME*, p. 10.

67 Herodotus, I, 163.

68 Herodotus, I, 164.

69 Strabo, IV, 1, 4, 179.

70 Richardson, p. 233; A. Stibbe, *Herakles in Etrurien* (1978); A. J. Pfiffig, *Herakles in der Bilderkunst der etruskischen Spiegel* (1978).

71 Caere and Veii sculptures, Vulci bronzes etc.

72 Brendel, p. 134: e.g. the revetments that covered the exposed part of the roof construction.

73 M. Moretti, *Tarquinia* (1977), pp. 12f.; J. Boardman, *Pre-Classical* (1967), pp. 164, 166. But these imports from Ionia are much less common in Etruria than their imitations; Brendel, p. 116 (for example, the refugees could not bring very much with them).

74 *Inscriptiones Graecae*, XII, 8, 1 (Kaminia). The reliefs of Avle Feluske at Vetulonia and Avle Tite at Volaterrae are not dissimilar. For other Lemnian fragments see Richardson, p. 8.

75 Pallottino, *Etr*, pp. 72f.; M. Gras, *Mél. Heurgon*, pp. 352ff. For philological differences see M. Lejeune, *CR*, XXI (1971), p. 459.

76 Thucydides, IV, 109, 4, ('Pelasgians'). For Lemnian links with Etruria, see

Anticleides in Strabo, V, 2, 4, 221; Pallottino, *Etr*, p. 64; R. Bloch, *Atti del primo Simposio internazionale di protostoria* (Orvieto, 1967), (1969), p. 214. Cremation urns at Volaterrae depicted the myth of Philoctetes whom the Greeks, on their way to the Trojan War, left behind on Lemnos.

77 M. Gras, *Mél. Heurgon*, p. 360.

78 G. P. Carratelli, *PP*, XVII (1962), p. 9.

79 Pliny, *NH*, XXXVI, 90.

80 *Homeric Hymns*, VII, 8; F. Jacoby, *Die Fragmente der griechischen Historiker*, 137, 52a (Strabo, VI, 2, 2, 267, from Ephorus).

81 For Etruscan finds in Greece see F. W. von Hase, *GICW*, p. 187. I owe the suggestion about the nature of these exchanges to Professor A. E. Raubitschek.

82 S. Boriskovskaya, *GICW*, pp. 194f.

83 Athens's struggle with its strategically located island neighbours at Aegina began *c.* 506 BC and ended in 457. Aegina sent a trader, Sostratus, to Tarquinii, influenced the architecture of a temple at Pyrgi, and played a leading part in the foundation of Etrusco-Greek Atria.

84 A. J. N. W. Prag, *GICW*, p. 214.

85 Pallottino, *Etr*, p. 182.

86 T. Rasmussen, *GICW*, p. 214.

87 Brendel, p. 195, believed the Etruscans also had a technical objection to the 'red-figure' process.

CHAPTER 4
The 'Origin' of the Etruscans

1 L. Bonfante, *Etruscan Dress* (1976), pp. 20f.

2 Brendel, pp. 52f., 59, 72, 314.

3 Brendel, p. 305; M. I. Finley, *Aspects of Antiquity* (1968), p. 110.

4 C. Hopkins, *Hommages à M. Renard*, III (1969), p. 304.

5 Hopkins (as above, p. 307) suggests that the Etruscans, unlike the Greeks, preferred metal utensils to ceramics for their most valued vessels. Certainly very few Greek examples have survived.

6 Athenaeus, I, 28, 15, 700.

7 B. Berenson, *Aesthetics and History in the Visual Arts* (1948), p. 171.

8 L. Bonfante, *Etruscan Dress* (1976), pp. 20, 49, 76, 91ff.; Pollux, VII, 22, 86.

9 Livy, I, 34, 9, 41.5.

10 E. Macnamara, *The Daily Life of the Etruscans* (1973), p. 170.

11 Brendel, p. 146.

12 Seneca the Younger, *Naturales Quaestiones*, II, 32, 2; Pallottino, *Etr*, p. 147.

13 T. J. Cornell, *JRS*, LXVIII (1978), pp. 172f.

14 Hus, *SO*, p. 199. Horns and trumpets were Etruscan inventions; Athenaeus, IV, 184.

15 Dennis, I, pp. 306, 326.

16 Banti, pp. 137f.; Richardson, p. 224; A. J. N. W. Prag, *GICW*, p. 214.

17 Brendel, p. 365.

18 Pallottino, *Etr*, pp. 189f. The wrapping of an Egyptian mummy at Zagreb and a tile

from Capua; Richardson, pp. 217f.

19 M. Pallottino, *SE*, XXXIV (1966), p. 468.

20 Described as the etymological, combinatory and bilingual methods.

21 Pallottino, *Etr*, p. 53. For Italian and Greek loan-words and borrowed names see Cristofani, *Etr*, p. 75. For a survey of recent researches see Cristofani, *IBR*, pp. 373–412.

22 *DH*, I. 29, 1, 1.

23 G. Radke, *Klio*, LVI (1974), p. 303. The name originated from north-eastern Etruria; see J. Heurgon, *Archeologica: scritti in onore di Aldo Neppi Modona*, pp. 353–8.

24 Three Indo-European groups: Latin and Sicel (eastern Sicily), Umbro-Sabellian, and Messapian (south-eastern Italy). There was also an Indo-European pocket at the head of the Adriatic, where Venetic was spoken.

25 Pallottino, *Etr*, pp. 50ff.

26 Pindar, *Pythians*, I, 72.

27 W. Randall-McIver, *The Etruscans* (1927), p. 6; R. Girod, *Caesarodunum*, VI (1971), pp. 225–32.

28 Greeks: *Homeric Hymn* VII, Alcimus, Theopompus, Heraclides Ponticus, Timaeus. Roman period: Athenaeus, IV, 153d, VII, 51, 7ff.; cf. W. V. Harris, *Rome in Etruria and Umbria* (1971), pp. 14ff.; Strong, p. 80; Pfiffig, *Gymnasium*, LXXI (1964), pp. 17f.; M. Grant, *Proceedings of the Classical Association*, LXXV (1978), p. 11.

29 M. Gras, *Mél. Heurgon*, I, pp. 341ff.

30 Plautus, *Cistellaria*, 562.

31 E. Macnamara, *Everyday Life of the Etruscans* (1973), pp. 168f.; Dennis, I, p. 310.

32 T. Mommsen, *Römische Geschichte*, 12th ed. (1920), p. 337 (*History of Rome*, 1894 ed., pp. 435f.).

33 *DH*, ix, 16, 8.

34 Pallottino, *Etr*, p. 79; Banti, p. 211. Thus Cristofani, *Etr*, pp. 122f., even places his discussion of origins at the end of his book as an epilogue; cf. D. Ridgway in Pallottino, *Etr*, p. 5.

35 Herodotus, 1, 94.

36 Polybius, IX, 2, 1; E. J. Bickermann, *Classical Philology*, XLVII (1952), pp. 65–81.

37 For various Varronian etymologies see N. Horsfall, *JRS*, LXII (1973), p. 79, n. 93.

38 Virgil, *Aeneid*, VIII, 54. In fact, 'Palatine' comes from the same root as the name of the goddess (or god) of shepherds Pales (cf. Palilia, Parilia).

39 Ovid, *Fasti*, II, 279ff.

40 M. Torelli, *EC*, p. 13.

41 Pallottino, *Etr*, p. 70 (A. Neppi Modona, *Cortona etrusca e romana*, 2nd ed., p. 19, n. 82, concedes the connection). Secondly, Gyges's legendary forerunner Atys was credited with a son named Torrhebus or Torebus (after whom a town (Tyrrha?) was said to have been called), and this could also have prompted the story quoted by

Herodotus; F. de Sanctis, *Storia dei Romani*, I, 2nd ed. (1956), pp. 126f.; T. Mommsen, *Römische Geschichte*, 12th ed. (1920), p. 120.

42 Virgil, *Aeneid*, VII, 484f., 508, 532; IX, 28.

43 J. Gagé, *Mélanges de l'Ecole Française de Rome* (1976), pp. 15, 18; *Revue des études latines*, LV (1977/8), pp. 84, 97, 104, 106, 111f.

44 Herodotus, I, 26ff.

45 Mopsuestia (now Misis) in Cilicia and Ascalon (Ashkelon) in Palestine.

46 *DH*, I. 28.

47 M. Gras, *Mél. Heurgon*, I, p. 361.

48 Tacitus, *Annals*, IV, 55; cf. E. Rawson, *JRS*, LXVIII (1978), p. 134.

49 Herodotus, I, 163.

50 Horace, *Odes*, IV, 15, 30; Pliny, *NH*, XVI, 66; Pallottino, *Etr*, p. 156.

51 M. Demus-Quatember, *Etruskische Grabarchitektur* (1958), pp. 63, 75, sees close links with Caria (south-western Asia Minor).

52 M. Torelli, *PP*, CLXXVII (1977), p. 407.

53 Pallottino, *Etr*, pp. 73, 246 n. 19.

54 *DH*, I, 30, 1.

55 *DH*, I, 30, 4; cf. W. V. Harris, *Rome in Etruria and Umbria* (1971), pp. 25f., 121. *DH*, I, 27, 3 misquotes Herodotus; E. Cary, Loeb ed., I, 1960, p. 87 n. 1.

56 Herodotus I, 7 (on Atys); *DH*, I, 27, 1 and 28, 1; cf. H. Hencken, *Tarquinia and Etruscan Origins* (1968), pp. 152, 153 (suggesting that Herodotus may have

telescoped two traditions relating to different epochs), 160.

57 N. K. Sandars, *The Sea-Peoples* (1978), pp. 111, 165, 200; M. Guido, *Sardinia* (1963), p. 189; M. Torelli, *EC*, p. 14.

58 Discussions by H. Hencken, *Tarquinia and Etruscan Origins* (1968), pp. 142ff.; C. F. C. Hawkes, *SE*, XXXVI (1968), pp. 368ff. Sardinia and Sicily have been suggested as such staging-points.

59 Censorinus, *De Die Natali*, 17, 5ff.

60 M. I. Finley, *Aspects of Antiquity* (1968), p. 35.

61 The earliest Etruscan urn-fields were concentrated in the Tolfa-Allumiere region; Potter, pp. 48f.

62 Strong, p. 19; Richardson, pp. 304.

63 C. F. C. Hawkes, *SE*, XXXVI (1968), p. 372; cf. Heurgon, p. 19.

64 Pliny, *NH*, III, 133; Livy, V, 33, 1. Discussed by G. Kahl-Furthmann, *Die Frage nach dem Ursprung der Etrusker* (1976), p. 16; R. M. Ogilvie, *Commentary on Livy Books 1–5* (1965), p. 706; Pallottino, *Etr*, p. 98.

65 H. Hencken, *Tarquinia and Etruscan Origins* (1968), op. cit., p. 165.

66 The first 'Etruscans' are dated at the end of the eighth century by R. M. Cook, *Ciba Foundation Symposium on Medical Biology and Etruscan Origins* (1959), p. 7.

67 M. Pallottino, *SE*, XXXVI (1968), p. 500. Though language does not necessarily coincide with race or racial movements,

the presence of many Italian loan-words and names in Etruscan suggests that the Etruscan language was at home in Italy for some time before *c.* 700 BC; see Cristofani, *Etr*, p. 75.

68 Cristofani, *Etr*, p. 123.

69 G. Matteucig, *Hommages à M. Renard*, III (1969), p. 432; G. Kahl-Furthmann, *Die Frage nach dem Ursprung der Etrusker* (1976), p. 91, also detects a series of small waves of immigrants (which, however, he traces back to Lydia).

70 J. B. Ward-Perkins, *Landscape and History in Central Italy* (1963), p. 8, M. Torelli, *EC*, p. 14.

71 N. G. L. Hammond, *Migrations and Invasions in Greece and Adjacent Areas* (1976), p. 46. Comparison with the immigrations of the Angles, Saxons, Jutes and Frisians into England can also be suggestive.

72 Brendel, p. 111.

CHAPTER 5
Expansion to the South

1 Velleius Paterculus, I, 7, 2–4. Probably such foundations were 'partly by force and partly by persuasion'; M. Frederiksen, *IBR*, p. 305.

2 Vases of Tarquinii of *c.* 800 circulated widely in Campania; L. K. Poppi, *ME*, p. 24.

3 Virgil, *Georgics*, II, 225: 'unkind to forlorn Acerrae', which it flooded; cf. M. Frederiksen, *IBR*, p. 278.

4 Strabo, V, 3, 6, 233; Pliny, *NH*, III, 5, 59.

5 M. Frederiksen, *IBR*, pp. 299, 301, 303.

6 For Miletus see Strong, p. 45. J. B. Ward-Perkins, *Cities of Ancient Greece and Italy* (1974), p. 25.

7 D. Ridgway, *GCR*, pp. 23, 25; A. Alföldi, *Early Rome and the Latins* (1965), p. 155.

8 The coastline of Campania (like that of Etruria) was very different in antiquity; see M. Guido, *Southern Italy* (1972), p. 47.

9 Velleius Paterculus, I, 7, 3. An important Etruscan tomb (*c.* 635–25 BC) has also been found at Cales (Calvi Vecchia); M. Frederiksen, *AR* (1976–7), p. 45; cf. P. Defosse, *Latomus*, XXXIV (1975), p. 1076. The first known Etruscan ruler in Campania may have been at Cales in *c.* 640–620 BC; M. Frederiksen, *IBR*, p. 298.

10 For Pompeii see Strabo, V, 4, 8, 247; M. Frederiksen, *IBR*, p. 297, S. Ferraro, *Antiqua*, II, 4 (1977), pp. 64ff. For other Etruscan sites on the Sarno see W. Johannowsky in A. Alföldi, *Early Rome and the Latins* (1965), p. 420, and M. Frederiksen, *IBR*, p. 278 (S. Marzano, S. Valentino Torio); p. 297 (Greek influences).

11 Brendel, p. 468, n. 6.

12 Strabo, V, 4, 13, 251; M. Frederiksen, *IBR*, p. 279. A Greek vase of *c.* 580 BC has been found there.

13 On recent evidence see D. Ridgway, *JRS*, LXVI (1976), p. 209; M. Frederiksen, *AR* (1976–7), p. 47; *IBR*, pp. 279 (identification with Picentia),

28of.; A. Rathje, ibid. pp. 152ff.

14 Pliny, *NH*, III, 5, 70.

15 G. Colonna, *CISME*, p. 7; M. Frederiksen, *AR* (1976–7), p. 47, A. Rathje, *IBR*, pp. 152ff. (resemblances to Caere and Praeneste tombs).

16 The Sele debouched at Sybaris's colony Posidonia (Paestum); see Ch. 3 n. 44.

17 H. H. Scullard, *The Elephant in the Greek and Roman World* (1974), pp. 172, 277 n. 113.

18 For Uri-Urina see N. K. Rutter, *The Coinage of Campania* (in the press). For Nola and Hyria see Pallottino, *Etr*, p. 95. For the link between Urina and Aurinia see Pfiffig, p. 93. Velsu; A. Sambon, *Les monnaies antiques de l'Italie*, 1903–4, p. 40 no. 10. Rutter also reports that another Campanian coinage with what seems to be an Etruscan name, 'Irnthi', is represented in a Pompeii hoard. But there is a river Irno farther south from which the name of Salernum (Salerno) is believed to have been derived. The mint of coins inscribed Velznani or Velzpapi and described in T. Hackens, *CISME*, p. 261 and n. 69, is probably distinct from that of the Velsu pieces, but is likewise unidentifiable.

19 Strabo, V, 4, 3, 242.

20 *DH*, VII, 6, 1–2.

21 Diodorus, XI, 88, 4.

22 E. Peruzzi, *Assimilation*, p. 175.

23 M. Grant, *History of Rome* (1978), Weidenfeld ed. p. 11, Scribner ed. p. 10. The approximate coincidence with the trading settlements at Pithecusae and Cumae is merely fortuitous.

24 F. Coarelli, *Guida archeologica di Roma*, 2nd ed. (1975), p. 9.

25 E. la Rocca, *DA*, VIII (1974–5), pp. 86–103; F. Canciani, ibid. pp. 79–85; A. S. Mura, *PP*, XXXII (1977), p. 63. Important new excavations of the adjacent Roman docks began in 1979. On Roman origins see M. Pallottino, *IBR*, pp. 197–222.

26 The Romans imported horses from Etruria; Livy, I, 35, 9 (Tarquinius Priscus). B. Andreae, *The Art of Rome* (1978), p. 39, has suggested that Rome was founded by an Etruscan city (he proposes Caere or Veii).

27 F. Castagnoli, *PP*, XXXII (1977), p. 343.

28 *L'area sacra di S. Omobono* (various authors), *PP*, XXXII (1977), pp. 9–128; M. Cristofani, *Prospettiva*, IX (1977), pp. 2–7; G. Colonna, *IBR*, pp. 227f.

29 Brendel, p. 463, n. 27; O.-W. von Vacano, *Aufstieg*, I, 4 (1973), pp. 582f.

30 Plutarch, *Camillus*, 22; *DH*, I, 29, 2.

31 E. Peruzzi, *Assimilation*, pp. 175–180.

32 M. Grant, *Roman Myths*, rev. ed. (1973), pp. 111ff.

33 Naevius, *Praetextae*, frgs. 2–3; M. Grant, *Roman Myths*, rev. ed. (1973), p. 120. Amulius was also the name of a legendary King of Rome.

34 F. Coarelli (ed.), *Studi su Praeneste* (1978); L. Quilici, *La Via Prenestina* (1977).

35 A. Bedini and F. Cordano, *PP*, XXXII (1977), p. 304. But the urbanization of Praeneste may not have been completed until a hundred years later; see A. Hus, *Revue des études latines*, LV (1977), p. 549.

36 On the three-fold character of the Latian culture see Heurgon, p. 23. On the Greek impact see D. Ridgway, *IBR*, p. 194.

37 M. Torelli, *EC*, p. 18; F. R. Ridgway, *CR*, XXVIII (1978), p. 113; *Civiltà del Lazio primitivo* (1976), p. 374, no. 127.

38 For Praeneste's remarkable series of mirrors (from *c.* 490?) and bronze boxes (*cistae*) see Brendel, pp. 202, 353, 360. For Etruscan mirrors in general see D. Rebuffat-Emmanuel, *Le miroir étrusque* (1973), and Vacano, pp. 8ff.

39 M. Cristofani, *Aufstieg* I, 2 (1972), p. 476.

40 Tusculum: a less probable interpretation regards its name as non- and pre-Etruscan. Tarracina: R. Rebuffat, *Mélanges de l'Ecole Française de Rome*, LXXVIII (1966), p. 35.

41 Hus, *SO*, p. 223 and n. 58; M. Frederiksen, *IBR*, p. 295.

42 C. Ampolo, *DA*, VIII, 1 (1974–5), pp. 161f., cf. Virgil, *Aeneid*, VIII, 146; X, 688; XII, 723, etc. (The Ardeans were also known as Rutulians).

43 In early times the Apulians were only called Daunians by themselves, Strabo, VI, 6, 3, 8, 283.

44 A. Bedini and F. Cordano, *PP*, XXXII (1977), pp. 310f. On neighbouring Ficana see T. Fischer Hansen, *XI Int. Congr.*, p. 40.

45 It shows the union of a goddess (Aphrodite, Venus, Turan) with a mortal (Anchises, the father of Aeneas). Later, a memorial mound (before 600) and shrine of Aeneas have been identified at the regional sanctuary of Lavinium (Pratica del Mare). M. Torelli, *DA*, VII (1973), pp. 396ff., ibid., VIII, 1 (1974–5), p. 43; P. Castagnoli, *PP*, XXXII (1977), pp. 351ff.

46 M. Crawford, *Mél. Heurgon*, I, p. 202, n. 25. The foundation of Ostia traditionally occurred at just about the date of the destruction of Politorium. The foundation has not yet received archaeological confirmation, but that may only be because the right area has not been explored. The Romans were not, at this stage, aiming at founding a port, because they still relied on Etruscan Caere for their fleet.

47 *DH*, I, 25, 5 ('the several nations of which it had been composed having lost their distinctive appellation' – cf. the spread of the tribal name 'Achaea' to comprise all Greece).

48 Servius on Virgil, *Georgics*, II, 533.

49 Livy, V, 33, 7f.

CHAPTER 6
Expansion to the North

1 Polybius, II, 17, 1 synchronizes the two.

2 Pliny, *NH*, III, 15, 115.

3 G. Colonna, *CISME*, p. 5 (also amber).

4 Heurgon, p. 17.

5 S. Sorda, *CISME*, pp. 67f., 70.

6 Pallottino, *Etr*, p. 92.

7 C. Sassatelli, *ME*, p. 38. Between the first quarter of the seventh and middle of the sixth centuries BC cremation still prevails but inhumation increases, C. M. Govi, ibid., Suppl.; cf. L. K. Poppi, ibid., p. 24.

8 L. Bonfante, *Prospettiva*, XVII (April 1979), p. 31 (map). For relations with Este (Ateste), see also M. Cristofani, *Aufstieg*, I, 2 (1972), p. 482; P. Bocchi, *Studi Banti*, pp. 69–80; F. R. Ridgway, *IBR*, pp. 430, 432, 435ff.

9 Brendel, pp. 181ff.

10 Brendel, p. 282 ('steles'). The horseshoe form persisted for 150 years.

11 Vacano, p. 151.

12 S. Tovoli, *Contributi per la carta archeologica*: *Etruria padana*, pp. 341–56.

13 Pfiffig, p. 92.

14 G. A. Mansuelli, *IBR*, pp. 354ff. For the 'Hippodamian' grid see A. Boethius and J. B. Ward-Perkins, *Greek and Roman Architecture* (1970), pp. 60f.

15 Hus, *SO*, p. 255; *EC*, p. 307.

16 Brendel, p. 296, Cristofani, *Etr*, p. 108 (Monte Acuto Ragazza, Monteguragazza).

17 Pfiffig, p. 92.

18 Virgil, *Aeneid*, X, 201–3.

19 A. Rosenberg, *Der Staat der alten Italiker* (1913), pp. 52ff., G. Radke, *Klio*, LV (1974), p. 53.

20 J. Heurgon, *Trois études sur le ver sacrum* (*Latomus*, XXVI (1957), p. 11). The traditional figure twelve is suspect here.

21 M. L. Gordon, *JRS*, XXIV (1934), p. 188.

22 Servius on Virgil, *Aeneid*, X, 203; G. Colonna, *SE*, XLII (1974), p. 10.

23 Pliny, *NH*, III, 19, 130.

24 Heurgon, p. 45; G. Colonna, *SE*, XLII (1974), p. 11, n. 46. The Arusnates had a cult of Cuslanus or Culsans; cf. at Cortona, Cristofani, *Etr*, p. 107.

25 Strabo, V, 4, 8, 247.

26 Pallottino, *Etr*, p. 97. Melpum: J. Bayet, *Tite Live: Histoire romaine* (Budé ed.), V, p. 163. Mutina: R. Bianchi Bandinelli and A. Giuliano, *Etruschi e Italici*, 2nd ed. (1976), p. 219. Regium (also Scandiano, S. Polo): *Quaderni d'archeologia reggiana*, II (1973), pp. 125–50; L. Barfield, *North Italy Before Rome* (1971), p. 112.

27 Pallottino, *Etr*, p. 123. Perhaps there was an Etruscan temple at Persolino (Faenza, the Roman Faventia); L. Barfield, *North Italy Before Rome* (1971), p. 112.

28 D. Ridgway, *AR* (1973–4), p. 58; L. K. Poppi, *ME*, p. 24.

29 G. V. Gentili, *Studi romagnoli*, XX (1969), pp. 295–331.

30 M. Zuffa, *Studi Banti*, pp. 354f.

31 Vetulonia, Tarquinii, Bisenzio, Perusia: e.g. M. Camporeale, *I commerci di Vetulonia in età orientalizzante* (1969), pp. 41 n. 9, 59f.

32 L. K. Poppi, *ME*, p. 22; L. Braccesi, *Grecità adriatica*, 2nd ed. (1977), pp. 85–8.

33 G. Colonna, *CISME*, p. 5.
34 Hus, *SO*, pp. 208f., 211, 258.
35 Strabo, V, 1, 11, 217, Pallottino, *Etr*, p. 123.
36 Name: Pfiffig, p. 92. Umbrian hillmen took Ravenna over; see Brendel, p. 256. Strabo, V, 4, 2, 241 also describes another Etruscan foundation on the coast much farther south at Cupra (Grottamare in the Marche), but its Etruscan character is doubtful; cf. B. F. Mostardi, *Cupra*, 1977.
37 M. Pallottino, *GICW*, p. 62; L. Braccesi, *Grecità adriatica*, 2nd ed. (1977), pp. 37f.
38 Pliny, *NH*, III, 16, 120: the Eridanus or Spineticus mouth, described as the Padus Vetus (Old Po) on medieval maps. The sea lagoon was the Vatrenus.
39 Probably Umbrian; see N. Alfieri and P. E. Arias, *Spina* (1960), p. 24.
40 G. Colonna, *CISME*, p. 12.
41 L. Braccesi, *Grecità adriatica*, 2nd ed. (1977), p. 56; S. Patitucci, *GICW*, p. 239, mostly from last quarter of the fifth century BC. Rhodian pottery is particularly prominent.
42 G. Colonna, *Rivista storica dell'antichità*, IV (1974) (1975), pp. 1ff., H. Jucker, *Gnomon*, XXXVII (1965), p. 297.
43 M. Zuffa, *Emilia preromana*, VII (1971–4) (1975), pp. 151–79.
44 *DH*, I, 26. He identifies them with the 'Pelasgians', a shifting, amorphous, blanket designation both for 'aboriginal' Aegean populations and northern immigrant elements.
45 From Herodotus, I, 27, who was, however, referring to Creston in Thrace, H. Hencken, *Tarquinia and Etruscan Origins* (1968), pp. 154f.; Richardson, pp. 2f., A. Neppi Modona, *Cortona etrusca e romana*, 2nd ed. (1977), pp. 6ff.
46 See, on Spina's contacts, C. Sassatelli, *SE*, XLV (1977), p. 145. Marbles – for instance an Athenian boy's head – presumably came direct from Greece.
47 F. Benoit and W. Kimmig, *Actes du Collège de Dijon* (1957) (1958), pp. 15–20.
48 Greece: Cristofani, *Etr*, p. 67 (Athens, Corcyra). Etruria: R. Chevallier, *Mél. Heurgon*, I, p. 152, n. 24; G. Colonna, *CISME*, p. 5; *Ambra: oro del nord* (Venice exhibition, 1978). The Brenner Pass provided another route.
49 Brendel, p. 256; A. J. Pfiffig, *Sprache*, VIII (1962), pp. 149–53.
50 Horses and amber: Cristofani, *Etr*, p. 67. Policing of sea: N. Alfieri and P. E. Arias, *Spina* (1960), p. 25; M. Zuffa, *Atti del I Convegno di Studi Etruschi*; *SE*, XXV, Suppl. (1959), pp. 133–43.
51 Venetian or Umbrian; see N. Alfieri and P. E. Arias, *Spina* (1960), p. 24.
52 G. Colonna, *Rivista storica dell'antichità*, IV (1974), pp. 1ff. Among the Greeks, Aeginetans were prominent.
53 From the Sagis mouth: see Pliny, *NH*, III, 16, 120.
54 *DH*, VII, 3, 1; G. Colonna,

Aspetti, pp. 258ff.; M. Frederiksen, *IBR*, p. 304.

55 'Condottieri' from Spina according to G. Radke, *Klio*, LV (1974), p. 50 and n. 192.

56 Pallottino, *Etr*, p. 98; J. Bayet, *Tite Live: Histoire romaine* (Budé ed.), V, p. 161.

57 V. J. Bruno, *Archaeology*, XXVI (1973), pp. 208–11.

58 Strabo, V, 2, 5, 223.

59 Hus, *SO*, p. 73; cf. Banti, p. 157; reserves by M. Cristofani, *Aspetti*, pp. 67ff.

60 Virgil, *Aeneid*, X, 179; Strabo, V, 2, 5, 222; Pliny, *NH*, III, 5, 50; G. Radke, *Klio*, LV (1974), p. 34. Based on a false derivation from Pisa in the Peloponnese.

61 Servius on Virgil, *Aeneid*, X, 179 (from Cato the Elder); cf. R. F. Paget, *Central Italy* (1973), p. 137.

62 L. Banti, *BE*, XX, 2, 1768; cf. M. Cristofani, *Aspetti*, pp. 67ff.

63 Banti, p. 157. Minor Etruscan finds have also occurred nearby; at Querceta, Camaiore and Torre del Lago, P. Mencacci and M. Zecchini, *Lucca preistorica* (1976), p. 226.

64 See *SE*, XXXIX (1971), p. 151.

65 D. Ridgway, *AR* (1973–4), p. 56.

66 P. Mencacci and M. Zecchini, op. cit., C. Scavone, *Princeton Encyclopaedia of Classical Sites* (1976), p. 527. Arruns was an Etruscan seer from 'deserted' Luca according to Lucan, *Civil War*, I, 588.

67 G. d'Achiardi, *SE*, I (1927), p. 414; M. Boni and F. Ippolito, *CISME*, p. 52; Cristofani, *Etr*, p. 54. The coastal plain is the Versilia.

68 M. Zecchini, *Gli Etruschi all' isola d'Elba* (1978), pp. 88, 115, 149 (sources). The site is Campo Casali.

69 Beside the River Magra, which was often regarded as the boundary between Etruria and Liguria; Strabo V, 2, 5, 222.

70 Livy, XLI, 13. 5: the Ager Lunensis (now the Lunigiana).

71 Strabo, V, 2, 5, 222; V. J. Bruno, *Archaeology*, XXVI (1973), pp. 202f.

72 Gold ship-like objects from Chiavari resemble Etruscan and near-eastern pieces; see P. G. Guzzi, *Hamburger Beiträge zur Archäologie*, V (1975) (1977), pp. 183–91.

73 *ME*, p. 81; G. Colonna, *CISME*, p. 10. Etruscan objects are also found at Vauvenargues (on Mont S. Victoire).

74 W. Dehn and O.-H. Frey, *IBR*, p. 493; Brendel, pp. 186, 457 n. 15 (p. 453 n. 13: cf. a chariot from Castel S. Mariano); Heurgon p. 74. Vix commanded not only the Rhône–Saône route but that of the Seine to the north and Alpine passes to the south-east. There have also been Etruscan finds at Gorge-Meillet (Marne) and Motte S. Valentin (Haute Marne), *ME*, p. 88; at Mercey-sur-Saône and Conliège, W. Dehn and O.-H. Frey, *IBR*, p. 500, and near Tours, R. Chevalier, *Homenaje Garcia Bellido*, II (1976) (1977), pp. 131–57.

75 Pallottino, *Etr*, pp. 83, 248 n. 3; J.-P. Morel, *EM*. in press.

76 B. Cunliffe, *The Celtic World*

(1979), pp. 35, 38, 40, 129; *ME*, pp. 88, 90; S. Piggott, *Ancient Europe* (1965), pp. 195, 212. A mould found on the Heuneburg was used for imitating Etruscan bronze handles, W. Dehn and O.-H. Frey, *IBR*, p. 500. The wheel had perhaps spread from the eastern Mediterranean to central Europe via Etruria by the seventh century BC; Cunliffe, p. 117.

77 B. Cunliffe, *The Celtic World* (1979), pp. 86, 100, 104.

CHAPTER 7
Disunity

1 G. Colonna, *CISME*, pp. 14f.
2 M. Pallottino, *SE*, XXII (1952–3), pp. 193ff.; G. V. Gentili and G. A. Mansuelli, *Aspetti*, p. 231; G. Colonna, *CISME*, p. 13.
3 C. Ampolo, *DA*, IV–V (1970–1), pp. 37–68. For the slaves (*lautni*) as integral members of the family see Cristofani, *Etr*, p. 41.
4 *DH*, IX, 5, 4 (*penestai*, of Thessaly); Cristofani, *Etr*, p. 41; W. V. Harris, *Rome in Etruria and Umbria* (1971), p. 121.
5 A. Momigliano, *JRS*, LIII (1963), p. 119.
6 M. Rostovtzeff, *Social and Economic History of the Roman Empire*, 2nd ed. (ed. P. M. Fraser) (1957), p. 23.
7 M. Torelli, *DA*, VIII, 1 (1974–5), pp. 27f.
8 Strong, p. 56; G. Radke, *Klio*, LV (1974), pp. 50f.
9 M. Torelli, *DA*, VIII, pp. 53f.;

T. J. Cornell, *JRS*, LXVIII (1978), p. 172.
10 Varro, *De Lingua Latina*, V, 8, 46; R. Turcan, *Mél. Heurgon*, II, p. 1016.
11 Banti, p. 207. Inscriptions referring to the headship of the league are all doubtful; Pallottino, *Etr*, p. 126; cf. T. J. Cornell, *JRS*, LXVIII (1978), p. 171; M. Grant, *Proceedings of the Classical Association*, LXXV (1978), p. 12.
12 P. J. Riis, *Introduction to Etruscan Art* (1953), p. 24; Cristofani, *AE*, p. 81; Heurgon, p. 44. Livy only refers to the twelve in relation to 434 BC; IV, 23, 5. Servius on Virgil, *Aeneid*, VIII, 475, refers to twelve chiefs (*lucumones*) or kings, of whom one presided.
13 The 'alliance' of five Etruscan states (Clusium, Arretium, Volaterrae, Rusellae, Vetulonia) against Tarquinius Priscus reported by *DH*, III, 51, 4 is cautiously accepted by G. Colonna, *SE*, XLI (1973), p. 69, but doubted as an anachronism by Banti, p. 128 – probably rightly, since Arretium and Rusellae scarcely existed as substantial city-states at that period.
14 At most there may have been times when one city or another, notably Tarquinii in the first instance, was important enough to establish a temporary measure of reluctant unity by dominating its neighbours. This is perhaps the meaning of the tradition that reached Strabo, V, 2, 2, 219 ('The Tyrrheni were

at first subject to only one ruler').

15 Strabo, V, 4, 3, 242.

16 Livy, V, 33.

17 Virgil, *Aeneid*, X, 691f., etc.

18 Banti, p. 207; cf. Vacano, pp. 129, 134.

19 Brendel, p. 111. Probably there were several distinct Etruscan leagues in the sixth century BC; L. R. Taylor, *Proceedings of the American Academy at Rome*, II (1923), p. 13.

20 M. Pallottino, *Atti del VII Convegno di studi sulla Magna Grecia* (1969), p. 45.

21 D. H. Lawrence, *Etruscan Places* (1932, Penguin ed. 1950), p. 168.

22 Cf. (to a lesser extent?) in Greece, A. M. Snodgrass, *Archaeology and the Rise of the Greek State* (1977), p. 13.

23 V. Bartlett, *Etruscan Retreat* (1964), pp. 64ff.

CHAPTER 8
Tarquinii

1 E. H. Richardson, *Memoirs of the American Academy at Rome*, XXVII (1962), p. 159; Brendel, pp. 26, 436 n. 4.

2 There is a similar example at Carthaginian Motya; Brendel, p. 440 n. 7. The Tomb of the Warriors (*c.* 730 BC?) is less reliable for dating; see Chapter 3 n. 54.

3 M. Cataldi and F. Boitani, *EC*, pp. 187f.

4 Pliny, *NH*, XXXV, 16, 152.

5 Brendel, p. 95.

6 D. Ridgway, *AR* (1976–7), p. 71 (Camarina).

7 *DH*, III, 46, 5.

8 G. Colonna, *CISME*, p. 9; M. Pallottino, *GICW*, p. 69.

9 Perhaps Ionian refugee artists came to Tarquinii via the Nile delta (Naucratis, etc.). M. Cristofani, *Prospettiva*, VII (Oct. 1976), pp. 2ff.

10 M. Moretti, *Tarquinia* (1974), p. 11. One of the artists was a Greek slave, Tarq Aranth (slave of Hercnas), G. Colonna, *Röm. Mitt.*, LXXXII (1975), p. 185; M. Torelli, *Archaeological News*, V, 4 (1976), p. 137.

11 Richardson, p. 229.

12 Brendel, pp. 168, 170 (Phrygia, Lycia).

13 Å. Åkerstrom, *GICW*, p. 214 (Hittite).

14 Banti, p. 79; Pallottino, *Etr*, pp. 112f. Tarquinii produced a great painted terracotta relief, the Winged Horses, *c.* 300 BC. M. Moretti, *Tarquinia* (1975), pl. 26.

15 G. Buchner, *AR* (1971), p. 67.

16 Banti, p. 105.

17 Banti, pp. 106f., M. Cristofani Martelli, *Le tombe di Tuscania nel Museo archeologico di Firenze* (1979). Cf. Manturanum nearby.

18 J. B. Ward-Perkins, *Harvard Studies in Classical Philology*, LXIV (1959), pp. 1–26.

19 Pliny, *NH*, XXXVI, 29.

20 G. Schmiedt, *Il livello antico del Mar Tirreno* (1972).

21 The earliest known Etruscan inscription (*c.* 700) may come from Tarquinii. M. Cristofani, *IBR*, p. 378, but this priority could be fortuitous.

22 A. Alföldi, *Römische Frühgeschichte* (1976), p. 170.

23 M. Torelli, *PP*, XXVI (1971), pp. 44–67; *SE*, XLV (1977), p. 448.

24 G. Lilliu, *NS* (1971), pp. 289ff.

25 E. D. Oren, V. S. Webb, *GICW*, pp. 199, 200f.; also Stratopeda (Migdol, *c.* 650) and frontier-post at Daphne (Tell Defenneh). The Pharaohs were Psammetichus I (Psamtik, *c.* 663–610 BC) and Amasis (Ahmose, *c.* 569–526).

26 Herodotus, IV, 52; F. D. Harvey, *PP*, XXXI (1976), pp. 206ff.; Cristofani, *AE*, pp. 79, 82, 113n, 153; Pallottino, *Etr*, p. 112; D. Ridgway, *AR* (1973–4), p. 50, fig. 9.

27 H. Dessau, *Inscriptiones Latinae Selectae*, 212.

28 R. M. Ogilvie, *Commentary on Livy Books 1–5* (1965), p. 141.

29 Discussed by T. N. Gantz, *Historia*, XXIV (1975), pp. 541f. and n. 12.

30 Strabo, V, 2, 2, 220.

31 *Corpus Inscriptionum Latinarum*, II, 3626–34; G. Radke, *Klio*, LVI (1974), pp. 44, 46; F. Defosse, *Revue belge de philologie et d'histoire* (1970), p. 1035.

32 Livy I, 34, 9, *DH*, III, 47, 2.

33 Torelli, *ET*, pp. 32–8.

34 Torelli, *ET*, pp. 72, 80ff.

35 Torelli, *ET*, pp. 87f.: he suggests the Septem Pagi (north of the Tiber mouth), Nepet (Nepi) and Sutrium (Sutri).

36 Torelli, *ET*, pp. 82ff.; G. Baffioni, *SE*, XXXV (1967), p. 133.

37 Treaties: W. V. Harris, *Rome in Etruria and Umbria* (1971), pp. 85–146; truces: A. J. Pfiffig, *Die Ausbreitung des römischen Stadtwesens in Etrurien* (1966), pp. 9–16.

CHAPTER 9
Caere

1 Banti, p. 48.

2 P. Mingazzini, *Rendiconti dell' Accademia dei Lincei*, Ser. 8, XXXI (1976) (1977), pp. 145–9; Cristofani, *AE*, pp. 45, 55, 58; M. Torelli, *Archaeological News*, V, 4 (1976), p. 135; Vacano, pp. 77ff.

3 M. Cataldi and F. Boitani, *EC*, p. 161. The Caeritans carry massive body-shields reaching almost to their ankles.

4 Brendel, p. 77; Potter, p. 72.

5 Banti, p. 40.

6 M. Cataldi and F. Boitani, *EC*, p. 172. This is different from the 'Tuscan' order, which has Doric capitals but a smooth shaft and footings (Pallottino, *Etr*, p. 162), and may have been introduced from Rhodes. For stone replicas of furniture in these tombs see S. Steingräber, *Etruskische Möbel* (1979), pp. 67ff.

7 Virgil, *Aeneid*, VIII, 606.

8 Brendel, pp. 172f.; J. M. Hemelrijk, *De Caeretanse Hydriae* (1957).

9 S. Haynes, *Etruscan Sculpture* (1971), pp. 11ff.; Banti, p. 220 and pl. 8(d).

10 Brendel, pp. 229, 231.

11 K. Hanell in A. Boethius (ed.), *Etruscan Culture, Land and People* (1962), pp. 279ff.; M. Cataldi and F. Boitani, *EC*, pp. 251–4; Potter, p. 55.

NOTES

12 S. Quilici Gigli, *Blera* (1976);
Potter, pp. 81f.

13 Dennis, I, p. 176.

14 For a map of its distribution see
Cristofani, *Etr*, p. 68.

15 Strabo, V, 3, 220.

16 Virgil, *Aeneid*, VIII, 597; cf.
Strong, p. 32.

17 Pallottino, *Etr*, p. 95; M. Torelli,
ET, p. 312. Also Cales (Calvi
Vecchia): P. Defosse, *Latomus*,
XXXIV (1975), p. 1076; M.
Frederiksen, *IBR*, p. 298.

18 Pallottino, *Etr*, p. 251.

19 J. MacIntosh Turfa, *AJA*,
LXXXI (1977), pp. 368–74.

20 J. Jehasse, *Les dernières leçons
d'Aléria*, in *Assimilation*, pp.
523ff.; J. and L. Jehasse, *IBR*,
pp. 313f., 340.

21 S. Moscati, *I Cartaginesi in Italia*
(1977), pp. 18, 29f., 134ff., R. C.
Raspi, *Storia della Sardegna*, 3rd
ed. (1977), pp. 183f.

22 Caere's other name, Agylla,
reportedly Greek (cf. Herodotus,
I, 167), may instead have been
Carthaginian. A. J. Pfiffig,
*Österreichische Akademie der
Wissenschaften, Philos-hist. kl.*
LXXXVIII, 2 (1965), p. 42.

23 Aristotle, *Politics*, III, 9, 1280a,
36.

24 Herodotus, I, 166–7; Pallottino,
Etr, p. 89. The Phoenicians
moved to Hyele or Elea (Velia).

25 Perhaps Arimnestus, King of the
'Etruscans', the first barbarian
ever to give a dedication to Zeus
at Olympia (Pausanias, V, 12,
4), was also Caeritan.

26 'When they were taking
possession of the islands lying off
the Tyrrhenian Sea': Diodorus

Siculus, V, 13, 4 and L. Jehasse,
IBR, p. 325. Diodorus, XI, 88, 5
describes Corsica as Etruscan
in 454–3 BC. The
Carthaginian–Etruscan alliance
may at this time have become
less commercial and more purely
political.

27 Strabo, V, 2, 7, 225; M. Guido,
Sardinia (1963), p. 33; F. Lo
Schiavo, *EM* (in press).

28 D. Ridgway, *AR* (1967–8), pp.
39f. (Castrum Novum was a
staging point on the Via
Aurelia).

29 M. Cataldi and F. Boitani, *EC*,
p. 214; Banti, p. 51 (Punta della
Vipera).

30 Silius Italicus, *Punica*, VIII, 476
(Alaesus, Halaesus).

31 J. P. Oleson, *Journal of Field
Archaeology*, IV (1977), pp.
297–308.

32 G. Colonna, *CISME*, p. 7; for
the site, see G. Kahl-
Furthmann, *Die Frage nach dem
Ursprung der Etrusker* (1976), p.
106; Potter, p. 55.

33 Pallottino, *Etr*, pp. 90, 93, 132,
190, 195f., 197f., 200, 207, 221,
272. The language of the first
inscription is probably Punic,
not Phoenicio-Cypriot as had
also been suggested.

34 The word *atranes* in the longer of
the two Etruscan inscriptions
(M. Pallottino, *Testimonia Linguae
Etruscae*, 2nd ed. (1968), p. 109,
no. 874) is related by M.
Zecchini, *Gli Etruschi all'isola
d'Elba* (1978), pp. 95, 99, to Le
Trane (formerly Latrani) on the
island of Elba, but alternative
interpretations are cited by Hus,

281

SO, p. 160, and Zecchini, op. cit., p. 96.

35 M. Cataldi and F. Boitani, *EC*, pp. 177f. ('Temple B').

36 G. P. Carratelli, *PP*, XVII (1962), p. 11 and n. 14; Cristofani, *Etr*, p. 18.

37 M. Pallottino, *SE*, XXXIV (1966), pp. 175–209.

38 R. Carpenter, *Beyond the Pillars of Hercules* (1966), pp. 65, 67, V. I. Kozlovskaya, *Vjestnik Drevnei Istorii*, CXXV (1973), pp. 93–104; M. Tarradell, *El impacto greco-fenicio en el extremo occidente*, in *Assimilation*, pp. 343–55; J. M. Blazquez, *Tartessos y los origenes de la colonizacian fenicia en occidente*, 2nd ed. (1975).

39 Diodorus Siculus, V, 20, 4.

40 Banti, pp. 73ff.

41 It has been suggested that Rome may have had Caeritan or Veientine founders.

42 G. Radke, *Klio*, LVI (1974), p. 46.

43 J. Gagé, *Mélanges de l'Ecole Française a Rome*, XLVI (1929), p. 127.

44 Cato, *fr.* 9–12 (Macrobius, *Saturnalia*, III, 5, 1); G. Dumézil, *Mél. Heurgon*, I, pp. 253ff.

45 The later Via Cornelia and Via Praenestina.

46 A. Bedini and F. Cordano, *PP*. XXXII (1977), p. 306; also Ficana.

47 E. D. van Buren, *Figurative Terracotta Revetments in Etruria and Latium* (1921), pp. 60, 70.

48 A. Alföldi, *Römische Frühgeschichte* (1976), p. 150.

49 D. Ridgway, *JRS*, LXVI (1976), p. 210.

50 Livy, I, 2, 2–3.

51 Heurgon, p. 138.

52 M. Sordi, *Aufstieg* I, 2 (1972), p. 791.

53 Diodorus Siculus, XV, 27, 4; Theophrastus, *History of Plants*, V, 8, 2; M. Sordi, *I rapporti romano-ceriti e l'origine della civitas sine suffragio* (1960), pp. 95f.

54 Livy, IX, 36, 3; Brendel, p. 408.

CHAPTER 10
Vulci

1 J. Wellard, *The Search for the Etruscans* (1973), p. 53.

2 Richardson, p. 11 (to Capalbio).

3 G. Buchner, *AR* (1970–1), p. 67; F. Canciani, *DA*, VIII (1974–5), pp. 79–85. A bronze sword from Vulci shows the influence of Greek modelling of the same period.

4 R. A. Higgins, *Greek and Roman Jewellery* (1961), p. 136.

5 S. Haynes, *Etruscan Sculpture* (1971), pp. 11f.

6 Richardson, p. 94.

7 Banti, p. 89.

8 M. Cataldi and F. Boitani, *EC*, p. 222.

9 G. Dennis, I, pp. 452f.

10 M. Cristofani Martelli, *Prospettiva*, IV (Nov. 1975), p. 44. For the successive Greek schools at Vulci, see A. Guiliano, *Prospettiva*, III (Oct. 1975), p. 4.

11 Richardson, p. 120; Brendel, p. 452, n. 1. They have, in fact, nothing whatever to do with Pontus (north-eastern Asia Minor) or with the Black Sea after which it was named.

12 L. Hannestad, *The Paris Painter* (1974), and *The Followers of the Paris Painter* (1976).

13 M. Moltesen, *SE*, XLVI (1978), p. 72.

14 S. Haynes, *Etruscan Bronze Utensils*, 2nd ed. (1974), pp. 18ff.

15 Pallottino, *Etr*, p. 182.

16 Brendel, p. 215. Vulcentine bronze-work was distributed around a commercial circuit directed by Sparta, with Sparta's southern Italian colony Taras (Tarentum, Taranto) serving as intermediary.

17 H. Jucker, *Gnomon*, XXXVII (1965), p. 297.

18 E.g. a fragment of a handle decorated with a frontal bearded figure, found at Heuneburg (Württemberg), comes from Vulci or shows a knowledge of its work.

19 Cristofani, *Etr*, p. 51, 7; H. Hencken, *Tarquinia and Etruscan Origins* (1968), p. 17.

20 V. Bracco, *Forma Italiae*, Regio III, Vol. 2, Volcei (1978).

21 G. Matteucig, *Hommages à M. Renaud*, III (1969), p. 439. A little to the east of Poggio Buco was another subsidiary centre that served the same purpose on a slightly more southerly route, Ischia del Castro, on a tributary of the Fiora. A cemetery to its west (Castro) has disclosed a bronze-covered chariot of wood and iron and the finest known collection of Etruscan animal sculpture (early sixth century BC). M. Cataldi and F. Boitani, *EC*, p. 226; M. Moltesen, *SE*, XLVI (1978), pp. 71f.

22 M. Pasquinucci, *EC*, p. 140.

23 Pfiffig, p. 93.

24 The region bears this name of the Silver Mountain not because it contained silver mines in ancient times, as it apparently did not (according to information from Dr Carmelo Latino, Chief Engineer of the Mineral District of Grosseto), but either (1) because of the colour of its rocks, or (2) because, after Etruscan independence was ended, the great Roman land-owning family of the Domitii had their bankers (*argentarii*) there. For other metals on the Argentario, see Cristofani, *Etr*, p. 54. For a cremation tomb of the tenth or ninth century BC see *L'età del ferro nell'Etruria marittima* (1965), p. 28, no. 4.

25 A. Mori, *Bollettino della Reale Società Geografica Italiana*, Ser. 6, VIII (1931), p. 534. Today an embankment links the Argentario with Orbetello. The more westerly of the two complete sandbar isthmuses ends at the mouth of the Albegna.

26 E.g. maps of 1573 (Siena), 1617 (Amsterdam, Hondius), 1815 (Bayerische Stadtbibliothek, Munich), F. W. Hase, *Röm. Mitt.* LXXIX (1972), pl. 81.

27 Pfiffig, p. 92.

28 M. Pasquinucci, *EC*, pp. 120, 128.

29 M. Pasquinucci, *EC*, p. 119.

30 P. Bocci-Pacino, *Princeton Encyclopaedia of Ancient Sites* (1976), p. 653. Pliny, *NH*, III, 5, 51 speaks of *Cosa Volcientium*.

31 Strabo, V, 2, 8, 225; Cristofani, *AE*, p. 84; M. Cristofani Martelli, *GICW*, p. 213, M. Torelli, *EC*, p. 13. Montalto Marina, on the estuary itself, has provided a few Roman remains, but nothing earlier.

32 Forum Aurelii was near the modern Montalto di Castro.

33 R. T. Ridley, *Klio*, LVII (1975), pp. 147–77; F. Zevi, *Omaggio a P. Bianchi Bandinelli* (1970), pp. 65–73.

34 Cristofani, *Etr*, p. 95. A portrait-painting of a woman that was on the opposite wall is missing, Brendel, p. 412.

35 G. Radke, *Klio* LVI (1974), p. 46; T. N. Gantz, *Historia*, XXIV (1975), pp. 552f. For the variant tradition, see n. 37.

36 J. Heurgon, *Comptes-rendus de l'Académie des Inscriptions* (1953), pp. 92ff.; *Latomus*, XII (1953), pp. 402–17; W. V. Harris, *Rome in Etruria and Umbria* (1971), pp. 26ff.; A. Garzetti, *From Tiberius to the Antonines* (1974), pp. 589, 739.

37 H. Dessau, *Inscriptiones Latinae Selectae*, 212 (paraphrased and altered by Tacitus, *Annals*, XI, 23–35).

38 M. Grant, *Roman Myths*, rev. ed. (1973), pp. 159f.

39 M. Pallottino, *Comptes-rendus de l'Académie des Inscriptions* (1977), pp. 216–35.

40 E. Benveniste, *Revue des études latines*, X (1932), pp. 429f., 436; L. Bonfante, *AJA*, LXXIII (1969), p. 253.

41 Livy, IV, 3, 12; *DH*, IV, 2, 2 (Tanaquil).

42 Similar names, such as Masterna, are recorded among Etruscans who later served in the Roman army. Perhaps, however, Macstrna is the title of a city-state official (cf. Lars and Porsenna ?) – especially as he is the only person among those mentioned in the François tomb paintings to lack a first name. If so, the word may be related to the Roman *magister* or Greek *mestor* (coordinator), R. T. Ridley, *Klio*, LVII (1975), pp. 164f.

43 J. Gagé, *Latomus*, XXXII (1973), pp. 6f.

44 Festus (W. M. Lindsey ed., 1913), p. 486.

45 M. Pallottino, *SE*, XIII (1939), pp. 456ff. (Veii, too, had a king with a similar name, Vibe). Possibly Vibenna visited the Veii sanctuary on his way towards Rome.

46 Arnobius, VI, 7; M. Grant, *Roman Myths*, rev. ed. (1973), p. 183. Arnobius wildly adds that the Capitolium was named after his head (*caput*).

47 Brendel, p. 413; A. de Agostino, *Il Museo Archeologico di Firenze* (1968), pp. 104f. The story is one of many variants on a well-known theme of the capture of a holy prophet in order to force him to make useful disclosures.

48 *Chronographia Urbis Romae* (AD 354); T. Mommsen, *Chronica Minora*, I (1892).

49 Pliny *NH*, III, 5, 52 (*Volcentani cognomine Etrusci*).

50 Richardson, p. 149.

51 Brendel, p. 380; Torelli, *ET*, p. 85.

52 This is preferable to the alternative view that the Vulcentines' Roman victims are being compared with the Trojan victims of Achilles – the Romans being allegedly of Trojan origin.

53 R. Carpenter, *Folktale, Fiction and Saga in the Homeric Epics* (1962), pp. 63–7; discussed by G. K. Galinsky, *Aeneas, Sicily and Rome* (1969), pp. 121f. and n. 48.

54 W. Fuchs, *Aufstieg*, I, 4 (1973), p. 63. On these stories see also N. Horsfall, *JRS* (1973), pp. 78f.

55 Lycophron, *Alexandra*, 1238–9; Plutarch, *Romulus*, 21.

56 M. Torelli, *DA*, VII (1973), p. 400; F. Castagnoli, *PP*, XXXII (1977), p. 355; J. Riis, *Entretiens Hardt*, XIII (1966), p. 71. There was an early manifestation at Politorium.

57 J. Gagé, *Mélanges de l'Ecole Francaise à Rome*, XLVI (1929), p. 130.

58 L. Pareti, *SE*, V (1931), pp. 154f.

59 D. Ridgway, *JRS*, LXVI (1976), p. 209; *Aspetti* p. 291.

60 Virgil, *Aeneid*, X, 168.

61 Pfiffig, p. 97.

62 B. d'Agostino, *SE*, XXXIII (1965), pp. 676f.

63 C. Battisti, *SE*, XXXII (1964), pp. 24ff.

64 The type of an elephant suggests that this was an anti-Roman issue under Hannibal. H. H. Scullard, *The Elephant in the Greek and Roman World* (1974), p. 72.

65 Scullard, pp. 211f.

66 Cristofani, *AE*, p. 62. A gilded ostrich egg from Vulci appeared near Quinto Fiorentino before 600 BC.

67 W. V. Harris, *Rome in Etruria and Umbria* (1971), pp. 82f. (Tiberius Coruncanius).

CHAPTER 11
Vetulonia

1 The Massa Marittima necropolis depended on Vetulonia. G. Camporeale, *I commerci di Vetulonia, in età orientalizzante* (1969), p. 11, n. 1.

2 Brendel, p. 44.

3 M. Pasquinucci, *EC*, p. 109.

4 Banti, pp. 56, 86, 149 n. 16.

5 F. M. von Hase, *Röm. Mitt.* LXXIX (1972), pp. 153ff.

6 Brendel, p. 462, n. 9.

7 J. Jully, *Opuscula Romana*, VI (1968), p. 52.

8 Banti, p. 134. Territorial overlaps between the two techniques occur.

9 R. A. Higgins, *Greek and Roman Jewellery* (1961), pp. 18f., 135, 138.

10 A. Boethius and J. B. Ward-Perkins, *Greek and Roman Architecture* (1970), pp. 57, 91.

11 G. Buonamici, *SE*, V (1931), p. 393 (references); M. Pallottino, *Testimonia Linguae Etruscae*, 2nd ed. (1968), p. 59, no. 363 (for the dedication formulas see Pallottino *Etr*, pp. 220, 230; Hus, *SO*, p. 162). For the Hirumina interpretation see Scullard, p. 223.

12 M. del Chiaro, *Etruscan Ghiaccio Forte* (1976), p. 36, n. 58.

13 M. Cristofani, *Aufstieg*, I, 2 (1972), p. 469.

14 Banti, p. 112, M. Pasquinucci, *EC*, p. 131. A pot from Marsiliana on which an alphabet is incised (Banti pp. 116f., Hus, *SO*. pl. 49) is now dated to *c*. 670–650.

15 Strong, p. 35.

16 M. del Chiaro, *Etruscan Ghiaccio Forte* (1976), pp. 17, 35, 38.

17 Pliny, *NH*, III, 5, 51; Cristofani, *AE*, p. 137.

18 G. Colonna, *SE*, XLI (1973), p. 45.

19 G. Colonna, *Mél. Heurgon*, p. 151.

20 G. Camporeale, *I commerci di Vetulonia in età orientalizzante* (1969), pp. 28ff.

21 Coins: F. Catalli, *CISME*, pp. 142ff. Monument: G. Camporeale, *I commerci di Vetulonia in età orientalizzante* (1969), p. 118; L. Banti, *SE*, V (1931), p. 185 and pl. 14. Moreover, Nethuns (Poseidon, Neptune), the god of water, was especially revered at Vetulonia. E. Macnamara, *The Everyday Life of the Etruscans* (1973), pp. 155f.

22 R. Bianchi Bandinelli and A. Guiliano, *Etruschi e Italici prima del dominio di Roma*, 2nd ed., (1976), p. 65, fig. 70; M. Guido, *Sardinia* (1963), pp. 177f.; M. Pasquinucci, *EC*, p. 109; S. von Reden, *Die Etrusker* (1978), p. 239.

23 Strabo, V, 2, 7, 124, 225.

24 Between 600 BC and AD 100 the sea-level was one metre higher than it is now, Cristofani, *Etr*, p. 10. Ombrone: V. J. Bruno, *Archaeology*, XXVI (1973), pp. 198–212.

25 Cicero, *In Defence of Milo*, XXIV, 74.

26 C. B. Curri, *Forma Italiae*, Region VII, Vol. 5, Vetulonia I; cf. G. Camporeale, *I commerci di Vetulonia in età orientalizzante* (1969), p. 115. Castiglione de la Pescaia at the mouth of the Bruna may also have been a port belonging to Vetulonia.

27 Silius Italicus, *Punica*, VIII, 483ff. – but the axe on Avle Feluske's gravestone is double, whereas the Roman axe is single. G. Radke, *Klassische Sprache und Literatur*, VI (1971), p. 89, assigns the origins of these emblems to Rome itself, under Etruscan rule. It is unlikely that Vetulonia belonged to a north Italian alliance hostile to Rome in the sixth century BC (p. 278).

28 Politorium: A. Bedini and F. Cordano, *PP*, XXXII (1977), p. 305 (with caution, p. 309). Praeneste, etc.; Banti, p. 257. Similar vase-handles are also found at Marsiliana.

29 M. Cristofani Martelli, M. A. Fugazzola Delpino, and P. B. Pacini, *EM* (in press).

30 Strabo, V, 2, 6, 223; Pliny, *NH*, III, 5, 50.

31 M. Cristofani Martelli, *CISME*, pp. 103f.

32 Heurgon, p. 73.

33 M. Pasquinucci, *EC*, p. 99. At Populonia, tombs with plinths of late seventh and early sixth century date are approached by corridors preceded by paved vestibules. In the sixth century,

when inhumation largely replaced cremation (in belated imitation of southern Etruria), new types of tomb began to appear, including some that have the appearance of rectangular shrines.

34 *DH*, III, 51; Servius on Virgil, *Aeneid*, X, 172; discussed by C. Battisti, *SE*, XXVII (1959), pp. 391ff.

35 Hus, *SO*, p. 63.

36 J. Jehasse, *EM* (in press). For Populonia's links with the opposite (west) coast of Corsica see Cristofani, *Etr*, pp. 67f.

37 M. Cristofani Martelli, *CISME*, p. 103. Elba, too, had an early strong-point named Volterraio, M. Zecchini, *Gli Etruschi all 'isola d'Elba* (1978), pp. 51, 195, 199.

38 Hus, *SO*, p. 64.

39 Strong, p. 35.

40 G. Camporeale, *I commerci di Vetulonia in età orientalizzante* (1969), pp. 50f.

41 Quasi-monetary bronze objects: S. Sorda, *CISME*, pp. 61, 63, 67. For ingots of mid-sixth century with incised mark ('dry branch'), see Cristofani, *Etr*, p. 68. Private issues of coinage: ibid.

42 Vetulonia: L. Camilli, *CISME*, pp. 181ff. Volaterrae: F. Catalli, *CISME*, pp. 141ff. Populonia: T. Hackens, *CISME*, p. 220. Other silver coins of 'Auriol type' (thus named after the site of a French hoard) may be of Etruscan or Massalian mintage, M. Cristofani Martelli, *CISME*, p. 87.

43 L. Breglia, *CISME*, p. 85, and other discussions in the same volume.

44 M. Boni and F. Ippolito, *CISME*, pp. 52ff.

45 T. Hackens, *CISME*, p. 264.

46 E.g. Lampsacus on the Propontis (Sea of Marmara), M. Cristofani Martelli, *CISME*, pp. 99, 100, 104.

47 The name 'Vetalu', associated with 'Pupluna' (Populonia) on coins of the third century BC, may not, as supposed, denote Vetulonia (M. Cristofani, *Mél. Heurgon*, I, pp. 209ff.) – which is 'Vatl' on other coins – but the Etruscan equivalent of 'Aethalia' (Elba). M. Pallottino, *CISME*, p. 367. However, U. Coli, *Nuovo saggio di lingua etrusca* (1966), p.36; M. Zecchini, *Gli Etruschi all'isola d'Elba* (1978), pp. 9, 95, 99, instead see 'Eitale, on a Caeritan inscription as the Etruscan name of Elba. For the considerable number of Etruscan sites see Zecchini, pp. 8ff.

48 Diodorus Siculus, XI, 88, 4f.

49 M. Zecchini, *Gli Etruschi all'isola d'Elba* (1978), p. 12.

50 D. Ridgway, *AR* (1967–8), p. 45; V. Melani and M. Vergari, *Roselle*, I (1974), p. 15.

51 M. Pasquinucci, *EC*, p. 112.

52 Brendel, p. 447, n. 2. Rusellae perhaps also took over from Vetulonia the Etruscan settlement of Heba (Magliano), seven miles inland, M. Pasquinucci, *EC*, p. 129.

53 Livy, XXVIII, 45, 18 (contribution to Scipio Africanus in Second Punic War, 205 BC).

54 T. Hackens, *CISME*, pp. 230–3; M. Pallottino, *CISME*, p. 367.

55 T. Hackens, *CISME*, pp. 262f.; compare plate 35 no. 5 with *JHS* (1946), pl. 5, nos. 2 and 3. A metrological connection with Corcyra was suggested by M. Segrè, *Metrologia e circolazione monetaria* (1928), p. 307; cf. a Corcyra–Naxos link in C. T. Seltman, *Greek Coins*, 2nd ed. (1955), p. 71.

56 On the relations of early Etruscan mints to metal supplies see A. Stazio, *EM* (in press). T. Hackens points to some find-evidence for Thezi-Thezle at Vulci (*CISME*, p. 231) but is prepared to envisage more than one mint (p. 266) – though mint-unity is suggested by the almost uniform inscriptions. M. Cristofani, *CISME*, p. 359 notes epigraphic resemblances to Vulci and Caere. Find-evidence and epigraphic evidence from the Lake Prilius area, however, might reveal similar analogies.

57 The numismatic evidence for an Etruscan name Tlamu(n) is now uncertain. M. Cristofani, *CISME*, p. 356, against W. V. Harris, *Rome in Etruria and Umbria* (1971), p. 206, n. 8.

58 R. Naumann, *Röm. Mitt.* LXX (1963), pp. 39–43. Coins of Vetulonia, Populonia and (Roman) Cosa are also found at Telamon. M. Cristofani, *CISME*, p. 356.

59 Cristofani, *ETR*, p. 15.

60 Livy, X, 37, 3; W. V. Harris, *Rome in Etruria and Umbria* (1971), p. 75.

CHAPTER 12
Volaterrae

1 M. Pasquinucci, *EC*, p. 72.

2 D. Ridgway, *AR* (1973–4), p. 55.

3 M. Pasquinucci, *EC*, p. 77. M. Pallottino, *Etudes étrusco-italiques* (1963), pp. 145f., detects a precedent at Xanthus in Lycia (southern Asia Minor).

4 The Lorenzini head: see M. Cristofani, *XI Int. Congr.*, p. 46.

5 'Quasi-portraits', scarcely individualized, Brendel, pp. 387, 393, 395.

6 For the famous (later) gates see E. Fiume, *Volterra* (1977), pp. 16, 19.

7 Brendel, p. 351.

8 J. Oleson, *Latomus*, XXXIII (1974), pp. 870–3.

9 Casale Marittimo (Cassalmarittimo): Banti, pp. 152, 261, pl. 71a; P. Bargellini, *L'arte etrusca*, 3rd ed. (1958), pls. 5 and 22. Montescudaio: Banti, pp. 152, 262, pl. 72a; F. Nicosia, *SE*, XXXVII (1969), pp. 369ff. To north: Casaglia with false-domed tomb, M. Pasquinucci, *EC*, p. 92.

10 Rutilius Namatianus, *On His Return*, 457ff.

11 At Ghinchia and Le Pompe. G. Monaco, *Princeton Encyclopaedia of Classical Sites* (1967), p. 210. An Etruscan burial-place has also been found at Belora near the sea. Castiglioncello: M. Pasquinucci, *EC*, p. 90.

12 Polybius, III, 79, 8.

13 Finds near the River Era: Laiatico (sixth-century gravestone), Terricciola (tombs),

Lari (a few seventh-century tombs). Bientina: La Nazione 10/3/79; M. Zecchini, *Gli Etruschi all'isola d'Elba* (1978), pp. 217f., 223f., 229.

14 R. A. Higgins, *Greek and Roman Jewellery* (1961), pp. 138, 141f., 144.

15 G. d'Achiardi, *SE*, I (1927), p. 414 regarded Luca as a mining settlement. Etruscan objects have been found in the Serchio valley at Ponte a Moriano. P. Mencacci and M. Zecchini, op. cit., p. 205, and in 1979 excavations Etruscan tunnels have been found at Coreglia Antelminelli.

16 Banti, pp. 5, 155, from Busca (Pinerolo).

17 Cristofani, *AE*, p. 122.

18 At Montecalvario, I Krauskopf, *Der Thebanische Sagenkreis* (1974), pp. 14–17, Brendel, p. 451.

19 J. J. Reich, *GICW*, p. 255.

20 M. Pasquinucci, *EC*, p. 77.

21 The Padule di Fucecchio. This was where Hannibal took four days to cross in 217 BC.

22 A. Tracchi, *SE*, XXXIX (1971), pp. 153f. – 66 localities of the upper Arno, Val d'Ambra and upper valley of the Ombrone Pistoiese (see next note).

23 V. S. Tacconi, *Territorio e architettura etrusca a Sesto Fiorentino* (1978), pp. 39f. 47, 50. The River Ombrone Pistoiese (distinct from the Ombrone of central Italy), beside Mount Albano Fiorentino (distinct from Mount Albano in Latium), joined the Arno at Pistoria (Pistoia).

24 Tacconi, pp. 39f., 61; M. Pasquinucci, *EC*, pp. 39f; Cristofani, *HE*, pl. 111 (gravestone similar to that of Avle Tite at Volaterrae).

25 According to a suggested textual emendation of Cicero, *Letters to Atticus*, I, 19, 4, he referred to its people as the *Artemini*. F. Nicosia, *Il tumulo di Montefortini e la Tomba dei Boschetti a Comeana* (1966); D. Ridgway, *AR* (1967–8), p. 44.

26 Tacconi, pp. 88ff.; F. Chiostri and M. Mannini, *Le tombe a tholos di Quinto* (1969).

27 Banti, pp. 155, 157.

28 Tacconi, pp. 65, 68 n. 72.

29 M. Pasquinucci, *EC*, p. 31.

30 Hus, *SO*, p. 72.

31 Banti, p. 159.

32 L. B. Curri, *NS* (1976/7), pp. 93–112; Tacconi, p. 58. The Mugello was the basin of the upper Sieve river. Another route led up to the Mugello a little to the west, not far from the River Bisenzio (nothing to do with the town of the same name on Lake Bolsena).

33 F. Nicosia, *Aspetti*, pp. 55f.

34 Brendel, pp. 282, 373.

35 Scullard, p. 169; Banti, p. 8 (cf. p. 159).

36 W. V. Harris, *Rome in Etruria and Umbria* (1971), pp. 61, 66.

CHAPTER 13
Clusium

1 Brendel, pp. 64ff.

2 M. Cristofani Martelli, *SE*, XLI (1973), pp. 117f.

3 Cristofani, *AE*, p. 46.

4 Banti, p. 163; Richardson, p. 141. The main cemetery of Clusium is Poggio Renzo.

5 R. D. Gempler von Diemtigen, *Die etruskischen Kanopen* (1975). The jars are misleadingly known as *canopi* owing to a fortuitous resemblance to jars from Canopus in Lower Egypt which contained the internal organs taken from mummified bodies.

6 Brendel, pp. 109, 130.

7 Another important centre of bronze-work in the territory of Clusium was Brolio. A. Hus, *Les bronzes étrusques* (1975), pp. 72ff.

8 Brendel, pp. 95ff; perhaps the first examples are a little earlier. For a fifth-century branch of this school at Chianciano see Pallottino, *Etr*, pl. 65 and p. 287; Mansuelli, fig. 50 and p. 130.

9 Brendel, pp. 207f.

10 At first there is Cretan influence, filtered through various intermediaries. On this, see L. Bonfante, *Studi Banti*, pp. 81ff.

11 Brendel, p. 137. There were also a few provincial variants.

12 Banti, p. 171. Caere's wares are *bucchero sottile*, those of Clusium *bucchero pesante*.

13 Varro in Pliny, XXXVI, 19, 91ff.; G. A. Mansuelli, *Mél. Heurgon*, II, p. 626.

14 Tomba di Arunte or degli Orazi or degli Orazi e Curiazi.

15 A. B. Cook, *JHS*, XXII (1902), p. 19.

16 M. H. Crawford, *Roman Republican Coinage*, I (1974), pp. 242f. (The Minucian Column, dubiously attributed to 439 BC, but perhaps later).

17 M. Pasquinucci, *EC*, p. 59.

18 Hus, *SO*, p. 59.

19 E.g. Pania Tomb, Brendel, pp. 64ff., 205, 459 n. 4.

20 Columella, II, 6, 3; Livy, XXVIII, 45, 18; Strabo, V, 2, 9; Cristofani, *Etr*, p. 51.

21 G. Bonfante, *Arezzo e gli Etruschi* (1976).

22 Strabo, V, 2, 9, 226. For drainage see Tacitus, *Annals*, I, 79.

23 Banti, p. 173.

24 Cristofani, *AE*, p. 128; Richardson, pp. 6of. (statuettes).

25 G. Colonna, *CISME*, p. 19. Arretium was the only Etruscan city to supply metal to Scipio Africans in 205 BC. Livy, XXVIII, 45.

26 Brendel, p. 327.

27 M. Pasquinucci, *EC*, p. 42; M. Cristofani, *XI Int. Congr.*, p. 46. The Ionian style at Clusium displays a time-lag in comparison with centres nearer the sea.

28 According to Torelli, *ET*, 44.

29 Livy, X, 3, 2; W. V. Harris, *Rome in Etruria and Umbria* (1971), p. 115.

30 Hus, *SO*, p. 60; Richardson, p. 2; N. Horsfall, *JRS*, LXIII (1973), pp. 68ff.; L. R. Taylor, *Proceedings of the American Academy at Rome*, II (1923), p. 191; A. Neppi Modona, *Cortona etrusca e romana nella storia e nell'arte*, new ed. (1977), pp. 3–8. Confusion with Croton was the cause of the strange story that the Greek philosopher Pythagoras of Samos came to Cortona (Vacano, p. 50; Hus, *SO*, p. 241).

31 The largest mound tomb is the Melone di Camucia, with a variant style of false vault. M. Pasquinucci, *EC*, pp. 51f.

32 M. Pasquinucci, *EC*, p. 48.

33 Brendel, p. 289; P. Bruschetti, *Il lampadario di Cortona* (1979).

34 Livy, IV, 52, 6. Up to Orte or even Orvieto or beyond: Strong, p. 12; Banti, p. 122.

35 Pliny, *NH*, III, 14, 113; Pallottino, *Etr*, p. 93.

36 Strabo, V, 1, 10, 216; Pallottino, *Etr*, p. 93. Sethlans, of Phoenician origin, was worshipped at Perusia.

37 Etruscanization at Tuder (Todi), Vettona (Bettona) and Cagli: Pallottino, *Etr*, p. 101.

38 The 'Loeb tripods' from Marsciano show Umbrian Etruscanization: Brendel, p. 162. Excellent reliefs on an Etruscan chariot from Monteleone di Spoleto combine Corinthian and Ionian elements; Brendel, p. 151.

39 M. Pasquinucci, *EC*, p. 67. Perusia's walls are made of travertine stone.

40 E.g. the Ipogeo dei Volumni, which first roused George Dennis's love of the Etruscan civilization, later displayed in his *Cities and Cemeteries of Etruria*.

41 D. Ridgway, *AR* (1973–4), p. 52; cf. R. A. Staccioli, *Aspetti*, pp. 207–15.

42 Pliny, *NH*, II, 54, 140. Richardson, p. 223, doubts if the same person is referred to.

43 R. Turcan, *Mél. Heurgon*, II, p. 1016. Volsinii possessed the important shrine of a goddess named Nortia: Banti, pp. 119,

121; Vacano, pp. 12, 18, 40, 83. The place specialized in underworld cults; Cristofani, *Etr*, p. 104.

44 G. Colonna, *CISME*, p. 13.

45 G. Colonna, *SE*, XLII (1974), pp. 3–24. Umbrian objects are also found there.

46 W. Johannowsky, *SE*, XXXIII (1965), p. 698; J. Heurgon, *Recherches sur l'histoire de la religion et la civilisation de Capoue préromaine* (1942), pp. 70ff., 130ff.

47 J. Hackens, *CISME*, p. 261.

48 Zonaras, VIII, 7, 4. An inscription from the Golini tomb may commemorate a Volsinian's appointment to an official post (*legatus*) by the Romans: J. Heurgon, *Colloquio su Roma medio-repubblicana* (Rome, April 1973).

49 North-west of Volsinii was Etruscan Acquapendente (above the Paglia), with very similar pottery. Bomarzo on the River Vezza also shows strong Volsinian influence. Viterbo (Vicus Elbii) was perhaps the Etruscan Sur(i)na and the Roman Surrina. Ferento was first an Etruscan town and then the Roman Ferentium or Ferentinum.

50 D. Ridgway, *AR* (1973–4), p. 51; Cristofani, *AE*, p. 64. It was only slightly later, under Ionian influences, that such ornaments became common in Etruria.

51 M. Cataldi and F. Boitani, *EC*, p. 263.

52 There is a Miniera di Murlo a little to the south of there.

53 Banti, p. 174; L. Bonfante,

Prospettiva, XVII (April 1979), p. 33.

54 M. Cristofani, *Prospettiva*, I (April 1975), p. 10; *AE*, p. 63; R. A. Staccioli, *Mél. Heurgon*, II, pp. 96of. K. J. Philips, *Poggio Civitate: Catalogo della Mostra* (Florence-Siena) (1970), p. 21, saw the building as a temple.

55 M. Pasquinucci, *EC*, p. 85.

56 R. Bianchi Bandinelli, *DA*, VI (1972), pp. 236–47; K. J. Phillips, *Poggio Civitate*, pp. 25ff. T. N. Gantz, *SE*, XXXIX (1971), pp. 3f., identifies two triads of divinities, but the figures could also be human.

57 L. Bonfante, *Archaeological News*, V, 4 (1976), p. 99; *Etruscan Dress* (1976), pp. 88, 153 n. 24.

58 Cristofani, *Etr*, p. 30.

59 J. P. Small, *SE*, XXXIX (1971), pp. 26–61.

60 Livy, I, 35; R. C. Bronson, *Studi Banti*, p. 104.

61 L. Bonfante, *Archaeological News*, V, 4 (1976), p. 99; Brendel, p. 457, nn. 13 and 14, points to Cypriot precedents.

62 M. Pasquinucci, *EC*, p. 85.

63 Servius on Virgil, *Aeneid*, X, 198. The founders of Bononia and Mantua on the one hand, and Perusia on the other, are here named as Ocnus and Aulestes respectively.

64 G. Camporeale, *Aspetti*, p. 124; L. Bonfante, *Archaeological News*, V, 4 (1976), p. 104.

65 L. Bonfante, *Prospettiva*, XVII (April 1979), p. 32. M. Cristofani, *Atti del Colloquio sul tema l'Etrusco arcaico* (1974) (1976), p. 26; *IBR*, pp. 378, 388.

66 Brendel, p. 281.

67 Banti, p. 247.

68 Cf. L. Bonfante, *GICW*, p. 194 (the northern *situla* [bucket] art). Sanctuaries at Bononia and Arretium seem related.

69 Livy, V, 33, 2.

70 J. Gagé, *Mélanges d'archéologie et d'histoire de l'Ecole Française de Rome* (1976), p. 23; R. M. Ogilvie, *Commentary on Livy, Books 1–5* (1965), p. 255.

71 Velleius Paterculus, I, 7.

72 Strabo, V, 3, 6, 233; Pliny, *NH*, III, 5, 59.

73 Virgil, *Aeneid*, X, 655 and 167–8f.

74 M. Pallottino, *SE*, XXXIV (1966), p. 427; G. Colonna, *SE*, XLI (1973), p. 69.

75 A. G. McKay, *Vergil's Italy* (1970), p. 88.

76 G. Radke, *Klio*, LVI (1974), p. 47; doubted by Pallottino, *Etr*, p. 129 (but cf. p. 134).

77 T. B. Macaulay, *Horatius*, XXII.

78 *DH*, V, 36, 1; Pliny, *NH*, II, 54, 140; Vacano, p. 126.

79 Tacitus, *Histories*, III, 72; Pliny, *NH*, XXXIV, 39, 139; *DH*, V, 35, 1.

80 E. Gjerstad, *Opuscula Romana*, VII (1967–9), p. 417.

81 R. M. Ogilvie, op. cit.

82 DH, V, 34, 2 (or his source), noting this difficulty, invents a quarrel between them.

83 Heurgon, p. 159.

84 Plutarch, *Poplicola*, 19, 11; M. Grant, *Roman Myths*, rev. ed. (1973), p. 200.

85 DH, V. 36, 3; 37, 1. This resulted in the death of Porsenna's son Arruns.

86 Livy, V, 35, 4.

87 Livy, V, 33, 3; M. Sordi, *Rivista storica dell'antichità*, VI–VII (1976–7), pp. 111ff.

88 Heurgon, p. 182. The Gauls may have been subsidized by Syracuse in their attacks on Etruria and Rome.

89 M. Grant, *Roman Myths*, rev. ed. (1973), p. 76.

90 R. M. Ogilvie, *Commentary on Livy, Books 1–5* (1965), p. 699. Heurgon accepts a Clusine–Roman connection but not a Clusine appeal to Rome.

CHAPTER 14
Veii

1 Potter, p. 78.

2 H. Jucker, *Gnomon*, XXXVII (1965), p. 305. The false vault shows an approach to true vaulting in the later Etruscan and Roman manner.

3 Brendel, p. 122.

4 Banti, p. 54.

5 *DH*, II, 54.

6 L. Vagnetti, *Il depositivo votivo di Campetti a Veio* (1971), p. 185 (reclassification of styles).

7 Brendel, p. 242. The Apollo's right arm, discovered thirty years ago, has given the figure unsuspected poise.

8 O. W. von Vacano, *Aufstieg*, I, 4 (1973), p. 528. Whether this was his personal or family name is uncertain.

9 Pliny, *NH*, XXXV, 157 (Varro).

10 Cristofani, *AE*, pp. 95, 102.

11 Potter, pp. 85, 87; Cristofani, *Etr*, p. 48. The Ponte Sodo separated Etruscan Veii from the Monte Michele to the north. It had holes in the roof to draw off water from above.

12 Potter, p. 86. The Romans knew these channels as *cuniculi*.

13 Strabo, V, 2, 6, 223 may have been thinking of Veii when he over-generalized about a lack of Etruscan harbours. Portus Ostiensis on the north bank lay far in the future, in Roman imperial times.

14 *Saline* near Volaterrae and at the mouths of the Albegna and Mignone, if already worked, were much less extensive; salt from Taras (Tarentum) was particularly valued (R. J. Forbes, *Studies in Ancient Technology*, VII (1963), p. 161); there were also some in Sardinia (R. C. Raspi, *Storia della Sardegna*, 3rd ed. (1977), p. 135).

15 Forbes, p. 161.

16 *DH*, II, 55, 5.

17 Strabo, V, 2, 9, 226.

18 Potter, p. 54.

19 Pliny, *NH*, III, 51; cf. Strabo, V, 2, 9, 226.

20 Brendel, p. 247. For links with the Salernum area see R. Bianchi Bandinelli and A. Giuliano, *Etruschi e Italici*, 2nd ed. (1976), p. 22.

21 Virgil, *Aeneid*, VII, 695 (Aequi Falisci).

22 E.g. Temple of Aphaea (a goddess similar to Artemis) at Aegina (510–490 BC); also south-Italian influence, notably from Taras (Tarentum): M. Cataldi and F. Boitani, *EC*, p. 278. Corinthian craftsmen, too, had worked at Falerii.

23 Pliny, *NH*, III, 5, 51 (Cato).

24 Servius on Virgil, *Aeneid*, VIII, 285. Halaesus (or Alaesus) was said to be from Argos, the son of Neptune (Poseidon, Nethuns).

25 Potter, p. 42; Potter, *A Faliscan Town in Southern Etruria: Excavations at Narce 1966–1971* (1976).

26 Brendel, p. 40.

27 Servius on Virgil, *Aeneid*, VII, 695f.

28 E. T. Salmon, *Samnium and the Samnites* (1967), pp. 35f., 54, 67, 145, 167, 178, 189; Livy, V, 34, 3f. (Gauls).

29 J. Heurgon, *Latomus*, XXVI (1957), p. 18; Scullard, p. 111; Banti, p. 62; Potter, p. 74.

30 J. Heurgon, *Latomus*, XXVI (1957), p. 13 ('without *ver sacrum*').

31 E.g. the successive colonizations of Corcyra by Euboeans and Corinthians.

32 Livy, V, 8, 5.

33 T. N. Gantz, *Opuscula Romana*, X (1974), pp. 1–22.

34 Potter, p. 80.

35 Since the cult of Aeneas is recorded at nearby Politorium, it may have come to Rome *via* Veii rather than direct from its principal Etruscan centre Vulci. It is possible that a famous piece of Roman bronze-work, the Capitoline wolf, was made by a pupil of Vulca in the second quarter of the fifth century BC: O. W. von Vacano, *Aufstieg*, I, 4 (1973), p. 573; Brendel, p. 253 – but the work seems un-Etruscan to B. Andreae, *The Art of Rome* (1978), p. 37.

36 Doubted by Varro, *De Lingua Latina*, V, 30; M. Sordi, *Aufstieg*, I, 2 (1972), p. 787.

37 According to Livy, I, 33, 9, they established salt-pans of their own after founding Ostia. But, if so, they were inferior to those on the Veientine bank.

38 On the disputed Septem Pagi on the right bank, see Livy, II, 55, 5 (antedating the struggle); J. Heurgon, *SE*, XLVI (1978), p. 621.

39 Livy, II, 15, 6.

40 R. M. Ogilvie, *Commentary on Livy, Books 1–5* (1965), p. 359; contrarily E. Badian, *JRS*, LII (1962), p. 201.

41 Livy, IV, 19, 5; Propertius, IV, 10; R. Hirata, *Annuario dell'Istituto Giapponese di Cultura in Roma*, X (1972–3), pp. 7–31.

42 Livy, V, 1, 4–5, discounted by R. M. Ogilvie, *Commentary on Livy, Books 1–5* (1965), p. 632; E. Rawson, *JRS*, LXVIII (1978), p. 134, n. 26 doubts the former explanation.

BIBLIOGRAPHY

Ancient Sources

The unsatisfactory character of the ancient literary sources relating to the Etruscans is summed up by Massimo Pallottino:

> In many of its aspects, we are forced to regard and study the civilization of Etruria as if it were a prehistoric civilization, although it belongs to full historical times; for we are often almost wholly limited to its external and material manifestations. We have not, in fact, the direct light thrown by a great literary tradition to help us penetrate into the thoughts, feelings and way of life of its creators, as is possible with the other great peoples of the classical world.[1]

Such Etruscan literature as did exist – including most of the extant inscriptions in the language – was mainly of a religious and ritual character. It included a famous corpus of doctrine, the detailed and complex *Disciplina Etrusca*. The Greeks and Romans sometimes suggested that this was of venerable origin, and some parts of it may have been ancient,[2] but the collection was apparently only entrusted to writing between the fourth and the second centuries BC,[3] when the infiltration of later Greek (Hellenistic) and Babylonian influences had already taken place. The *Disciplina Etrusca* has not, however, survived, though a good many references to its contents are made by Greek and Latin authors.

Etruscan poetry was apparently only a late and derivative development, modelled on Greek drama,[4] and the same was probably true of Etruscan historiography as a literary art, including the 'Tuscan histories' to which Varro referred in the first century BC.[5] Nevertheless, Etruscan historical and legendary traditions, quite independent of those of Greece and Rome, had been preserved and handed down from the past. This is strikingly revealed by the paintings from the François tomb at Vulci and inscriptions from Tarquinii (*elogia Tarquiniensia*). Such traditions were probably based on family histories and archives;[6] the Etruscan poet Persius (AD 34–62), from Volaterrae, reminds us how his aristocratic compatriots cherished their genealogical trees.[7] Maecenas and Sejanus,[8] leading advisers of Augustus (31 BC–AD 14) and Tiberius (AD 14–37), were both Etruscans, from Arretium and Volsinii respectively; their fame and influence helped to make sure that, although the Romanization of Etruria was by that time complete, its past glories were by no means forgotten. Moreover, the Emperor Claudius, one of whose wives, Plautia Urgulanilla, was Etruscan, wrote a massive Greek work on her people in twenty books and received honours from the Etruscans[9] – but this work, too, is lost.

In consequence, our literary information about the Etruscans depends instead on more-or-less incidental references by Greek and Latin authors. Those quoted or referred to in the present volume are the following:

GREEK

ALCIMUS, fourth century BC. Historian. Born in Sicily. His writings, of which only fragments survive, include criticisms of Etruscan extravagance and an assertion that Aeneas married a woman called Tyrrhenia.

ARISTOTLE, 384–322 BC. Philosopher. Born at Stagira in Chalcidice (Macedonia). Author of numerous treatises, including the *Politics*. A work on *Etruscan Customs (Turrhenon Nomima)* was attributed to him.

ARISTOXENUS, born 378/360 BC. Philosopher, musical theorist and biographer, born at Taras (Tarentum, Taranto, in south-eastern Italy).

ATHENAEUS, wrote about AD 200. Born at Naucratis (Nabira) in Egypt. Author of the encyclopaedic *Learned Banquet (Deipnosophistae)*.

DIODORUS SICULUS, later first century BC. Historian. Born at Agyrium (Agira) in Sicily. Author of *The Library (Bibliotheke)*, a world history from the earliest times.

DIONYSIUS OF HALICARNASSUS, later first century BC. Rhetorician and historian. Born at Halicarnassus (Bodrum) in Caria (south-western Asia Minor). Author of treatises on literary criticism and *History of Early Rome (Romaike Archaiologia)*. He claimed some special knowledge of the Etruscans and planned a monograph about them.

EPHORUS, *c.* 405–330 BC. Historian. Born at Cyme (Namurtköy) in Aeolis (western Asia Minor). His works included *Histories*, a universal history in thirty books, of which the greater part is lost.

HERACLIDES PONTICUS, fourth century BC. Philosopher. His numerous works, now surviving only in fragments, included *Constitutions*, in which he wrote disapprovingly about Etruscan luxury.

HERODOTUS, *c.* 480–425 BC. Historian. Born at Halicarnassus (Bodrum) in Caria (south-western Asia Minor). His pioneer *History* in nine books describes the Greco-Persian wars and their background, and quotes Lydian stories indicating that the Etruscans were of Lydian origin.

HESIOD, *c.* 700 BC. Epic poet. Born at Ascra in Boeotia (central Greece). Believed to have composed and sung the *Works and Days* and *Theogony*.

HOMER, probably eighth century BC. Epic poet. Perhaps born at Chios or Smyrna (Izmir) in Ionia (western Asia Minor). Believed to have composed and sung the *Iliad* and *Odyssey*.

HOMERIC HYMNS, a collection of hymns, literary rather than devotional, written between the eighth and sixth centuries BC and wrongly attributed to Homer.

LYCOPHRON, born *c.* 320 BC. Poet. Born at Chalcis on the island of Euboea (central Greece). Reputedly author of the *Alexandra*, a dramatic prophecy by the seer Cassandra of the Trojan War and subsequent events.

PAUSANIAS, wrote in about AD 150. Geographer and traveller. Born near Mount Sipylus in Lydia (western Asia Minor). Author of *Description of Greece (Periegesis tes Hellados)*.

PINDAR, 518–438 BC. Lyric poet. Born at Cynoscephalae in Boeotia (central Greece). His poems included *Odes* for victors in the Olympian, Pythian, Nemean and Isthmian Games.

PLATO, *c.* 429–347 BC. Philosopher. Born at Athens. Pupil of Socrates and author of twenty-five *Dialogues*, the *Apology*, and letters and poems.

PLUTARCH, (Lucius Mestrius Plutarchus), before AD 50–after 120. Biographer, philosopher and antiquarian. Works include numerous treatises (the *Moralia*) and poems of Greek and Latin biographies.

POLLUX (Julius Pollux), wrote in about AD 180. Lexicographer and rhetorician. Born at Naucratis (Nabira) in Egypt. Author of *Onomasticon*, a list of Attic words and technical terms.

POLYBIUS, *c.* 200–after 118 BC. Historian. Born at Megalopolis in Arcadia (Peloponnese, southern Greece). Author of *Histories* of the Roman world in forty books (of which five, and excerpts from others, have survived), covering the period from 220 to 146 BC.

PYTHAGORAS, born *c.* 580 BC. Philosopher, mathematician, and founder of a religious society. Born at Samos (Ionia, western Asia Minor), but worked at Croton (south-eastern Italy). It is doubtful if he left any writings.

STRABO, *c.* 64 BC–AD 19. Geographer and historian. Born at Amaseia (Amasra) in Pontus (north-eastern Asia Minor). His works included the extant *Geography* in seventeen books.

THEOPHRASTUS, *c.* 370–288 BC. Philosopher and biologist: successor of Aristotle. Born at Eresus on the island of Lesbos (Aeolis, off western Asia Minor). Works included *History of (Enquiry into) Plants* and *Growth of Plants*.

THEOPOMPUS, born 378 BC. Historian. Born on the island of Chios (Ionia, off western Asia Minor). Author of *Greek Histories (Hellenica)* and *History of Philip (Philippica*, on Philip II of Macedonia). He displayed a strong bias against the Etruscans.

THUCYDIDES, 460/55–*c.* 400 BC. Athenian historian. Author of (incomplete) history of the Peloponnesian War (431–404 BC).

TIMAEUS, *c.* 356–260 BC. Historian. Born at Tauromenium (Taormina) in Sicily. Author of *History* in thirty-eight books (of which fragments survive). The work is primarily concerned with Sicily but includes censure of Etruscan luxury.

XANTHUS, fifth century BC. Historian. Born in Lydia (western Asia Minor). Author of history of Lydia (*Lydiaca*), including much legendary material. Except for fragments it is lost, but we are told that it denied the Etruscans a Lydian origin.

ZONARAS, (Johannes Zonaras), twelfth century AD. Byzantine historian, high official, and monk. Author of *Epitome of Histories* from the Creation to AD 1118.

LATIN

ARNOBIUS, wrote AD 296. Rhetorician and theologian. Born at Sicca Veneria in Numidia (El Kef in Tunisia). Author of *Against the Nations (Adversus Nationes)*, attacking paganism.

CAECINA (Aulus Caecina), first century BC. Orator and expert on Etruscan lore. Born at Volaterrae (Volterra) in Etruria. Author of a version of *The Etruscan Discipline (Disciplina Etrusca)*.

CATO THE ELDER (THE CENSOR) (Marcus Porcius Cato Censorius), 234–149 BC. Public figure, historian, antiquarian, agriculturalist. Born at Tusculum (near Frascati) in Latium (Lazio). His works included *Origines (Origins)* in seven books (mainly lost) and *On Agriculture (De Agricultura)*.

CENSORINUS, third century AD. Grammarian. His writings included an encyclopaedic work *On His Birthday (De Die Natali)*, a birthday gift to a contemporary.

CHRONOGRAPHIA URBIS ROMAE, AD 354. An anonymous illustrated Christian handbook of the City of Rome, including chronicles, calendars and lists of consuls and bishops.

CICERO (Marcus Tullius), 106–43 BC. Public figure and orator, rhetorician, popular philosopher, poet. Born at Arpino (Arpinum) in Latium (Lazio). Many speeches, treatises and letters *To Atticus* and *To Friends*.

COLUMELLA (Lucius Junius Moderatus Columella), first century AD. Agricultural writer. Born at Gades (Cadiz) in Spain. Author of *On Agriculture (De Re Rustica)* in twelve books (one in verse).

FESTUS (Sextus Pompeius Festus), late second century AD. Scholar. Wrote an epitome (summary) of the treatise *On the Significance of Words (De Significatu Verborum)* of Verrius Flaccus, scholar of the early first century AD.

ITINERARIUM MARITIMUM, a description of sea routes, is preserved with the *Itinerarium Antoninianum*, which in its present form comprises a late third century AD collection of routes used for troop movements.

LIVY (Titus Livius), 59 BC–AD 17 or 64 BC–AD 12. Historian. Born at Patavium (Padua) in Cisalpine Gaul (northern Italy). Wrote *History of Rome (Ab Urbe Condita)* down to 9 BC in 142 books, of which 35 are extant.

LUCAN (Marcus Annaeus Lucanus), AD 39–68. Epic poet. Born at Corduba (Cordova) in Spain. Author of epic poem, the *Civil War (Bellum Civile)* or 'Pharsalia', in ten books, about the war between Caesar and Pompey.

NAMATIANUS (Rutilius Claudius Namatianus), early fourth century AD. Public figure and poet. Born at Tolosa (Toulouse) in south-western Gaul. Author of *De Reditu Suo (On his Return)*, a poetical itinerary (the last part is lost).

OVID (Publius Ovidius Naso), 43 BC–AD 17. Poet. Born at Sulmo (Sulmona) in central Italy. His collections of elegiac verse, and the *Metamorphoses* in hexameters, contain references to Etruscan religion and mythology.

PERSIUS (Aulus Persius Flaccus), AD 34–62. Satirical and philosophical poet from Volaterrae (Volterra) in Etruria. A book of six satires has survived.

PLAUTUS (Titus Maccius Plautus), c. 254–184 BC. Comic dramatist. Born at Sarsina (Mercato Saraceno) in Umbria (central Italy). Twenty of his verse plays, and fragments of another, have survived. One, the *Cistellaria*, comments scathingly on the morals of Etruscan women.

PLINY THE ELDER (Gaius Plinius Secundus), AD 23/24–79. Historian and encyclopaedic scientist. Born at Comum (Como) in Cisalpine Gaul (northern Italy). His works included a *History* (now lost) and *Natural History*, in thirty-one and thirty-seven books respectively. Among the Etruscan authorities of whom he made use, perhaps at second hand, was Tarquinius Priscus.

PROPERTIUS (Sextus Propertius), 54/48–after 16 BC. Elegiac poet. Born at Asisium (Assisi) in Umbria (central Italy). Author of four books of poetry.

SENECA THE YOUNGER (Lucius Annaeus Seneca), 5/4 BC–AD 65. Philosopher and dramatic poet. Born at Corduba (Cordova) in Spain. His numerous works included a scientific treatise, *Natural Questions*, which drew on the *Disciplina Etrusca* of Aulus Caecina.

SERVIUS (Marius or Maurus Servius Honoratus), *c.* AD 400. Grammarian and commentator. His most important work was a commentary on Virgil, which has survived both in the original and in an enlarged form (Servius Auctus or Servius Danielis).

SILIUS ITALICUS (Tiberius Catius Asconius Silius Italicus), *c.* AD 26–101. Epic poet. Probably born at Patavium (Padua) in Cisalpine Gaul (northern Italy). Author of *Punica*, a historical epic poem in seventeen books on the Second Punic War (218–201 BC).

TACITUS (Publius Cornelius Tacitus), *c.* AD 56–*c.* 117. Senator and historian. Probably of Gallic or north Italian origin. Author of histories of the Roman Principate, the *Histories* and *Annals* (of which a total of two-thirds survives); also the *Agricola* (biography), *Germania*, and *Dialogue on Orators (Dialogus de Oratoribus)*.

VARRO (Marcus Terentius Varro), 116–27 BC. Encyclopaedic scholar. Born at Reate (Rieti) in the Sabine country (central Italy). Author of numerous works, of which *On the Latin Language (De Lingua Latina)* – in part – and *On Agriculture (Res Rusticae)* survive.

VELLEIUS PATERCULUS (Gaius Velleius Paterculus), *c.* 10 BC–after AD 30. Officer and historian. Born in Campania (south-western Italy). Author of *Roman Histories* in two books down to AD 30.

VERRIUS FLACCUS, an ex-slave (freedman), later first century BC. The most learned of Augustan scholars. Author of lost work *On the Significance of Words (De Significatu Verborum)* and antiquarian writings including a study of the Etruscans *(Libri Rerum Etruscarum)*.

VIRGIL (Publius Vergilius Maro), 70–10 BC. Poet. Born at Andes near Mantua (Mantova) in Cisalpine Gaul (northern Italy). Author of *Eclogues* or *Bucolics* (10 poems), *Georgics* (4 books), and *Aeneid* (12 books). See also Servius.

VITRUVIUS (Vitruvius Pollio), later first century BC. Architect and military engineer. Author of *On Architecture (De Architectura)* in 10 books.

In collecting information about the Etruscans we have to rely not only on the more or less fragmentary allusions by all these writers but also, to a very great extent, as Massimo Pallottino observed, on the 'external and material manifestations' of their own culture. Among these, artistic and domestic and funerary objects and architectural remains are of course prominent. But inscriptions and coins (though these start relatively late) also require scrutiny, and so do the traces of roads and irrigation works.

Since all these objects relate to technical disciplines, we have to examine them in conjunction with the comments of their modern interpreters. A list of some of these modern writings follows. It includes only books and not articles, since the useful articles devoted to the subject are much too numerous to list.

Nor can the very many studies of individual sites[10] or catalogues of museums be enumerated,[11] though some of them are cited in the notes.

As the character of this book-list will suggest, Etruscan studies are a bibliographical nightmare. In particular, full-scale writings recording researches of the most significant nature are frequently entombed in the reports of congresses and in *Festschrifts*, so that these studies are extremely hard for librarians and students to track down.

Some Books

Acts of the VIIIth International Congress of Prehistoric and Protohistoric Sciences (1966) (Prague 1970).

ALFÖLDI, A., *Römische Frühgeschichte: Kritik und Forschung seit 1964* (Heidelberg 1976).

Archaeologica: Scritti in onore di A. Neppi Modona (Florence 1975).

Art and Culture of the Etruscans (Conference) (Leningrad 1972).

Aspetti e problemi dell' Etruria interna (Atti dell' VIII Convegno nazionale di studi etruschi e italici, Orvieto–Perugia, 1972) (Florence 1974).

Assimilation et résistance à la culture gréco-romaine dans le monde ancien (Travaux du VIᵉ Congrès International d'Etudes Classiques) (Madrid 1974).

Atti dei Convegni di studi etruschi, I (Convegno nazionale etrusco) – XI (1958–76) (1959–77) (see also Aspetti, above).

Atti del Colloquio sul tema l'Etrusco arcaico (1974) (Florence 1976).

Atti del VIII Convegno di studi sulla Magna Grecia (1969) (Naples 1971).

Atti del primo Simposio internazionale di protostoria italiana (Rome 1969).

BANTI, L., *The Etruscan Cities and their Culture* (London 1973).

BARGELLINI, P., *L' arte etrusca*, 3rd ed. (Florence 1958).

BIANCHI BANDINELLI, R., *Arte etrusca e arte italica* (Rome 1963).

—— and GIULIANO, A., *Etruschi e Italici prima del dominio di Roma* (Milan 1972).

BIZZARI, M., and CURRI, C., *Magica Etruria* (Florence 1968).

BLOCH, R., *Etruscan Art* (London 1966) (and *Die Kunst der Etrusker*, 3rd ed., 1977)

——*The Etruscans*, rev. ed. (London and New York 1961).

BOARDMAN, J., and VOLLENWEIDER, M.-L., *Catalogue of Engraved Gems and Finger-Rings in the Ashmolean Museum*, vol. I (Greek and Etruscan) (Oxford 1979).

BOETHIUS, A., *Etruscan and Early Roman Architecture* (Harmondsworth 1979).

—— (etc.), *Etruscan Culture, Land and People* (New York 1962).

—— and WARD-PERKINS, J. B., *Etruscan and Roman Architecture* (Harmondsworth 1970).

BOITANI, F., CATALDI, M., and PASQUINUCCI, M. (intr. by TORELLI, M.), *Etruscan Cities* (London 1978).

BONAMICI, M., *I buccheri con figurazioni graffite* (Florence 1974).

BONFANTE, L., *Etruscan Dress* (London and Baltimore 1978).

BORISKOVSKAYA, S. P., *Production Centres of Etruscan Bucchero* (in Russian) (Moscow 1975).

BRENDEL, O. J., *Etruscan Art* (ed. E. H. Richardson) (Harmondsworth 1978).

BROWN, W. L., *The Etruscan Lion* (Oxford 1960).

BRUUN, P., HOHTI, P. (etc.), *Studies in the Romanization of Etruria* (Rome 1975).

BUCHNER, G., 'Nuovi aspetti e problemi posti dagli scavi di Pitecusa', in *Contribution a l'étude de la société et de la colonisation eubéennes* (1975).

—— and RIDGWAY, D., on Pithecusae (Ischia) excavations, in *Monumenti Antichi*, vol. 1 (Rome, in press).

BUONAMICI, G., *Fonti di storia etrusca tratte dagli autori classici* (Florence 1939).

CAMERINI, E., *Il bucchero etrusco* (Rome 1977).

CAMPOREALE, G., *I commerci di Vetulonia in età orientalizzante* (Rome 1969).

CIATTINI, A., MELANI, V., and NICOSIA, F., *Itinerari etruschi* (Pistoia 1971).

Contributi introduttivi allo studio della monetazione etrusca (Atti del V Convegno del Centro Internazionale di studi numismatici 1975) (Naples 1976).

Corpus Inscriptionum Etruscarum (Leipzig 1898–).

Corpus Speculorum Etruscorum, vol. 1 fasc. 1 (Bologna 1979).

CRISTOFANI, M., *Città e campagna nell'Etruria settentrionale* (Arezzo 1976).

—— *Introduzione allo studio di etrusco* (1973, reprint 1977).

—— *L'arte degli Etruschi: produzione e consumo* (Turin 1978).

—— *The Etruscans* (London 1979).

CUNLIFFE, B., *The Celtic World* (Lucerne 1979).

DAL MASO, L. B., and VIGHI, R., *Southern Etruria* (Florence 1975).

DEL CHIARO, M., *Etruscan Art from West Coast Collections* (Exhibition) (Santa Barbara 1967).

DEMUS-QUATEMBER, F., *Etruskische Grabarchitektur* (Baden-Baden 1958).

DENNIS, G., *Cities and Cemeteries of Etruria* (London 1848, 2nd edition 1878, reprint 1968).

DE PALMA, C., *Testimonianze etrusche* (Florence 1974).

DUMEZIL, G., *La religion romaine archaïque: avec un appendice sur la religion des Etrusques*, rev. ed. (1974).

XIth International Congress of Classical Archaeology (Programme) (London 1978).

ELSTE, R., *Zur Frage der Proto-Etrusker* (Hamburg 1977).

FORBES, R. J., *Studies in Ancient Technology*, 9 vols. (1955–72).

FORESTI, L. A., *Testi, ipotesi e considerazioni sull' origine degli Etruschi* (Graz dissertation) (Vienna 1974).

GAGÉ, J., *Enquêtes sur les structures sociales et religieuses de la Rome primitive* (Brussels 1977).

GATTI, E., *Gli Etruschi* (Chiaravalle Centrale 1979).

GAUDIO, A., *Les étrusques: une civilisation retrouvée* (Paris 1969).

GEMPLER VON DIEMTIGEN, R. D., *Die etruskischen Kanopen* (Küsnacht-Einsiedeln 1974).

GRANT, M., *History of Rome*, rev. ed. (New York 1978).

—— *Roman Myths*, 3rd ed. (Harmondsworth 1973).

Greece and Italy in the Classical World (Acta of the XIth International Congress of Classical Archaeology, 1978) (London 1979).

GRÖTEKE, F., *Etruskerland: Geschichte, Kunst, Kultur* (Stuttgart 1973).

GUZZO, P. G., *Le fibule in Etruria dal VI al I secolo* (Rome 1973).

HAMPTON, C., *The Etruscans and the Survival of Etruria* (London 1969) (*The Etruscan Survival*, New York 1970).

HARREL-COURTÈS, H., *Etruscan Italy* (Edinburgh and London 1964).

HARRIS, W. V., *Rome in Etruria and Umbria* (Oxford 1971).

HAWKES, C. and S. (eds.), *Archaeology and History*, vol. I: *Greeks, Celts, and Romans* (London 1973).

HAYNES, S., *Etruscan Bronze Utensils*, rev. ed. (London 1974).

——*Etruscan Sculpture* (London 1971).

HEALY, J. F., *Mining and Metallurgy in the Greek and Roman World* (London 1978).

HENCKEN, H., *Tarquinia and Etruscan Origins* (London 1968).

——*Tarquinia, Villanovans and Etruscans* (Cambridge, Mass. 1968).

HESS, R., *Das etruskische Italien*, 2nd ed. (Cologne 1974).

HEURGON, J., *The Daily Life of the Etruscans* (London 1964).

——*Recherches sur les structures sociales dans l'antiquité classique* (Paris 1970).

——*The Rise of Rome to 264 BC* (London 1973). (see also *L'Italie préromaine et la Rome républicaine*)

HIGGINS, R. A., *Greek and Roman Jewellery* (London 1961).

HUS, A., *Les bronzes étrusques* (Brussels 1975).

——*Les siècles d'or de l'histoire étrusque (675–475 avant JC)* (Brussels 1976).

KAHL-FURTHMANN, G., *Die Frage nach dem Ursprung der Etrusker* (Meisenheim am Glan 1976).

KELLER, W., *The Etruscans* (1975).

LATTANZI, M. S., *Le antiche città dell' Etruria; saggio di geografia urbana* (Florence 1974).

LAWRENCE, D. H., *Etruscan Places* (London 1932).

Le monde étrusque (exhibition) (Marseille 1977).

LERICI, C. M., *Italia sepolta* (Milan 1962).

L' età del ferro nell'Etruria marittima (Grosseto 1965).

L' Italie préromaine et la Rome républicaine (Mélanges offerts à Jacques Heurgon) (Paris 1976).

LOPES REGINA, M., *Problemi di storia e di topografia etrusca* (Florence 1967).

MACINTOSH, J., *Etruscan–Punic Relations* (Dissertation) (Bryn Mawr 1975).

MACIVER, D. RANDALL-, *The Etruscans* (Oxford 1927).

MACNAMARA, E., *The Everyday Life of the Etruscans* (London 1973).

MANSUELLI, G. A., *Etruria and Early Rome* (London 1966).

MASSA, A., *The World of the Etruscans* (1973).

MAZZOLAI, A., *Gli Etruschi della costa tirrenica* (Florence 1977).

MORETTI, M., *Nuove scoperte e acquisizioni nell'Etruria meridionale* (Rome 1975).

——*Nuovi monumenti della pittura* (1966).

—— *The National Museum of the Villa Giulia* (1975).

—— and MAETZKE, G., *The Art of the Etruscans* (London 1970).

MOSCATI, S., *I Cartaginesi in Italia* (Milan 1977).

NEPPI MODONA, A., *Guida alle antichità etrusche*, 6th ed. (Florence 1973).

OGILVIE, R. M., *Early Rome and the Etruscans* (Hassocks and London 1976).

PAGET, R. F., *Central Italy: An Archaeological Guide* (London 1973).

PALLOTTINO, M., *La civiltà artistica etrusco-italica* (Florence 1971).

——*La langue étrusque: problèmes et perspectives* (Paris 1978).

—— *Saggi di antichità* (Rome 1979).

——*Testimonia Linguae Etruscae*, 2nd ed. (Florence 1968).

——*The Etruscans* (rev. ed. by D. Ridgway) (London 1974) (and *Etruscologia*, 6th ed., 1977).

——(etc., ed.), *Popoli e civiltà dell'Italia antica*, vols. 1–7 (Rome 1974–8).

PERUZZI, E., *Aspetti culturali del Lazio primitivo* (Florence 1978).

——*Origini di Roma* (Bologna 1970).

PFIFFIG, A. J., *Einführung in die Etruskologie* (Darmstadt 1972).

——*Religio etrusca* (Graz 1975).

POTTER, T. W., *The Changing Landscape of South Etruria* (London 1979).

POULSEN, V., *Etruskische Kunst* (Königstein 1969).

PRAYON, F., *Frühetruskische Grab- und Hausarchitektur* (Heidelberg 1975).

——*L'oriente e la statuaria etrusca arcaica* (1977).

QUILICI, L. (etc.), *Civiltà del Lazio primitivo* (Exhibition) (Rome 1976).

QUILICI GIGLI, S., *Archeologia laziale* (Quaderni di studio per l'archeologia etrusco-italica, I) (Rome 1978).

RASMUSSEN, T. B., *Bucchero Pottery from Southern Etruria* (1979).

RASPI, R. C., *Storia della Sardegna*, 3rd ed. (Milan 1977).

RENARD, M., *Initiation a l'étruscologie* (Brussels 1941).

RHODES, D. E., *Dennis of Etruria* (London 1973).

RICHARDSON, E. H., *Etruscan Sculptures* (London 1966).

——*The Etruscans: Their Art and their Civilization* (Chicago 1964, reprint 1976). (See also Brendel, O. J.)

RIDGWAY, D. and F. R. (eds.), *Italy Before the Romans* (London and New York 1979).

RIECHE, A., *Das antike Italien aus der Luft* (Bergisch Gladbach 1978).

RIIS, P. S., *An Introduction to Etruscan Art* (Copenhagen 1953).

SAVELLI, A., *Nuove interpretazioni etrusche* (Bologna 1970).

SCHMIEDT, G., *Il livello antico del Mar Tirreno* (Florence 1972).

SCULLARD, H. H., *The Etruscan Cities and Rome* (London 1967) (and *Le città etrusche*, 2nd ed., Milan 1976).

SOLARI, A., *Topografia storica di Etruria* (Rome 1976).

SPRENGER, M., *Die etruskische Plastik des fünften Jahrhunderts und ihr Verhältnis zur griechischen Kunst* (Rome 1972).

——and BARTOLINI, G., *Die Etrusker: Kunst und Geschichte* (Munich 1978).

STACCIOLI, R. A., *Il 'mistero' della lingua etrusca* (Rome 1977).

STEINGRÄBER, S., *Etruskische Möbel* (Rome 1979).

STIBBE, C. M., *Pontische Vasenmaler* (in press).

STRØM, I., *Problems Concerning the Origin and Early Development of the Etruscan Orientalizing Style* (Odense 1971).

STRONG, D. E., *The Early Etruscans* (London 1968).

Studi in onore di L. Banti (Rome 1965).

Studi sulla città antica (Atti del Convegno di studi sulla città etrusca e italica preromana, Bologna–Florence, 1966) (1970).

STÜTZER, H., *Die Etrusker und ihre Welt* (Cologne 1975).

SZILAGYI, J. G., *Etrusko-Korinthosi Vàzafestészet* (Budapest 1975).

TEITZ, R. S., *Masterpieces of Etruscan Art* (Worcester, Mass. 1967).

TORELLI, M., *Elogia Tarquiniensia* (Rome 1975).

——*Lazio arcaico e mondo greco*, vols. 1–5 (La Parola del Passato), (Naples 1977).

——and BIANCHI BANDINELLI, R., *L'arte dell'antichità classica*, vol. 2.) (Etruria–Roma) (Turin 1976).

TRUMP, D., *Central and South Italy Before Rome* (London 1966).

Tyrrhenica: Saggi di studi etruschi (Milan 1957).

VAN BUREN, E. D., *Figurative Revetments in Etruria and Latium in the Sixth and Fifth Centuries* BC (London 1921).

VAN DEN DRIESSCHE, B., and HACKENS, T., *Antiquités italiques, étrusques et romaines: choix de documents graphiques*, vol. 1 (Louvain 1977).

VAN DER MEER, L. B., *De Etrusken* (The Hague 1977).

VON REDEN, S., *Die Etrusker* (Bergisch Gladbach 1978).

VON VACANO, O.-W., *The Etruscans in the Ancient World*, 2nd ed. (Bloomington 1965).

WARD-PERKINS, J. B., *Cities of Ancient Greece and Italy* (New York 1974).

WEEBER, K.-W., *Geschichte der Etrusker* (Stuttgart 1979).

WELLARD, J., *The Search for the Etruscans* (London 1973).

ZECCHINI, M., *Gli Etruschi all' isola d'Elba* (Portoferraio 1978).

ZSCHIETZSCHMANN, W., *Etruskische Kunst* (Frankfurt 1969).

NOTES TO BIBLIOGRAPHY

1 Pallottino, *Etr*, p. 153.
2 Banti, p. 154.
3 Banti, p. 180; Vacano, pp. 13,
  41; Hus, *SO*, p. 166 M. Grant,
  Roman Myths, rev. ed. (1973), pp.
  27, 29. The Etruscan writers
  Tarquitius Priscus and Aulus
  Caecina were among the
  intermediaries in the
  transmission of Etruscan lore
  to the Romans; Grant, pp. 25f.,
  74.
4 Banti, p. 155; R. Bloch, *The
  Etruscans*, rev. ed. (1961), p. 140;
  Grant, p. 28.
5 Censorinus, *De Die Natali*, 17, 6;
  Banti, p. 155; Bloch, p. 141;
  E. Macnamara, *Everyday Life of
  the Etruscans* (1973), p. 188.
6 Torelli, *ET*, pp. 93f.; Cristofani,
  Etr, p. 83; W. V. Harris, *Rome in
  Etruria and Umbria* (1971), p. 30.
  Umbria (1971), p. 30.
7 Persius, *Satires*, III, 28.
8 Maecenas's mother belonged to
  the noble house of the Cilnii
  from Arretium. R. Syme, *The
  Roman Revolution* (1939), p. 129
  and no. 4; W. V. Harris, *Rome in
  Etruria and Umbria* (1971), pp.
  320f. Sejanus: Tacitus, *Annals*,
  IV, 3; Harris, pp. 314f.
9 The states of Etruria seem to
  have set up a monument to
  Claudius; Harris, p. 28. Among
  subsequent Roman emperors,
  Otho (AD 69) and Trebonianus
  Gallus (251–3) were Etruscan,
  from Ferentium and Perusia
  respectively.
10 Recorded in the annual *Studi
  Etruschi*. These excavations are
  conducted under the auspices of
  the various Italian Soprin-
  tendenze Archeologiche, of
  which the most important for the
  present purpose are those at
  Florence (Etruria), Rome
  (Etruria Meridionale; Lazio;
  Roma), Naples (Campania),
  Bologna, Padua, Cagliari
  (southern Sardinia) and Sassari
  (northern Sardinia).
11 An exception may be made,
  however, in favour of the two
  most important museums of all,
  the Museo Nazionale di Villa
  Giulia, Rome (M. Moretti, *The
  National Museum of Villa Giulia*,
  undated) and the Museo
  Archeologico at Florence (A. de
  Agostino, *Il Museo Archeologico di
  Firenze* [Florence, 1968]). But
  Etruscan objects exist in an
  enormous number of museums.
  Mario del Chiaro is preparing
  an inventory of those in
  American collections.

INDEX

307

9931850   GRANT, M.

937.5   THE ETRUSCANS

24/09/80   £17.50

Please renew/return this item by the last date shown.

So that your telephone call is charged at local rate, please call the numbers as set out below:

	From Area codes 01923 or 0208:	From the rest of Herts:
Renewals:	01923 471373	01438 737373
Enquiries:	01923 471333	01438 737333
Minicom:	01923 471599	01438 737599

L32b

Hertfordshire
COUNTY COUNCIL
Community Information

25 APR

- 4 MAR 2004
- 9 FEB 2005

15 OCT 2005

- 8 SEP 2008

20 OCT 2008

2/12

L32a

L32/rev79